Discover
Australia

Experience the best of Australia

This edition written and researched by

Charles Rawlings-Way,
Brett Atkinson, Lindsay Brown, Jayne D'Arcy,
Anthony Ham, Shawn Low, Virginia Maxwell,
Tom Spurling, Steve Waters, Meg Worby

Contents

Plan Your Trip

Discover Australia

Melbourne &
the Great Ocean
Road

Contents

Discover Australia

This Is Australia

Island, country, continent...Australia is a big 'un whichever way you spin it. The essence of the place is diversity:
deserts, coral reefs, tall forests, snow-cloaked mountains
and multicultural melting-pot cities.

Most Australians live along the coast, and most of these folks live in cities.

In fact, Australia is the 18th-most urbanised country in the
world, with around 70% of Australians living in its 10 largest towns. It follows that the cities here are a whole lotta
fun! Sydney, the sun-kissed Harbour City, is a glamorous
collusion of beaches, boutiques and bars; Melbourne is
all arts, alleyways and Aussie Rules football; Brisbane is
a subtropical patchwork of urban villages on the way up.
Whichever city you're wheeling into, you'll never go wanting for an offbeat theatre production, a rockin' live band,
lofty art gallery opening or sweaty music festival mosh pit.

Hungry? Australia's celebrated chefs fuse together

European techniques and fresh Pacific Rim ingredients.
'Mod Oz' (or Modern Australian) is what the locals call it,
and seafood plays a starring role: from succulent Moreton
Bay bugs to delicate King George whiting, there's a lot of
variety in the ocean's bounty. And, of course, beer in hand,
you'll still find beef, lamb and chicken sizzling on traditional Aussie barbecues. Not into beer? From Barossa
Valley shiraz to Hunter Valley semillon, Australian wines
are world-beaters. Need a caffeine hit? These days there
are espresso coffee machines in pubs and petrol stations,
and baristas stationed at downtown coffee carts – you're
never far from a double-shot, day or night.

There's a heck of a lot of tarmac across this wide brown land. The temptation is to hit

the open road and explore, but remember that Australia is
reeeally big! An outback road trip will require some serious
planning and the luxury of time. Alternatively, state capitals
and regional centres are well connected by airlines: with
a little ground work you can cover a good chunk of the
country in just a few weeks.

> 66
>
> The
> temptation
> is to hit
> the open
> road and
> explore ...
>
> 99

Outback road near Alice Springs (p286)

Australia

INDONESIA

Dili
EAST
TIMOR

SAVU
SEA

TIMOR
SEA

ARAFURA
SEA

Melville
Island

Cobourg
Peninsula

Bathurst
Island

Darwin (15)

Nhulunbuy

Jabiru
Kakadu
National
Park

Arnhem
Land

Groote
Eylandt

INDIAN
OCEAN

Cape
Londonderry

Joseph
Bonaparte
Gulf

Katherine

Mataranka

Cape
Leveque

Wyndham

Kununurra

The
Kimberley

Derby

Fitzroy
Crossing

Tennant
Creek

NORTHERN
TERRITORY

Broome

Fitzroy River

Halls
Creek

Port Hedland

Dampier

Karratha

The
Pilbara

WESTERN
AUSTRALIA

MacDonnell Ranges

Alice Springs (22)

North
West
Cape

Exmouth

Newman

Little Sandy
Desert

Gibson
Desert

Uluru-
Kata Tjuta
National Park

(4) Yulara

Simpson

Carnarvon

Shark
Bay

Great
Victoria
Desert

Desert

Marla

Lake Eyre
North

SOUTH
AUSTRALIA

Coober
Pedy

Lake Eyre
South

INDIAN
OCEAN

Geraldton

Nullarbor Plain

Eucla

Ceduna

Port
Augusta

Kalgoorlie-
Boulder

Whyalla

Eyre
Peninsula

Port
Lincoln

Perth

Fremantle (16)

Norseman

Great Australian
Bight

Adelaide

Busselton

Bunbury

Esperance

Margaret River (18)

Cape
Leeuwin

Albany

Kangaroo
Island (14)

ELEVATION

2000m
1500m
1000m
750m
500m
250m
0

N 0 ———— 500 km
   0 ———— 250 miles

SOUTHERN
OCEAN

PAPUA NEW GUINEA

Torres Strait

Thursday Island

Cape York

Port Moresby ✪

SOLOMON ISLANDS

CORAL SEA

Cape York Peninsula

Cape Melville

Gulf of Carpentaria

Normanton

Cooktown

Port Douglas

Cairns

Great Barrier Reef Marine Park ⚓

Innisfail

SOUTH PACIFIC OCEAN

Mt Isa

Cloncurry

Ingham

Charters Towers

Townsville

Bowen

Airlie Beach

Whitsunday Islands

Mackay

Winton

Longreach

Barcaldine

Great Dividing Range

Rockhampton

Gladstone

Great Barrier Reef Marine Park ⚓

Tropic of Capricorn

Birdsville

QUEENSLAND

Charleville

Bundaberg

Hervey Bay

Fraser Island

Noosa

Maroochydore

Toowoomba

St George

Brisbane

Surfers Paradise

Coolangatta

Tweed Heads

Byron Bay

Gold Coast

Bourke

Grafton

Broken Hill

Nyngan

Tamworth

Armidale

Coffs Harbour

NEW SOUTH WALES

Dubbo

Port Macquarie

Flinders Ranges

Darling River

Mildura

Bathurst

Newcastle

Lord Howe Island (NSW)

Hay

Cowra

Katoomba

Sydney

Wagga Wagga

Wollongong

Murray Bridge

Swan Hill

VICTORIA

Murray River

Albury

Canberra

Batemans Bay

Mt Gambier

Horsham

Wodonga

Ballarat

Geelong

Melbourne

Warrnambool

Wilsons Promontory

King Island

Bass Strait

Flinders Island

TASMAN SEA

Devonport

Launceston

Queenstown

TASMANIA

Hobart

140°E 145°E 150°E 155°E 160°E

25 Top Highlights

1 Sydney Opera House

2 Great Barrier Reef

3 Melbourne

4 Uluru-Kata Tjuta National Park

5 MONA, Hobart

6 Daintree Rainforest

7 Byron Bay

8 Great Ocean Road

9 The Whitsundays

10 Bridge Climbing, Sydney

11 Gold Coast

12 Canberra's Museums & Galleries

13 Wilsons Promontory

14 Kangaroo Island

15 Darwin & Kakadu National Park

16 Perth & Fremantle

17 Learning to Surf, Byron Bay

18 Margaret River

19 Cradle Mountain

20 Sporting Obsessions, Melbourne

21 Native Wildlife, Phillip Island

22 Indigenous Art, Central Australia

23 Fraser Island

24 Bushwalking, Blue Mountains

25 Gourmet Food, Wine & Beer, Tasmania

25 Australia's Top Highlights

Sydney Opera House

Magnificent Sydney Opera House (p70) on Sydney Harbour is a headline act in itself. Jørn Utzon's building on Circular Quay's Bennelong Point more than holds its own amid the visual feast of the harbour's attention-grabbing bridge, shimmering blue waters and jaunty green ferries. Best of all, everyone can experience the magic on offer here – a waterside bar, acclaimed French restaurant, guided tours and star-studded performance schedule make sure of that.

JAMES R D. SCOTT/GETTY IMAGES ©

②

Great Barrier Reef

The Great Barrier Reef (p176) is jaw-droppingly beautiful. Stretching more than 2000km along the Queensland coastline, it's a complex ecosystem populated with dazzling coral, languid sea turtles, gliding rays, timid reef sharks and tropical fish of every colour and size. Whether you dive it, snorkel it or explore it via scenic flight or glass-bottom boat, this vivid undersea kingdom – and its coral-fringed islands – is unforgettable. Pink anemonefish

Melbourne

The next best restaurant/chef/cafe/barista/food truck may be the talk of the town, but there are things locals here would never change: the leafy parks and gardens in the inner city 'burbs; the clunky trams that whisk creative northerners to sea-breezy St Kilda; and the allegiances that living in such a sport-mad city brings. The city's (p216) famed street-art scene expresses Melburnians' fears, frustrations and joys. Centre Place

The Best...
Big-City Coffee Spots

FRATELLI PARADISO
Sydney-sexy staff and fab espresso: Rome ain't so far away... (p86)

PELLEGRINI'S ESPRESSO BAR
Melbourne's original (and still the best) espresso bar has serious cred (p233)

BREW
Caffeine fiends head down this Brisbane laneway (p146)

LITTLE WILLY'S
Our pick for a hip coffee hit in Perth (p312)

DAVID HILL/GETTY IMAGES ©

13

The Best...
Museums

4 Uluru-Kata Tjuta National Park

With its remote desert location, deep cultural significance and spectacular natural beauty, Uluru (Ayers Rock) is a pilgrimage well worth the hundreds of kilometres it takes to get here. But Uluru-Kata Tjuta National Park (p290) offers much more than the chance to see the Rock. Along with the equally captivating Kata Tjuta (the Olgas), there are mystical walks, sublime sunsets and ancient desert cultures to encounter. Uluru (Ayers Rock)

5 MONA, Hobart

A ferry ride from Hobart's harbourfront, the Museum of Old & New Art (MONA; p351) is an innovative world-class institution. Described as a 'subversive adult Disneyland', three levels of spectacular underground galleries showcase more than 400 often-challenging and controversial works of art. It's guaranteed that intense debate and conversation will be on the agenda after viewing one of Australia's unique arts experiences.

Daintree Rainforest

Lush green rainforest tumbles down towards brilliant white-sand coastline in the ancient World Heritage–listed Daintree Rainforest (p197). Upon entering the forest you'll be enveloped by birdsong and the buzz of insects. Continue exploring via wildlife-spotting tours, mountain treks, interpretive boardwalks, canopy walks, 4WD trips, horse riding, kayaking and cruises.

Byron Bay

Byron Bay (just Byron to its mates; p126) is one of the enduring icons of Australian culture. Families on school holidays, surfers and sun-seekers from around the globe gather by the foreshore at sunset, drawn to this spot by fabulous restaurants, a chilled pace of life, beaches and an astonishing range of activities. This is one of the most beautiful stretches of coast in the country. Wategos Beach

Great Ocean Road

The Twelve Apostles – rock formations jutting out of wild waters – are one of Victoria's most dramatic sights, but it's the 'getting there' road trip (p249) that doubles their impact. Curl along roads beside spectacular Bass Strait beaches, then whip inland through rainforests alive with small towns and big trees. Further along is maritime treasure Port Fairy.

Twelve Apostles, Port Campbell (p257)

8

The Best...
Beaches

BONDI BEACH
Big, wide and handsome, Bondi is Australia's most famous beach (p74)

AVALON
The pick of Sydney's northern beaches: a dreamy arc of orange sand with solid surf (p77)

COTTESLOE BEACH
Perth's best beach is a good time waiting to happen (p307)

LITTLE WATEGOS
A Byron Bay gem: mainland Australia's most easterly beach (p126)

BELLS BEACH
A wild Southern Ocean beach with brilliant (if unreliable) surf (p252)

MANFRED GOTTSCHALK/GETTY IMAGES ©

The Whitsundays

You can hop around a whole stack of tropical islands in this seafaring life and never find anywhere with the sheer tropical beauty of the Whitsundays (p179). Travellers of all monetary persuasions launch yachts from party town Airlie Beach and drift between these lush green isles in a slow search for paradise (you'll probably find it in more than one place). Wish you were here? Hamilton Island (p185)

The Best...
Markets

RICHARD I'ANSON/GETTY IMAGES ®

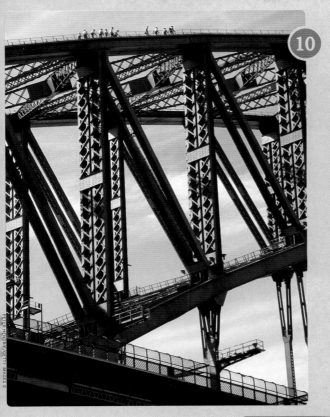

Bridge Climbing, Sydney

Got a good head for heights? Make a beeline for Sydney's iconic Harbour Bridge or Brisbane's Storey Bridge and climb above it all. Sydney's BridgeClimb (p62) has been sending intrepid visitors over the grand arch for more than a decade: the views from the top are predictably sublime. Story Bridge Adventure Climb (p145) is a newer experience but no less mesmerising. And it's not just about views – the bridges themselves are epic structures. Climbing Sydney Harbour Bridge

10

PETER HENDRIE/GETTY IMAGES ©

Gold Coast

Brash, trashy, hedonistic, over-hyped... Queensland's Gold Coast (p132) is all of these things, but if you're looking for a party, bring it on! Beyond the fray is the beach – an improbably gorgeous coastline of clean sand, warm water and peeling surf breaks. The bronzed gods of the surf, Australia's surf life-savers, patrol the sand and pit their skills against one another in surf carnivals. Also here are Australia's biggest theme parks – rollercoaster nirvana!

11

© GERARD/GETTY IMAGES ©

Canberra's Museums & Galleries

Though Canberra (p342) is only a century old, Australia's purpose-built capital has always been preoccupied with history. So it's not surprising that the major drawcards here are lavishly endowed museums and galleries that focus on recounting and interpreting the national narrative. Institutions such as the National Gallery of Australia, National Museum of Australia, National Portrait Gallery and Australian War Memorial offer visitors a fascinating insight into the country's history and culture. National Museum of Australia

Wilsons Promontory

Victoria's southernmost point and finest coastal national park, Wilsons Promontory (or just 'the Prom'; p258) is heaven for bushwalkers, wildlife watchers, surfers and photographers. The scenery here is out of this world: even short walks from the main base at Tidal River will reveal views of stunning beaches and bays. But with more than 80km of marked walking trails, the best of the Prom requires some serious footwork. Tidal River

Kangaroo Island

Kangaroo Island (or just 'KI'; p345) is a big place – 150km long and 57km wide. Plenty of room for the local wildlife to run amok! You'll see kangaroos (of course), plus wallabies, bandicoots, possums, koalas, platypuses, cockatoos, dolphins, whales, penguins and seals. After you're done wildlife spotting, there are country pubs, wineries and seafood shacks to keep you fed and watered. Flinders Chase National Park (p346)

14

The Best...
Eat Streets

BRUNSWICK ST, MELBOURNE
Wall-to-wall cafes and restaurants in inner-city Fitzroy. There are some great pubs around here too! (p229)

CHINATOWN, SYDNEY
Pan-Asian delights for just a few dollars (p85)

BOUNDARY ST, WEST END, BRISBANE
Cafes, bars and book-shops – the three pillars of society (p146)

MITCHELL ST, DARWIN
Backpacker bars and crowded street ter-races overflow with edibles (p276)

The Best...
Indigenous Cultural Experiences

KAKADU ROCK ART
Check out the amazing rock art galleries at Ubirr and Nourlangie in Kakadu National Park (p281)

ALICE SPRINGS
Explore 'the Alice' and nearby MacDonnell Ranges with a local Warlpiri guide (p286)

ULURU-KATA TJUTA CULTURAL CENTRE
Understand local Aboriginal law, custom and religion on Uluru's doorstep (p290)

INGAN TOURS
Aboriginal tours from Mission Beach in Tropical North Queensland (p186)

INDIGENOUS ART GALLERIES, DARWIN
Close to the source, Darwin's commercial art galleries sell gorgeous Indigenous art (p279)

15

Darwin & Kakadu National Park

This frontier city (p270) has emerged from the tropical steam to become a multicultural, hedonistic hotspot: the launch pad for trips into some of Australia's most remarkable wilderness. Two hours southeast down the highway, Kakadu National Park (p281) is the place to see Indigenous rock art under jagged escarpments and idyllic waterholes at the base of plummeting waterfalls. Raucous birdlife and saltwater crocodiles are guaranteed highlights. Left: Maguk (Barramundi Gorge), Kakadu National Park; Above: Mindil Beach Sunset Market, Darwin (p275)

ABOVE: DANITA DELIMONT/GETTY IMAGES ©; LEFT: BETHUNE CARMICHAEL/GETTY IMAGES ©

Perth & Fremantle

Perth (p306) may be isolated, but it's far from being a backwater. Sophisticated restaurants fly the flag for modern Australian cuisine and chic cocktail bars linger in hidden laneways. Perth's more bohemian inner suburbs echo with the thrum of guitars and the sizzle of woks. Just down the river, the pubs of laidback Fremantle (p319) serve some of Western Australia's finest craft beers, and colonial buildings punctuate a glorious Victorian townscape. Fremantle

Learning to Surf, Byron Bay

Whenever the swell is working, Australia's beaches fill with flotillas of rubber-suited people, bobbing around in the surf. Learning to surf is an Australian rite of passage – if you feel like joining in, Byron Bay (p126) has a few good learn-to-surf schools. You can also learn some skills at Noosa in Queensland, Bondi and Manly beaches in Sydney, and Anglesea on Victoria's Great Ocean Road. The Pass, Byron Bay

Margaret River

The joy of drifting from winery to winery along country roads shaded by tall gum trees is only one of the delights of Margaret River (p328) in Western Australia's south-west. There are also caves to explore, historic towns to visit and spring wildflowers to admire. Surfers flock to world-class breaks around 'Margs', but it's not unusual to find yourself on a brilliant white-sand beach and nobody else in sight.

The Best...
Live Music Venues

NORTHCOTE SOCIAL CLUB
A suburban Melbourne pub that's become the cty's best music venue (p242)

BENNETTS LANE
Hip, jazzy hot-spot down a central Melbourne laneway (p242)

MOJO'S
Timeless rock room in Fremantle, Western Australia (p325)

VENUE 505
Sydney's best little jazz bar (p98)

Cradle Mountain

A precipitous comb of rock carved out by millennia of ice and wind, crescent-shaped Cradle Mountain (p352) is Tasmania's most recognisable – and spectacular – mountain peak. It's an all-day walk (and boulder scramble) to the summit and back, for unbelievable panoramas over Tasmania's alpine heart. If the peak has disappeared in clouds or snow, warm yourself by the fire in one of the nearby lodges...and come back tomorrow.

JOHN WHITE PHOTOS/GETTY IMAGES ©

The Best...
Shopping

QUEEN VICTORIA BUILDING
Wow, what a beauty! Downtown Sydney's Victorian shopping masterpiece (p100)

QUEEN VICTORIA MARKET
Melbourne's freshest fish, meat and fruit 'n' veg, plus a fab night market on Wednesday in summer (p220)

PADDINGTON & WOOLLAHRA
Dandy designer duds along Sydney's Oxford St, Glenmore Rd and Queen St (p99)

ADELAIDE CENTRAL MARKET
Roam these indoor market aisles for dazzling foodie delights (p344)

TIM BARKER/GETTY IMAGES ©

20 Sporting Obsessions, Melbourne

Australia is sports mad! The pinnacle of the Australian Rules football season is the AFL (Australian Football League) Grand Final in Melbourne in late September. Melbourne (p216) also hosts the Australian Open tennis (January), the Australian Formula One Grand Prix (March) and the Melbourne Cup horse race (November). In Queensland and New South Wales, catch a National Rugby League (NRL) match. And – anywhere – watching big-screen sport in a pub is an essential experience. AFL match, Melbourne Cricket Ground (p221)

Native Wildlife, Phillip Island

Head to Phillip Island (p247) southeast of Melbourne for adorable little penguins and fur seals, and north for otherworldly cassowaries and dinosaur-like crocodiles. In between, you'll find a panoply of extraordinary animals found nowhere else on earth: koalas, kangaroos, wombats and platypuses. There's great whale watching along the coast, plus the omnipresent cackle of the laughing kookaburra. Blue-winged kookaburra

Indigenous Art, Central Australia

Indigenous art (p369) is a conduit between past and present, supernatural and earthly, people and land. Central Australian dot paintings are exquisite, as are Tiwi Island wood carvings and fabrics, Arnhem Land bark paintings and Torres Strait Islander prints, weavings and carvings. Most large galleries around Australia have Indigenous collections, or make an informed purchase at a commercial gallery. Central Land Council office mural, Tennant Creek

Fraser Island

Fraser Island (p159) is an ecological wonderland created by drifting sand, where wild dogs roam free and lush rainforest grows on sand. It's a primal island utopia, home to a profusion of wildlife. The best way to explore the island is in a 4WD – cruising up the seemingly endless Seventy-Five Mile Beach and bouncing along sandy inland tracks.

The Best...
Wildlife Spotting

GREAT BARRIER REEF
Turtles, dolphins, whales and fish, fish, fish... A reef trip is a submarine spectacular! (p197)

KAKADU NATIONAL PARK
Spot crocs here, plus more birds than you've had feather pillows (p281)

THE OTWAYS
Look for koalas in the Otway forests along Victoria's Great Ocean Road (p256)

AUSTRALIA ZOO
Short on time? Check out Australia's iconic animals at southeast Queensland's popular zoo (p156)

Bushwalking, Blue Mountains

Tramping, trekking, rambling and hiking are what you do overseas – here it's called bushwalking. Whether it's a stroll in the Blue Mountains (p107) or a hike through Tasmania's wilderness, Australia has it all. There are seriously long walks across the expanses of Western Australia and South Australia, and some seriously hard tracks (anywhere in the southwest Tasmanian wilderness). But on a short holiday, zoom in on the easy afternoon or day walks that can be reached by public transport from the cities. Hanging Rock, Blue Mountains

The Best...
National Parks

ULURU-KATA TJUTA NATIONAL PARK
Big rocks, big sky, big road trip! (p290)

KAKADU NATIONAL PARK
Top End tropical wilderness with birdlife, wetlands, crocodiles and Aboriginal rock-art galleries (p281)

SYDNEY HARBOUR NATIONAL PARK
Islands, sandstone cliffs and magical walking trails (p60)

DAINTREE NATIONAL PARK
Tropical jungle, butterflies and empty white-sand beaches (p202)

CRADLE MOUNTAIN-LAKE ST CLAIR NATIONAL PARK
Alpine wilderness with icy lakes, peaks and epic walking trails (p352)

RICHARD I'ANSON/GETTY IMAGES ©

25

Gourmet Food, Wine & Beer, Tasmania

Across Australia you'll find gourmet offerings for all budgets: cool-climate wines and cheeses in Tasmania (p349), coffee and fab Greek and Italian in Melbourne, oysters and seafood in Sydney, punchy wines in South Australia, marron in Western Australia, and native meats and bush tucker in the Northern Territory. Foodie heaven! The nation's many wine regions have spawned a culture of fine cuisine using regional ingredients. And if beer is your poison, the Aussie craft beer scene is brewing. Food festival, Hobart

Australia's Top Itineraries

Sydney to the Blue Mountains

5 DAYS

Big City, Big Wilderness

With only five days and jet lag weighing in, focus on Sydney's must-see sights, get out onto Sydney Harbour, unwind at the beach and taste the Australian bush in the Blue Mountains, west of Sydney.

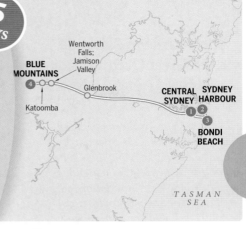

❶ Central Sydney (p60)

Arriving in Sydney, take a few days to get to know Australia's first city. Take a city tour and cross the Sydney Harbour Bridge. If you've booked ahead, tackle the famous BridgeClimb before exploring the historic Rocks and Circular Quay. Dine in a harbourside restaurant, then catch a show at the Sydney Opera House.

CENTRAL SYDNEY ➲ SYDNEY HARBOUR

🛥 **One to three hours** Harbour cruises. 🛥 **30 minutes** Ferry to Manly.

❷ Sydney Harbour (p60)

Find your sea legs on a harbour cruise past sandy coves, islands and harbourfront real estate. Catch the ferry to Manly for a swim, lunch or a surfing lesson. Check out shady Nielsen Park and Shark Bay in Vaucluse, then wander out to the Gap at the entrance to Sydney Harbour for some clifftop views.

SYDNEY HARBOUR ➲ BONDI BEACH

🚗 **30 minutes** From downtown Sydney along Oxford St, then Bondi Rd. 🚆 **15 minutes** To Bondi Junction, then 🚌 **15 minutes** to Bondi Beach.

❸ Bondi Beach (p74)

Cruise out to world-famous, glamorous Bondi Beach for a chilled-out day of sun, sand and surf. If you're feeling chipper, propel yourself along the Bondi to Coogee Coastal Walk (allow about two hours, with a few stops), featuring eye-popping coastal views and plenty of places for a swim, some lunch or a pick-me-up coffee.

BONDI BEACH ➲ BLUE MOUNTAINS

🚗 **Two hours** Along Parramatta Rd, then the M4 Western Motorway. 🚆 **2.5 hours** From Bondi Junction to Katoomba.

❹ Blue Mountains (p107)

The Blue Mountains are Sydney's over-grown backyard: hop on a tour, catch a train or hire a car for maximum flexibility. Stop in foothills town Glenbrook to see some Aboriginal hand stencils, then go camera crazy at Jamison Valley and Wentworth Falls. Continue to the moody Katoomba, with its gourmet delights and atmospheric accommodation. Scan the hazy horizon from Echo Point, or sign up for some hiking, canyoning or rock climbing.

Bondi Beach (p74)
RICHARD I'ANSON/GETTY IMAGES ©

33

5 DAYS

Melbourne to Adelaide via the Great Ocean Road
Southern Scenic

Melbourne, city of substance: gritty, arty, complex and unfailingly authentic. Spend a few days digging its vibe, then head south for a classic road trip along the Great Ocean Road. Beyond, refined Adelaide and world-class wine regions await.

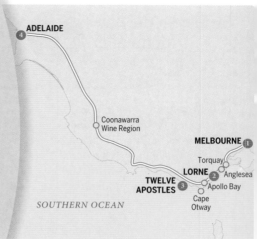

ADELAIDE

Coonawarra Wine Region

MELBOURNE

Torquay

LORNE

TWELVE APOSTLES

Anglesea

Apollo Bay

Cape Otway

SOUTHERN OCEAN

1 Melbourne (p216)

A burgeoning bayside city of four million-plus people, Melbourne is famous for the arts, Aussie Rules football and exemplary coffee. This is an introspective city: a place to visit bookshops, go to the theatre, eat, drink and talk. Spend a couple of days exploring the cafes and bars hidden in the downtown laneways, and the art galleries, shops and multicultural restaurants. Don't miss a night out on arty Brunswick St in Fitzroy, and another in tarty St Kilda by the bay.

MELBOURNE ○ LORNE

🚗 **Two hours** Along the Princes Fwy (M1) and the Great Ocean Road (B100), via Torquay. 🚌 **2.5 hours** Along the same route.

2 Lorne (p253)

The gateway to the scenic Great Ocean Road is Torquay, a hip surf town dotted with surf-apparel shops and a surf museum. Not far away is the legendary Bells Beach, which featured (in name only) alongside Keanu Reeves and Patrick Swayze in *Point Break*. Continuing west, you'll pass laid-back Anglesea, where you can launch into a surf lesson; and then Lorne, a long-time holiday spot for Melburnians. The beach here is perfect for a swim, after which have lunch at one of the eateries along the main drag.

LORNE ○ TWELVE APOSTLES

🚗 **Two hours** Head west along the Great Ocean Road (B100), via Apollo Bay. 🚌 **Three hours** Along the same route.

3 Twelve Apostles (p257)

Heading west, the Great Ocean Road turns on some sublime scenery, twisting and turning above the surf-strewn coastline. Apollo Bay is a thriving beach town with some decent eateries, a busy pub and solid surf – a good spot to stop for the night. The next day, continue west to Port Campbell National Park and the highlight of the Great Ocean Road – the jagged rock formations of the Twelve Apostles.

TWELVE APOSTLES ○ ADELAIDE

🚗 **Seven hours** Along the Great Ocean Road (B100) and the Dukes Hwy (A8). 🚌 **12 hours** Along the same route.

4 Adelaide (p344)

Truck west across the border into South Australia (SA), stopping to sip some cabernet sauvignon in the famed Coonawarra Wine Region. The Big Smoke here is Adelaide (population 1.26 million), a dignified capital famed for festivals and the arts, and central to some terrific wine regions including the Barossa Valley and McLaren Vale. Get a taste for SA wine at the excellent National Wine Centre of Australia in the city.

Federation Square (p229), Melbourne

10 DAYS

Sydney to Brisbane & the East Coast Beaches
Coastal Cruise

Fire-up the Kombi, strap your surfboard to the roof and cruise into an Endless Summer. This stretch of Australia's east coast has consistent waves and cheery surf communities. En route are quirky hinterland towns and fab national parks.

NOOSA **5**

BRISBANE **4**
Surfers Paradise
Springbrook National Park **3** GOLD COAST
Nimbin
Bangalow **2** BYRON BAY

SOUTH
PACIFIC
OCEAN

Hunter Valley

SYDNEY **1**

① Sydney (p60)

Start with the bright lights of Sydney: don't miss the sparkling harbour, gorgeous Sydney Opera House and impressive Sydney Harbour Bridge. For bird's-eye city views, tackle the BridgeClimb over the grand grey arch. Warm up your surfing muscles at the quintessentially Australian Bondi Beach. After two days, meander north along the coast or detour to the Hunter Valley for some vino-quaffing before wheeling north into Byron Bay.

SYDNEY ⊙ BYRON BAY

🚗 **10 hours** Along Sydney–Newcastle Fwy, then Pacific Hwy (Route 1). 🚃 **12.5 hours** Along the same route.

② Byron Bay (p126)

Despite big development arriving from the north and south, Byron Bay remains a happy hippie town with great pubs, restaurants, beaches and the famous Pass point break. Don't miss small-town detours inland to photogenic Bangalow and Australia's quasi-mythical alt-lifestyle hangout, Nimbin. Continue north a couple of hours to the glitzy Gold Coast.

BYRON BAY ⊙ GOLD COAST

🚗 **1.5 hours** Via Pacific Hwy (Route 1). 🚃 **Two hours** Along the same route.

③ Gold Coast (p132)

Crossing into Queensland you'll soon hit the glam Gold Coast. First stop is surf-lifesaving mecca Coolangatta, then beautiful Burleigh Heads – on the rocky headland south of town is the tiny but lush Burleigh Head National Park. Inland, detour to Springbrook National Park for high-plateau waterfalls and lookouts. Back down at sea level, Surfers Paradise looms as a slightly unnerving cityscape on the horizon. Stop if you like casinos and theme parks, or continue north to the easygoing river city of Brisbane.

GOLD COAST ⊙ BRISBANE

🚗 **1.25 hours** Via Pacific Motorway (M1). 🚃 **1.5 hours** Along the same route.

④ Brisbane (p139)

Once a sleepy country town, Brisbane (aka 'Brisvegas') is now a boom town, growing so fast that it can be difficult to navigate. Urban charms (great dining, nightlife, hip neighbourhoods and the arts) meld seamlessly with leafy riverside parks. Spend a day or two, then head north to the Sunshine Coast and jewel-like Noosa.

BRISBANE ⊙ NOOSA

🚗 **Two hours** Via Bruce Hwy (M1) then Eumundi–Noosa Rd (Route 12). 🚃 **2.5 hours** Along the same route.

⑤ Noosa (p155)

Noosa really is a paradise: fabulous restaurants along Hastings St, slow-rolling surf beaches and dense national park forest. Wind up your safari with a glass of wine and a toast to 'Huey', the God of Good Surf.

Noosa beach (p157)

Port Douglas ○
CAIRNS ④ ⑤ **GREAT BARRIER REEF**
CORAL SEA
Airlie Beach ○ ③ **WHITSUNDAY ISLANDS**
② **SYDNEY**
TASMAN SEA
① **MELBOURNE**

Melbourne to the Great Barrier Reef
East Coast Classic

This classic south–north run takes in thousands of kilometres of Aussie coastline. It could take a lifetime or, with a handful of airline tickets, you can sample the best of the east coast in just 10 days.

① Melbourne (p216)

Kick-start your trip in the southern capital of Melbourne, a hip city famous for its live music, multicultural mix and sporting obsessions. Dip into the inner city's bohemian arts scene, linger in cafe-colonised laneways, catch a live band or watch a game of Aussie Rules football during winter. Swing into Chinatown for some dumplings or play gourmand among the food stalls of the Queen Victoria Market.

MELBOURNE ⊙ SYDNEY

✈ **One hour** Melbourne's Tullamarine Airport to Sydney Airport.

② Sydney (p60)

Next stop is bright 'n' breezy Sydney: take a couple of days to do it justice. Must-dos include a Sydney Harbour cruise, a stroll around Darling Harbour and Chinatown, and a plunge into the famous waves of Bondi Beach. If you're feeling arty, check out the Art Gallery of NSW, or just snooze in the sun in the nearby Royal Botanic Gardens. On your final night, hit the bright lights and bars around Darlinghurst and Kings Cross, or book a restaurant with spotlit views of the Sydney Harbour Bridge and Sydney Opera House.

SYDNEY ⊙ WHITSUNDAY ISLANDS

✈ **2.5 hours** Sydney Airport to Hamilton Island.

③ Whitsunday Islands (p179)

To access the sublime Whitsunday Islands, hop a flight to Proserpine near party town

Airlie Beach, or fly direct to hedonistic Hamilton Island. Spend a day or two island-hopping under a billowing sail, reef diving or snorkelling, or just kicking back by a resort pool.

WHITSUNDAY ISLANDS ⊙ CAIRNS

✈ **1.5 hours** Hamilton Island to Cairns.

④ Cairns & Port Douglas (p188)

Catch another flight to Cairns, Far North Queensland's tourist mecca. All the urban trappings are here, or you can day-trip into the Daintree Rainforest, take a scenic railway ride through the rainforest to hippie Kuranda, or take a 90-minute drive further north to Port Douglas, a ritzy tropical town with top-notch eateries and accommodation.

CAIRNS/PORT DOUGLAS ⊙ GREAT BARRIER REEF

⚓ **8 hours** Return day-trip from Cairns or Port Douglas.

⑤ Great Barrier Reef (p176)

Of course, no visit to tropical Far North Queensland would be complete without visiting the Great Barrier Reef. From Cairns or Port Douglas you can boat-tour out to see the amazing coral and scuba dive, strap on a snorkel or just peer through a glass-bottomed boat. Astonishing!

Mossman Gorge (p203), Daintree National Park
RICHARD I'ANSON/GETTY IMAGES ©

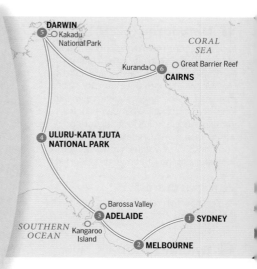

Sydney to the Great Barrier Reef
Cities, Deserts & Tropics

Domestic flights will cover the vast distances across Australia. This journey runs from the big east-coast cities through the red desert heart, up to the tropical Top End then across to Cairns and the Great Barrier Reef.

1 Sydney (p60)

Kick things off in show-stopping Sydney – bright lights, big city! A tour of Sydney Opera House will take you inside this iconic building, or see it from the water on a leisurely harbour cruise. Check out Darling Harbour with its swath of attractions, go shopping in Paddington, or take a guided city tour to see the big-ticket sights. History buffs will get a kick out of the Rocks, Hyde Park Barracks Museum and the Museum of Sydney, while those keen for a surf should head straight for the beaches: famous Bondi, low-key Manly or the chilled-out Northern Beaches.

SYDNEY ⟶ MELBOURNE

✈ **One hour** Sydney Airport to Melbourne's Tullamarine Airport.

2 Melbourne (p216)

Fly south to the Victorian capital of Melbourne: on one side a sophisticate, with leafy parks, elaborate Victorian architecture and distinguished theatres, museums and galleries; and on the other savvy and street-wise, with hip street art, an independent music scene and laneway coffee culture all its own.

MELBOURNE ⟶ ADELAIDE

✈ **One hour** Melbourne to Adelaide. 🚆 **11 hours** *The Overland* train Melbourne to Adelaide.

3 Adelaide (p344)

Winging into Adelaide in South Australia, spend a day exploring the elegantly spread-out sandstone capital, or detour an hour north to the legendary Barossa Valley, one of the world's great wine regions. Cellar doors offer tastings, and there's a slew of quality eateries here for lunch or dinner. An overnight trip south of Adelaide will deliver you to Kangaroo Island, an undeveloped and underrated haven for native wildlife.

ADELAIDE ⟶ ULURU-KATA TJUTA NATIONAL PARK

✈ **4.5 hours** Adelaide to Uluru (flights via Alice Springs). 🚆 **19 hours** *The Ghan* train from Adelaide to Alice Springs, then fly to Uluru (45 minutes).

4 Uluru-Kata Tjuta National Park (p290)

Enough of the wild things and wine? Jump on a flight to Uluru-Kata Tjuta National Park

⑤ **Darwin** (p270)

Wing your way north to the youthful, exuberant, tropical capital of Darwin, where you can eat a curry or a kebab at Mindil Beach Sunset Market, get wobbly on Mitchell St after dark, and organise an overnight tour to the World Heritage–listed Kakadu National Park, a wetland of international significance rich with Aboriginal rock art, birdlife and crocodiles.

DARWIN ➡ CAIRNS

✈ **2.5 hours** Darwin to Cairns.

⑥ **Cairns** (p188)

Flying back east, next stop is tropical Cairns, an effervescent base for the amazing sights and activities of Far North Queensland. Dangle above the rainforest on the Skyrail Rainforest Cableway en route to the markets at nearby Kuranda, or just let it all hang out on the local tropical beaches. Make the most of your day-trip to the Great Barrier Reef with a snorkel or scuba dive. Some international flights leave from Cairns, but chances are you'll have to backtrack to Sydney: time for one more swim at Bondi?

and be moved by the commanding bulk of monolithic Uluru. You've seen the photos and the TV shows, but there's nothing quite like seeing an Uluru sunset firsthand. Nearby Kata-Tjuta (the Olgas) is just as impressive (and, in fact, a taller geologic formation): walk among the imposing red domes through the Valley of the Winds.

ULURU-KATA TJUTA NATIONAL PARK ➡ DARWIN

✈ **45 minutes** Uluru to Alice Springs, then **two hours** Alice Springs to Darwin.

Month by Month

Top Events

⚝ **Adelaide Fringe**, February

⚝ **Sydney Gay & Lesbian Mardi Gras**, March

⚝ **Melbourne International Film Festival**, July

⚝ **Tropfest**, February

⚝ **AFL Grand Final**, September

January

⚝ Sydney Festival

(www.sydneyfestival.org.au) 'It's big' says the promo material. Indeed, sprawling over three summer weeks, this fab affiliation of music, dance, talks, theatre and visual arts (much of it free and family-focussed) is an artistic behemoth.

⚝ Big Day Out

(www.bigdayout.com) This touring one-day alt-rock festival visits Sydney, Melbourne, Adelaide, Perth and the Gold Coast. It features a huge line-up of big-name international artists (previously Metallica, The Killers and Red Hot Chili Peppers have appeared) and plenty of home-grown talent. Think moshing, sun and beer.

⚝ MONA FOMA

(www.mofo.net.au) Brian Ritchie, bass player with the Violent Femmes, pulls the curatorial strings as MONA's adventurous spirit inspires Tasmania's annual celebration of eclectic and exciting art, music and culture. Launched in June 2013, Dark MOFO is the festival's moody winter sibling.

⚝ Tamworth Country Music Festival

(www.tamworthcountrymusicfestival.com.au) This late-January hoedown in northern New South Wales (NSW) is all about big hats, golden guitars and some of the finest country music you'll hear this side of Nashville, Tennessee (mostly Australian acts, with a few world-class internationals).

⚝ Australia Day

(www.australia-day.com) Australia's 'birthday' (when the First Fleet landed in 1788) is 26 January, and Australians celebrate with picnics, barbecues, fireworks and, increasingly, nationalistic flag-waving, drunkenness and

March Sydney Gay & Lesbian Mardi Gras
RICHARD KENDALL/GETTY IMAGES ©

chest-beating. In less mood to celebrate are Indigenous Australians, who refer to it as Invasion Day or Survival Day.

 # February

Tropfest

(www.tropfest.com.au) The world's largest short-film festival happens on Sydney's grassy Domain one Sunday in late February. To discourage cheating and inspire creativity, a compulsory prop appears in each entry (eg kiss, sneeze, balloon). Free screenings and celeb judges (Joseph Fiennes, Salma Hayek).

Adelaide Fringe

(www.adelaidefringe.com.au) All the acts that don't make the cut (or don't want to) for the more highbrow Adelaide Festival end up in the month-long Fringe, second only to Edinburgh's version. Hyperactive comedy, music and circus acts spill from the Garden of Unearthly Delights in the parklands.

 # March

 Sydney Gay & Lesbian Mardi Gras

(www.mardigras.org.au) A month-long arts festival culminating in a flamboyant parade along Sydney's Oxford St on the first Saturday in March attracts 300,000 spectators. Gyms empty out, solariums darken, waxing emporiums tally their profits. After-party tickets are gold.

WOMADelaide

(www.womadelaide.com.au) Annual festival of world music, arts, food and dance, held over four days in Adelaide's luscious Botanic Park, attracting crowds from around Australia. Eight stages host hundreds of acts. It's very family friendly and you can get a cold beer too.

 # April

Apollo Bay Music Festival

(www.apollobaymusicfestival.com) On the gorgeous Great Ocean Road southwest of Melbourne (just far enough to make it an overnighter), this alt-pop, left-field fest spreads itself out along the foreshore. The town's churches, halls, and cafes become performance venues.

 # May

Whale Watching

Between May and October along the southeastern Australian coast, migrating southern right and humpback whales come close to shore to feed, breed and calf. See them at Hervey Bay (Queensland), Warrnambool (Victoria), Victor Harbor (South Australia), Albany (WA) and North Stradbroke Island (Queensland).

 # June

Laura Aboriginal Dance Festival

(www.lauradancefestival.com) Sleepy Laura, 330km north of Cairns on the Cape York Peninsula in Far North Queensland, hosts the largest traditional Indigenous gathering in Australia. Communities from the region come together for dance, song and ceremony. The Laura Races and Rodeo happen the following weekend.

Ski Season

(www.ski.com.au) When winter blows in (June to August), snow bunnies and powder hounds dust off their skis and snowboards and make for the mountains. Victoria and NSW have the key resorts; there are a couple of small runs in Tasmania too.

 # August

 Cairns Festival

(www.cairns.qld.gov.au/festival) Running for three weeks from late August to early September, this massive art-and-culture fest brings a stellar program of music, theatre, dance, comedy, film, Indigenous art and public exhibitions. Outdoor events held in public plazas, parks and gardens make good use of Cairns' tropical setting.

 # September

 Brisbane Festival

(www.brisbanefestival.com.au) One of Australia's largest and most diverse arts festivals runs for 22 days in September and features an impressive line-up of concerts, plays, dance performances and fringe events around the city. It finishes off with 'Riverfire', an elaborate fireworks show over the river.

 Aussie Rules Grand Final

(www.afl.com.au) The pinnacle of the Australian Rules football season is this high-flying spectacle in Melbourne, watched (on TV) by millions of impassioned Aussies. Tickets to the game are scarce, but at half-time everyone's neighbourhood BBQ moves into the local park for a little amateur kick-to-kick.

October

Jazz in the Vines

(www.jazzinthevines.com.au) There are lots of food-and-wine festivals like this across Australia's wine regions (Barossa, McLaren Vale, Yarra Valley...). The Hunter Valley's proximity to the Sydney jazz

 # July

 Melbourne International Film Festival

(MIFF; www.miff.com.au) Right up there with Toronto and Cannes, MIFF has been running since 1952 and has grown into a wildly popular event; tickets sell like piping-hot chestnuts in the inner city. Myriad short films, feature-length spectaculars and documentaries flicker across city screens every winter.

Beer Can Regatta

(www.beercanregatta.org.au) The Northern Territory festival calendar is studded with quirky gems like this one at Darwin's Mindil Beach, where hundreds of 'boats' constructed from empty beer cans race across the shallows. Much drinking and laughter: staying afloat is a secondary concern.

scene ensures a top line-up at Tyrrell's Vineyard.

November

Melbourne Cup

(www.melbournecup.com) On the first Tuesday in November, Australia's (if not the world's) premier horse race chews up the turf in Melbourne. Country towns schedule racing events to coincide with the day and the country does actually pause to watch the 'race that stops a nation'.

Margaret River Gourmet Escape

(www.gourmetescape.com.au) Western Australia's contribution to the national circuit of fine food-and-wine fests. The line-up of celebrity chefs is impressive: dozens of culinary doyens plating up seriously good food. But it's the Margaret River wines that really steal the show.

◉ Sculpture by the Sea

(www.sculpturebythesea.com) In mid-November the clifftop trail from Bondi Beach to Tamarama in Sydney transforms into an exquisite sculpture garden. Serious prize money is on offer for the most creative, curious or quizzical offerings from international and local sculptors. Also happens on Perth's Cottesloe Beach in March.

December

✈ Sydney to Hobart Yacht Race

(www.rolexsydneyhobart.com) On Boxing Day, Sydney Harbour churns with competitors and onlookers for the start of the world's most arduous open-ocean yacht race (628 nautical miles!). When the yachties hit Hobart a few days later, this small city celebrates with feasting, drinking and dancing sea-legs.

Far left: December Sydney to Hobart Yacht Race
Left: June Laura Aboriginal Dance Festival

PHOTOGRAPHERS:
(FAR LEFT) MICHAEL DUNNING/GETTY IMAGES ©;
(LEFT) PAUL DYMOND/GETTY IMAGES ©

What's New

For this new edition of Discover Australia, our authors hunted down the fresh, the transformed, the hot and the happening. Here are a few of our favourites. For up-to-the-minute recommendations, see lonelyplanet.com/australia.

1 MUSEUM OF CONTEMPORARY ART, SYDNEY

The $53-million renovation of MCA features a new entrance, exhibition spaces, rooftop cafe and sculpture terrace. Also new is ART-BAR, a hip performance event on the last Friday of the month. (p61)

2 NATIONAL LIBRARY OF AUSTRALIA, CANBERRA

The new Treasures Gallery at the National Library features prized items collected over the past 100 years, including Lieutenant James Cook's journal from the Endeavour. (02-6262 1111; www.nla.gov.au; Parkes Pl, Parkes; Treasures Gallery 10am-5pm)

3 PORT DOUGLAS MOONLIGHT CINEMA, QUEENSLAND

The latest addition to Australia's outdoor movie scene. Kick back in the tropical night with contemporary and classic flicks. (p204)

4 BRISBANE BARS

Brisbane has twigged to small-bar culture: there's a slew of sassy new booze rooms here. Top of our list are Super Whatnot in the city and The End in the West End. (p147 and p148)

5 GOURMANIA FOOD TOURS, HOBART

Explore Hobart's food scene on a walking tour: meet artisan producers, restaurateurs and wine experts, and make a list of places to return to later in your trip. (0419 180 113; www.gourmaniafoodtours.com.au; per person from $95)

6 WEST TERRACE CEMETERY, ADELAIDE

Creepy? Well, just a bit. But the new self-guided tours of this old boneyard on Adelaide's CBD fringe make a great escape from the busy streets. (www.aca.sa.gov.au; West Tce; 6.30am-6pm Nov-Apr, to 8.30pm May-Oct)

7 WATERFRONT PRECINCT, DARWIN

Darwin's ever-evolving Waterfront Precinct now hosts a wave lagoon and a seawater recreation lagoon, patrolled by lifesavers and surrounded by lawns and eateries. (p270)

8 BROOKFIELD PLACE, PERTH

With multiple restaurants, cafes and bars, Perth's hottest new precinct for eating and drinking centres on the thoughtful restoration of a row of downtown heritage buildings. (p311)

9 MARGARET RIVER GOURMET ESCAPE, WESTERN AUSTRALIA

Australia's – and the world's – best chefs, food writers and gourmands descend on Margaret River to celebrate the region's fine craft beers, wines and artisan produce. (p328)

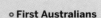

Get Inspired

 Books

o **Death of a River Guide** (Richard Flanagan; 1997) Thoughts of a man drowning in Tasmania.

o **Montebello** (Robert Drewe; 2012) British nuclear tests in WA: part memoir, part exposé.

o **Oscar & Lucinda** (Peter Carey; 1988) How to relocate a glass church.

o **Voss** (Patrick White; 1957) Contrasts the outback with Sydney colonial life.

o **The Secret River** (Kate Grenville; 2005) Nineteenth-century convict life near Sydney.

Films

o **Gallipoli** (director Peter Weir; 1981) Nationhood in the crucible of WWI.

o **Lantana** (director Ray Lawrence; 2001) A moving meditation on love, truth and grief.

o **Australia** (director Baz Luhrmann; 2008) Over-the-top period romance in northern Australia.

o **Ten Canoes** (directors Rolf de Heer & Peter Djigirr; 2006) Entirely in Aboriginal language.

o **Two Hands** (director Gregor Jordan; 1999) Black-humoured look at Sydney's underworld.

Music

o **Back in Black** (AC/DC; 1980) Essential rock; key track 'Back in Black'.

o **The Rubens** (The Rubens; 2012) Croony and catchy; key track 'Lay It Down'.

o **Internationalist** (Powderfinger; 1998) Brisbane's best; key track 'Passenger'.

o **Circus Animals** (Cold Chisel; 1982) Cold Chisel's peak; key track 'Bow River'.

o **Diorama** (Silverchair; 2002) Post-grunge splendour; key track 'The Greatest View'.

Websites

o **Lonely Planet** (www.lonelyplanet.com/australia) Destination info, hotels, travel forum.

o **The Australian** (www.theaustralian.com.au) National broadsheet.

o **Parks Australia** (www.environment.gov.au/parks) National parks info.

o **First Australians** (www.sbs.com.au/firstaustralians) TV series on indigenous Australia.

o **Coastalwatch** (www.coastalwatch.com) Surf reports.

 **Short on time?**

This list will give you an instant insight into Australia.

Read Dirt Music (Tim Winton; 2001) Guitar-strung Western Australian page turner.

Watch The Adventures of Priscilla, Queen of the Desert (director Stephan Elliot; 1994) Sydney drag queens go road-tripping.

Listen Diesel & Dust (Midnight Oil; 1987) Indigenous land rights hit the mainstream airwaves.

Log on Tourism Australia (www.australia.com) Official tourism site with nationwide visitor info.

Swimming race entrant, Bondi Beach (p74), Sydney
ANDREW WATSON/GETTY IMAGES ©

Need to Know

Currency
Australian dollars ($)

Language
English

Visas
All visitors to Australia need a visa, except New Zealanders. Apply online for an ETA or eVisitor visa.

Money
ATMs widely available. Credit cards accepted in most hotels and restaurants.

Mobile Phones
European phones work on Australia's network, but most American or Japanese phones do not. Use global roaming or a local SIM card.

Wi-Fi
Increasingly available in hotels, cafes and pubs.

Internet Access
Internet cafes in most cities and large towns, plus many public libraries.

Tipping
Not required, but tip 10% in restaurants and taxis if you're happy with the service.

When to Go

- Darwin
  GO Jun–Aug
- Cairns
  GO Sep–Nov
- Perth
  GO Oct–Dec
- Sydney
  GO Dec–Feb
- Hobart
  GO Jan–Mar

Desert, dry climate
Dry climate
Tropical climate, wet & dry seasons
Warm to hot summers. mild winters

High Season
(Dec–Feb)
- Summertime: local holidays, busy beaches and cricket.
- Prices jump 25% for big-city accommodation.
- Avoid the Red Centre, where temperatures soar north of 40°C.

Shoulder
(Sep–Nov & Mar–May)
- Spring sees warm sunshine, clear skies, shorter queues.
- Local business people are relaxed!
- Autumn is atmospheric and beautiful in Victoria and Tasmania.

Low Season
(Jun–Aug)
- Cool rainy days down south; mild and sunny up north.
- Lower tourist numbers; attractions keep shorter hours.
- Head for the desert, the tropical north or the ski resorts.

Advance Planning

- **Three months before** Look into visa requirements. What season will it be in Australia? Plan your trajectory to dodge the heat, humidity or chilly southern winter.

- **One month before** Book accommodation, internal flights, long-distance train travel and a bridge climb in Sydney or Brisbane.

- **One week before** Book a surfing lesson or reef dive, buy a sun hat and reserve a table at a Sydney harbourside restaurant.

Daily Costs

Budget Less than $130

o Dorm bed: $25–35

o Double room in a hostel: from $80

o Budget pizza or pasta meal: $10–15

o Short public-transport bus or tram ride: $4

Midrange $130–280

o Double room in a midrange hotel/motel: $100–200

o Breakfast or lunch in a cafe: $20–40

o Short taxi ride: $25

o Car hire per day: from $35

Top End More than $280

o Double room in a top-end hotel: from $200

o Three-course meal in a high-end restaurant: from $80

o Nightclub cover charge: $10–20

o Domestic flight Sydney to Melbourne: from $100

Exchange Rates

Canada	C$1	$1.04
China	Y1	$0.17
Euro zone	€1	$1.43
Japan	¥100	$1.08
New Zealand	NZ$1	$0.87
UK	UK£1	$1.70
USA	US$1	$1.08

For current exchange rates see www.xe.com.

What to Bring

o **Sunscreen** Plus sunglasses and a hat to deflect harsh southern rays.

o **Insect repellent** Especially for the tropical north.

o **Travel insurance** Ensure it covers 'risky' activities like surfing or scuba diving.

o **Electricity adapter** For all your digital gadgets.

o **A taste for cold beer and fine wine** Oceans of each await!

Arriving in Australia

o **Sydney Airport** AirportLink trains run to the city every 10 minutes, 4.50am to 12.40am. Prebooked shuttle buses service city hotels. A taxi costs $40 to $50 (30 minutes).

o **Melbourne Airport** SkyBus 24-hour services run to the city every 10 to 30 minutes. A taxi costs around $40 (25 minutes). If you're driving, the CityLink toll road is the fastest route.

o **Brisbane Airport** Airtrain trains run to the city every 15 to 30 minutes, 5.45am to 10pm. Prebooked shuttle buses service city hotels. A taxi costs $35 to $45 (25 minutes).

Getting Around

o **Air** Save time covering Australia's vast distances.

o **Car** Explore national parks and small-town Australia. Drive on the left.

o **Train** Cross the continent east–west on the *Indian Pacific* or south–north on the *Ghan*.

o **Bus** Private buses: cheaper than trains but less comfortable.

o **Boat** Cruise to tropical islands, coral-reefs and Tasmania.

Sleeping

o **Hotels** Three- to five-star hotels with high-standard amenities; in cities, towns and tourist hot-spots.

o **B&Bs** Homey bed-and-breakfasts across the country.

o **Motels** Sameness tempered by value, convenience and cleanliness.

o **Resorts** Luxury trimmings: pools, restaurants, spas, bars, golf courses...

o **Hostels** Sociable, low-cost affairs for under-30s party people.

o **Pubs** From friendly country pubs to downtown dives (inspect before you commit).

Be Forewarned

o **At the beach** Play it safe: swim between the flags.

o **Wild weather** Cyclones, floods, bushfires...it's all here, but heed local warnings and you'll be fine.

o **Summertime blues** Big-city price rises and crowds.

Sydney & the Blue Mountains

Sydney is the capital that every other Australian city loves to hate – but what that really means is that they all want to be just like it: sun-kissed, sophisticated and self-confident.

Built around one of the world's most beautiful natural harbours – a maze of lazy bays and sandstone headlands – Sydney hosts three of Australia's major icons: the Sydney Harbour Bridge, Sydney Opera House and Bondi Beach. But the attractions don't stop there...

The country's oldest, largest and most diverse city also houses magnificent museums and restaurants, a vivacious performing-arts scene and yet more sublime beaches. After dark, hip bars and clubs collide as Sydneysiders wage war against sleep... So wake up! Sydney is as good as it gets.

Don't miss a trip to the Blue Mountains, the city's hazy backdrop, with a slew of eye-popping lookouts, forests and quirky mountain towns.

Sydney Harbour (p60)

51

Sydney & the Blue Mountains

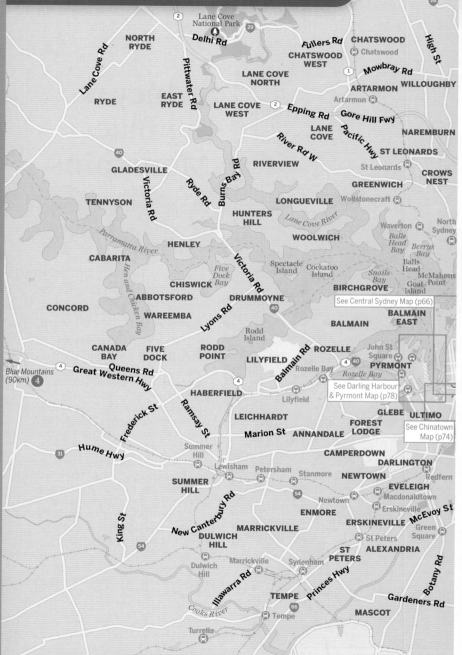

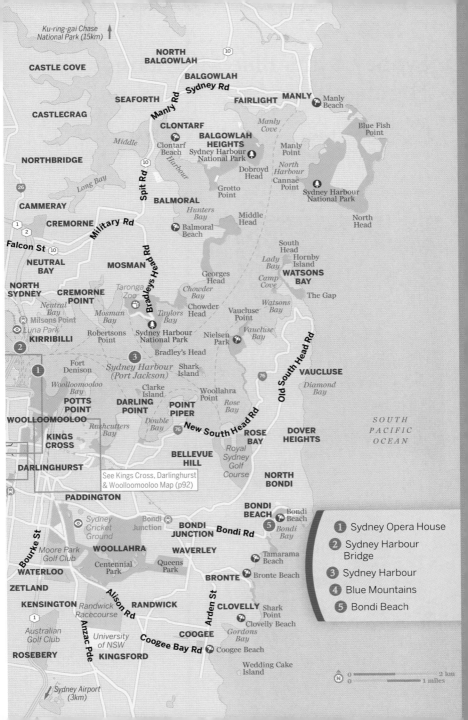

Sydney & the Blue Mountains Highlights

Sydney Opera House

Sydney's most recognisable icon is the Sydney Opera House (p70), its shell-like 'sails' shimmering on the blue harbour waters on a sunny Sydney day. Perfectly positioned on Bennelong Point, this curvy creation delights the eye from almost every angle and always makes a good photo. Get up close and examine the self-cleaning tiles or explore the interior on a guided tour. Better still, take in a show.

Sydney Harbour Bridge

The Sydney Harbour Bridge (p62) is a spookily big object – you'll catch sight of it in the corner of your eye and get a fright! Walking across it is the best way to check it out: start at Milsons Point and walk towards the city with Opera House views. Want to get higher? Try a knee-trembling BridgeClimb or scale the 200 stairs to the Pylon Lookout.

ANDREW WATSON/GETTY IMAGES ©

Sydney Harbour

3

Sydney Harbour is the essence of Sydney. Whether you're sitting down to lunch at a waterfront restaurant, exploring a shore-side park, island hopping, wandering the trails through Sydney Harbour National Park (p60), riding the ferry to Manly or kicking back on a leisurely harbour cruise, there's no better way to experience the beauty of Australia's biggest city.

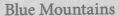

4

Blue Mountains

A hazy backdrop to greater Sydney, the magnificent Blue Mountains (p107) are a sublime natural creation, with precipitous sandstone cliffs, spectacular waterfalls, gaping canyons and character-laden mountain towns. It's a magical environment for adventure activities: try your hand at abseiling, canyoning, rock climbing, mountain biking or bushwalking, or just unwind over a long lunch in a hip mountain eatery.

5

Bondi Beach

An essential Sydney experience, sexy Bondi Beach (p84) offers munificent opportunities for lazing on the sand, lingering in bars and cafes, carving up the surf, splashing in the shallows and swimming in sheltered pools. Tightly arranged beach towels form a colourful mosaic; a wade in the water reveals multitudes of accents and languages. After dark, the action shifts to accomplished restaurants, wine bars and pubs.

Sydney & the Blue Mountains' Best...

Fresh-Air Factories

○ **Manly Ferry** Step onto the deck and suck in the sea air. (p102)

○ **Hyde Park** Sydney's lungs: a formal park with avenues of trees and swaths of lawn. (p63)

○ **Royal Botanic Gardens** A clean-breathing botany lesson. (p62)

○ **Blue Mountains** High above the big smoke. (p107)

Places to Look Down & Out

○ **Sydney Harbour Bridge** The sidewalk view is good, but from the BridgeClimb it's unbelievable! (p62)

○ **Sydney Tower** Scan from Sydney Harbour to the Blue Mountains. (p67)

○ **The Gap** Impressive clifftop lookout near the entrance to Sydney Harbour. (p73)

○ **Echo Point** Accessible Blue Mountains lookout, starring the rugged Three Sisters. (p109)

Places to Cool Off

○ **Bondi Beach** Plunge into the waves at Sydney's famous beach. (p96)

○ **Camp Cove** Sheltered, family-friendly Sydney Harbour beach. (p73)

○ **Northern Beaches** Sandy string of unpretentious surf beaches from Manly to Palm Beach. (p77)

○ **Katoomba** Beat the city heat with a day trip to this misty mountain town. (p109)

Places to Wander

o **The Rocks & Circular Quay** History and attractions between the Opera House and the Harbour Bridge. (p61)

o **Bondi to Coogee Clifftop Walk** Sandy beaches, cafe pit-stops and churning surf. (p74)

o **Darling Harbour** Traverse C-shaped Darling Harbour from King St Wharf to Pyrmont. (p69)

o **Royal National Park** Explore the world's second-oldest national park. (p104)

Left: Ferry ride past Sydney Harbour Bridge (p62); **Above:** Hyde Park (p63)

Need to Know

ADVANCE PLANNING

o **One month before** Book a Sydney Harbour BridgeClimb (p62).

o **Two weeks before** Book tickets for an Opera House show (p97) and Blue Mountains tour.

o **One week before** Book a harbour cruise and top restaurant table: try Chiswick Restaurant (p88) or Icebergs Dining Room (p89).

RESOURCES

o **Sydney City Council Information Kiosks** (www.cityofsydney.nsw.gov.au) At Circular Quay, Kings Cross, Chinatown and the Town Hall on George St.

o **Sydney Visitor Centres** (www.sydney.com) At the Rocks and Darling Harbour.

o **Blue Mountains Visitor Centres** (www.visitbluemountains.com.au) At Glenbrook and Katoomba.

o **Tourism New South Wales** (www.visitnsw.com.au) Statewide accommodation and travel advice.

o **National Roads & Motorists Association** (NRMA; www.nrma.com.au) Driving info and roadside assistance.

GETTING AROUND

o **Walk** Around Circular Quay, and the Bondi to Coogee Clifftop Walk.

o **Ferry** To Taronga Zoo, Manly, Darling Harbour and other harbourside destinations.

o **Bus** All around the city, including Bondi Beach.

o **Train** Around Sydney's outer suburbs, and to the Blue Mountains.

o **Airport Link** Trains between Sydney Airport and central Sydney.

BE FOREWARNED

o **Crowds** Summer (December to February) gets busy: queues, crowded surf and elevated accommodation prices.

Sydney Walking Tour

Down by Circular Quay, the Rocks was where European settlers set up shop in 1788: it remains the first port of call for many Sydney visitors. From here, wander around Circular Quay to the unmissable Sydney Opera House.

WALK FACTS

- **Start** Observatory Hill
- **Finish** Royal Botanic Gardens
- **Distance** 4km
- **Duration** 2½ hours

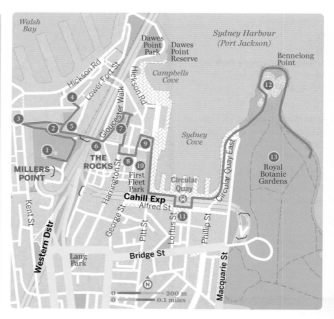

1 Observatory Hill

Kick start your walk atop the peaceful knoll of Observatory Hill. Check out the view, then head downhill.

2 Argyle Place

Follow the curvy path down to Argyle Place (p61), a quiet, English-style village green where any Australian is legally allowed to graze cattle!

3 Lord Nelson Brewery Hotel

Across the road and slightly west, the Lord Nelson Brewery Hotel (p81) contends for the title of Australia's oldest pub. Head back down Argyle Place; turn left into Lower Fort St.

4 Ferry Lane

Cross the road to teensy Ferry Lane and the foundations of Arthur Payne's house (the first victim of Sydney's 1900 bubonic plague outbreak).

5 Garrison Church

Double back along Lower Fort St to the handsome Garrison Church (1848; p61). Australia's first prime minister, Edmund Barton, went to school here.

6 Argyle Cut

Go left into Argyle St and through the impressive Argyle Cut, bored into the sandstone between Circular Quay and Millers Point.

⑦ Foundation Park

Just past the Cut take the stairs to the left; head along Gloucester Walk to Foundation Park and its 1870s ruins. Continue along Gloucester Walk, turn right into Atherden St, then right again, passing Playfair St's terraced houses.

⑧ Suez Canal

Cross Argyle St into Harrington St then jag left into Suez Canal, a narrow laneway once frequented by prostitutes and the notorious 'Rocks Push' gang.

⑨ Cadman's Cottage

Turn left into George St, Sydney's oldest road. Head down the stairs to the right to Cadman's Cottage, Sydney's oldest house (1816).

⑩ Museum of Contemporary Art

Follow Circular Quay past the engaging art-deco Museum of Contemporary Art (p61) and the ferry wharves.

⑪ Customs House

Cut underneath the train station to the fabulously renovated 1885 Customs House: there's a model of downtown Sydney set into the floor.

⑫ Sydney Opera House

Continue past the Opera Quays (aka 'The Toaster') complex on Circular Quay East towards the heaven-sent sails of the Sydney Opera House (p70). To the left is the unmissable Sydney Harbour Bridge (p62).

⑬ Royal Botanic Gardens

Circumnavigate Bennelong Point, following the water's edge to the gates of the Royal Botanic Gardens (p62): cool your boots on the grass.

Sydney & the Blue Mountains In...

TWO DAYS

Start with our Rocks and Circular Quay **walking tour**, then follow the harbourside walkway to the **Art Gallery of NSW** (p63). Catch an evening show at the **Sydney Opera House** (p70).

Next day, soak up the scene at **Bondi** (p74), take the Clifftop Walk to Coogee, then boot it back to Bondi for dinner at **Icebergs** (p89).

FOUR DAYS

Day three: jump on a ferry and chug across the harbour to **Manly** (p76) for a surf lesson. That night, head to stylin' **Surry Hills** (p72) for drinks and dinner.

Day four: dig into Sydney's convict heritage at the **Hyde Park Barracks Museum** (p68) then spend the afternoon shopping in **Paddington** (p72).

ONE WEEK

Spend a couple of days in the **Blue Mountains** (p107) with a full day's bushwalking and a gourmet dinner. Back in Sydney, visit **Taronga Zoo** (p75), yacht out on the harbour and delve into flashy/trashy **Kings Cross**.

Taronga Zoo (p75)
JULIET COOMBE/GETTY IMAGES ©

Discover Sydney & the Blue Mountains

SYDNEY

This is the country's oldest, largest and most diverse city, a sun-kissed settlement that is characterised by spectacular scenery and the cheeky, convict-derived charm of its residents.

 Sights

Sydney Harbour

Stretching 20km inland from the South Pacific Ocean to the mouth of the Parramatta River, this magnificent natural harbour is the city's shimmering soul and the focus of every visitor's stay. Exploring this vast and visually arresting area by ferry is one of Sydney's great joys. Forming the gateway to the harbour from the ocean are **North Head** and **South Head**. The former fishing village of **Watsons Bay** nestles on South Head's harbour side, and the city's favourite day-trip destination, **Manly**, occupies a promontory straddling harbour and ocean near North Head.

The focal point of the inner harbour and the city's major transport hub is **Circular Quay**, home to the Sydney Opera House and the recently renovated Museum of Modern Art (MCA).

Sydney Harbour National Park   Park

(www.npws.nsw.gov.au) Sydney Harbour National Park protects large swaths of bushland around the harbour shoreline, plus several **harbour islands**. In among the greenery you'll find walking tracks, scenic lookouts, Aboriginal carvings, beaches and

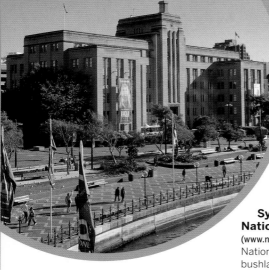

Museum of Contemporary Art
DAVID HILL/GETTY IMAGES ©

a handful of historic sites. Free brochures, including self-guided tours, are available from the Sydney Harbour National Park Information Centre (p101) in the Rocks.

The park also includes five harbour islands: Clark Island off Darling Point, Shark Island off Rose Bay, Rodd Island in Iron Cover near Birkenhead, Goat Island off Balmain and the small, fortified Fort Denison off Mrs Macquaries Point. Three of these can be visited on daily tours.

Circular Quay

Museum of Contemporary Art
Gallery

(MCA; Map p66; ☑02-9245 2400; www.mca. com.au; 140 George St; ◷10am-5pm Mon-Wed & Fri-Sun, to 9pm Thu; ☐Circular Quay, ☒Circular Quay, ☒Circular Quay) FREE This showcase of Australian and international contemporary art occupies a Gotham City–style art-deco frontage fronting Circular Quay West. Its recent $53-million redevelopment has seen the addition of impressive new exhibition spaces and an upstairs cafe/sculpture terrace with spectacular views. Volunteer-led guided tours are offered at 11am and 1pm daily, with extra tours at 7pm on Thursday and 3pm on weekends.

The Rocks

The site of Sydney's first European settlement has evolved unrecognisably from the days when its residents sloshed through open sewers and squalid alleyways.

The Rocks remained a commercial and maritime hub until shipping services moved from Circular Quay in the late 1800s.

It wasn't until the 1970s that the Rocks' cultural and architectural heritage was recognised. The ensuing tourism-driven redevelopment saved many old buildings, but has turned the area east of the bridge highway into a tourist trap where kitsch cafes and shops hocking stuffed koalas and ersatz didgeridoos reign supreme.

Nevertheless, it's a fascinating area to explore on foot.

Beyond the **Argyle Cut** (Map p66; Argyle St; ☒Circular Quay), an impressive tunnel excavated by convicts, is **Millers Point**, a charming district of early colonial homes; stroll here to enjoy everything the Rocks is not. **Argyle Place** (Map p66; Argyle St; ☒Circular Quay) is an English-style village green overlooked by **Garrison Church** (Map p66; ☑02-9247 1268; www. thegarrisonchurch.org.au; 62 Lower Fort St; ◷9am-5pm; ☒Circular Quay), Australia's oldest house of worship (1848).

The wharves around Dawes Point are rapidly emerging from prolonged decay. Walsh Bay's Pier 4 houses the renowned Sydney Theatre Company and several other performance troupes. The impressive Sydney Theatre is across the road.

The Rocks Discovery Museum
Museum

(Map p66; ☑02-9240 8680; www.rocksdisco verymuseum.com; 2-8 Kendall La; ◷10am-5pm; ☐Circular Quay, ☒Circular Quay, ☒Circular Quay) FREE Divided into four chronological displays – Warrane (pre-1788), Colony (1788–1820), Port (1820–1900) and Transformations (1900 to the present) – this excellent museum digs deep into the Rocks' history and leads you on an artefact-rich tour. Sensitive attention is given to the Rocks' original inhabitants, the Gadigal people.

Sydney Observatory
Observatory

(Map p66; ☑02-9921 3485; www.sydney observatory.com.au; Watson Rd; building & grounds free, telescope & 3D theatre adult/ concession & child $8/6, night telescope & 3D theatre adult/concession $18/14; ◷10am-5pm; ☐Circular Quay, ☒Circular Quay, ☒Circular Quay) Built in the 1850s, Sydney's copper-domed observatory sits in gardens overlooking Millers Point and the harbour. Inside is a collection of vintage apparatus, including Australia's oldest working telescope (1874). Bookings are essential for the night telescope and theatre sessions.

DANITA DELIMONT/GETTY IMAGES ©

★ Don't Miss
Sydney Harbour Bridge

Sydneysiders adore their 'coathanger'. Thousands of them drive, walk and rollerblade across it every day, others clamber over it on the wildly popular BridgeClimb tour or sail under it on a Sydney ferry.

The bridge's vital statistics are impressive: 134m high, 502m long, 49m wide and 53,000 tonnes.

The best way to experience the bridge is on foot – don't expect much of a view crossing by train or car (driving south there's a toll). Staircases access the bridge from both shores; a footpath runs along its eastern side. If this view gives you a taste for more, sign up for the **BridgeClimb** (Map p66; ☎02-8274 7777; www.bridgeclimb.com; 3 Cumberland St, the Rocks; adult $198-298, child $138-198; 🚇Circular Quay, ⛴Circular Quay). Don a headset, a safety cord and a dandy grey jumpsuit, and you'll be ready to embark on an exhilarating climb to the top of Sydney's famous harbour bridge. Safety is taken seriously, as is the money-making potential of the photographic sessions at the top (personal cameras aren't allowed).

Alternatively, you can scale the southeast pylon to the Pylon Lookout Museum – enter via the bridge stairs on Cumberland St.

NEED TO KNOW
Map p66; 🚇Circular Quay, ⛴Circular Quay, 🚆Circular Quay

City East

Royal Botanic Gardens   Gardens
(Map p66; ☎02-9231 8111; www.rbgsyd.nsw.
gov.au; Mrs Macquaries Rd; ☺7am-sunset;
🚇Circular Quay, ⛴Circular Quay, 🚆Circular Quay or Martin Pl) 🏷FREE Highlights of this 30-hectare urban oasis include the rose garden, rainforest walk and palm grove. The Cadi Jam Ora display tells the story

of the Gadigal people and features plants that grew on this site before European settlement – it's best explored on an **Aboriginal Heritage Tour** (☎02-9231 8134; adult/student & child $36.50/16.50; ◷10am Fri), which includes bush-food tastings. Advance bookings are essential.

At the northeastern tip of the gardens is a scenic lookout known as **Mrs Macquaries Point**. It was named in 1810 after Elizabeth, Governor Macquarie's wife, who ordered a chair chiselled into the rock from which she'd view the harbour. In summer the OpenAir Cinema (p96) operates here.

Volunteers conduct free 1½-hour **guided walks** of the gardens departing from the information counter at the garden shop at 10.30am daily; there are extra walks at 1pm on weekdays from March to November.

Art Gallery of NSW
Gallery

(Map p92; ☎1800 679 278; www.artgallery.nsw. gov.au; Art Gallery Rd, the Domain; ◷10am-5pm Thu-Tue, to 9pm Wed; ☒St James) FREE Magnificently located on an elevated site in The Domain, the state's flagship art gallery boasts an impressive collection of Australian and international art. Highlights include the Aboriginal and Torres Strait Islander art on display in the Yiribana Gallery on lower level 3, the contemporary galleries on lower level 2 and the Australian galleries on the ground floor.

Around Hyde Park

Located at the southern end of Macquarie St, this much-loved civic park has a grand avenue of trees and a series of delightful fountains.

Australian Museum
Museum

(Map p66; ☎02-9320 6000; http://australian museum.net.au; 6 College St; adult/child $12/8; ◷9.30am-5pm; ☒Museum) Occupying a prominent position opposite Hyde Park on the corner of William Street, this natural history museum stuffed its first animal and started collecting minerals just 40 years after the First Fleet dropped anchor and its curatorial philosophy and permanent exhibits don't appear to have changed much in the intervening centuries. The only exceptions are the changing exhibits in the Indigenous Australians gallery, which often showcases contemporary Aboriginal issues and art, and the blockbuster travelling exhibitions that the museum sources from overseas institutions.

Central Sydney

Sydney lacks a true civic centre, but **Martin Place** (Map p66; ☒Martin Place) comes close. This grand pedestrian mall extends from Macquarie St to George St, and is lined with monumental financial buildings and the Victorian colonnaded general post office.

The 1874 **Town Hall** (Map p66; ☎02-9265 9189; www.cityofsydney.nsw.gov.au/ sydneytownhall; 483 George St; ◷8am-6pm Mon-Fri; ☒Town Hall) is a few blocks south of Martin Pl on the corner of George and Druitt Sts. The elaborate chamber room and concert hall inside match the fabulously ornate exterior. The neighbouring Anglican **St Andrew's Cathedral** (Map p66; ☎02-9265 1661; www. cathedral.sydney.anglican.asn.au; cnr George & Bathurst Sts; ◷10am-4pm Mon, Tue, Fri & Sat, 8am-8pm Wed, 10am-6.30pm Thu, 7.30am-8pm Sun; ☒Town Hall) was built around the same time. Next to St Andrew's, occupying an entire city block, is the **Queen Victoria Building** (QVB; Map p66; ☎02-9264 9209; www.qvb.com.au; 455 George St; tours $15; ◷11am-5pm Sun, 9am-6pm Mon-Wed, Fri & Sat, to 9pm Thu; ☒Town Hall), Sydney's most sumptuous shopping complex. Running a close second is the elegant Strand Arcade (p100) running between Pitt St Mall and George St, which has a strong representation of Australian designer fashion. On the corner of Pitt and Market Sts is Westfield Sydney (p100), the city's glitziest shopping mall.

Breathing life into the southwestern zone is Sydney's much-loved **Chinatown**

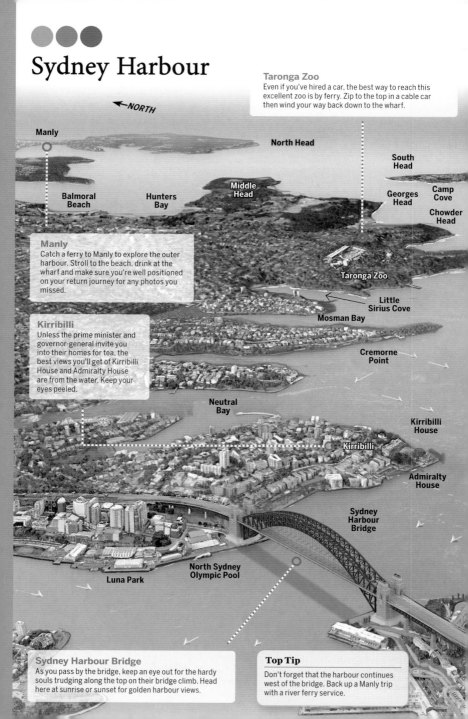

Sydney Harbour

←NORTH

Taronga Zoo
Even if you've hired a car, the best way to reach this excellent zoo is by ferry. Zip to the top in a cable car then wind your way back down to the wharf.

Manly

North Head

South Head

Camp Cove

Balmoral Beach

Hunters Bay

Middle Head

Georges Head

Chowder Head

Manly
Catch a ferry to Manly to explore the outer harbour. Stroll to the beach, drink at the wharf and make sure you're well positioned on your return journey for any photos you missed.

Taronga Zoo

Little Sirius Cove

Mosman Bay

Kirribilli
Unless the prime minister and governor-general invite you into their homes for tea, the best views you'll get of Kirribilli House and Admiralty House are from the water. Keep your eyes peeled.

Cremorne Point

Neutral Bay

Kirribilli House

Kirribilli

Admiralty House

Sydney Harbour Bridge

North Sydney Olympic Pool

Luna Park

Sydney Harbour Bridge
As you pass by the bridge, keep an eye out for the hardy souls trudging along the top on their bridge climb. Head here at sunrise or sunset for golden harbour views.

Top Tip
Don't forget that the harbour continues west of the bridge. Back up a Manly trip with a river ferry service.

Watsons Bay
Imagine Watsons Bay as the isolated fishing village it once was as you pull into its sheltered wharf. Stroll around South Head for views up the harbour and over ocean-battered cliffs.

Fort Denison
Known as Pinchgut, this fortified speck was once a place of fearsome punishment. The bodies of executed convicts were left to hang here as a grisly warning to all; the local Aborigines were horrified.

PETE DRAICEVICH ©

Ferries
Circular Quay is the hub for state-run Sydney Ferries; nine separate routes leave from here, journeying to 38 different wharves.

Vaucluse Bay

Watsons Bay

Shark Bay

Macquarie Lighthouse

Rose Bay

Shark Island

Point Piper

Bradleys Head

Double Bay

Darling Point

Clark Island

Garden Island

Naval Base

Elizabeth Bay

Fort Denison

Potts Point

Mrs Macquaries Point

Woolloomooloo Finger Wharf

Sydney Opera House

Government House

Farm Cove

Royal Botanic Gardens

Circular Quay

The Rocks

Sydney Opera House
You can clamber all over it and walk around it, but nothing beats the perspective you get as your ferry glides past the Opera House's dazzling sails. Have your camera at the ready.

Circular Quay
Circular Quay has been at the centre of Sydney life since the First Fleet dropped anchor here in 1788. Book your ferry ticket, check the indicator boards for the correct pier and get onboard.

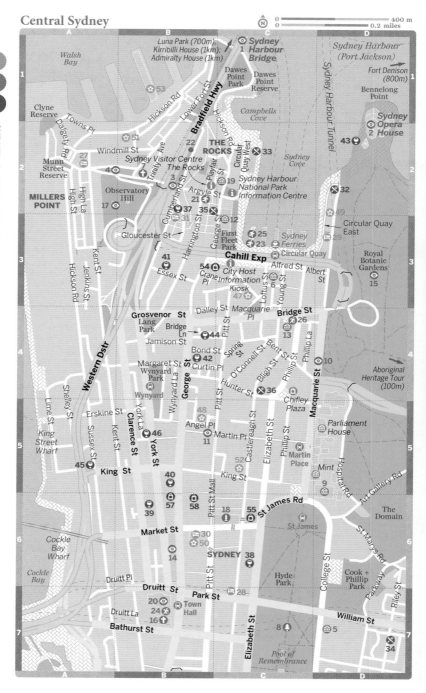

0   400 m
0   0.2 miles

SYDNEY & THE BLUE MOUNTAINS SYDNEY

Walsh
Bay

Luna Park (700m);
Kirribilli House (1km);
Admiralty House (1km)

Sydney
1 Harbour
Bridge

Sydney Harbour
(Port Jackson)

Fort Denison
(800m)

Dawes
Point
Park

Dawes
Point
Reserve

Bennelong
Point

Clyne
Reserve

53

Campbells
Cove

Sydney
2 Opera
House

51

Windmill St

22

THE
ROCKS

33

43

27

Sydney Visitor Centre
The Rocks

7

4

3

19

Circular Quay West

Sydney Cove

Sydney
Harbour

32

MILLERS
POINT

Munn
Street
Reserve

Observatory
Hill

17

Playfair

Sydney Harbour
National Park
Information Centre

49

Circular Quay
East

Argyle St

21

Gloucester St

37 35

31 12

George St

First
Fleet
Park

25

23

Sydney
Ferries

Circular Quay

29

Royal
Botanic
Gardens

15

Essex St

41

Harrington St

Cahill Exp

54

City Host
Information
Kiosk

Alfred St Albert
St

Crane
Pl

47

6

Dalley St Macquarie
Pl

Grosvenor St

Lang
Park

Bridge
Ln

44

Jamison St

Bond St

42

Curtin Pl

Spring
St

O'Connell St

Bridge St

26

13

Bent St

Phillip La

10

Margaret St
Wynyard
Park

George St

Wynyard La

Bligh St

Phillip St

Macquarie St

Aboriginal
Heritage Tour
(100m)

Wynyard

Hunter St

36

Chifley
Plaza

Lime St

Shelley St

Erskine St

York La

Pitt St

Castlereagh St

Elizabeth St

Parliament
House

King
Street
Wharf

46

York St

48

Angel Pl

11

Martin Pl

52

Martin
Place

9

Mint

45

King St

40

King St

57

39

58

Pitt St Mall

18

55

St James Rd

St James

The
Domain

Market St

30

50

14

SYDNEY

38

Hyde
Park

Cook +
Phillip
Park

Cockle
Bay
Wharf

Druitt Pl

Druitt St

28

Cockle
Bay

20

24

Town
Hall

Park St

College St

16

Bathurst St

Druitt La

8

5

William St

Riley St

Pool of
Remembrance

66

Central Sydney

(Map p74; www.chinatown.com.au/eng; Dixon St; ⑧Town Hall), a vibrant district of restaurants, shops, street art and aroma-filled alleyways.

Sydney Tower Eye Tower
(Map p66; ☑02-9333 9222; www.sydneytower eye.com.au; 100 Market St; adult/child $26/15, Skywalk adult/child $65/45; ☺9am-10.30pm; ⑧St James) The 309m-tall Sydney Tower offers unbeatable 360-degree views from its observation level 250m up in the sky.

On a clear day you'll see west to the Blue Mountains, south to Botany Bay, east across the harbour to the silvery Pacific and down onto the city streets.

Daredevils can don a spiffy 'skysuit' and take the **Skywalk**: shackle yourself to the safety rail and step onto two glass-floored viewing platforms outside Sydney Tower's observation deck, 268m above the street; it's even possible to sign up for one of the yoga classes held here – see the website for details.

Museum of Sydney   Museum

(MoS; Map p66; ☑ 02-9251 5988; www.hht.net.
au; cnr Phillip & Bridge Sts; adult/concession
$10/5; ⊙10am-5pm; ☐Circular Quay, ☎Circu-
lar Quay, ☒Circular Quay) Built on the site of
Sydney's first (and infamously pungent)
Government House, the museum offers
a modest array of permanent exhibits
documenting Sydney's early colonial
history – brought to life through oral
histories, artefacts and state-of-the-art
interactive installations – as well as a
changing exhibition program in its two
temporary galleries.

Macquarie Street   Historic Precinct

(Map p66) A swath of splendid sandstone
colonial buildings grace this street, defin-
ing the central city's eastern edge. Many
of these buildings were commissioned by
Lachlan Macquarie, the first NSW governor to envisage and plan for a settlement
that would rise above its convict origins
and become a place where prosperous fu-
tures could be forged. Macquarie enlisted
convict architect Francis Greenway to

help realise his plans, and together they
set a gold standard for architectural
excellence that the city has – alas – never
since managed to replicate.

Hyde Park Barracks Museum   Museum

(Map p66; ☑ 02-8239 2311; www.hht.net.
au; Queens Sq, Macquarie St; adult/conces-
sion$10/5; ⊙10am-5pm; ☒St James) Francis
Greenway designed this austerely elegant Georgian structure as housing for
male convicts in the early 19th century,
and 50,000 men and boys spent time
here between 1819 and 1848. From 1830
the building housed courts of General
Sessions at which convicts and their
employers put their complaints to visiting
magistrates, who determined various
penalties. The building housed new
female migrants as well as the colony's
destitute women from 1848, and then
was converted into government departments. In 1990 it was transformed into
this museum, which uses installations
and exhibits to give an absolutely

Left: SEA LIFE Sydney Aquarium; **Below:** Steps off Macquarie Street
(LEFT) ANDREW WATSON/GETTY IMAGES ©; (BELOW) OLIVER STREWE/GETTY IMAGES ©

fascinating insight into everyday convict life.

Darling Harbour & Around

Cockle Bay on the city's western edge was once an industrial dockland full of factories, warehouses and shipyards. These days it's a sprawling and exceptionally tacky waterfront tourist development (www.darlingharbour.com), the only redeeming features of which are an excellent aquarium and maritime museum.

If you're keen to find somewhere for a coffee or meal, we suggest skipping the overpriced and underwhelming outlets on **Cockle Bay Wharf** and **King St Wharf**, instead making your way to **Jones Bay Wharf**, home to the excellent Flying Fish Restaurant & Bar (p90).

Alternatively, stroll across the restored **Pyrmont Bridge**, which cuts over this mess with a timeless dignity. It leads to **Pyrmont**, home of the Sydney Fish Market (p71).

Darling Harbour and Pyrmont are serviced by ferry and Metro Light Rail (MLR).

SEA LIFE Sydney Aquarium
Aquarium

(Map p78; ☎02-8251 7800; www.sydney aquarium.com.au; Darling Harbour; adult/child $38/22; ◎9am-8pm; ◉Town Hall) This place brings in more paying visitors than any other attraction in NSW, and is particularly popular with children. Highlights include the Great Barrier Reef display, the slightly scary Shark Walk and Shark Valley, the South Coast Shipwreck display (complete with weedy sea dragons and a super-cute colony of little penguins) and the Sydney Harbour Habitat (home to the clown anemonefish, aka Little Nemo).

WILD LIFE Sydney Zoo
Zoo

(Map p78; ☎02-9333 9245; www.wildlifesydney. com.au; Darling Harbour; adult/child $36/20; ◎9am-5pm; ◉Town Hall) This indoor

69

BRIAN LAWRENCE/GETTY IMAGES ©

⭐ Don't Miss
Sydney Opera House

Designed by Danish architect Jørn Utzon, this World Heritage–listed building is Australia's most recognisable landmark. Visually referencing the billowing white sails of a seagoing yacht (but described by local wags as more accurately resembling the sexual congress of turtles), it's a commanding presence on Circular Quay.

The best way to experience the opera house is, of course, to book ahead so that you can attend a performance (there are more than 2000 of these annually), but you can also take a one-hour **guided tour** (☎02-9250 7777; adult/child/family $35/25/90; ⊙9am-5pm) of the building. There's also a two-hour 'access all areas' **backstage tour** ($155; ⊙7am daily) that includes breakfast in the Green Room. Check the website for details.

NEED TO KNOW

Map p66; ☎02-9250 7111; www.sydneyoperahouse.com; Bennelong Point; 🚇Circular Quay, 🚢Circular Quay, 🚌Circular Quay

wildlife zoo next to the aquarium offers the chance to get up close to local critters, including koalas, kangaroos, rock wallabies, echidnas, Tasmanian devils, a hairy-nosed wombat, scrub pythons and plenty of bugs.

Powerhouse Museum 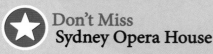 Museum

(Map p74; ☎02-9217 0111; www.powerhouse museum.com; 500 Harris St, Ultimo; adult/

child $12/6; ⊙10am-5pm; 🚌Paddy's Markets) A short walk from Darling Harbour, this museum is housed in the former power station for Sydney's once-extensive tram network. A sensational showcase for science and design, it's inevitably a huge hit with children but is equally popular with adults.

Australian National Maritime Museum   Museum

(Map p78; ☏ 02-9298 3777; www.anmm.gov.au; 2 Murray St, Darling Harbour; adult/concession & child $7/3.50; ⏱ 9.30am-5pm; 🚌 Pyrmont Bay) Housed under a roof resembling a seagoing vessel's sails, this museum examines Australia's inextricable relationship with the sea through exhibits that are arranged thematically. Exhibition subjects range from indigenous islander culture to the surf scene, commercial ocean liners to the navy. There are free volunteer tours on most days (call ahead for times) and kids' activities on Sundays.

Chinese Garden of Friendship   Gardens

(Map p78; ☏ 02-9240 8888; Darling Harbour; adult/child $6/3; ⏱ 9.30am-5pm; 🚌 Town Hall) Built according to Taoist principles, this tranquil garden was designed by architects from Guangzhou (Sydney's sister city) for Australia's bicentenary in 1988. It features pavilions, waterfalls, lakes, paths and lush plant life.

Sydney Fish Market   Market

(Map p78; ☏ 02-9004 1100; www.sydneyfish market.com.au; Bank St, Pyrmont; ⏱ 7am-4pm; 🚌 Fish Market) This piscatorial precinct on Blackwattle Bay shifts over 15 million kilograms of seafood annually, and has retail outlets, restaurants, a sushi bar, an oyster bar and a highly regarded cooking school. Go on a behind-the-scenes **tour** (☏ 02-9004 1163/8; adult/child 10-13 $25/10; ⏱ 6.40am Mon, Thu & Fri), or sign up for a cooking class with a celebrity chef; see the website for details.

Kings Cross

Crowned by a huge illuminated **Coca-Cola sign** (Map p92) – Sydney's equivalent of LA's iconic Hollywood sign – 'the Cross' has long been the home of Sydney's vice industry. In the 19th and early 20th centuries the suburb was home to grand estates and stylish apartments, but it underwent a radical change in 1930s when wine-soaked intellectuals, artists, musicians, pleasure-seekers and ne'er-do-wells rowdily claimed the streets for their own. Its reputation was sealed during the Vietnam War, when American sailors based at the nearby Garden Island naval base flooded the Cross with a tide of drug-fuelled debauchery.

Although the streets retain an air of seedy hedonism, the neighbourhood has recently undergone something of a cultural renaissance. Sleazy one minute and sophisticated the next, it's well worth a visit.

Possibly the only word in the world with eight 'o's, the suburb of **Woolloomooloo**, down **McElhone Stairs** (Map p92; Victoria St; 🚌 Kings Cross) from the Cross, was once a slum full of drunks and sailors (a fair few of whom were drunken sailors). Things are more genteel these days –

Sydney Fish Market
ANDREW WATSON/GETTY IMAGES ©

the pubs are relaxed and **Woolloomooloo Wharf** is now home to a boutique hotel and a swath of upmarket restaurants. Outside the wharf is the famous **Harry's Cafe de Wheels** (Map p92; 📞02-9347 3074; www.harryscafedewheels.com.au; Cowper Wharf Rd; pies $3-4; 🕑9am-1am Sun, 8.30am-3am Mon-Sat; 🚌311), where generations of Sydneysiders have stopped to sober up over a late-night 'Tiger' (beef pie served with mushy peas, mashed potato and gravy) on the way home from a big night at the Cross.

It's a 15-minute walk to the Cross from the city, or you could hop on a train. Buses 311 and 323-6 from the city also pass through here.

Inner East

Once the heart of Sydney's entertainment and shopping scenes, **Oxford Street** is now sadly tawdry. Most shopping action has moved onto side streets such as Glenmore Rd in Paddington and Queen St in Woollahra, while bars and restaurants have migrated to neighbouring **Surry Hills**. Despite this, the area around **Taylor Square** (Map p92; cnr Oxford & Bourke Sts; 🚇Museum) is still the decadent nucleus for the city's gay community – the Sydney Gay & Lesbian Mardi Gras famously gyrates through here every February, and gay-centric pubs and clubs do a brisk trade every weekend.

Wedged between Oxford and William Sts, **Darlinghurst** is home to cafes, pubs, restaurants and boutique hotels.

Paddington, aka 'Paddo', is an upmarket residential suburb of restored Victorian-era terrace houses, many with attractive iron 'lace' detailing.

The best time to explore Paddington's jacaranda-lined streets and laneways is on Saturday, when the Paddington Markets (p99) are held.

East of Paddington is the ritzy residential suburb of **Woollahra**. Just southeast, at the top end of Oxford St, is the 220-hectare **Centennial Park** (📞02-9339 6699; www.centennialparklands.com.au; Oxford St; 🕑vehicles sunrise-sunset; 🚇Bondi Junction), which has running, cycling, skating and horse-riding tracks, duck ponds, barbecue sites and sports pitches.

Beach at Lady Bay

Sydney Jewish Museum
Museum

(Map p92; ☎02-9360 7999; www.sydney jewishmuseum.com.au; 148 Darlinghurst Rd, Darlinghurst; adult/child $10/6; ☉10am-4pm Sun-Thu, to 2pm Fri; ☒Kings Cross) Created largely as a Holocaust memorial, this museum also has a modest display examining Australian Jewish history, culture and tradition from the time of the First Fleet (which included 16 known Jews) to the immediate aftermath of WWII (when Australia became home to the largest number of Holocaust survivors per capita after Israel) to the present day.

Eastern Suburbs

Handsome **Rushcutters Bay** is a five-minute walk east of Kings Cross; its harbourside park is a lovely spot for a walk or jog. The eastern suburbs extend out from here – a conservative conglomeration of elite private schools, European sedans, overpriced boutiques and heavily mortgaged waterside mansions. The harbour-hugging New South Head Rd passes through **Double Bay** and **Rose Bay**, and then climbs east into the gorgeous enclave of **Vaucluse**, where shady **Nielsen Park** (Vaucluse Rd; ☉daylight hr; ▣325) is home to one of Sydney's best harbour beaches, complete with a netted swimming enclosure, crescent-shaped stretch of sand, picnic facilities and a popular cafe-restaurant.

At the entrance to the harbour is **Watsons Bay**, where you can enjoy blissful briny breezes and a postcard-perfect view of the city skyline while eating takeaway fish and chips from Doyles on the Wharf (p89) or taking tea in the genteel surrounds of **Dunbar House** (☎02-9337 1226; www.dunbarhouse.com.au; 9 Marine Pde, Watsons Bay; breakfast dishes $10-16; ☉8am-3.30pm; ☒Watsons Bay). Nearby **Camp Cove** is a lovely beach, and there's a nude beach (mostly male) near South Head at **Lady Bay**. **South Head** has great views across the harbour entrance to North Head and Middle Head. The **Gap** is an epic clifftop lookout where sunrises,

Local Knowledge

Sydney Harbour

BY TONY ZRILIC, HOSPITALITY MANAGER, CAPTAIN COOK CRUISES

1 FERRY TO MANLY
The Manly Ferry (p102) departs Circular Quay every half hour or so. When you get to Manly, walk the Corso from the harbour beach to the ocean beach. Be sure to buy a gelato or have a cold beer while watching the mass of sun lovers enjoying this unique part of Sydney.

2 FORESHORE WALK FROM BRADLEY'S HEAD
The harbour is lined with fabulous foreshore walks. Take the ferry from Circular Quay to Taronga Zoo (p75), then walk around the headland to Chowder Bay. Stop for breakfast or lunch at a foreshore brasserie.

3 WATSONS BAY & THE GAP
Catch a hop-on/hop-off cruise to Watsons Bay (p73) and have fish and chips at **Doyles on the Beach** (☎02-9337 2007; www.doyles.com.au; 11 Marine Pde; mains $30-60; ☉lunch & dinner; ▣325, ☒Watsons Bay). Walk to the Gap for great views of the Pacific and the Blue Mountains.

4 LUNCH AT FORT DENISON
Take the ferry from Circular Quay to **Fort Denison** (ferry & tour adult/child $27/17; ☉tours 12.15pm & 2.30pm daily, plus 10.45am Wed-Sun; ☒Captain Cook Cruises), the heritage-listed island in the middle of the harbour. Enjoy a meal in the midst of Sydney's amazing icons: the Opera House and the Harbour Bridge.

5 SWIM AT NIELSEN PARK
Nielsen Park (p73) is one of the many netted harbour beaches where you can swim as yachts glide by. Catch a bus from Circular Quay.

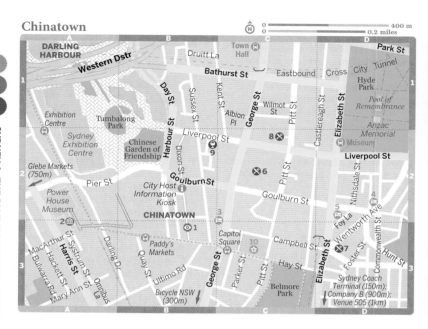

Chinatown

sunsets, canoodling and suicide leaps transpire with similar frequency.

Buses 324 and 325 from Circular Quay service the eastern suburbs via Kings Cross (grab a seat on the left heading east to snare the best views) and bus 380 travels from Circular Quay via Paddington, North Bondi and Watsons Bay. The Watsons Bay ferry leaves from Wharf 4 at Circular Quay, stopping at Double Bay and Rose Bay en route.

Bondi

Flanked by rugged rocks and multimillion-dollar apartments, Bondi's famous golden crescent of sand and surf attracts a daily cast of sunburned backpackers and bronzed locals who swarm over the sand, surrounding clifftop paths and beachfront park.

The simply sensational 5.5km **Bondi to Coogee Clifftop Walk** leads south from Bondi Beach along the clifftops to Coogee via Tamarama, Bronte and Clovelly, interweaving panoramic views, patrolled beaches, sea baths, waterside parks and plaques recounting local Aboriginal myths and stories.

To get here, take bus 389, 380 or 333 from Circular Quay. Alternatively, take a bus or train to the transport interchange at Bondi Junction and transfer to bus 382, 381, X84, X89 or one of the previously mentioned services there.

Inner West

West of the city centre is the pretty peninsula suburb of **Balmain**, once a notoriously rough neighbourhood of dockyard workers but now an arty enclave flush with beautifully restored Victorian houses, welcoming pubs, cafes and trendy shops. To get to Balmain, catch a ferry from Wharf 5 at Circular Quay to the wharf at East Balmain or hop on bus 433 at George St in the Rocks or bus 442 from the QVB; both buses stop in Rozelle en route.

South of Sydney University is **Newtown**, a melting pot of social and sexual subcultures. King St, its main drag, is full of hip boutiques, bookshops, cafes and bars. Take the train, or bus 422, 423, 426 or 428 from Circular Quay or Castlereagh St to King St.

North Shore

At the northern end of the Harbour Bridge you'll find the unexpectedly tranquil waterside suburbs of **Milsons Point** and **McMahons Point**.

Just east of the bridge is the stately suburb of **Kirribilli**, home to **Admiralty House** and **Kirribilli House**, the Sydney residences of the governor-general and prime minister respectively.

You can walk across the bridge to access Milsons Point, McMahons Point, Lavender Bay and Kirribilli, or take the short ferry ride from Wharves 4 and 5 at Circular Quay.

Taronga Zoo

Zoo

(☎ 02-9969 2777; www.taronga.org.au; Bradleys Head Rd, Mosman; adult/child 4-15 $44/22; ⌚ 9.30am-4.30pm May-Aug, to 5pm Sep-Apr; 🐨 Taronga Zoo) Sydneysiders often joke that the animals here are housed on the best tract of real estate in the city. Highlights include the nocturnal platypus habitat, the Great Southern Oceans section, the Asian elephant display and the seals.

Animal displays, feedings and 'encounters' happen throughout the day. Twilight concerts jazz things up in summer, and you can even sign up for a 'Roar and Snore' overnight camping experience. See the website for details.

Admiralty House, Kirribilli Point

Guided tours include **Nura Diya** (☎ 02-9978 4782; 90min tour adult/child $99/69; ⏱ 9.45am Mon, Wed & Fri), where Indigenous guides introduce you to native animals and share Dreaming stories about them, while giving an insight into traditional Aboriginal life. Advance bookings are essential.

From the ferry wharf, the Sky Safari cable car will whisk you to the main entrance, from where you can traverse the zoo downhill back to the ferry. This is included in the cost of your entrance ticket. A Zoo Pass (adult/child/family $51.50/25.50/144.50) includes a return ferry ride from Circular Quay plus zoo admission.

Luna Park
Amusement Park

(☎ 02-9922 6644; www.lunaparksydney.com; 1 Olympic Dr, Milsons Point; single-ride tickets $10, ride pass $20-50; ⏱ 11am-10pm Fri & Sat, 10am-6pm Sun, 11am-4pm Mon; ⛴ Milsons Point/Luna Park) A demented-looking clown sculpture forms the entrance to this amusement park overlooking Sydney Harbour and is one of a number of original 1930s features. Others include the Coney Island funhouse, a pretty carousel and the nausea-inducing rotor.

Manly

Refreshingly relaxed Manly occupies a narrow isthmus between ocean and harbour beaches near North Head. It's the only place in Sydney where you can catch a harbour ferry to swim in the ocean.

Other than the beach, the suburb's greatest attraction is the **Manly Scenic Walkway** (🚌 140, 143, 144; ⛴ Manly). This has two major components: the 10km western stretch between Manly Cove and Spit Bridge in Mosman, and the 9.5km eastern loop from Manly Cove to North Head and back.

Go to www.manly.nsw.gov.au/attractions/walking-tracks/manly-scenic-walkway to download a map of the full route. Information is also available from the helpful visitor centre in front of Manly Wharf.

Regular ferries travel between Circular Quay and Manly – it's one of Sydney's best-loved journeys.

Manly Quarantine Station
Historic Site

(☎ 02-9466 1500; www.qstation.com.au; North Head Scenic Dr; ⏱ visitor centre 10am-2pm Mon-Thu, to 4pm Sun, to 8pm Fri & Sat) Between 1832 and 1984 migrants suspected of carrying contagious diseases were isolated at this facility, and it's now a popular tourist attraction complete with visitor centre, cafe, bar and restaurant. Take a two-hour **Quarantine Station Story Tour** (adult/child $35/25; ⏱ 2pm Sat & Sun), a spooky adults-only **Ghost Tour** (Wed-Fri & Sun $44, Sat $52; ⏱ 8pm Wed-Sun) or a **'Family**

Luna Park
THIEN DO/GETTY IMAGES ©

Ghosty' Tour (adult/child/family $36/28/120; ⏰7pm Fri & Sat summer, 6pm Fri & Sat winter). Bookings are essential for all three.

To get here, walk or take bus 135 from Stand J outside Manly Wharf.

······································

Northern Beaches

The 20km-stretch of coast between Manly and well-heeled **Palm Beach** (where TV soap *Home and Away* is filmed) is often described as the most impressive urban surfing landscape in the world, and the sun-bronzed locals who swim and catch the waves at Manly, Collaroy, Freshwater, Dee Why, Narrabeen, Mona Vale, Newport, Bilgola, Avalon, Whale and Palm Beaches are uniformly proud to agree.

To get to Collaroy, North Narrabeen (for Narrabeen), Mona Vale, Newport, Bilgola, Avalon, Whale and Palm Beaches from the CBD, catch bus L90 or 190 from the Queen Victoria Building. From Manly Wharf, bus 136 goes to Chatswood via Curl Curl, and Dee Why; bus 156 goes to McCarrs Creek via Dee Why, Collaroy, North Narrabeen and Mona Vale.

Ku-ring-gai Chase National Park
National Park

(www.nationalparks.nsw.gov.au; admission per car per day $11, landing fee by boat adult/child $3/2) This spectacular, 14,928-hectare park, 24km from the city centre, forms Sydney's northern boundary. It's a classic mix of sandstone, bushland and water vistas, taking in over 100km of coastline along the southern edge of Broken Bay where it heads into the Hawkesbury River.

Remnants of Aboriginal life are visible today thanks to the preservation of more than 800 sites, including rock paintings, middens and cave art. To learn about these sites and about the park's flora and fauna, enter the park through the Mt Colah entrance and visit the **Kalkari Discovery Centre** (✆02-9472 9300; Ku-ring-gai Chase Rd; ⏰9am-5pm) `FREE`, which has displays and videos on Australian fauna and Aboriginal culture.

For information about the park, stop at the **Bobbin Inn Visitor Centre** (✆02-9472 8949; Bobbin Head, Bobbin Inn; ⏰10am-noon &

12.30-4pm), which is operated by the NSW Parks and Wildlife Service. EcoTreasures (p80) runs highly regarded guided tours in the park.

Access to the park is by car or the **Palm Beach Ferry** (✆02-9974 2411; www. palmbeachferry.com.au; adult/child $7.50/3.70; ⏰9am-7pm Mon-Fri, to 6pm Sat & Sun) run by Fantasea. This runs hourly from Palm Beach to Mackerel Beach, via the Basin (20 minutes).

If you are arriving by car, you can enter Ku-ring-gai Chase Rd off Pacific Hwy, Mt Colah; Bobbin Head Rd, North Turramurra; or McCarrs Creek Rd, Terrey Hills.

Activities

CYCLING

Bicycle NSW (✆02-9218 5400; www.bicycle nsw.org.au; Level 5, 822 George St; ⏰9am-5pm Mon-Fri; 🚆Central) publishes *Cycling Around Sydney*, a book detailing 30 city routes and paths; purchase it through the website. Sydney City Council offers cycling maps, a list of shops offering bike hire and plenty of other information on its excellent Sydney Cycleways (http://sydneycycleways.net) website.

DIVING & SNORKELLING

Sydney's best shore dives are at Gordons Bay, north of Coogee; Shark Point, Clovelly; and Ship Rock, Cronulla. Other destinations include North Bondi, Camp Cove and Bare Island. Popular boat-dive sites are Wedding Cake Island off Coogee, Sydney Heads, and off Royal National Park.

There's good snorkelling off Clovelly and Manly Beaches. EcoTreasures (p80), a company specialising in ecotourism, runs a popular Snorkel Walk & Talk tour in Manly.

Dive Centre Bondi
Diving

(✆02-9369 3855; www.divebondi.com.au; 198 Bondi Rd, Bondi; ⏰9am-6pm Mon-Fri, 7.30am-6pm Sat & Sun) This Professional Association of Diving Instructors (PADI) five-star centre offers learn-to-dive courses (one day $225, three days $495), guided shore dives

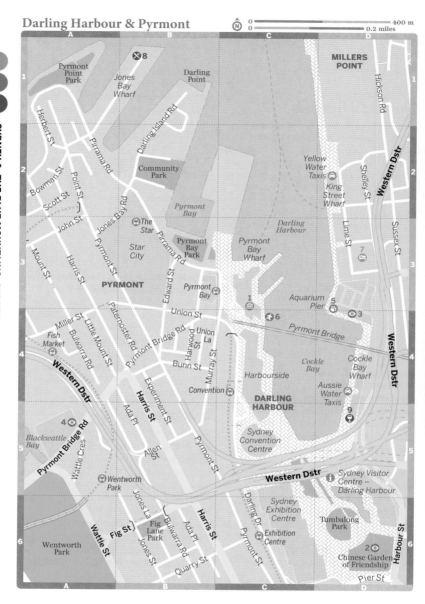

($120 for two dives) and fortnightly boat dives ($225).

Dive Centre Manly   Diving

(☏02-9977 4355; www.divesydney.com.au; 10 Belgrave St, Manly; ◷9am-6pm Mon-Fri,

8am-6pm Sat & Sun) One of the largest dive shops in Sydney. A two-day learn-to-dive PADI adventure costs $495, daily guided shore dives cost $115/125 for one/two dives, and Friday, Saturday and Sunday boat dives cost $175.

Darling Harbour & Pyrmont

SAILING

EastSail
Sailing

(☏02-9327 1166; www.eastsail.com.au; d'Albora Marina, New Beach Rd, Rushcutters Bay) Nobody ever said that yachting was a cheap sport. Take the two-day, live-aboard Start Yachting course for $575, or arrange a charter.

Sydney by Sail
Sailing

(Map p78; ☏02-9280 1110; www.sydneybysail.com; 2 Murray St, Darling Harbour) Departing daily from outside the Maritime Museum, Sydney by Sail offers harbour cruises (three hours $165, children half-price) and coastal sailing adventures on weekends (six hours, adult/child $190/80).

SURFING

On the South Shore, get tubed at Bondi, Tamarama, Coogee, Maroubra and Cronulla. The North Shore is home to a dozen surf beaches between Manly and Palm Beach, including Curl Curl, Dee Why, Narrabeen, Mona Vale and Newport.

Let's Go Surfing
Surfing

(☏02-9365 1800; www.letsgosurfing.com.au; 128 Ramsgate Ave, North Bondi) You can hire gear (board and wetsuit one hour/two hours/day/week $25/30/50/150) or learn to surf with this well-established

school. It caters to practically everyone, with classes for grommets aged seven to 16 (1½ hours $49), adults (two hours $99, women-only classes available) and private tuition (1½ hours $175).

Manly Surf School
Surfing

(☏02-9977 6977; www.manlysurfschool.com; North Steyne Surf Club, Manly) Offers group surf lessons (one/two lessons adult $70/110, child $55/90) as well as private tuition (adult/child $90/70 one hour lesson).

SWIMMING

There are 100-plus public swimming pools in Sydney, and many beaches have protected rock pools. Harbour beaches offer sheltered and shark-netted swimming, but nothing beats Pacific Ocean waves.

Andrew 'Boy' Charlton Pool
Swimming

(☏02-9358 6686; www.abcpool.org; 1c Mrs Macquaries Rd, The Domain; adult/child $6/4.50; ☉6am-8pm mid-Sep–Apr) Sydney's best saltwater pool – smack bang next to the harbour – is a magnet for water-loving gays, straights, mums and fashionistas. Serious lap swimmers rule the scene.

Bondi Icebergs Swimming Club
Swimming

(☏02-9130 4804; www.icebergs.com.au; 1 Notts Ave, Bondi; adult/child $5.50/3.50; ☉6am-6.30pm Mon-Wed & Fri, 6.30am-6.30pm Sat & Sun) The city's most famous pool commands the best view in Bondi and has a cute little cafe.

North Sydney Olympic Pool
Swimming

(☏02-9955 2309; www.northsydney.nsw.gov.au; Alfred St South, Milsons Point ; adult/child $6.70/3.40; ☉5.30am-9pm Mon-Fri, 7am-7pm Sat & Sun, creche 9am-noon Mon, Wed & Fri) Next to Luna Park, with fantastic harbour views.

Tours

BICYCLE TOURS

Bike Buffs
Cycling

(☏0414 960 332; www.bikebuffs.com.au) Offers a four-hour, two-wheeled tour (adult/child/family $95/70/290) around the harbourside sights (including jaunts over the Harbour Bridge), departing from its meeting point on the corner of Argyle and Lower Fort Sts in the Rocks at 10.30am every day. Bookings essential.

Bonza Bike Tours   Cycling
(Map p66; ☎02-9247 8800; www.bonza biketours.com; 30 Harrington St, the Rocks; ☒Circular Quay) These bike boffins run a 2½ hour City Highlights tour on Tuesday, Wednesday, Thursday and Sunday, and a four-hour Sydney Classic tour on Monday, Wednesday, Friday and Saturday. Both cost adult/child/family $99/79/290. Other tours tackle the Harbour Bridge, Manly and the city highlights.

ECO TOURS

EcoTreasures   Tour, Snorkelling
(☎0415 121 648; www.ecotreasures.com.au) ⚐ Small group tours include the Sydney Coastal Experience (eight hours, adult/ child $145/125), which involves a one-hour paddleboard lesson, a guided 5km bushwalk in Ku-ring-gai Chase National Park, a swim, whale watching (in season) and lunch. Also offers coastal walks, a Snorkel Walk & Talk in Manly and a range of Aboriginal heritage tours lead by Indigenous guides.

HARBOUR CRUISES

Captain Cook Cruises   Cruise
(Map p66; ☎02-9206 1111, 1800 804 843; www. captaincook.com.au) This crew offers a Harbour Highlights cruise (adult/child/ family $32/16/66) plus a 24-hour Harbour Explorer pass (adult/child/family $42/24/84) that is the aquatic version of a hop-on, hop-off bus tour stopping at Watsons Bay, Shark Island, Taronga Zoo, Fort Denison, Circular Quay, Luna Park and Darling Harbour. Both leave from Circular Quay's Wharf 6.

Matilda Cruises   Cruise
(Map p66; ☎02-8270 5188; www.matilda.com. au) Matilda offers a variety of cruise options on sailing catamarans, motorised catamarans and high-speed executive rockets. It also runs a 24-hour hop-on, hop-off harbour circuit pass (adult/child $42/24) departing from Pier 26 at Darling Harbour before picking up more passengers at Circular Quay's Wharf 6.

Powerhouse Museum (p70)

Sydney for Children

Organised kids' activities ramp up during school holidays (December/January, April, July and September); check www.sydneyforkids.com.au, www.kidfriendly.com.au, www.au.timeout.com/sydney/kids and www.webchild.com.au/sydneyschild/your-community for listings.

Most kids love the **SEA LIFE Sydney Aquarium** (p69), **WILD LIFE Sydney Zoo** (p69) and **Australian National Maritime Museum** (p71) at Darling Harbour, and the **Powerhouse Museum** (p70) at neighbouring Ultimo. Also worth investigating are the 'Tours for Tots' and 'GalleryKids Sunday Performance Program' at the **Art Gallery of NSW** (p63) – details are on the gallery's website.

Elsewhere, **Taronga Zoo** (p75) and **Luna Park** (p76) are sure to please.

KAYAK TOURS

Natural Wanders
Kayaking

(📞0427 225 072; www.kayaksydney.com; tours $65-150) Offers exhilarating morning tours around the Harbour Bridge, Lavender Bay, Balmain, Birchgrove, Kirribilli, Neutral Bay and Mosman for both novices and experiences kayakers. A private 2¼-hour tour costs $150 for one person or $240 for two; group tours start at $65 per person.

WALKING TOURS

I'm Free
Walking

(Map p66; www.imfree.com.au; ⏲10.30am & 2.30pm) FREE These tours are nominally free, but in reality are run by enthusiastic young guides for tips. There's a three-hour tour of the city departing from the anchor beside Sydney Town Hall at 10.30am and 2.30pm, and a 1½-hour tour of the Rocks departing from Cadman's Cottage at 6pm. No bookings taken – just show up and look for the guide in a bright green T-shirt. Check the website for time-table changes.

Sydney Architecture Walks
Walking, Cycling

(Map p66; 📞0403 888 390; www.sydney architecture.org; walk adult/concession $35/25, cycle $120/110) These bright young archi-buffs run a five-hour cycling tour and three themed two-hour walking tours (the city; Utzon and the Sydney Opera House;

and harbour-edge architecture). The tours depart from the Museum of Sydney; call or email info@sydneyarchitecture.org for bookings and departure times.

 Sleeping

Circular Quay & the Rocks

Sydney Harbour YHA
Hostel $

(Map p66; 📞02-8272 0900; www.yha.com.au; 110 Cumberland St, the Rocks; dm $48-50, d $168-185, f $205; ✳@🛜; 🚊Circular Quay, ⛴Circular Quay, 🚌Circular Quay) The view from the rooftop terrace and deluxe rooms at this relatively new and exceptionally well-run YHA hostel is fabulous – right over Circular Quay to the Opera House. The modern four- and six-bed dorms and the private rooms are neat and comfortable; all come with private bathrooms. The building was designed to be environmentally sustainable and incorporates a major archaeological dig into its footprint.

Lord Nelson Brewery Hotel
Historic Hotel $$

(Map p66; 📞02-9251 4044; www.lordnelson.com.au; 19 Kent St, Millers Point; r with/without bathroom $190/130; ✳🛜; 🚌Circular Quay) Pulling beers since 1841, this boutique sandstone pub has nine upstairs rooms with exposed stone walls and dormer

81

windows. Most are spacious and have en suites; there are also cheaper, smaller rooms with shared facilities.

Pullman Quay Grand Sydney Harbour   Apartment $$$

(Map p66; ☎02-9256 4000; www.mirvachotels. com; 61 Macquarie St, Circular Quay East; 1-/2 bedroom apt from $409/699; ❄️🛜; 🚇Circular Quay, ⛴️Circular Quay, 🚊Circular Quay) Known locally as 'the Toaster', the architecturally uninspired building housing this apartment hotel has the city's best location – right next to the Opera House. Each of the apartments has contemporary decor and features a balcony, separate lounge and dining areas, bathroom with spa bath, and kitchen with integrated laundry.

City Centre

Pensione Hotel   Boutique Hotel $$

(Map p74; ☎02-9265 8888; www.pensione.com. au; 631-635 George St; s from $110, d from $135; ❄️🛜; 🚊Central) This tastefully reworked post office features smart, neutrally

shaded rooms with tea/coffee facilities and fridges. Guests can also use the laundry and communal lounge-kitchenette. It's a busy location, and even though the windows facing George St are double-glazed you should expect street noise.

Adina Apartment Hotel Sydney Harbourside   Apartment $$

(Map p78; ☎02-9249 7000; www.adinahotels. com.au; 55 Shelley St, Kings Street Wharf, Darling Harbour; studio from $170, 1-bedroom apt from $200; 🅿️❄️🛜♨️; ⛴️Darling Harbour) A newish low-rise development just off King St Wharf where all apartments have kitchens, and all but the studios have laundry facilities and balconies. There's also a pool, a gym and a sauna.

Vibe Hotel Sydney   Hotel $$

(Map p74; ☎02-8272 3300; www.vibehotels. com.au; 111 Goulburn St; d/ste from $180/210; ❄️@🛜♨️; 🚊Central) The rooms are spacious and well priced at this handy midrange hotel near Museum and Central train stations and on the fringe of Surry Hills. All have a seating area, flat-screen TV, work desk and large closet. It has a ground-floor cafe and a gym, a sauna and a good-sized pool on the outdoor deck.

Travelodge Sydney   Hotel $$

(Map p74; ☎02-8267 1700; www.travelodge. com.au/travelodge-sydney-hotel/home; cnr Wentworth Ave & Goulburn St; d from $110; ❄️@🛜; 🚊Museum, Central) A great location near Hyde Park (equidistant between Museum Station and Central Station) plus clean, comfortable and well-set-up rooms with basic kitchenette mean that this is a compelling albeit characterless choice, particularly if you can score one of the internet specials (look for the three- or five-night packages).

Lord Nelson Brewery Hotel (p81)

QT Sydney
Boutique Hotel $$$

(Map p66; 🕿 02-8262 0000; www.qtsydney.com. au; 49 Market St; rm from $380; ❄ 🛜; 🚇 Town Hall) Nothing's being kept on the QT at this new boutique hotel. The ultra-theatrical decor and gregarious staff perfectly suit the location in the historic State Theatre buildings, and quirky touches such as the DIY martini kit in every room deserve applause.

Park8
Boutique Hotel $$$

(Map p66; 🕿 02-9283 2488; www.8hotels.com; 185 Castlereagh St; r $225-275; ❄ 🛜; 🚇 Town Hall) Hidden in plain sight behind a hole-in-the-wall cafe, this offering close to the city's major shopping action gets the balance of comfort and style just right.

Kings Cross, Potts Point & Woolloomooloo

Blue Parrot
Hostel $

(Map p92; 🕿 02-9356 4888; www.blueparrot. com.au; 87 Macleay St, Potts Point; dm $34-40; @ 🛜; 🚇 Kings Cross) If you're looking for a home away from home, this cracker of a hostel will fit the bill. Away from the seedy epicentre of the Cross, it's surrounded by the alluring cafes, bars and restaurants that Potts Point is known for, but is so comfortable that you'll probably decide to stay in, cook in the communal kitchen and then chill out in one of the hammocks strung between trees in the leafy rear courtyard.

Diamant
Hotel $$

(Map p92; 🕿 02-9295 8888; www.diamant.com. au; 14 Kings Cross Rd, Kings Cross; r $159-375, ste $315-425, apts $500-$3200; P ❄ 🛜; 🚇 Kings Cross) Riding high behind the iconic Coca-Cola sign is this well-priced designer hotel. Rooms and apartments are slick and spacious, with king-size beds, quality linen, work desks, huge plasma screens and iPod docks; some are set up for disabled guests. Choose from bridge, harbour or city views.

Regents Court
Apartment $$

(Map p92; 🕿 02-9331 2099; www.8hotels. com; 18 Springfield Ave, Kings Cross; studio apt from $185; ❄ 🛜; 🚇 Kings Cross) Nestled on a slowly gentrifying back street in the centre of the Cross, this apartment block has been reinvented as a boutique apartment hotel by Sydney stylemeisters 8 Hotels. There are 26 sparsely furnished, self-contained studio apartments up for grabs, all with cooking facilities.

BLUE Sydney
Luxury Hotel $$$

(Map p92; 🕿 02-9331 9000; www.tajhotels.com/ sydney; 6 Cowper Wharf Rdwy, Woolloomooloo; r from $252; ❄ @ 🛜 🏊; 🚌 311) Originally opened by the chic W Hotels chain but now operated by the ultra-professional Taj Group, this outstanding hotel occupies the front section of the Woolloomooloo finger wharf. Although the common areas lack allure, most guests couldn't care less – they're too busy relaxing in their spacious, lavishly appointed rooms, swimming in the indoor pool, using the gym or wining and dining in one of the wharf's excellent restaurants.

Simpsons of Potts Point
B&B $$$

(Map p92; 🕿 02-9356 2199; www.simpsons hotel.com; 8 Challis Ave, Potts Point; r from $235; P ❄ @ 🛜; 🚇 Kings Cross) Occupying an 1892 red-brick villa at the quiet end of a busy cafe strip, this perennially popular place has an endearingly old-fashioned interior decoration. The downstairs lounge and breakfast room are lovely, and rooms are both comfortable and impeccably clean.

Inner East

Medusa
Boutique Hotel $$

(Map p92; 🕿 02-9331 1000; www.medusa. com.au; 267 Darlinghurst Rd, Darlinghurst; r $210-420; ❄ @ 🛜; 🚇 Kings Cross) There's not a serpent in sight at this theatrically decorated, gay-friendly designer hotel. Eighteen stylish and comfortable rooms with basic kitchenette are arranged around an internal courtyard featuring a surprisingly noisy water feature (fortunately, it's turned off at night). Staff will happily welcome your chihuahua, but don't encourage child guests.

Below: Medusa (p83); **Right:** Ravesi's

(LEFT) LONELY PLANET/GETTY IMAGES ©; (BELOW) OLIVER STREWE/GETTY IMAGES ©

Adina Apartment Hotel Sydney
Apartment $$

(Map p92; ☏02-8302 1000; www.adinahotels. com.au; 359 Crown St, Surry Hills; apt from $190; P✳@🛜🏊; ☒Central) As one of the main pastimes in Surry Hills is eating out, you may find the well-equipped kitch-enette of your spacious, well-appointed apartment doesn't get a lot of use – there are three highly regarded restaurants in the same complex.

Kirketon Hotel
Boutique Hotel $$

(Map p92; ☏02-9332 2011; www.kirketon.com. au; 229 Darlinghurst Rd; r $160-280; ✳🛜; ☒Kings Cross) You might feel like you're in a David Lynch movie as you wander the darkened, mirror-lined corridors to your room, one of 40 spread over two levels. Even the cramped standard rooms have classy trimmings such as gilt-edged mir-rors, superior linen and plasma screens.

Hotel Altamont
Boutique Hotel $$

(Map p92; ☏02-9360 6000; www.altamont. com.au; 207 Darlinghurst Rd, Darlinghurst; d $99-190; ✳🛜; ☒Kings Cross) Altamont flagged the end of '60s peace and love, but here in Darlinghurst the good times continue unabated. Sixteen well-priced rooms have a pleasant but slightly worn decor – opt for a deluxe version if possible. Staff are welcoming and the location is close – but not too close – to the Cross. Breakfast is included in the room rate.

Bondi

Bondi Beach House
Guesthouse $$

(☏0417 336 444; www.bondibeachhouse.com. au; 28 Sir Thomas Mitchell Rd; s $80-135, d $120-300, ste $185-325; ✳🛜; ☐389, 380 or 333) Tucked away in a tranquil pocket behind Campbell Pde, this charming place offers a real home-away-from-home atmosphere. Six of the nine rooms have

private bathrooms; of these, the suites are the nicest. No children under 12 and DIY breakfast.

Ravesi's Boutique Hotel **$$$**
(☑02-9365 4422; www.ravesis.com.au; 118 Campbell Pde; d $209-389, ste $289-549; ❄ ☎; 🚌389, 380 or 333) Ravesi's fits into Bondi's shaggy surfer scene like a briefcase on a beach, but it's a popular choice for romantic weekends. The sleek chocolate-and-grey rooms are well sized, but their location above one of Campbell Pde's busiest bars means that they can be noisy. The best have deep balconies with five-star ocean views.

Manly

101 Addison Road B&B **$$**
(☑02-9977 6216; www.bb-manly.com; 101 Addison Rd; r $160-170; P ☎; 🚢Manly) At the risk of sounding like a Victorian matron, the only word to describe this 1880 cottage on a quiet street near Shelley Beach is 'delightful'. Two rooms are available, but

single-group bookings are the name of the game (from one to four people) – meaning you'll have free reign of the antique-strewn accommodation, including a private lounge with grand piano and open fireplace.

Eating

City Centre, the Rocks & Circular Quay

Din Tai Fung Chinese **$**
(Map p74; www.dintaifungaustralia.com.au; L1, World Sq, 644 George St; dumplings $11-20, steamed buns $3, noodles $12-19; ⏰11.30am-2.30pm & 5.30-9pm; 🚉Museum) It also does noodles and buns, but it's the dumplings that have made this Taiwanese chain famous, delivering an explosion of fabulously flavoursome broth as you bite into their delicate casings (opt for the Xiao Long Bao).

Sydney Madang   Korean $

(Map p74; 371a Pitt St; soups $12-17, pancakes $13-22, steam bowl $40-55; ⏰11.30am-1am; 🚇Museum) Down a teensy Little Korea laneway is this backdoor gem – an authentic barbecue joint that's low on interior charisma but high on quality and quantity. Noisy, cramped and chaotic, yes, but the chilli seafood soup, korean pancakes and steam bowl banquets will have you coming back the next day.

Quay   Modern Australian $$$

(Map p66; 📞02-9251 5600; www.quay.com. au; L3, Overseas Passenger Terminal; set menu lunch/dinner from $125/175; ⏰noon-2.30pm Tue-Fri, 6-10pm daily; 🚇Circular Quay, 🚢Circular Quay, 🚆Circular Quay) Quay is shamelessly guilty of breaking the rule that good views make for bad food. Chef Peter Gilmore has achieved international recognition for his exquisite mod-Oz food (Quay is in the San Pellegrino Top 50 list) and the view is simply extraordinary – as long as there's not a cruise ship in the way. Bookings essential.

Rockpool
Bar & Grill   Steakhouse $$$

(Map p66; 📞02-8078 1900; www.rockpool. com; 66 Hunter St; mains $25-115; ⏰noon-3pm Mon-Fri, 6-11pm Mon-Sat; 🚆Martin Pl) You'll feel like a 1930s Manhattan stockbroker when you dine at this sleek operation in the art-deco City Mutual Building. The bar is famous for its dry-aged, full-blood wagyu burger (make sure you order a side of the hand-cut fat chips), and the grill specialises in succulent steaks cooked on the wood-fired grill and seafood dishes cooked in a charcoal oven.

Kings Cross, Potts Point & Woolloomooloo

Room 10   Cafe $

(Map p92; 10 Llankelly Pl, Kings Cross; mains $8-12; ⏰7am-4pm Mon-Fri, 8am-4pm Sat, 9am-2pm Sun; 🚇Kings Cross) An exemplar of the current crop of hip cafes taking Sydney by storm (tiny space, laneway location, uncomfortable seating, excellent coffee, simple but delicious food), Room 10 is also a standout contributor when it comes to the reinvention of the Cross. Queue for a stool, or order your coffee to go.

Fratelli Paradiso   Italian $$

(Map p92; www.fratelliparadiso.com; 12-16 Challis Ave, Potts Point; mains $22-31; ⏰7am-11pm Mon-Sat, to 6pm Sun; 🚇Kings Cross) This underlit trattoria has them queuing at the door (especially on weekends). Showcasing perfectly cooked, seasonally inspired Italian dishes and serving excellent espresso coffee, it has plenty of Italian-style va va voom. No bookings.

Apollo   Greek $$

(Map p92; 📞02-8354 0888; www.theapollo.com. au; 44 Macleay St, Potts Point; meze $5-22, mains $16-34; ⏰6-10.30pm Mon-Thu, noon-10.30pm Fri & Sat, noon-9.30pm Sun; 🚇Kings Cross) An exemplar of modern Greek cooking, this taverna has fashionably minimalist decor, a well-priced menu of share plates and a bustling vibe.

Tilbury Hotel   Gastropub $$

(Map p92; www.tilburyhotel.com.au; 12-18 Nicholson St, Woolloomooloo; restaurant mains $28-36, bar mains $12-18; ⏰restaurant noon-3pm & 6-10pm Tue-Sat, noon-5pm Sun, bar 11am-11pm Mon-Thu, 11am-midnight Fri & Sat, noon-10pm Sun ; 🚌311) Once the dank domain of burly sailors and visiting ne'er-do-wells, the Tilbury now sparkles as one of the city's best gastropubs. It attracts a well-heeled crowd that eats mod-Med dishes in the airy restaurant and outdoor courtyard (lunch only) or noshes on steaks, gourmet burgers and fish and chips in the front bar.

Inner East

Reuben Hills   Cafe $

(http://reubenhills.com.au; 61 Albion St, Surry Hills; eggs & sandwiches $11-16, mains $11-18; ⏰7am-4pm Mon-Sat, 8am-4pm Sun; 🚇Central) An industrial fitout and Latin American menu await here at Reuben Hills (aka hipster central). Fantastic single-origin coffee and fried chicken star, but the eggs, tacos and *baleadas* (sandwiches) are no slouches either.

Spice I Am
Thai $

(Map p74; www.spiceiam.com; 90 Wentworth Ave, Surry Hills; mains $8-26; 11.30am-3.30pm & 5.45-10pm; Central) The signature dishes at this mega-popular BYO eatery on the city edge of Surry Hills are fragrant, flavoursome and cheap, meaning that queues are inevitable. It's been so successful that it's opened other, more upmarket and licensed branches in **Balmain** (237 Darling St, Balmain; 5.45-10.30pm Mon-Wed, 11.30am-3.30pm & 5.45-10.30pm Thu-Sun; East Balmain) and **Darlinghurst** (Map p92; 02-9280 0928; 296-300 Victoria St, Darlinghurst; mains $28-38; 11.30am-3.30pm & 5.45-10.30pm; ; Kings Cross).

Carrington
Spanish $$

(02-9360 4714; http://the-carrington.com.au/; 563 Bourke St, Surry Hills; breakfast dishes $6-20, tapas $8-19, mains $18-28; noon-10pm Mon-Fri, 9am-10pm Sat & Sun; Central) Many consider this to be Sydney's best gastropub, and there's no denying that the classic Iberian menu offerings deserve a heartfelt *olé*! Weekend breakfast might be a tortilla or baked egg, lunch could be a sandwich or salad and dinner can be chosen from an array of tapas, *pintxos* and mains.

Red Lantern
Vietnamese $$

(02-9698 4355; www.redlantern.com.au; 545 Crown St, Surry Hills; mains $28-40; 6-10pm Mon, Sat & Sun, noon-3pm & 6-10pm Tue-Fri; ; Central) Run by popular television presenter Luke Nguyen, this atmospheric eatery serves modern takes on classic Vietnamese dishes, and is deservedly popular. There's another branch in **East Sydney** (Map p66; 02-9698 4355; www.redlantern.com.au/riley/; 60 Riley St, Darlinghurst; noon-3pm & 6-10pm Tue-Fri, 6-10pm Sat & Sun; Museum or Kings Cross).

bills
Cafe $

(Map p92; www.bills.com.au; 433 Liverpool St, Darlinghurst; breakfast $5.50-18.50, lunch $7.50-26; 7.30am-3pm Mon-Sat, 8.30am-3pm Sun) Bill Granger almost single-handedly kicked off the Sydney craze for stylish brunch. His two most famous dishes – ricotta hotcakes and sweetcorn fritters – have legions of fans. This is where it all started, but there are also branches in **Surry Hills** (Map p92; 02-9360 4762; 359 Crown St, Surrey Hills; 7am-10pm; Central) and **Woollahra** (02-9328 7997; 118 Queen St, Woollahra; mains $14-26; breakfast & lunch; 389).

Billy Kwong
Chinese $$

(Map p92; 02-9332 3300; www.kyliekwong.org; 3/355 Crown St, Surry Hills; mains $24-49; 6-10pm Mon-Thu, to 11pm Fri & Sat, to 9pm Sun; ; Central) BK's sets aside most of its tables for walk-in customers, which

Dumplings at Din Tai Fung (p85)
SATOSHI KAWASE/GETTY IMAGES ©

is perfect for travellers who don't have the luxury of booking weeks ahead. Chef Kylie Kwong cooks up modern Chinese dishes using the best organic, sustainable and fair-trade ingredients (try the duck with orange sauce) and serves them in a cramped, noisy but convivial environment.

Paddington & Woollahra

Chiswick Restaurant
Modern Australian **$$**

(✆02-8388 8688; www.chiswickrestaurant.com.au; 65 Ocean St, Woollahra; mains $28-38; ⊙noon-2.30pm & 6-10pm Mon-Thu, noon-3pm & 5.30-10pm Fri-Sun; 🚍389) There may be a celebrity at centre stage (TV regular Matt Moran), but the real star of this show is the pretty kitchen garden, which wraps around the dining room and dictates what's on the menu. There are a decent number of options for vegetarians, but meat from the Moran family farm and local seafood feature prominently.

Bistro Moncur
French **$$**

(✆02-9327 9713; www.bistromoncur.com.au; 116 Queen St, Woollahra; mains $30-45; ⊙noon-3pm & 6-10.30pm Tue-Sun, 6-10.30pm Mon; 🚍389) Mini-moguls and lunching ladies while away long afternoons beneath Bistro Moncur's vaulted ceilings and monochromatic mural. The menu changes seasonally but signature dishes such as grilled sirloin Cafe de Paris delight diners year-round. No bookings.

Bondi & Bronte

Bondi Picnic
Cafe **$**

(101 Hall St, Bondi; breakfast $9-15, sandwiches $10; ⊙6.30am-4pm; 🛜; 🚍389, 380 or 333) The indoor/outdoor window seats give this cruisy corner cafe a suitably alfresco feel, and the laid-back locals who breakfast here give it a big-thumbs up. Simple fresh food, free wi-fi and excellent coffee are on offer.

North Bondi Italian Food
Italian **$$**

(118-120 Ramsgate Ave, North Bondi; pastas $18-38, mains $18-34; ⊙6pm-midnight Mon-Thu, noon-midnight Fri-Sun, open from noon Thu summer only; 🚍389, 380 or 333) As noisy as it is fashionable, this terrific trattoria in the North Bondi RSL building has a

Oxford Street, Paddington (p72)

The Cult of the Celebrity Chef

There is a veritable constellation of chefs cooking around town who have attained local and international stardom courtesy of television cooking programs or cookbooks. They include the following:

○ **Bill Granger**: bills (p87) Lifestyle chef and author of 10 cookbooks whose food and style are thought by many to be quintessentially Sydney.

○ **Kylie Kwong**: Billy Kwong (p87) Presents her own television programs (*My China* etc) and has written a number of cookbooks.

○ **Luke Nguyen**: Red Lantern (p87) Presents his own television programs (*Luke Nguyen's Vietnam, The Songs of Sapa, Luke Nguyen's Greater Mekong*) and has written a number of cookbooks.

○ **Matt Moran**: **Aria** (Map p66; ☎ 02-9252 2555; www.ariarestaurant.com; 1 Macquarie St; mains $48; ⊙ lunch Mon-Fri, dinner daily; ☒ Circular Quay), Chiswick Restaurant (p88) Matt's portrait is on show at the National Portrait Gallery in Canberra and he is known to millions of Australians through regular appearances on *MasterChef Australia*.

○ **Neil Perry**: Rockpool Bar & Grill (p86), **Rockpool** (Map p66; ☎ 02-9252 1888; www.rockpool.com; 107 George St; 2 courses $100; ⊙ lunch Fri & Sat, dinner Tue-Sat; ☒ Circular Quay) and **Spice Temple** (Map p66; ☎ 02-8078 1088; www.rockpool.com; 10 Bligh St; dishes $15-45; ⊙ lunch Mon-Fri, dinner Mon-Sat; ☒ Martin Place) The city's original rock-star chef (with ponytail to match) has a long list of cookbooks and appearances on television cooking programs to his credit.

casual vibe, simple but *molto delizioso* food and a democratic no-booking policy. Come early to snaffle a table overlooking the beach. The owners also operate a Paddington offshoot, **Neild Avenue** (Map p92; ☎ 02-8353 4400; 10 Neild Ave, Paddington; mains $35-42; ⊙ noon-4pm & 6-10pm Fri-Sun, 6-10pm Mon-Thu; ☒ Edgecliff).

Icebergs
Dining Room
Italian $$$

(☎ 02-9365 9000; www.idrb.com; 1 Notts Ave, Bondi; mains $36-95; ⊙ noon-4.30pm & 6.30pm-midnight Tue-Sun; ☒ 389, 380 or 333) Icebergs' million-dollar view sweeps across the Bondi Beach arc to the sea. The menu features modern takes on classic Italian dishes and a dedicated menu of aged beef, perfectly cooked. Come for lunch so as to make the most of the view, or arrive in time to enjoy a sunset cocktail at the bar before your meal.

Eastern Beaches

Doyles on the Wharf   Fish & Chips $

(www.doyles.com.au; Fisherman's Wharf, Watsons Bay; fish & chips $14-19, half-dozen oysters $13.50; ⊙ 10.30am-5pm Sun-Thu, to 7pm Fri & Sat; ☒ Watsons Bay) The million-dollar view comes free of charge when you buy lunch from this kiosk at the front of Watsons Bay Warf, and there are plenty of vantage points in the adjoining park.

Inner West

Bloodwood   International $$

(www.bloodwoodnewtown.com; 416 King St, Newtown; mains $25-30; ⊙ 5pm-late Mon, Wed & Thu, noon-late Fri & Sat, noon-10pm Sun; ☒ Newtown) Relax over a few drinks and a progression of globally inspired shared plates at this popular bar-bistro. The decor is industrial

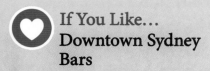

If You Like...
Downtown Sydney Bars

1 **GRASSHOPPER**
(Map p66; www.thegrasshopper.com.au; 1 Temperance Lane; ⏰4pm-late Mon-Thu & Sat, noon-late Fri; 🚉St James) The first of many grungy laneway bars to open in the inner city couldn't have chosen a more darkly ironic location than Temperance Lane. The heart of the operation is the cool downstairs bar; hop upstairs for food.

2 **PALMER & CO**
(Map p66; www.merivale.com.au/palmerandco; Abercrombie Lane; ⏰5pm-late Sat-Wed, 4pm-late Thu, noon-late Fri; 🚉Wynyard) Another self-consciously hip member of Sydney's speakeasy brigade, this 'legitimate importer of bracing tonics and fortifying liquid' is part of Justin Hemmes' trend-setting hospitality empire and has the cashed-up and fashionable clientele that this inevitably entails.

3 **O BAR**
(Map p66; www.summitrestaurant.com.au; Level 47, Australia Sq, 264 George St; ⏰5pm-late Sat-Tue, noon-late Wed-Fri; 🚉Wynyard) Shoot up to this murderously cool revolving *Goldfinger*-esque bar, offering killer cocktails, comfortable chairs and views to die for.

4 **ASH STREET CELLAR**
(www.merivale.com/ashstcellar; 1 Ash St; ⏰8.30am-11pm Mon-Fri) Part of the frighteningly fashionable Ivy complex, this European-flavoured wine bar in a pedestrianised laneway off George St largely caters to suits, but makes everyone feel welcome. There's excellent coffee during the day, and even better tapas ($8 to $32) and wine at night.

chic and the vibe is alternative – very Newtown.

Flying Fish
Seafood $$$
(Map p78; 📞02-9518 6677; www.flyingfish.com.au; Jones Bay Wharf; mains around $40; ⏰noon-5pm Sun, 6-10.30pm Mon-Sat; 🚉The Star)

Fancy the idea of a Sri Lankan–style barramundi curry eaten in a glamorous loft-style restaurant overlooking the water? Or maybe a glass of champagne enjoyed with freshly shucked oysters or A-grade sashimi in an outdoor bar? Flying Fish offers both options, and even has a kids' menu ($25).

North Shore & Manly
Bower Restaurant
Cafe, Modern Australian $$
(📞02-9977 5451; www.thebowerrestaurant.com.au; cnr Marine Pde & Bower La, Manly; breakfast $7.50-23.50, lunch $20-33; ⏰8am-3pm; 🚢Manly) Follow the scenic promenade east from Manly's ocean beach towards Shelly Beach and you will soon arrive at this cute cafe within spray's breath of the sea. Eat in, or grab take-out fish & chips ($16) or panini ($8).

Drinking & Nightlife

The Rocks & Circular Quay
Opera Bar
Bar, Live Music
(Map p66; www.operabar.com.au; lower concourse, Sydney Opera House, Circular Quay; ⏰11.30am-midnight Sun-Thu, to 1am Fri & Sat; 🚉Circular Quay, 🚢Circular Quay, 🚉Circular Quay) Putting a totally different – and mighty sophisticated – spin on the concept of a beer garden, Sydney's most spectacularly sited bar is the perfect place to be on balmy evenings. There's live music from 8.30pm weekdays and 2pm on weekends.

Harts Pub
Pub
(Map p66; www.hartspub.com; cnr Essex and Gloucester Sts, the Rocks; ⏰noon-midnight Mon-Wed, to 1am Thu-Sat, to 11pm Sun; 🚉Circular Quay, 🚢Circular Quay) Pouring a range of craft beers (small batch beer brewed using traditional methods), Harts is

frequented by locals drawn by the beer, the rugby tipping competition and some of Sydney's best pub food.

Australian Hotel   Pub

(Map p66; www.australianheritagehotel.com; 100 Cumberland St, the Rocks; 🚊 Circular Quay, 🚢 Circular Quay, 🚇 Circular Quay) Boasting a bonza selection of fair dinkum ocker beer and wine, the Australian keeps to the antipodean theme with its pizzas, which feature kangaroo, emu, saltwater crocodile and other unorthodox toppings ($17 to $26).

City Centre

Stitch   Bar

(Map p66; www.stitchbar.com; 61 York St; ⏱ 4pm-midnight Mon-Wed, noon-2am Thu-Sat; 🚇 Wynyard) The finest exemplar of Sydney's penchant for ersatz speakeasys, Stitch is accessed via swinging doors at the rear of what looks like a tailor's workshop. Hidden beneath is a surprisingly large but perpetually crowded space decorated with sewing patterns and wooden Singer sewing-machine cases.

Baxter Inn   Bar

(Map p66; www.thebaxterinn.com; 152-156 Clarence St; ⏱ 4pm-1am Mon-Sat; 🚇 Town Hall) Yes, it really is down that dark lane and through that unmarked door (it's easier to find if there's a queue; otherwise look for the bouncer lurking nearby). Whisky's the poison at this self-proclaimed and highly fashionable swillhouse.

Bambini Wine Room   Wine Bar

(Map p66; www.bambinitrust.com.au; 185 Elizabeth St; ⏱ 3-10pm Mon-Fri, 5.30-11pm Sat; 🚇 St James) Don't worry, this bar doesn't sell wine to *bambini* – it's a very grown-up, European affair. The tiny dark-wood-panelled room is the sort of place where you'd expect to see Oscar Wilde holding court in the corner.

Chinatown & Darling Harbour

Good God Small Club   Club, Live Music

(Map p74; www.goodgodgoodgod.com; 55 Liverpool St, Chinatown; front bar free, club free-$20; ⏱ 5pm-1am Wed, to 2am Thu, to 5am Fri,

View from the Opera Bar

91

SYDNEY & THE BLUE MOUNTAINS SYDNEY

Kings Cross, Darlinghurst & Woolloomooloo

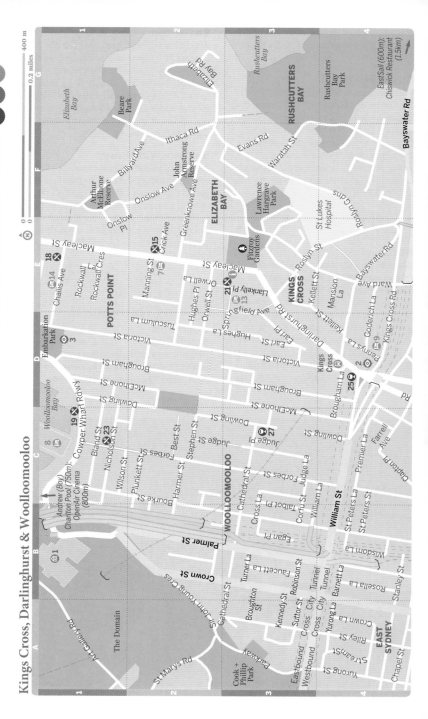

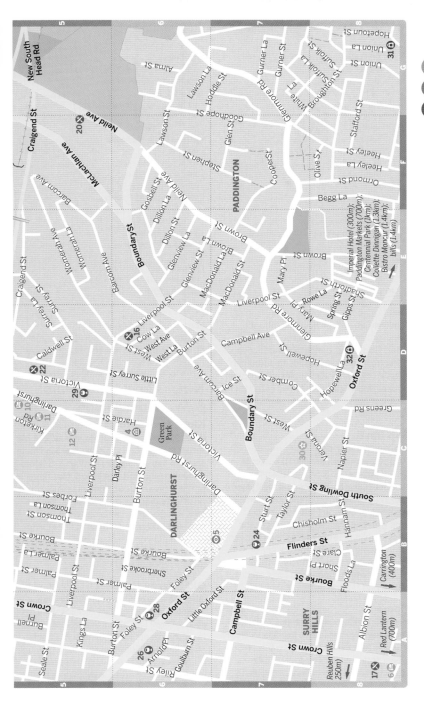

6pm-5am Sat; 🚇Town Hall) In a defunct underground taverna near Chinatown, Good God's rear dancetaria hosts everything from live indie bands to Jamaican reggae, '50s soul, rockabilly and tropical house music. Its success lies in the focus on great music rather than glamorous surrounds.

Slip Inn & Chinese Laundry
Bar, Club

(Map p66; www.merivale.com; 111 Sussex St, Central Sydney; club $15-25; ⏱10am-midnight Mon-Thu, to 2am Fri, 5pm-2am Sat; 🚇Wynyard) Slip in to this warren of moody rooms on the edge of Darling Harbour and bump hips with the kids. On Friday night the bass cranks up at the attached Chinese Laundry nightclub on the corner of King and Sussex Sts; on Saturdays there's a roster of international and local electro, house and techno DJs.

Home
Club, Live Music

(Map p78; www.homesydney.com; 1 Wheat Rd, Cockle Bay Wharf; admission free-$55; ⏱club Fri & Sat; 🚇Town Hall) Welcome to the pleasuredome: a three-level, 2100-capacity timber and glass 'prow' that's home to a dance floor, countless bars, outdoor balconies, and sonics that make other clubs sound like transistor radios.

Kings Cross, Potts Point & Woolloomooloo

Kings Cross Hotel
Pub, Live Music

(Map p92; www.kingscrosshotel.com.au; 244-248 William St, Kings Cross; ⏱noon-3am Sun-Thu, to 6am Fri & Sat; 🚇Kings Cross) With five floors above ground and one below, this huge pub is a hive of boozy entertainment that positively swarms on weekends. Best of all is FBi Social, an alternative radio station—led takeover of the 2nd floor bringing with it an edgy roster of live music. The roof bar has DJs on weekends and awesome city views.

Old Fitzroy Hotel
Pub

(Map p92; www.oldfitzroy.com.au; 129 Dowling St, Woolloomooloo; ⏱11am-midnight Mon-Fri, noon-midnight Sat, 3-10pm Sun; 🚇Kings Cross) Islington meets Melbourne in the back streets of Woolloomooloo: this totally unpretentious theatre pub is also a decent old-fashioned boozer in its own right.

There are airy street-side tables, and an upstairs area with a pool table and scruffy lounges.

Inner East

Shady Pines Saloon   Bar

(Map p92; www.shadypinessaloon.com; shop 4, 256 Crown St, East Sydney; ⊙4pm-midnight; 🚇Museum) With no sign or street number on the door and an entry from a shady back lane (look for the white door before Bikram Yoga on Foley St), this subterranean honky-tonk caters to the urban boho. Sip whisky-and-rye with the good old hipster boys amid Western memorabilia and taxidermy.

Imperial Hotel   Pub

(www.imperialhotelpaddington.com.au; 252 Oxford St, Paddington; ⊙10am-midnight Mon-Sat, to 10pm Sun; 🚌380) Paddington is one of Sydney's golden suburbs, blessed with a great location, leafy streets, pretty houses and wonderful pubs. This is the best of the neighbourhood watering holes, offering a stylish interior, solicitous service, an extensive list of regional wines, live acoustic music on Sunday afternoons and simply sensational pub grub (mains $17 to $29).

Victoria Room   Cocktail Bar

(Map p92; ☎02-9357 4488; www.thevictoria room.com; Level 1, 235 Victoria St, Darlinghurst; ⊙6pm-midnight Tue-Thu, to 1am Fri & Sat, high tea noon-5pm Sat & Sun; 🚇Kings Cross) Claim a chesterfield and relax over an expertly prepared cocktail or two at this sultry, Raj-style drinking den or book ahead to enjoy the weekend high tea ($45 to $65).

Newtown

Courthouse Hotel   Pub

(202 Australia St; ⊙10am-midnight Mon-Sat, to 10pm Sun; 🚇Newtown) What a brilliant pub! A block back from the King St fray, the 150-year-old Courthouse is the kind of place where everyone from pool-playing goth lesbians to magistrates can have a beer and feel right at home. A beer garden, beer specials, decent house red and good pub grub, too.

Jester Seeds   Cocktail Bar

(www.jesterseeds.com; 127 King St; ⊙4pm-midnight Tue-Sat, to 10pm Sun; 🚇Newtown) Jester

Entrance to Chinatown (p63)

信 屨 德 通

ROB REICHENFELD/GETTY IMAGES ©

Seeds is very Newtown. By that we mean a bit gloomy, a little grungy and very hip, with the requisite thrift-shop furniture, graffiti, obtuse name, astroturf 'garden' and classic but credible soundtrack.

Bondi

Icebergs Bar   Bar
(www.idrb.com; 1 Notts Ave, Bondi; ☉noon-midnight Tue-Sat, to 10pm Sun; ☐380, 389, 333) Most folks come here to eat in the attached restaurant, but the bar is a brilliant place for a drink. The hanging chairs, colourful sofas and ritzy cocktails are fab, but the view looking north across Bondi Beach is the absolute killer.

Manly

Manly Wharf Hotel   Pub
(www.manlywharfhotel.com.au; Manly Wharf; ☉11.30am-midnight Mon-Sat, 11am-10pm Sun; ☀Manly) Tuck away a few schooners after a hard day in the surf, then pour yourself onto the ferry. Sports games draw a crowd and DJs liven up Sunday after-noons. Great pub food, too, with specials throughout the week.

Entertainment

CINEMAS

OpenAir Cinema   Cinema
(☎1300 366 649; www.stgeorgeopenair.com.au; Mrs Macquaries Rd, Royal Botanic Gardens; tickets $35; ☉Jan & Feb; ☐Circular Quay, ☀Circular Quay, ☒Circular Quay) Right on the harbour, the outdoor three-storey screen here comes with surround sound, sunsets, skyline and swanky food and wine. Most tickets are purchased in advance, but a limited number of tickets go on sale at the door each night at 6.30pm – check the website for details.

Dendy Opera Quays   Cinema
(Map p66; ☎02-9247 3800; www.dendy.com.au; 2 Circular Quay East; 2-/3D adult $18/19; ☉sessions 10am-9pm; ☐Circular Quay, ☀Circular Quay, ☒Circular Quay) When the harbour glare and squawking seagulls get too much, follow the scent of popcorn into the dark folds of this plush cinema. Screening first-run, independent world films, it's augmented by friendly attend-

Manly Wharf Hotel

Gay & Lesbian Sydney

Gay and lesbian culture forms a vocal and vital part of Sydney's social fabric. **Taylor Square** on Oxford St is the centre of arguably the second-largest gay community in the world (after San Francisco); Newtown is home to Sydney's lesbian scene.

Sydney's famous **Gay & Lesbian Mardi Gras** (www.mardigras.org.au) draws more than 300,000 spectators and involves over 10,000 participants; the Mardi Gras also runs the annual **Sleaze Ball** (✆02-9568 8600; www.mardigras.org.au; 1 Driver Ave, Hordern Pavilion; 🚌339) held in late September/early October at the Horden Pavilion in Moore Park.

Free gay media includes *SX* (www.gaynewsnetwork.com.au), the *Star Observer* (www.starobserver.com.au), *Lesbians on the Loose* (www.lotl.com) and *DNA* (www.dnamagazine.com.au).

Most hotels, restaurants and bars in Darlinghurst and Surry Hills are very gay-friendly. To party, go for a wander along the city end of Oxford St or check out the following:

Arq (Map p92; ✆02-9380 8700; www.arqsydney.com.au; 16 Flinders St; admission free-$25; 🕐9pm-late Thu-Sun; 🚇Museum) Drag shows on Thursday from 9pm, clubbing over two floors on Friday and Saturday, cabaret on Sunday (the main event of the week).

Imperial Hotel (www.theimperialhotel.com.au; 35 Erskineville Rd; front bar free, cellar club before/after 10pm free/$10, cabaret bar Fri/Sat $10/15; 🕐3pm-late; 🚇Erskineville) The drag acts at this art-deco pub inspired *Priscilla, Queen of the Desert* (the opening scene was filmed here).

Midnight Shift (Map p92; ✆02-9358 3848; www.themidnightshift.com.au; 85 Oxford St; admission free-$10; 🕐4pm-late Mon-Fri, 2pm-late Sat & Sun; 🚇Museum) The grande dame of the Oxford St scene.

ants, a cafe and a bar. There's another branch in King St, Newtown.

Moonlight Cinema
Cinema

(✆1300 551 908; www.moonlight.com.au; Belvedere Amphitheatre, cnr Loch & Broome Aves; adult $18; 🕐Dec-Mar; 🚇Bondi Junction) Take a picnic and join the bats under the stars in magnificent Centennial Park; enter via Woollahra Gate on Oxford St. A mix of new-release blockbusters, art house and classics is programmed.

Palace Verona
Cinema

(Map p92; ✆02-9360 6099; www.palace cinemas.com.au; 17 Oxford St, Paddington; adult $11-18.50; 🕐sessions 10am-9.30pm; 🚌380) This urbane cinema has a wine and espresso bar where you can debate the

artistic merits of the nonblockbuster flick you've just seen.

LIVE MUSIC

Sydney Opera House
Performing Arts

(Map p66; ✆02-9250 7777; www.sydneyopera house.com; Bennelong Point, Circular Quay; 🕐box office 9am-8.30pm Mon-Sat; 🚌Circular Quay, ⛴Circular Quay, 🚇Circular Quay) Yes, it's more than a landmark. In addition to theatre and dance, there are performances by Opera Australia, the Australian Ballet, the Sydney Symphony and Bangarra Dance Theatre.

City Recital Hall
Classical Music

(Map p66; ✆02-8256 2222; www.cityrecital hall.com; 2 Angel Pl, City Centre; 🕐box office

9am-5pm Mon-Fri; 🚇Martin Pl) Based on the classic configuration of the 19th-century European concert hall, this custom-built 1200-seat venue boasts near-perfect acoustics. Catch top-flight companies such as Musica Viva, the Australian Brandenburg Orchestra and the Australian Chamber Orchestra here.

Venue 505 — Live Music

(www.venue505.com; 280 Cleveland St, Surry Hills; ⏰from 7.30pm Mon-Sat; 🚇Central) Focusing on jazz, roots, reggae, funk, gypsy and Latin music, this small, relaxed venue is artist-run and thoughtfully programmed. The space features comfortable couches and murals by a local artist.

Basement — Live Music

(Map p66; 📞02-9251 2797; www.thebasement.com.au; 7 Macquarie Pl, Circular Quay; 🚌Circular Quay; ⛴Circular Quay, 🚇Circular Quay) Once solely a jazz venue, the Basement now hosts international and local musicians working in many disciplines and genres. Dinner-and-show tickets net

you a table by the stage, guaranteeing a better view than the standing-only area by the bar.

Annandale Hotel — Live Music

(📞02-9550 1078; www.annandalehotel.com; 17 Parramatta Rd, Annandale; ⏰box office 9.30am-5.30pm Tue-Fri; 🚌436-440) Long at the forefront of Sydney's live music scene, the Annandale coughs up alt-rock, metal, punk and electronica.

SPECTATOR SPORTS

Sydneysiders are passionate about the **National Rugby League** (NRL; www.nrl.com.au; tickets through Ticketek from $25), the season kicking off in March in suburban stadiums and the ANZ Stadium, with September finals.

Over the same period, hometown favourites the Sydney Swans and Greater Western Sydney (the Giants) play in the **Australian Football League** (AFL; www.afl.com.au; tickets $20-40). The Swans play at the Sydney Cricket Ground (SCG) and the Giants at the Sydney Showground Stadium in Sydney's Olympic Park.

The **cricket** (http://cricket.com.au) season runs from October to March, the SCG hosting interstate Sheffield Shield and sell-out international Test, Twenty20 and One Day International matches.

THEATRE

For theatre performances, head to the **Sydney Theatre** (Map p66; 📞02-9250 1999; www.sydneytheatre.org; 22 Hickson Rd; 🚇Wynyard), **Wharf Theatre** (Map p66; 📞02-9250 1777; www.sydneytheatre.com.au; Pier 4/5, 15 Hickson Rd; 🚇Wynyard) 🚶 and **Company B** (📞02-9699 3444; www.belvoir.com.au; 25 Belvoir St). For musicals and other stage events, go to the **Capitol Theatre**

NRL match, Cronulla Sharks vs Wests Tigers
ADAM PRETTY/GETTY IMAGES ©

(Map p74; ☏02-9320 5000; www.capitoltheatre.com.au; 13 Campbell St; ⓇCentral), **Theatre Royal** (Map p66; www.theatreroyal.net.au; 108 King St, MLC Centre) and **State Theatre** (Map p66; ☏136 100; www.statetheatre.com.au; 49 Market St; ⓇSt James).

 Shopping

Aboriginal & Pacific Art
Art & Craft

(www.2danksstreet.com.au; 2 Danks St, Waterloo; ⏱11am-5pm Tue-Sat; 🚍M20, 355) One of a number of commercial galleries under the same roof; this one represents community-based Aboriginal and Pacific Islander art.

Australian Wine Centre
Wine

(Map p66; www.australianwinecentre.com; Goldfields House, 1 Alfred St, Circular Quay; ⓇCircular Quay) This multilingual basement store is packed with quality Australian wine, beer and spirits. Pick up some Hunter Valley semillon or organise a shipment back home.

Collette Dinnigan
Clothing

(www.collettedinnigan.com.au; 104 Queen St, Woollahra; 🚍380) The queen of Aussie couture delivers fabulously feminine frocks with exquisite trimmings.

David Jones
Department Store

(Map p66; www.davidjones.com.au; 86-108 Castlereagh St, Central Sydney; ⓇSt James) DJs is Sydney's premier department store. The Castlereagh St store has women's and children's clothing; Market St has menswear and a high-brow food court. There's another store at **Westfield Bondi Junction** (☏02-9947 8000; www.westfield.com.au; 500 Oxford St; ⏱9.30am-6pm Fri-Wed, to 9pm Thu; ⓇBondi Junction).

Leona Edmiston
Clothing, Accessories

(Map p92; www.leonaedmiston.com; 88 William St, Paddington; 🚍380) Leona Edmiston knows frocks – from little and black to whimsically floral or all-out sexy. Also at Westfield Bondi Junction, Westfield Sydney, Chifley Plaza and the Strand Arcade.

If You Like…
Weekend Markets

1 BONDI MARKETS
(☏02-9315 8988; www.bondimarkets.com.au; Bondi Beach Public School, Campbell Pde; ⏱9am-1pm Sat, 10am-4pm Sun; 🚍380) The kids are at the beach on Sunday while their school fills up with Bondi characters rummaging through tie-dyed secondhand clothes and books, beads and earrings, aromatherapy oils, candles, old records and more.

2 EVELEIGH MARKET
(www.eveleighmarket.com.au; 243 Wilson St, Darlington; ⏱farmers market 8am-1pm Sat, artisans' market 10am-3pm 1st Sun of month, closed 1st half of Jan; ⓇRedfern) More than 70 regular stallholders sell their home-grown produce at Sydney's best farmers market, which is held in a heritage-listed railway workshop in the Eveleigh Railyards.

3 GLEBE MARKETS
(www.glebemarkets.com.au; Glebe Public School, cnr Glebe Point Rd & Derby Pl; ⏱10am-4pm Sat; 🚍Glebe) Sydney's dreadlocked, shoeless, inner-city contingent beats an aimless course to this crowded hippy-ish market.

4 PADDINGTON MARKETS
(www.paddingtonmarkets.com.au; Paddington Public School, 395 Oxford St, Paddington; ⏱10am-4pm Sat; 🚍380) Originating in the 1970s when it was beloved by the alternative set, this market is considerably more mainstream these days, but is still worth checking out for its new and vintage clothing, creative crafts and jewellery.

5 ROZELLE MARKETS
(☏02-9818 5373; www.rozellemarkets.com.au; cnr Darling & National Sts; ⏱9am-4pm Sat & Sun; 🚍432-4) One of Sydney's best bargain-hunter markets, with very few tourists. Sift through hippie jewellery, vintage clothes, books and knick-knacks, with live folk music, palm readings and exotic food stalls as a backdrop.

Below: Strand Arcade; **Right:** Queen Victoria Building

Queen Victoria Building
Shopping Centre

(QVB; Map p66; www.qvb.com.au; 455 George St, Central Sydney; 🚇 Town Hall) The magnificent QVB takes up a whole block and boasts nearly 200 shops on five levels. It's a high-Victorian masterpiece – without doubt Sydney's most beautiful shopping centre.

RM Williams
Clothing, Accessories

(Map p66; www.rmwilliams.com.au; 389 George St, Central Sydney; 🚇 Wynyard) Urban cowboys and country folk can't get enough of this hard-wearing Aussie outback gear.

Strand Arcade
Shopping Centre

(Map p66; www.strandarcade.com.au; 412 George St, Central Sydney; 🚇 St James) Constructed in 1891, the Strand competes with the QVB for the title of the city's most beautiful shopping centre. It has a particularly strong range of Australian designer fashion, and is home to Strand Hatters, a Sydney institution.

Westfield Sydney
Mall

(Map p66; www.westfield.com.au/sydney; cnr Pitt St Mall & Market St, Central Sydney) This huge shopping mall incorporates Sydney Tower and has an excellent food court plus main-street retailers such as Zara and Gap.

Zimmermann
Clothing

(Map p92; www.zimmermannwear.com; 2-16 Glenmore Rd, Paddington; 🚌 380) Chic and cheeky women's street clothes and swimwear from sisters Nicky and Simone Zimmermann. There are other stores in Westfield Sydney and Westfield Bondi Junction.

ℹ️ Information

Medical Services

Kings Cross Clinic (☎ 02-9358 3066; www.kingscrossclinic.com.au; 13 Springfield Ave, Kings Cross; ⏲ 9am-1pm & 2-6pm Mon-Fri, 10am-1pm Sat; 🚇 Kings Cross) General practitioners with a travel medicine focus, offering vaccinations, dive medicals and sexual health advice.

St Vincent's Hospital (☎02-8382 1111; www.stvincents.com.au; 390 Victoria St, Darlinghurst; ☺24hr emergency dept; 🚆Kings Cross)

Sydney Hospital (☎02-9382 7111; www.seslhd.health.nsw.gov.au/SHSEH; 8 Macquarie St, Central Sydney; ☺24hr emergency dept)

Tourist Information

City Host Information Kiosks (www.cityofsydney.nsw.gov.au) Circular Quay (Map p66; cnr Pitt & Alfred Sts; ☺9am-5pm; 🚆Circular Quay); Town Hall (p63); Haymarket (Map p74; Dixon St; ☺11am-7pm; 🚆Town Hall) Friendly and helpful staff supply maps, brochures and information.

Kings Cross Tourist Information Kiosk (Map p92; crn Darlinghurst Rd & Macleay St, Kings Cross; ☺9am-5pm Sun-Thu,to 11pm Fri & Sat; 🚆Kings Cross) Supplies maps, brochures, walking-tour maps and transport information.

Manly Visitor Information Centre (☎02-9977 1430; www.manlytourism.com.au; Manly Wharf; ☺9am-5pm Mon-Fri, 10am-4pm Sat & Sun; 🚢Manly) Extremely helpful volunteer staff supply brochures, maps and transport information.

Sydney Harbour National Park Information Centre (Map p66; ☎02-9253 0888; www.environment.nsw.gov.au; Cadman's Cottage, 110 George St; ☺9.30am-4.30pm Mon-Fri, 10am-4.30pm Sat & Sun; 🚆Circular Quay) Has maps of walks in different parts of the park and organises tours of the harbour islands.

Sydney Visitor Centres (☎02-9240 8788; www.sydneyvisitorcentre.com) Darling Harbour (Map p78; ☎02-9240 8788; www.darlingharbour.com; ☺9.30am-5.30pm; 🚆Town Hall); the Rocks (Map p66; ☎02-9240 8788; www.sydneyvisitorcentre.com; cnr Argyle & Playfair Sts; ☺9.30am-5.30pm; 🚆Circular Quay) Both branches have a wide range of brochures and staff can book accommodation, tours and attractions.

🛈 Getting There & Away

Air

Sydney Airport (SYD; www.sydneyairport.com.au) is Australia's busiest, so don't be surprised if there are delays. It's only 10km south of the city centre, making access relatively easy. The

T1 (international) and T2 and T3 (domestic) terminals are a 4km bus ($5.50, 10 minutes) or train ($5, two minutes) ride apart (the airport is privately run so transferring terminals – a service that's free in most of the world – is seen as a profit opportunity).

Bus

All private interstate and regional bus travellers arrive at the **Sydney Coach Terminal** (☎02-9281 9366; Eddy Ave, Central Station; ⊙6am-6pm Mon-Fri, 8am-6pm Sat & Sun) on the corner of Eddy Ave and Pitt St in front of Central Station.

Train

CountryLink (☎13 22 32; www.countrylink.info) runs services connecting Sydney with regional and interstate destinations. The major train hub is **Central Station** (☎24hr transport information 13 15 00, bookings 13 22 32; www.countrylink. info; Eddy Ave; ⊙staffed ticket booths 6.15am-8.45pm, ticket machines 24hr).

ⓘ Getting Around

For information on government-operated buses, ferries and trains try the **Transport Infoline** (☎13 15 00; www.131500.com.au).

MyZone Tickets & Passes

There are three discount options for travelling on Sydney's public transport network: MyMulti day passes, MyMulti weekly passes and TravelTen Tickets. You can purchase these at newsagencies, newsstands and bus/ferry/train ticket offices. For information, see www.myzone.nsw.gov.au.

MyMulti Day Pass This pass (adult/child $22/11) gives unlimited transport on government-operated buses, ferries, MLR and trains within Sydney, the Blue Mountains, Hunter Valley, Central Coast, Newcastle and Illawarra.

MyMulti Passes Gives unlimited transport in the metropolitan area for one week (adult $44 to $52, child $22 to $26), or across Sydney, the Blue Mountains, Hunter Valley, Central Coast, Newcastle, South Coast, Southern Highlands and Port Stephens (adult/child $61/30.50).

MyBus, MyTrain and MyFerry TravelTen Tickets These offer 10 discounted rides but can only be used on one mode of transport.

To/From the Airport

One of the easiest ways to get to and from the airport is with a shuttle company – most hotels and hostels will be able to organise this for you.

Airport Link (☎13 15 00; www.airportlink. com.au; one-way adult/child Domestic Station to Central Sydney $15.90/11.40, International Station to Central Sydney $16.70/11.80; ⊙4.30am-12.40am) is a strange service: it's a normal commuter train line, but you pay through the nose to use the airport stations (punters going to Wolli Creek, the next stop *beyond* the airport, pay $3.60). The trip from Central Station takes a mere 10 minutes or so.

Taxi fares from the airport are approximately $40 to the city centre ($45 between 10pm and 6am), $39 to Bondi ($45 between 10pm and 6am) and $75 to Manly ($88 between 10pm and 6am).

Boat

Ferry Harbour ferries and RiverCats (to Parramatta) operated by **Sydney Ferries** (Map p66; www.sydneyferries.info) depart from Circular Quay. Most ferries operate between 6am and midnight; those servicing tourist attractions operate shorter hours.

A one-way inner-harbour ride on a regular ferry costs adult/concession $5.80/2.90. A one-way ride to Manly or Parramatta costs $7.20/$3.60.

A one-way trip to Manly with **Manly Fast Ferry** (☎02-9583 1199; www.manlyfastferry.com.au) costs adult/child $9/6 one way. Services depart from Circular Quay's Wharf 6 between 6.40am and 7.30pm weekdays, 10.10am and 6.40pm weekends.

Water taxis ply dedicated shuttle routes; rides to/from other harbour venues can be booked. **Aussie Water Taxis** (Map p78; ☎02-9211 7730; www.aussiewatertaxis.com; Cockle Bay Wharf) Darling Harbour to Circular Quay single/return adult $15/25, child $10/15; Darling Harbour to Taronga Zoo single/return adult $25/40, child $15/25; 45-minute Harbour and Nightlights Tours adult/child $35/25.

Yellow Water Taxis (Map p78; ☎02-9299 0199; www.yellowwatertaxis.com.au) Circular Quay to Darling Harbour adult/child $15/10; set price per four people for other trips – see the website for details.

Bus

Sydney Buses (☎131 500; www.sydneybuses. info) has an extensive network; you can check route and timetable information online. Nightrider buses operate infrequently after regular services cease around midnight.

The main city bus stops are Circular Quay, Wynyard Park (York St), the Queen Victoria Building (QVB; York St) and Railway Sq. Many services are prepay-only during the week – buy tickets from newsagents or Bus TransitShops. On weekends you can usually purchase your ticket on the bus. There are three fare zones: $2.20/3.60/4.60. There's a Bus TransitShop booth at Circular Quay, and there are others at the Queen Victoria Building, Railway Sq and Wynyard Station.

Car & Motorcycle

Cars are good for day trips out of town, but driving one in the city is like having an anchor around your neck. Traffic is heavy and parking is both elusive and very expensive (expect $30 per day).

Road Tolls

There's a $4 southbound toll on the Sydney Harbour Bridge and Tunnel; a $6 northbound toll on the Eastern Distributor; tolls of $2.30 to $4.90 on the Cross City Tunnel; and a $3 toll on the Lane Cove Tunnel. Sydney's main motorways (M2, M5 South-West and M7) are also tolled ($0.62 to $7.30). For information about the system, go to www.sydneymotorways.com.

The tolling system is electronic, meaning that it's up to you to organise an electronic tag or visitors' pass through any of the following websites: www.roamcom.au, www.roamexpress.com.au or www.myetoll.com.au. Note that most car-hire companies now supply etags.

Metro Light Rail (MLR)

The **Metro Light Rail** (MLR; www.metrolightrail.com.au) operates tram services between Central Station and the Sydney Convention Centre in Darling Harbour via Chinatown (zone 1) and then beyond Darling Harbour to Lilyfield via Pyrmont, Star City Casino, the Fish Markets, Glebe and Rozelle (zone 2). Services between Central and Star City run every 10 to 15 minutes

24 hours per day; others operate from 6am to 11pm (midnight on Friday and Saturday).

Taxi

Taxis and cab ranks proliferate in Sydney. Flag fall is $3.50, then it's $2.14 per kilometre (plus 20% from 10pm to 6am). The waiting charge is $0.92 per minute. Passengers must pay bridge, tunnel and road tolls (even if you don't incur them 'outbound', the returning driver will incur them 'inbound').

Major taxi companies offering phone bookings ($2.40 fee):

Legion (☏13 14 51; www.legioncabs.com.au)

Premier Cabs (☏13 10 17; www.premiercabs.com.au)

Taxis Combined (☏13 33 00; www.taxiscombined.com.au)

Train

Sydney's suburban rail network is operated by **CityRail** (☏131 500; www.cityrail.info). Lines radiate from the underground City Circle (seven city-centre stations plus Kings Cross) but don't service the northern, southern or eastern beaches, Balmain/Rozelle or Glebe. All suburban

Central Station

trains stop at Central Station, and usually one or more of the other City Circle stations, too.

Trains run from around 5am to midnight. After 9am on weekdays you can buy an off-peak return ticket, valid until midnight, for 30% less than the standard fare.

Twenty-four-hour ticket machines occupy most stations, but customer service officers are usually available if you need help with the fares. If you have to change trains, buy a ticket to your ultimate destination, but don't exit the transfer station en route or your ticket will be invalid.

AROUND SYDNEY

Royal National Park

The 15,080-hectare **Royal National Park** (☎02-9542 0648; www.environment.nsw.gov.au; cars $11, pedestrians & cyclists free; ⏰gates to park areas locked at 8.30pm daily) was established in 1879, making it the oldest national park in the world after Yellowstone in the USA. Here you'll find pockets of subtropical rainforest, wind-blown coastal scrub, sandstone gullies dominated by gum trees, fresh- and saltwater wetlands, and isolated beaches. Traditionally the

Winifred Falls, Royal National Park

home of the Dharawal people, there are also numerous Aboriginal sites and artefacts.

Within the park there's sheltered saltwater swimming at Wattamolla, Jibbon, Little Marley and Bonnie Vale, and freshwater swimming holes at Karloo Pool (around 2km east of Heathcote Station), Deer Pool and Curracurrang. Surfers should head for Garie Beach, North Era, South Era and Burning Palms on the park's southern coastline. At the historic **Audley Boat Shed** (☎02-9545 4967; www.audleyboatshed.com; 6 Farnell Ave) you can hire rowboats, canoes and kayaks ($20/45 per hour/day), aqua bikes ($15 per 30 minutes) and bicycles ($16/34 per hour/day) and make your way up Kangaroo Creek or the Hacking River.

The **park office** (☎02-9542 0648; 159 Farnell Ave, Audley Heights; ⏰9am-4.30pm Mon-Fri) can assist with maps, brochures, camping permits and bushwalking details.

❶ Getting There & Away

From Sydney, take the Princes Hwy south and turn off at Farnell Ave, south of Loftus, to the park's northern end – it's about a 45-minute drive from the city.

YURY PROKOPENKO/GETTY IMAGES ©

The most scenic route into the park is to take the CityRail train (Eastern Suburbs and Illawarra line) to Cronulla (one way adult/child $5/2.50), and then jump aboard a **Cronulla National Park Ferry** (☎02-9523 2990; www.cronullaferries.com.au; Cronulla Wharf; adult/child one way $6.30/$3.15; ⊙hourly between 5.30am-6.30pm Mon-Fri, 8.30am-6.30pm Sat, 8.30am-5.30pm Sun) to Bundeena.

Alternatively, Loftus, Engadine, Heathcote, Waterfall and Otford train stations are on the park boundary and have trails leading into the park. Loftus is closest to the park office (6km).

Hawkesbury River

Less than an hour from Sydney, the tranquil Hawkesbury River is a favourite weekend destination for stressed-out city folk. The river – one of the longest in eastern Australia – flows past honeycomb-coloured cliffs, historic townships and riverside hamlets into bays and inlets and between a series of national parks.

The **Riverboat Postman** (☎02-9985 9900, 0400 600 111; www.riverboatpostman.com.au; Brooklyn Public Wharf, Dangar Rd; adult/child/seniors $50/15/44; ⊙10am Mon-Fri), Australia's last operating mail boat, departs from the Brooklyn Wharf, beside the Hawkesbury River Railway Station, and chugs 40km up the Lower Hawkesbury as far as Marlow, returning to Brooklyn at 1.15pm.

Further upstream a narrow forested waterway diverts from the Hawkesbury and peters down to the chilled-out river town of **Berowra Waters**, where a handful of businesses, boat sheds and residences cluster around the free, 24-hour ferry across Berowra Creek.

CityRail trains run from Sydney's Central Station to Berowra (one way adult/child $6.60/3.30, 45 minutes, roughly hourly) and on to Brooklyn's Hawkesbury River Station (one way adult/child $6.60/3.30, one hour). Note that Berowra train station is a solid 6km trudge from Berowra Waters. **Hawkesbury Water Taxis** (☎0400 600 111; www.hawkesburycruises.com.au; trips from $80) will take you anywhere along the river.

The lively riverside hamlet of **Wisemans Ferry** spills over a bow of the Hawkesbury River where it slides east towards Brooklyn. The surrounding area retains remnants of the convict-built **Great North Road**, originally constructed to link Sydney with the Hunter Valley and now part of the Australian Convict Sites listing on Unesco's World Heritage List. To download a self-guided tour brochure, go to www.rta.nsw.gov.au and type 'convict trail' into the search box.

The **Hawkesbury Visitor Information Centre** (☎02-4578 0233; www.hawkesburytourism.com.au; Ham Common, Hawkesbury Valley Way, Clarendon, Ham Common Park, Clarendon; ⊙9am-5pm Mon-Fri, to 4pm Sat & Sun) opposite the RAAF base at Clarendon, between the towns of Richmond and Windsor, can supply information about the region.

Hunter Valley

A filigree of narrow country lanes criss-crosses this verdant valley, but a pleasant country drive isn't the main motivator for visitors – sheer decadence is. The Hunter Valley is one big gorge-fest: fine wine, boutique beer, chocolate, cheese, olives, you name it.

The oldest wine region in Australia, the Hunter is known for its semillon and shiraz. Even those with only a casual interest in wine should be sure to tour around – it's a lovely area, surrounded by national parks and chock-full of things to do.

◉ Sights & Activities

WINERIES

The valley's 140-plus wineries range from small-scale family-run affairs to massive commercial operations.

Brokenwood   Winery
(www.brokenwood.com.au; 401-427 McDonalds Rd, Pokolbin; ⊙9.30am-5pm Mon-Sat, 10am-5pm Sun) One of the Hunter's most acclaimed wineries.

Hawkesbury Houseboats

The best way to experience the Hawkesbury is on a fully equipped houseboat. Rates skyrocket during summer and school holidays, but most outfits offer affordable low-season, midweek and long-term rental specials. To give a very rough guide, a two-/four-/six-berth boat for three nights costs from $650/740/1100 from September to early December, with prices doubling during the Christmas/New Year period and on weekends and holidays throughout the year.

Companies are based in Brooklyn, Wisemans Ferry and Lower Portland.

Able Hawkesbury River Houseboats (02-4566 4308, 1800 024 979; www.hawkesbury houseboats.com.au; 3008 River Rd, Wisemans Ferry)

Brooklyn Marina (02-9985 7722; www.brooklynmarina.com.au; 45 Brooklyn Rd, Brooklyn)

Holidays Afloat (02-9985 5555; www.holidaysafloat.com.au; 87 Brooklyn Rd, Brooklyn)

Ripples Houseboats (02-9985 5555; www.ripples.com.au; 87 Brooklyn Rd, Brooklyn)

Hungerford Hill
Winery

(www.hungerfordhill.com.au; 2450 Broke Rd, Pokolbin; 10am-5pm Sun-Thu, to 6pm Fri & Sat) Shaped like a big barrel, with its 'lid' permanently propped open, this winery stands sentinel at the entry to Broke Rd. It houses the highly regarded **Muse Restaurant** (02-4998 6777; www.musedining.com.au; Hungerford Hill Vineyard, 1 Broke Rd, Pokolbin; lunch mains $26-36, set 2-/3-course dinner $75/95, 5-course tasting menu $110; 10am-5pm & 6.30-10pm Wed-Sat, 10am-5pm Sun).

Margan
Winery

(www.margan.com.au; 1238 Millbrodale Rd, Broke; 10am-5pm) Gorgeous setting, classy tasting room and the fabulous **Margan restaurant** (02-6579 1372; www.margan.com.au; 1238 Milbrodale Rd, Broke; breakfast dishes $12-18, lunch mains $36-38, 2-/4-/5-course tasting menu $65/80/95; noon-3pm & 6-9.30pm Fri & Sat, 9-11am & noon-3pm Sun).

Small Winemakers Centre
Cellar Door

(www.smallwinemakerscentre.com.au; 426 McDonalds Rd, Pokolbin; 10am-5pm) Acts as a cellar door for six boutique winemakers plus the Australian Regional Food Store.

Tamburlaine
Winery

(www.tamburlaine.com.au; 358 McDonalds Rd, Pokolbin; 9am-5pm) An excellent producer focusing on sustainable viticulture.

Tours

Some operators will collect you in Sydney or Newcastle for a lengthy day trip.

Hunter Valley Boutique Wine Tours
Wine

(02-4990 8989; www.huntervalleytours.com.au) Small-group tours; from $65 per person for a half-day tour and from $99 for a full-day tour including lunch.

Hunter Valley Wine Tasting Tours
Wine

(02-9357 5511; www.huntervalleywinetasting tours.com.au) These full-day minivan tours from Sydney ($110 to $153), Newcastle ($80 to $105) or the valley ($75 to $100) visit five wineries.

Wine Rover
Wine

(02-4990 1699; www.rovercoaches.com.au) Coaches will pick you up in Cessnock or Pokolbin ($45/55 weekdays/weekends), Branxton ($55/65), Newcastle ($60/70) or Morisset train station ($55/65) for a day spent visiting wineries and other attractions.

❶ Information

Hunter Valley Visitor Information Centre
(☏ 02-4990 0900; www.winecountry.com.au; 455 Wine Country Dr, Pokolbin; ⊘ 9am-5pm Mon-Sat, to 4pm Sun) The visitor centre has a huge stock of leaflets as well as information on valley accommodation, attractions and dining.

❶ Getting There & Away

If you're driving from Sydney, consider exiting north from the M1 at the Peats Ridge Rd exit and making your way along the convict-built Great North Rd to the charming colonial town of Wollombi and then heading north to Broke or east to Cessnock via Wollombi Rd.

CityRail has a line heading through the Hunter Valley from Newcastle (adult/child $6.60/3.30, 55 minutes); get off at Morisset and catch a conecting Rover Coaches service to Cessnock (adult/child $4.50/2.20, 50 minutes). Trains from Sydney (adult/child $8.40/4.20, 3¾ hours) also stop at Morisset.

Rover Coaches (☏ 02-4990 1699; www.rovercoaches.com.au) has regular services between Cessnock and Newcastle ($4.50, 1½

hours). **Hunter Valley Day Tours** (☏ 02-4951 4574; www.huntervalleydaytours.com.au) operates a shuttle service from Newcastle Airport to Hunter Valley hotels ($125 for one to two persons).

BLUE MOUNTAINS

A region with more than its fair share of natural beauty, the Blue Mountains was an obvious contender when Unesco called for Australian nominations to the World Heritage List, and its inclusion was ratified in 2000. The slate-coloured haze that gives the mountains their name comes from a fine mist of oil exuded by the huge eucalyptus gums that form a dense canopy across the landscape of deep, often-inaccessible valleys and chiselled sandstone outcrops.

The foothills begin 65km inland from Sydney, rising to an 1100m-high sandstone plateau riddled with valleys eroded into the stone over thousands of years. There are eight connected conservation areas in the region, including the **Blue Mountains National Park** (☏ 02-4787 8877; www.environment.nsw.

Hunter Valley vineyard

gov.au/nationalparks; per car $7 in the Glenbrook area only), which has some truly fantastic scenery, excellent bushwalks, Aboriginal engravings and all the canyons and cliffs you could ask for.

Although it's possible to visit on a day trip from Sydney, we strongly recommend that you stay at least one night so that you can explore a few of the towns, do at least one bushwalk and enjoy a dinner at one of the excellent restaurants in Blackheath or Leura.

◎ Sights

Glenbrook to Blackheath

Arriving from Sydney, the first of the Blue Mountains town you will encounter is Glenbrook (population 4945). From here, you can drive or walk into the Blue Mountains National Park; this is the only part of the park where entry fees apply. Six kilometres from the park entrance gate is the **Mt Portal Lookout**, which

has panoramic views into the Glenbrook Gorge, over the Nepean River and back to Sydney.

Artist, author and bon vivant Norman Lindsay, infamous for his racy artworks (imagine an unfortunate conflation of Boucher and Beardsley) but much loved for his children's tale *The Magic Pudding*, lived in Faulconbridge, 14km up the mountain from Glenbrook, from 1912 until his death in 1969. His home and studio have been preserved and are maintained by the National Trust as the **Norman Lindsay Gallery and Museum** (✎ 02-4751 1067; www.normanlindsay.com.au; 14 Norman Lindsay Cres, Faulconbridge; adult/child $12/6; ⊙ 10am-4pm), with a significant collection of his paintings, watercolours, drawings and sculptures.

Further up the mountain, the town of **Wentworth Falls** (population 5934) commands views to the south across the majestic Jamison Valley. One of the best bushwalks in the Blue Mountains – the National Pass Walk – has its starting point at the **Conservation Hut** (www.conservationhut.com.au; Fletcher St; lunch mains $21-29, sandwiches $8.50-18; ⊙ 9am-4pm Mon-Fri, to 5pm Sat & Sun), where maps, information, water and food are available. The track passes Queen Victoria lookout and then heads into the sublimely beautiful Valley of the Waters, home to the Empress, Silvia and Lodore waterfalls. It then leads up the historic Grand Stairway, built by hand in the early 1900s, and arrives at the Wentworth Falls and Jamison lookouts, both of which offer magnificent views.

Nearby **Leura** (population 4365) is a genteel town of undulating streets, heritage houses and lush gardens. At its centre is the Mall, a tree-

Three Sisters, Blue Mountains National Park

lined main street with boutiques, galleries and cafes.

Just outside town is **Gordon Falls Reserve**, an idyllic picnic spot complete with barbeques. From here you can trek the steep Prince Henry Cliff Walk, or take the Cliff Drive 4km west past Leura Cascades to **Katoomba** (population 8016), the region's main town. The often-misty steep streets are lined with art-deco buildings and the local population is an odd mix of country battlers, hippies, mortgage refugees from the big smoke (Sydney) and members of a Tennessee-based messianic Christian sect called the Twelve Tribes (aka the Community of Believers), who live communally, believe in traditional lifestyle and operate the Common Ground Café in the main street. Extraordinarily, all of these locals seem to live together harmoniously. They also seem to cope with the huge numbers of tour buses and tourists who come here to ooh and aah at the spectacular view of the Jamison Valley and **Three Sisters** rock formation towers from the **Echo Point** viewing platforms.

Three kilometres from the centre of Katoomba you'll find **Scenic World** (☎02-4780 0200; www.scenicworld.com.au; cnr Violet St & Cliff Dr, Katoomba; cableway, walkway & skyway adult/child/family $28/14/70; ☺9am-5pm), with a megaplex vibe and modern cable car descending the 52-degree incline to the valley floor. Also here is a glass-floored Scenic Skyway, a cable car floating out across the valley.

To the north of Katoomba are the towns of **Medlow Bath** (population 517) and **Blackheath** (population 4353). Blackheath is a good base for visiting the Grose, Kanimbla and Megalong Valleys.

East of town are lookouts at **Govetts Leap** (comparable to the Three Sisters in terms of 'wow' factor but nowhere near as crowded), **Bridal Veil Falls** (the highest in the Blue Mountains) and **Evans Lookout**. To the northeast, via Hat Hill Rd, are **Pulpit Rock**, **Perrys Lookdown** and **Anvil Rock**.

Mt Victoria & Hartley

Mt Victoria (population 896) sits at 1043m and is the highest town in the mountains. Historic buildings in town include **St Peter's Church** (1874) and the **Toll Keepers Cottage** (1849).

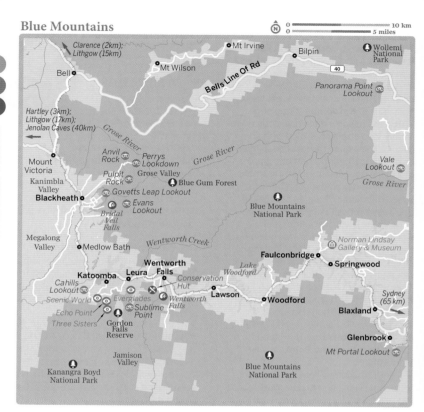

About 12km past Mt Victoria, on the western slopes of the range, is the tiny, sandstone 'ghost' town of **Hartley** (population 299), which flourished from the 1830s but declined when bypassed by the railway in 1887. It's been well preserved and a number of historic buildings remain, including several private homes and inns.

 Activities

BUSHWALKING

Explorers Wentworth, Blaxland and Lawson set off a craze for exploring the area when they became the first Europeans to traverse these majestic mountains in 1813. Fortunately, there are walks of every possible duration and level of difficulty on offer, so everyone can participate. The two most popular bushwalking areas are the Jamison Valley, south of Katoomba, and the Grose Valley, northeast of Katoomba and east of Blackheath. Other great walking opportunities can be found in the area south of Glenbrook, the Kanangra-Boyd National Park (accessible from Oberon or Jenolan Caves) and the Wollemi National Park, north of Bells Line of Road.

The extraordinarily helpful **NPWS Visitor Centre** (☏02-4787 8877; bluemountains.heritagecentre@environment.nsw. gov.au; Govetts Leap Rd, Blackheath; ☺9am-4.30pm) at Blackheath, about 2.5km off the Great Western Hwy and 10km north of Katoomba, can help you pick a hike, offer safety tips and advise about camping. Always leave your name and walk plan with the Katoomba Police, at the NPWS office or at one of the visitor centres;

the Katoomba police station, Echo Point Visitor Centre and NPWS office also offer free use of personal locator beacons. It's important to carry clean drinking water with you – the mountain streams are polluted due to their proximity to urban areas.

A range of NPWS walks pamphlets and maps ($3 to $7) are available from the NPWS office and from the visitor information centres at Glenbrook and Katoomba. All three centres also sell the Hema *Blue Mountains* walking map ($10.50) and Veechi Stuart's well-regarded *Blue Mountains: Best Bushwalks* ($32) book.

CYCLING

The mountains are also a popular cycling destination, with many people taking their bikes on the train to Woodford and then cycling downhill to Glenbrook, which is a ride of two to three hours. Cycling maps ($7) are available from the visitor information centres located at Glenbrook and Katoomba.

ADVENTURE ACTIVITIES & TOURS

Most operators have offices in Katoomba, and competition is fierce, so shop around for the best deal.

Australian School of Mountaineering   Adventure Sports
(ASM; ☎ 02-4782 2014; www.asmguides.com; 166 Katoomba St, Katoomba) Full-day rock climbs ($195) and canyoning ($180 to $220), plus abseiling courses.

Blue Mountains Walkabout   Cultural Tour
(☎ 0408 443 822; www.bluemountainswalk about.com; $95) Full-day Indigenous-owned and -guided adventurous trek with a spiritual theme; starts at Faulconbridge train station and ends at Springwood station.

High 'n' Wild Mountain Adventures   Adventure Sports
(☎ 02-4782 6224; www.highandwild.com.au; 3/5 Katoomba St, Katoomba) Organises guided abseiling ($125 to $189), rock climbing ($249 to $349) and canyoning ($179 to $225) trips.

Overcliff-Undercliff track near Wentworth Falls (p108)

DANITA DELIMONT/GETTY IMAGES ©

Muggadah Indigenous Tours
Cultural Tour

(☎02-4782 2413, 0423 573 909; kathleen@muggadahtours.com.au; adult/child $50/25) Indigenous-operated guided walks viewing significant cultural sites on traditional land around Echo Point.

River Deep Mountain High
Adventure Sports

(☎02-4782 6109; www.rdmh.com.au; 2/187 Katoomba St, Katoomba) Offers half-day abseiling ($130), full-day canyoning ($190) and full-day canyoning and abseiling ($180) packages, plus a range of guided hikes and 4WD tours.

Tread Lightly Eco Tours
Ecotours

(☎02-4788 1229; www.treadlightly.com.au) Has a wide range of day and night walks ($65 to $135) that emphasise the ecology of the region.

Sleeping

Glenella Guesthouse
Guesthouse $$

(☎02-4787 8352; www.glenellabluemountains hotel.com.au; 56-60 Govetts Leap Rd; r $110-170, f $220-260; ☎) Graceful Glenella has been

functioning as a guesthouse since 1912 and is now operated with enthusiasm and expertise by a young couple who make guests feel very welcome. There are seven comfortable bedrooms, an attractive lounge and a stunning dining room where a truly excellent breakfast is served.

Waldorf Leura Gardens
Hotel $$

(☎02-4784 4000; www.leuragardensresort.com. au; 20-28 Fitzroy St, Leura; d $107-199; ❄🛜🏊) Resort facilities (heated pool and spa, table tennis, gym, squash courts, pool table and gym), a garden setting and a location opposite Leura's 18-hole golf course make this motel-style place a popular choice for families and retirees. Rooms are comfortable and clean, service is friendly and both advance-purchase and last-minute rates are highly affordable.

Broomelea Bed & Breakfast
B&B $$

(☎02-4784 2940; www.broomelea.com.au; 273 Leura Mall, Leura; r $160-225; @🛜) Leafy Leura gets a bum rap for being snooty, but when B&Bs are as plush as this 1909 Edwardian specimen, who cares? Manicured gardens, cane furniture on the verandah, an open fire and a snug lounge

Devil's Coach House Cave, Jenolan Caves

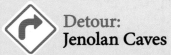

Detour:
Jenolan Caves

The story behind the discovery of **Jenolan Caves** (☏1300 763 311; www.jenolancaves. org.au; Jenolan Caves Rd; admission with tour adult/child from $30/21; ☉tours 9am-5.30pm) is the stuff of legends: local pastoralist James Whalan stumbled across the prehistoric caves while tracking the escaped convict and cattle rustler James McKeown, who is thought to have used the caves as a hideout.

Originally named Binoomea or 'Dark Places' by the Gundungurra people, the caves took shape more than 400 million years ago and are one of the most extensive and complex limestone cave systems in the world.

There are more than 350 caves in the region, although only a handful are open to the public. You must take a **tour** to see them; there's a bewildering array of options at different levels of difficulty; staff at the ticket office are happy to explain them all. You can also don a boiler suit and squeeze yourself through narrow tunnels with only a headlamp to guide you on a **Plughole Adventure Tour** ($80; ☉1.15pm daily).

The caves are 30km from the Great Western Hwy (Rte 4), a 1¼-hour drive from Katoomba. The narrow Jenolan Caves Rd becomes a one-way system between 11.45am and 1.15pm daily, running clockwise from the caves out through Oberon.

are just a few of Broomelea's bonuses. There's also a self-contained cottage for families ($160 to $205).

Lilianfels Luxury Hotel **$$$**
(☏02-4780 1200; www.lilianfels.com.au; Lilianfels Ave, Katoomba; d $250-715, ste $425-725; ❋@☎☒) Ah, if life could always be this sweet! This luxury resort offers 85 rooms, the region's best restaurant (Darley's; three-courses $125) and an indulgent array of facilities including a spa, heated indoor and outdoor pools, tennis court, billiard/games room, library and gym. Located in a historic homestead in manicured gardens next to Echo Point, it is regularly nominated as one of Australia's top hotels.

 Eating

Anonymous Cafe **$**
(www.anonymouscafe.com.au; 237-238 Great Western Hwy, Blackheath; sandwiches $10, ploughman's lunch $14-17; ☉6am-4pm Mon-Fri, 7am-5pm Sat & Sun) The groovy inner-city Sydney coffee thang has kicked off here in Blackheath courtesy of this cute cafe

opposite the train station in Blackheath, and the locals are lovin' it. The coffee (blend and single origin) is made with care and expertise, and the menu changes each week according to what local produce is in season.

Solitary Modern Australian **$$**
(☏02-4782 1164; www.solitary.com.au; 90 Cliff Dr, Leura Falls; lunch dishes $15-32, sandwiches $14-18, scones $13; ☉10.30am-4.30pm Wed, Thu, Sun & Mon, 10.30am-4.30pm & 6.30-10pm Fri & Sat, closed 2 weeks Jan) The seasonally driven menu tries hard to live up to this restaurant's setting atop the Leura Cascades. Sit in the old-fashioned dining spaces or on the front lawn to enjoy lunch or a Devonshire tea.

Leura Garage Mediterranean **$$**
(☏02-4784 3391; www.leuragarage.com.au; 84 Railway Pde, Leura; breakfast $9-19, shared plates $9-31, pizzas $21-29; ☉11.30am-late Mon, Thu & Fri, 8am-late Sat & Sun) Suspended mufflers and stacks of old tires signal the occupation of the former tenant of this hugely popular place off the top end of Leura Mall. The vibe is hipster-ish, the

house wine is perfectly quaffable and the shared plates, including deli-laden pizza, are hefty in size.

Silk's Brasserie   Modern Australian $$

(☏02-4784 2534; www.silksleura.com; 128 Leura Mall, Leura; lunch mains $24-39, dinner mains $30-39; ☺noon-2.30pm & 6-9pm Mon-Sat) A warm welcome awaits at Leura's long-standing fine diner. Although the dishes can sometimes be overworked, the serves are generous and the flavours harmonious.There's a two-course minimum on Friday and Saturday nights.

Drinking & Entertainment

Alexandra Hotel   Pub

(www.alexandrahotel.com.au; 62 Great Western Hwy, Leura; ☺meals noon-2pm & 5.30-9pm) The Alex is a gem. Join the punters at the pool comp on Monday, poker night on Wednesday, gay night on Friday and DJ on Saturday. For a rest, relax over an excellent pub meal in the restaurant (mains $18 to $27) or bar ($15 to $19).

Edge Cinema   Cinema

(www.edgecinema.com.au; 225 Great Western Hwy, Katoomba; tickets $16; ☺9.30am-late) A giant screen (and we mean humongous!) shows mainstream movies. Budget Tuesdays feature flicks for $10 per person.

ℹ Information

There are visitor information centres on the Great Western Hwy at Glenbrook (☏1300 653 408; www.visitbluemountains.org; Great Western Highway; ☺8.30am-4pm Mon-Sat, to 3pm Sun) and at Echo Point in Katoomba (☏1300 653 408; www.visitbluemountains.com.au; Echo Point, Katoomba; ☺9am-5pm). Both can provide plenty of information and will book accommodation, tours and attractions.

The Blue Mountains District Anzac Memorial Hospital (☏02-4784 6500; www.wsahs. nsw.gov.au/bluemountains/index.htm; cnr Woodlands Rd & Great Western Hwy, Katoomba; ☺24hr emergency) in Katoomba has a 24-hour emergency department.

ℹ Getting There & Around

To reach the Blue Mountains by road, leave Sydney via Parramatta Rd. At Strathfield detour onto the toll-free M4, which becomes the Great Western Hwy west of Penrith and takes you to all of the Blue Mountains towns. It takes approximately 1½ hours to drive from central Sydney to Katoomba.

Blue Mountains Bus (☏02-4751 1077; www.bmbc.com.au) Local buses travel from Katoomba to Wentworth Falls (buses 685 and 690K), Scenic World (bus 686), Leura (buses 685 and 690K) and Blackheath (bus 698). Fares cost between $2 and $4.30.

Blue Mountains Explorer Bus (☏1300 300 915; www.explorerbus.com. au; 283 Bathurst Rd, Katoomba; adult/child

Canyoning in the Blue Mountains National Park (p109)
CARSTEN PETER/GETTY IMAGES ©

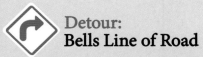

Detour:
Bells Line of Road

This stretch of road between Richmond and Lithgow is the most scenic route across the Blue Mountains and is highly recommended if you have your own transport. There are fine views towards the coast from Kurrajong Heights on the eastern slopes of the range, there are orchards (mainly apple) around Bilpin, and there's sandstone-cliff and bush scenery all the way to Lithgow.

Midway between Bilpin and Bell, the delightful **Blue Mountains Botanic Garden Mount Tomah** (☎02-4567 3000; www.rbgsyd.nsw.gov.au; Bells Line of Road; ⏰9am-5.30pm Mon-Fri, 9.30am-5.30pm Sat & Sun) FREE is a cool-climate annexe of Sydney's Royal Botanic Gardens. In addition to native plants there are displays of exotic cold-climate species, including some magnificent rhododendrons.

To access Bells Line of Road, head out on Parramatta Rd from Sydney, and from Parramatta drive northwest on Windsor Rd to Windsor. Richmond Rd from Windsor becomes the Bells Line of Road west of Richmond. The road meets State Route 69 at Kurrajong, which can be followed through the Wollemi and Yengo National Parks to the Hunter Valley.

$38/19; ⏰9.45am-4.54pm) Offers hop-on/hop-off service on a 26-stop Katoomba–Leura loop. Leaves from Katoomba station every 30 minutes to one hour.

Blue Mountains ExplorerLink (☎13 15 00; www.cityrail.info/tickets/which/explorerlink; 1-day pass adult/child from $49.60/24.80, 3-day pass adult/child from $71.60/35.80) Gives return train travel from Sydney to the Blue Mountains, plus access to the Explorer Bus service.

CityRail (☎13 15 00; www.cityrail.info) Runs to the mountains from Sydney's Central Station (one way adult/child $8.40/4.20, two hours, hourly). Off-peak return tickets cost $11.60/5.80. There are stations at towns along the Great Western Hwy, including Glenbrook, Faulconbridge, Wentworth Falls, Leura, Katoomba, Medlow Bath, Blackheath, Mt Victoria, Zig Zag and Lithgow.

Trolley Tours (☎4782 7999; www.trolleytours.com.au; 76 Bathurst Rd, Katoomba; ticket $25; ⏰9.45am-5.42pm) Runs a hop-on, hop-off bus barely disguised as a trolley, looping around 29 stops in Katoomba and Leura.

Brisbane & the East Coast Beaches

From northern New South Wales to Queensland's Sunshine Coast, this section of Australia's east coast demands attention. Score some serious holiday points: the in-your-face seductions of the Gold Coast, hippie hinterland towns, and Brisbane, Australia's third-largest city... all caressed by surf and dappled with 300 days of sunshine a year.

Byron Bay, Australia's most easterly town, is a haven for surfers, foodies and festival-goers. Further north the Gold Coast sparkles with amusement parks, surf carnivals and nocturnal glitz. Brisbane engages city slickers with its upbeat, confident vibe, while the Sunshine Coast is criminally underrated: a relaxed span of holiday towns, white-sand beaches and wildlife-watching possibilities. Offshore, World Heritage–listed Fraser Island is studded with gorgeous forests and lakes.

Queenslander hospitality is the order of the day: down-to-earth and uncynical, the locals really know how to let it all hang out.

Kids' lifesaving drill at Burleigh Heads (p135), Gold Coast

Riverside view of Brisbane (p139)

Brisbane & the East Coast Beaches

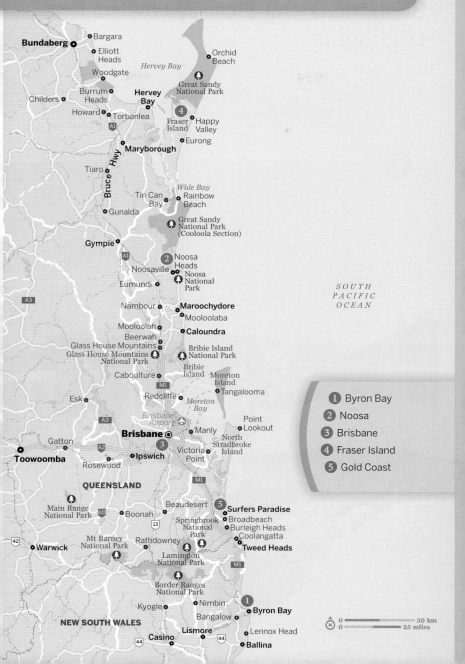

Bundaberg
Bargara
Elliott Heads
Woodgate
Hervey Bay
Orchid Beach
Childers
Burrum Heads
Hervey Bay
Great Sandy National Park
Howard
Torbanlea
4
Fraser Island
Happy Valley
Maryborough
Eurong
Tiaro
Bruce Hwy
Wide Bay
Tin Can Bay
Rainbow Beach
Gunalda
Great Sandy National Park (Cooloola Section)
Gympie
2 Noosa Heads
Noosaville
Noosa National Park
Eumundi
Nambour
Maroochydore
Mooloolaba
Mooloolah
Beerwah
Caloundra
Glass House Mountains
Glass House Mountains National Park
Bribie Island National Park
Caboolture
Bribie Island
Moreton Island
Redcliffe
Tangalooma
Moreton Bay
Brisbane Airport
Esk
Point Lookout
Brisbane
Manly
North Stradbroke Island
Gatton
Victoria Point
Toowoomba
3
Ipswich
Rosewood
QUEENSLAND
Beaudesert
5 Surfers Paradise
Main Range National Park
Boonah
Springbrook National Park
Broadbeach
Burleigh Heads
Coolangatta
Mt Barney National Park
Rathdowney
Tweed Heads
Warwick
Lamington National Park
Border Ranges National Park
Nimbin
Kyogle
Bangalow
1
Byron Bay
Lismore
Lennox Head
NEW SOUTH WALES
Casino
Ballina

SOUTH PACIFIC OCEAN

1 Byron Bay
2 Noosa
3 Brisbane
4 Fraser Island
5 Gold Coast

0   50 km
0   25 miles

Brisbane & the East Coast Beaches Highlights

Byron Bay

Byron Bay (p126) – the town adjacent to Cape Byron, Australia's most easterly point – scores points for its laid-back lifestyle, international vibe and beautiful beaches and surf breaks. It's the kind of place where people come for a week and stay six months. Twenty minutes inland, the hinterland is a maze of hills, valleys, waterfalls and hippie towns.

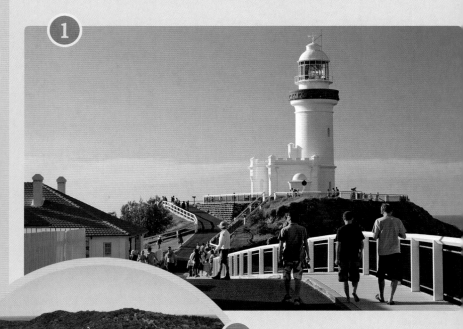

1

2 ## Noosa

It just keeps getting better at Noosa (p157), the Sunshine Coast's premier resort town, where style meets surf, or chic meets surfie chick. Noosa is developed, but the little luxuries of the well-heeled mingle effortlessly with free-of-charge natural attributes – the beach and the bush. Enjoy the culinary and shopping delights of Hastings St, take a surfing lesson, or just kick back and sip a coffee or a cocktail.

PETER HARRISON/GETTY IMAGES ©

MANFRED GOTTSCHALK/GETTY IMAGES ©

Brisbane

3

Australia's third-largest city is a booming metropolis engraved with a hypnotically meandering river. Exploring Brisbane (p139) by river ferry and passing under the sturdy Story Bridge will give you a wonderful appreciation of this prosperous city. Along the river banks are subtropical gardens and vestiges of colonial architecture, the superb Gallery of Modern Art and an intricate network or urban enclaves full of cafes, bars and restaurants. Story Bridge (p145)

DAVID WALL PHOTO/GETTY IMAGES ©

4

Fraser Island

They broke the mould when they made Fraser Island (p159): the world's largest sand island (120km long!) isn't like anywhere else on the planet. Birds, dingoes and marine life enjoy tropical forests, dunes, freshwater lakes and beaches (...the latter they also share with humans in 4WDs). It's a brilliant place to escape for a day or two in the wilds. Kingfisher Bay

5

Gold Coast

Love it or loathe it, the Gold Coast (p132) never fails to elicit an opinion. It's undeniably dynamic: high-rise apartments jostle for views over the gorgeous sandy coast, while club-fuelled nightlife goes berserk in the backstreets. But the amazing Gold Coast theme parks are what many are here for: a half-dozen adrenalin-charged excuses to stay another day. Sea World theme park (p138)

121

Brisbane & the East Coast Beaches' Best...

Beaches

⊙ **Little Wategos** Byron Bay's (and mainland Australia's) most easterly stretch of sand. (p126)

⊙ **Coolangatta** Check the surf at Kirra or just snooze on the sand. (p137)

⊙ **Cylinder Beach** Lovely family-friendly beach on North Stradbroke Island. (p153)

⊙ **Surfers Paradise** The name says it all. Face the ocean and forget the high-rise backdrop. (p132)

Outdoor Activities

⊙ **Gold Coast surfing** Ride the Gold Coast surf on a surfboard or, for an extra lift, attach a kite and power across the waves. (p132)

⊙ **Noosa bushwalking** Take a stroll through lush Noosa National Park to golden-sand beaches. (p157)

⊙ **Tangalooma dolphin feeding** Wade into the Moreton Island waters and hand-feed Flipper. (p154)

⊙ **Fraser Island 4WD beaches** It's a cliché, but it's great fun! (Consider carbon offsetting...) (p162)

Kids' Stuff

⊙ **Gold Coast theme parks** Adventure on tap for thrill seekers and restless teens. (p138)

⊙ **Australia Zoo** Take the kids for a day-trip to this fabulous wildlife park. (p156)

⊙ **South Bank, Brisbane** Galleries, museum, science centre: terrific scientific and artistic education. And a beach! (p139)

⊙ **Lone Pine Koala Sanctuary** Boat along the Brisbane River to meet some koalas (just don't call them 'bears'). (p142)

Crowd-Dodging Hideaways

○ **Bangalow** Just 10 minutes from Byron Bay, Bangalow keeps things happily low-key. (p131)

○ **Rainbow Beach** A relaxed, unpretentious little town that's the departure point for Fraser Island... We hate to blow its cover! (p163)

○ **Burleigh Heads** Great surf and beachfront eateries with little of the Gold Coast hype. (p135)

○ **Springbrook National Park** Plateaus, waterfalls and rock formations in the Gold Coast hinterland. (p137)

Left: SkyPoint Observation Deck (p133), Surfers Paradise; **Above:** Springbrook National Park (p137)
(LEFT) MANFRED GOTTSCHALK/GETTY IMAGES ©;
(ABOVE) OLIVER STREWE/GETTY IMAGES ©

ADVANCE PLANNING

○ **One month before** Organise internal flights, resort accommodation and a Story Bridge Adventure Climb (p145) in Brisbane.

○ **Two weeks before** Book a Fraser Island trip or some Moreton Bay dolphin-spotting.

○ **One week before** Book a Byron Bay surfing lesson and a classy Brisbane restaurant table: try E'cco (p146) or Ortiga (p147).

RESOURCES

○ **Queensland Holidays** (www.queenslandholidays.com.au) Great for planning your trip.

○ **Tourism Queensland** (www.tq.com.au) Government-run body promoting Queensland.

○ **Visit Brisbane** (www.visitbrisbane.com.au) All things 'Brizzy'.

○ **Visit Byron Bay** (www.visitbyronbay.com) Tourism info for Byron and around.

○ **Royal Automobile Club of Queensland** (RACQ; www.racq.com.au) Driving info and emergency roadside assistance.

GETTING AROUND

○ **Walk** Through Noosa National Park and to the Cape Byron lighthouse.

○ **Drive** Around the Byron Bay and Gold Coast hinterland.

○ **Train** From Brisbane Airport into the city.

○ **Ferry** Along the Brisbane River and out to North Stradbroke Island, Moreton Island and Fraser Island.

BE FOREWARNED

○ **Crowds & Festivals** Gold Coast peak seasons: January, early July and early October (theme park queues). Easter is festival time in Byron Bay, which means tight accommodation (also between Christmas and late January).

○ **Box jellyfish** Occasionally occur as far south as Fraser Island (October to April).

○ **Fraser Island's dingoes** Keep your distance.

Brisbane & the East Coast Beaches Itineraries

It's not far, but there's lots to see from Byron Bay to Brisbane. If you have more time, head north to explore islands, whale-filled bays and the Sunshine Coast.

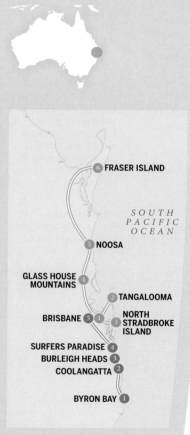

FRASER ISLAND 6

SOUTH PACIFIC OCEAN

NOOSA 5

GLASS HOUSE MOUNTAINS 1

TANGALOOMA 2

BRISBANE 5 1

NORTH STRADBROKE ISLAND

SURFERS PARADISE 4

BURLEIGH HEADS 3

COOLANGATTA 2

BYRON BAY 1

3 DAYS

BYRON BAY TO BRISBANE
Surf to City

It might be hard to leave the point breaks, cafes and chilled-out vibes of ❶ **Byron Bay** (p126) behind, but point your radar north and cross the state line into Queensland. Pit-stop for a night at sandy ❷ **Coolangatta** (p137) or ❸ **Burleigh Heads** (p135) for some uncomplicated beach life and a relaxed surfside dinner. Get some sleep too – glitzy ❹ **Surfers Paradise** (p132) awaits: parade your wares on the sand or succumb to the after-dark decadence. If the kids (or you) are eager for a rollercoaster rush, swing by the Gold Coast's hugely popular theme parks.

Turn inland to ❺ **Brisbane** (p139), take in a show and explore the sights along the Brisbane River. Check out the bars, bookshops and cafes in the West End, mooch around the eateries in New Farm, or dissolve the evening in the bars and clubs in Fortitude Valley. There are some superb markets here, too: the Saturday-morning Davies Park Market (p150) is in the West End by the river. Climb the Story Bridge for sparkling city views, or jump on a slow boat to the Lone Pine Koala Sanctuary (p142) to cuddle a koala and get photo proof of the event.

Top Left: Lone Pine Koala Sanctuary (p142), Brisbane; **Top Right:** Tangalooma (p154), Moreton Island
(TOP LEFT) YUKI NAKANO/GETTY IMAGES ©; (TOP RIGHT) PHILIP GAME/GETTY IMAGES ©

5 DAYS

BRISBANE TO FRASER ISLAND

Most of the Sunshine Coast

Galleries, bars, restaurants... Big-city ❶**Brisbane** (p139) oozes urban cool, but there's plenty to see surrounding the big smoke and to the north along the Sunshine Coast. Spend a day cooling off on a hinterland tour, or take a ferry to Moreton Island to feed the dolphins at ❷**Tangalooma** (p154). Alternatively, spend a night on chilled-out ❸**North Stradbroke Island** (p153) with an early-morning surf.

Back on the mainland, navigate through the peaky ❹**Glass House Mountains** (p159) and check out the world-famous Australia Zoo.

Continue through languid Sunshine Coast towns to elegant beachside ❺**Noosa** (p157) and resurrect your board-riding skills, go kayaking, explore national park rainforest or gorge on multicultural cuisine.

If you've got any energy left, consider a 4WD exploration of sandy ❻**Fraser Island** (p159), dotted with lakes, dunes and rambunctious wildlife.

Discover Brisbane & the East Coast Beaches

BYRON BAY

The reputation of this iconic Aussie beach town precedes it: it's a gorgeous town where the trademark laid-back, New Age populace lives an escapist, organic lifestyle against a backdrop of evergreen hinterland and endlessly surfable coastline.

◉ Sights

Main Beach, immediately in front of town, is terrific for people-watching and swimming. At the western edge of town, **Belongil Beach** is clothing-optional. **Clarkes Beach**, at the eastern end of Main Beach, is good for surfing, but the best surf is at the next few beaches: **Pass**, **Wategos** and **Little Wategos**.

Tallow Beach is an amazing stretch that extends 7km south of Cape Byron to a rockier patch around **Broken Head**, where a succession of small beaches dots the coast before opening onto **Seven Mile Beach**, which goes all the way to Lennox Head.

Cape Byron

The grandfather of the poet Lord Byron was a renowned navigator in the 1760s, and Captain Cook named this spot, mainland Australia's most easterly, after him.

The views from the summit are spectacular, particularly if you've just burnt breakfast off on the climbing track from Clarkes Beach. The surrounding ocean also jumps to the tune of dolphins and migrating humpback whales in June and July. Towering over all is the 1901 **lighthouse** (☎ 02-6685 6585; Lighthouse Rd;

Cape Byron
HOLGER LEUE/GETTY IMAGES ©

⊘8am-sunset), Australia's most easterly and a powerful landmark.

 # Activities

Black Dog Surfing
Surfing

(☏02-6680 9828; www.blackdogsurfing.com; 4/5-11 Bryon St) Intimate group lessons and women's courses.

Surfing Byron Bay
Surfing

(☏02-6685 7099; www.gosurfingbyronbay.com; 84 Jonson St) Has courses for kids and, unlike some other operators, they surf in Byron Bay, not Ballina.

Sundive
Diving

(☏02-6685 7755; www.sundive.com.au; 8 Middleton St; snorkelling tour $55; ⊘tours 8am, 10.45am & 1pm) Scuba diving plus daily snorkelling.

Blue Bay Divers
Diving, Snorkelling

(☏1800 858 155; www.bluebaydivers.com.au; double dive with tank hire $115) Small groups and the chance to dive or snorkel with dolphins and turtles.

Bikram Yoga
Yoga

(☏02-6685 6334; www.bikramyogabyronbay. com.au; 8 Grevillea St; casual 90min class $20) One of the more respected yoga schools in Byron.

Relax Haven
Health & Fitness

(☏02-6685 8304; www.relaxhaven.com.au; 3/107 Jonson St; ⊘9am-8.30pm) Massages, kinesiology and floatation tanks that get rave reviews from travellers.

Cape Byron Kayaks
Kayaking

(☏02-6680 9555; www.capebyronkayaks.com; adult/child $69/59; ⊘tours 8.30am & 1pm) Cape Byron Kayaks offers great half-day kayaking tours in and around Cape Byron Marine Park. Exhibitionist dolphins are the main attraction (if you don't see one you get a free second trip).

Bay Beach Hire
Bicycle Rental

(☏1800 089 699; 3/14 Bay St; half-/full-day bike or surfboard rental $20/30) Bikes, surfboards, stand-up paddle boards, wetsuits and snorkels for hire.

 # Tours

Aboriginal Cultural Concepts
Cultural Tour

(☏0405 654 280; www.aboriginalcultural concepts.com; half-/full-day tours $80/160; ⊘10am-1pm Wed-Sat) Heritage tours exploring mythological sights along Bundjalung Coast. Highly recommended.

Byron Bay Eco Tours
Ecotour

(☏02-6685 4030; www.byron-bay.com/ ecotours; tours $85; ⊘9am) Full-day tours to nearby rainforests with excellent commentary.

Mountain Bike Tours
Mountain Biking

(☏0429 122 504; www.mountainbiketours. com.au; half-/full-day tours $75/125; ⊘9am) Environmentally friendly bike tours into the rainforest and along the coast.

 # Sleeping

The accommodation booking office, run by the visitor centre (p130), is a great service for booking in advance.

Nomads Arts Factory Lodge
Hostel, Campground $

(☏02-6685 7709; www.nomadsworld.com/arts -factory; Skinners Shoot Rd; camp sites $18, dm/d from $35/80; @ 🛜 🛋) For an archetypal Byron experience, bunker down here. The complex has didgeridoo lessons and yoga and meditation workshops delivered in a serene hippie-esque setting on a picturesque swamp. Choose from colourful six- to 10-bed dorms, a cottage, tepees or wagons. Couples can opt for aptly titled 'cube' rooms, island retreat canvas huts or the pricier love shack with bathroom.

Atlantic
Guesthouse $$

(☏02-6685 5118; www.atlanticbyronbay.com. au; 13 Marvell St; r from $155; ❄ 🛜 🛋) What a difference a facelift makes. This little residential compound has been transformed into a shiny white seaside haven where Byron surf culture meets Caribbean style.

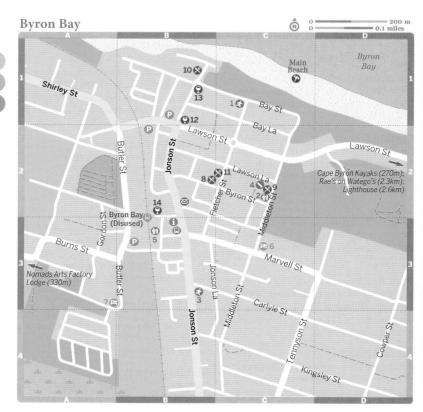

Byron Bay

✪ Activities, Courses & Tours
1 Bay Beach Hire	C1
2 Black Dog Surfing	C2
3 Relax Haven	B3
4 Sundive	C2
5 Surfing Byron Bay	B3

😴 Sleeping
6 Atlantic	C3
7 Bamboo Cottage	A3

✖ Eating
8 Earth 'n' Sea	B2
9 Espressohead	C2
10 Fishheads	B1
11 St Elmo	C2

🍷 Drinking & Nightlife
12 Balcony	B1
13 Beach Hotel	B1
14 Railway Friendly Bar	B2

Bamboo Cottage Guesthouse **$$**
(☎ 02-6685 5509; www.byron-bay.com/
bamboocottage; 76 Butler St; r from $120; 🛜)
Featuring global charm and wall hang-
ings, Bamboo Cottage treats guests to a
choice of three individually styled rooms
with Asian and Pacific island overtones in
a home-away-from-home atmosphere.
It's on the quiet side of the tracks. The
cheaper rooms have shared bathrooms.

Byron at Byron Resort **$$$**
(☎ 02-6639 2000, 1300 554 362; www.thebyron
atbyron.com.au; r from $305; ❄ @ 🛜 ≋) For
the ultimate in luxury this 92-suite resort
is set within 45 acres of subtropical rainforest. It is a hive of wildlife and endangered species and the resort maintains
its sympathy for the environment with
eco credentials listed online. When you're

not lounging by the infinity pool take the 10-minute stroll to Tallow Beach via a series of wonderful boardwalks.

Rae's on Watego's Hotel $$$

(☎02-6685 5366; www.raes.com.au; Marine Pde; r from $540; ❄@🛜🏊) This dazzlingly white Mediterranean villa was once rated one of the world's top 25 hotels. It's definitely one of Australia's. Rooms here have an artistic and casual elegance that lets the luxury sneak up on you. The restaurant is worth the trip alone.

🍴 Eating

Fishheads Seafood, Fish & Chips $

(www.restaurantbyronbay.com; 1 Jonson St; mains $9.50-22; ⏱7.30am-9pm; 🛜) Right on the beach, this fabulous takeaway shop sells traditional battered fish and chips ($9.80) or take it up a notch with chilli and garlic squid with Asian coleslaw. The restaurant is fine too, but why wouldn't you dine on the beach?

Espressohead Cafe $

(Shop 7, Middleton St) Locals flock to this place for its excellent coffees, bagels, fresh pasta and salads.

St Elmo Mediterranean, Bar $$

(☎02-6680 7426; www.stelmodining.com; cnr Fletcher St & Lawson Lane; mains $14.50-26; ⏱4pm-late Mon-Thu, noon-late Fri-Sun) Kartell stools nod to just how much design work it takes to get bums on seats. Sit on one to be served gourmet cocktails by extremely fit, bronzed and accented bar staff, or settle in for dinner; the shared plates ($23) make great date fodder. Dishes might include seared scallops with peppers stuffed with chorizo and prawn paella.

Earth 'n' Sea Italian $$

(☎02-6685 6029; www.earthnsea.com.au; cnr Fletcher & Byron Sts; pasta $15-18, pizza from $17.50; ⏱noon-2.30pm & 5-9pm Mon-Fri, noon-9pm Sat & Sun) The pizza list at this old favourite is long and full of flavour. Pasta is on the menu too. Beers include several excellent microbrews from the Northern Rivers Brewing Co.

Local Knowledge

Byron Bay

BY DEAN JOHNSTON, INSTRUCTOR, BLACK DOG SURFING

1 SURF SPOTS

The Pass is my number-one spot: an awesome right-hand point break – great for beginners – with some really long rides. I also love Tallows, a beach break for experienced surfers, with a bit more power. There are so many spots, and it's so consistent – you can surf here pretty much every day.

2 CAPE BYRON LIGHTHOUSE

Venture up to the lighthouse on Cape Byron (p126), about a half-hour walk from town: either go through the rainforest, or hug the coast and walk up along the cliffs. It's a great place to spot whales and dolphins.

3 FESTIVALS

The **East Coast International Blues & Roots Music Festival** (www.bluesfest.com. au) and **Byron Bay Writers' Festival** (www. byronbaywritersfestival.com.au) are huge here every year. It can get crowded out in the surf, but it's such a mellow atmosphere.

4 EATING & DRINKING

You can't go past the Beach Hotel (p130) for a beer – it pumps! Espressohead does the best coffee in town. Food-wise, Earth 'n' Sea is great for a pizza after a three-hour surf session.

5 HINTERLAND

The Byron Bay hinterland is really beautiful. Bangalow (p131) is just 10 minutes away – a really cool little town. Backpackers love Nimbin (p131): local tour companies can drive you out there and back, stopping at special places like Minyon Falls along the way.

🍷 Drinking & Nightlife

Balcony Bar

(www.balcony.com.au; cnr Lawson & Jonson Sts; ⏱8am-11pm) With its verandah poking out

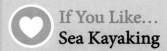

If You Like...
Sea Kayaking

1 REDLANDS KAYAK TOURS
(1300 529 258; www.redlandskayaktours.com.au; per person/family $69/246) Three-hour guided kayak tours of Moreton Bay for grown-ups and kids, departing various mainland locations. Shorter paddles are also available.

2 GOSEA KAYAKS
(0416 222 344; www.goseakayakbyronbay.com.au; adult/child $69/59; tours 9.30am & 2pm) If you don't see a whale, turtle or dolphin, you kayak for free. Some tours have Aboriginal guides. At Byron Bay.

3 STRADDIE ADVENTURES
(0417 741 963, 07-3409 8414; www.straddieadventures.com.au; 132 Dickson Way, Point Lookout; daily) Hires out surfboards, snorkelling equipment and bicycles, and runs sea-kayaking trips (adult/child $60/45) and sandboarding sessions ($30/25). Located on North Stradbroke Island.

4 ADVENTURE OUTLET
(07-5571 2929; www.adventureoutlet.com.au; Shop 5, 3 Jackman St, Southport; half-day tours incl transfers $89) Tour includes kayaking, snorkelling, fish feeding, bushwalking and morning or afternoon tea. On the Gold Coast.

amid the palm trees, this fine bar-cum-restaurant is the place to park yourself. Choose from stools, chairs or sofas while working through a cocktail list that will make you giddy just looking at it.

Railway Friendly Bar   Pub
(Jonson St; 11am-late) This indoor-outdoor pub draws everyone from lobster-red British tourists to acid-soaked hippies and high-on-life earth mothers. Its cosy interior is the old railway station. The front beer garden, conducive to boozy afternoons, has live music most nights.

Beach Hotel   Pub
(www.beachhotel.com.au; cnr Jonson & Bay Sts; 11am-late) The mothership of all pubs is close to the main beach and is shot through with a fabulously infectious atmosphere that makes everyone your best mate. There's live music and DJs some nights.

🛈 Information
Medical Services
Byron Bay Hospital (02-6685 6200; www.ncahs.nsw.gov.au; cnr Wordsworth & Shirley Sts; 24hr) For medical emergencies.

Tourist Information
Visitor Centre (02-6680 8558; www.visitbyronbay.com; Stationmaster's Cottage, Jonson St; 9am-5pm) Ground zero for tourist information. It can get a little overwhelmed during peak periods.

🛈 Getting There & Away
Air
The closest airport is at Ballina and with its rapidly expanding service it is the best airport for Byron.

Coolangatta airport on the Gold Coast has a greater range of services but can involve a traffic-clogged drive. **Byron Bay Shuttle** (www.byronbayshuttle.com.au) serves both Coolangatta ($36.10) and Ballina ($17.10) airports.

Bus
Long-distance buses for **Greyhound** (1300 4739 46863; www.greyhound.com.au) and **Premier** (13 34 10; www.premierms.com.au) stop on Jonson St.

Other services include the following:
Byron Easy Bus (02-6685 7447; www.byronbayshuttle.com.au) Byron Bay to Brisbane ($54) or Gold Coast ($39) airports.
Express Bus Service (1300 363 123; www.byronbayexpress.com.au) Byron Bay to Coolangatta and Surfers Paradise (one way/return $30/55).

🛈 Getting Around
Byron Bay Taxis (02-6685 5008; www.byronbaytaxis.com.au) On call 24 hours.

Earth Car Rentals (02-6685 7472; www.earthcar.com.au; 3a/1 Byron St) Claims to be Australia's first carbon-neutral car rental company

FAR NORTH COAST HINTERLAND

Bangalow

Boutiques, fine eateries, bookshops and an excellent pub, all a mere 14km from Byron Bay. Beautiful Bangalow (population 1520), with its character-laden main street, is the kind of place that turns Sydneysiders into tree-changers.

There's a good weekly **farmers market** (Byron St; ⊗8-11am Sat) and a praised **cooking school** (02-6687 2799; www.leahroland.com/bangalow-cooking-school).

Stately old **Bangalow Guesthouse** (02-6687 1317; bangalowguesthouse.com.au; 99 Byron St; r $165-285) sits on the river's edge ensuring guests see platypuses and oversized lizards as they eat breakfast. It's the stuff of B&B dreams.

Uptown (02-6687 2555; www.townbangalow.com.au; 33 Byron St; five-course set menu $85; ⊗6.30-9.30pm Thu-Sat) is one of coastal NSW's best restaurants with a designer set menu with seasonal local produce. Book ahead.

Blanch's Bus Service (02-6686 2144; www.blanchs.com.au) operates a service to Ballina ($9) and Byron Bay ($7.80).

Nimbin

Welcome to Australia's hippie capital, a strange little place and an ageing social experiment where anything goes. Reefers included.

◎ Sights & Activities

Hemp Embassy   Novelty Shop
(www.hempembassy.net; 51 Cullen St) This place raises consciousness about marijuana legalisation, as well as providing all the tools and fashion items you'll need to get high (or at least attract more police raids). The embassy leads the Mardi Grass festival each May.

Nimbin Museum   Museum
(www.nimbinmuseum.com; 62 Cullen St; admission by $2 donation) An interpretive and expressionistic museum that packs an eclectic collection of local art into a modest space. It's far more a work of art than of history.

ⓘ Information

Visitor Centre (02-6689 1388; www.visitnimbin.com.au; 46 Cullen St; ⊗10am-4pm) Has great local info.

ⓘ Getting There & Away

Companies in Byron Bay offer day tours to Nimbin, sometimes with stops in the region.
Nimbin Shuttle (0413 217 153; www.nimbintours.com.au; one way/same-day return $14/25, open return $26)

The Nimbin Story

Until the 1970s, Nimbin was a pretty if otherwise unremarkable village like so many in the hinterland of the northern New South Wales coast. That changed forever in May 1973 when the third (and final) Aquarius Festival was held here, drawing large numbers of students, hippies and devotees of sustainable living and alternative lifestyles. After the 10-day festival ended, some of the festival attendees stayed on in an attempt to live out the ideals expressed during the festival – Nimbin hasn't been the same since.

Grasshoppers (☏0438 269 076; www.
grasshoppers.com.au; return incl BBQ lunch $45)
Jim's Alternative Tours (☏0401 592 247; www.
jimsalternativetours.com; tours $40; ☉10am)

GOLD COAST

You might rub your eyes and do a double-
take as you approach the Gold Goast
from afar: fronting onto this iconic ribbon
of surf beaches is a towering city of high-
rise apartments, totally at odds with the
natural landscape. Down at street level
are eateries, bars and theme parks that
attract a perpetual stream of sunburnt
holidaymakers. The undisputed fun
capital is Surfers Paradise, where dizzying
nightlife sucks you in and spits you back
out exhausted. But the hype diminishes
drastically away from Surfers: Broadbeach's chic style and Burleigh Heads'
seaside charm mellow into Coolangatta's
laid-back surfer ethos.

ⓘ Getting There & Around

The international/national Gold Coast Airport
(www.goldcoastairport.com.au) is at Coolangatta,
25km south of Surfers Paradise.

The Gold Coast Tourist Shuttle (☏07-5574
5111, 1300 655 655; www.gcshuttle.com.au; one-
way per adult/child $20/12) will meet your flight
and drop you at most Gold Coast accommodation;
book in advance. Con-X-ion Airport Transfers
(☏1300 266 946; www.cxn.com.au; one-way per
adult/child from $20/12) runs a similar service.

Coachtrans (☏07-3358 9700, 1300 664
700; www.coachtrans.com.au) runs transfers
between Brisbane airport and most Gold Coast
accommodation (one way adult/child $46/230).

Surfers Paradise
& Broadbeach

Some say the surfers prefer beaches
elsewhere and paradise has been tragi-
cally lost, but there's no denying this wild
and trashy party zone attracts a phenomenal number of visitors (20,000 per day!).

Left: Gold Coast City; Below: Nimbin Museum (p131)
(LEFT) PATRICK OBEREM/GETTY IMAGES ©; (BELOW) MATTHEW MICAH WRIGHT/GETTY IMAGES ©

The decibel level is considerably lower directly south in Broadbeach (population 4650), which offers some chic restaurants and a gorgeous stretch of golden shore.

Sights & Activities

SkyPoint Observation Deck
Lookout

(www.skypoint.com.au; Level 77, Q1 Bldg, Hamilton Ave, Surfers Paradise; adult/child/family $21/12.50/54.50; ⏰7am-8.30pm Sun-Thu, to 11.30am Fri & Sat) Surfers' sights are usually spread across beach towels, but for an eagle-eye scope, zip up to this 230m-high observation deck near the top of Q1, the 27th tallest building in the world! You can also tackle the **SkyPoint Climb** up the spire to 270m high (adult/child from $69/49).

Cheyne Horan School of Surf
Surfing

(☎1800 227 873; www.cheynehoran.com.au; 2hr lesson $49, 3/5 lessons $129/189; ⏰10am & 2pm) Learn to carve up the waves with former pro surfer Cheyne Horan. Board hire $30 per day.

Tours

Aqua Duck
Boat Tour

(☎07-5539 0222; www.aquaduck.com.au; 36 Cavill Ave, Surfers Paradise; adult/child/family $35/26/95; ⏰every 75min 10am-5.30pm) Check out Surfers by land and water in a boat with wheels. One-hour tours depart from Surfers Paradise Blvd outside Centre Arcade.

🛏 Sleeping

Vibe Hotel
Hotel $$

(☎07-5539 0444, 13 84 23; www.vibehotels. com.au; 42 Ferny Ave, Surfers Paradise; d $100-250; ✱@🛜☎) Slick but affordable, this chocolate and lime-green high-rise on the Nerang River is a vibrant gem amongst Surfers' bland plethora of hotels and

133

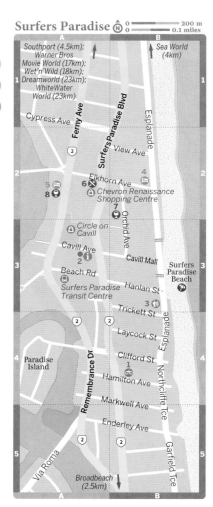

ocean views and the 18m pool is a bonus. Minimum two-night stay.

Eating

Baritalia
Italian $$

(07-5592 4700; www.baritaliagoldcoast.com. au; Shop 15, Chevron Renaissance Bldg, cnr Elkhorn Ave & Surfers Paradise Blvd, Surfers Paradise; mains $15-35; 7.30am-late) Perfect for people-watching, this Italian bar and restaurant has a fab outdoor terrace and hip international staff. Go for the chilli seafood broth with Moreton Bay bugs, saffron and capers, or excellent pastas, pizzas and risotto.

Moo Moo
Steakhouse $$$

(07-5539 9952; www.moomoorestaurant. com; Broadbeach on the Park, 2486 Gold Coast Hwy, Broadbeach; mains $29-69; noon-3pm & 6pm-late) A carnivorous mecca, Moo Moo's winning steaks include lots of wagyu and a 400g, 50-day dry-aged rib eye on the bone. There's also seafood and pasta on the menu. Love the cowhide-clad bar!

Drinking & Nightlife

Titanium Bar
Bar

(www.titaniumbar.com.au; 30-34 Ferny Ave, Surfers Paradise; 10am-late) Unless you like Irish pubs, this metallic-looking bar is the best drinking spot in town, perfect for a beer or six as the sun sets over the Nerang River.

apartments. The rooms are subtle-chic and the pool is a top spot for sundowners.

Chateau Beachside Resort
Apartment $$

(07-5538 1022; www.chateaubeachside.com. au; cnr Elkhorn Ave & Esplanade, Surfers Paradise; d/1-bedroom apt from $170/200;) Less Loire Valley, more Las Vegas, this seaside 'chateau' (actually an 18-storey tower) is an excellent choice. All the renovated studios and apartments have

Sin City
Club

(www.sincitynightclub.com.au; 22 Orchid Ave, Surfers Paradise; ⏰9pm-late) This Vegas-style sin pit is the place for wrongdoings: sexy staff, big-name DJs and visiting celebs trying not to get photographed.

ⓘ Information

Gold Coast Information & Booking Centre
(☎1300 309 440; www.visitgoldcoast.com; Cavill Ave, Surfers Paradise; ⏰8.30am-5pm Mon-Sat, 9am-4pm Sun) The main GC tourist information booth; also sells theme-park tickets and has public transport info.

Gold Coast Hospital (☎07-5519 8211; www.health.qld.gov.au/goldcoasthealth; 108 Nerang St, Southport)

ⓘ Getting There & Around

Long-distance buses stop at the **Surfers Paradise Transit Centre** (10 Beach Rd, Surfers Paradise). **Greyhound** (www.greyhound.com.au) and **Premier Motor Service** (www.premierms.com.au) have frequent services to/from Brisbane ($26, 90 minutes), Byron Bay ($30, 2½ hours) and beyond.
Bike Hire Gold Coast (☎1800 130 140; www.bikehiregoldcoast.com.au; bike hire per half/full day $25/30) Quality mountain bikes delivered to your door.

Gold Coast Cabs (☎13 10 08; www.gccabs.com.au)

Burleigh Heads

The true, sandy essence of the Gold Coast permeates the chilled-out surfie town of Burleigh Heads. With its cheery cafes and beachfront restaurants, famous right-hand point break, beautiful beach and little national park on the rocky headland, Burleigh charms everyone.

◉ Sights & Activities

Burleigh Head National Park
National Park

(www.nprsr.qld.gov.au/parks/burleigh-head; Goodwin Tce; ⏰24hr) **FREE** A walk around the headland through Burleigh Head National Park is a must for any visitor – it's a 27-hectare rainforest reserve with plenty of bird life and several walking trails.

Currumbin Wildlife Sanctuary
Wildlife Reserve

(☎07-5534 1266, 1300 886 511; www.cws.org.au; 28 Tomewin St, Currumbin; adult/child/family $49/33/131; ⏰8am-5pm) Currumbin Wildlife Sanctuary has Australia's biggest rainforest aviary, where you can hand-feed a technicolour blur of rainbow lorikeets. There's also kangaroo feeding, photo ops with koalas and crocodiles, reptile shows and Aboriginal dance displays.

Jellurgal Cultural Centre
Indigenous Culture

(☎07-5525 5955; www.jellurgal.com.au; 1711 Gold Coast Hwy; ⏰8am-4pm Mon-Sat, 9am-2pm

Rainbow lorikeets, Currumbin Wildlife Sanctuary
BOB CHARLTON/GETTY IMAGES ©

Sun) **FREE** This new Aboriginal cultural centre at the base of Burleigh's headland sheds some light on life here hundreds of years ago. There's lots of art and artefacts to look at, plus an interpretive multimedia boardwalk.

Sleeping

Burleigh Palms Holiday Apartments
Apartment **$$**

(☏07-5576 3955; www.burleighpalms.com; 1849 Gold Coast Hwy; 1-bedroom apt per night/week from $150/550, 2-bedroom apt from $180/660; ❄️🛜♨️) Even though they're on the highway, these large and comfortable self-contained units – a quick dash to the beach through the back alley – are solid value.

Hillhaven Holiday Apartments
Apartment **$$**

(☏07-5535 1055; www.hillhaven.com.au; 2 Goodwin Tce; 2-bedroom apt from $180; @🛜) Right on the headland adjacent to the national park, these renovated apartments – the pick of which is the gold deluxe room at $300 per night – have awesome views

of Burleigh Heads and the surf. It's ultra quiet and only 150m to the beach.

🍴 Eating & Drinking

Borough Barista
Cafe **$**

(www.facebook.com/pages/borough-barista/236745933011462; 14 The Esplanade; mains $10-17; ⏱6am-2.30pm) A little open-walled caffeine shack with a simple menu of burgers and salads and an unmistakable panache when it comes to coffee. The grilled haloumi burger with mushrooms, caramelised onions and chutney will turn you vegetarian. Cool tunes and friendly vibes.

Fish House
Seafood **$$$**

(☏07-5535 7725; www.thefishhouse.com.au; 50 Goodwin Tce; mains $36-46; ⏱noon-3pm & 6-9pm Wed-Sun) This stylish red-brick box across the road from the beach goes heavy on the underwater stuff: whiting, swordfish, trevalla, John Dory...all locally caught or imported fresh from interstate. Dress in decent duds and be prepared to speak loudly (lots of hard surfaces).

Purling Brook Falls, Springbrook National Park

OLIVER STREWE/GETTY IMAGES ©

Detour:
Springbrook National Park

About a 40-minute drive west of Burleigh Heads, **Springbrook National Park** (www.nprsr.qld.gov.au/parks/springbrook) is a steep remnant of the huge Tweed Shield volcano that centred on nearby Mt Warning in NSW more than 20 million years ago. It's a wonderland for hikers, with excellent trails through cool-temperate, subtropical and eucalypt forests offering a mosaic of gorges, cliffs and waterfalls.

The park is divided into four sections. The 900m-high **Springbrook Plateau** section is laced with waterfalls and eye-popping lookouts, including the 106m Purling Brook Falls, Canyon Lookout and Best of All Lookout. There's an unstaffed **visitor information centre** at the end of Old School Rd.

The scenic **Natural Bridge** section, off the Nerang–Murwillumbah road, has a 1km walking circuit leading to a huge rock arch spanning a water-formed cave – home to a luminous colony of glow-worms.

The **Mt Cougal** section, accessed via Currumbin Creek Rd, has several waterfalls and swimming holes (watch out for submerged logs and slippery rocks). The heavily forested **Numinbah** section to the north is the fourth section of the park.

Coolangatta

A laid-back seaside town on Queensland's southern border, Coolangatta has quality surf beaches and a tight-knit community. If you want to bypass the glam and party scene, catch some great waves or just kick back on the beach, 'Cooly' is for you!

Activities

Cooly Surf Surfing
(☑07-5536 1470; www.surfshopaustralia.com.au; cnr Marine Pde & Dutton St; ⊗9am-5pm) Cooly Surf hires out surfboards (half/full day $30/45) and stand-up paddleboards ($40/55), and it runs two-hour surfing lessons ($45).

Sleeping

Komune Hotel, Hostel $
(☑07-5536 6764; www.komuneresorts.com; 146 Marine Pde; dm from $45, 1-/2-bedroom apt from $105/145, penthouse from $245; 🖥🛏) With beach-funk decor, Bali-esque pool area and an ultra laid-back vibe, this eight-storey converted apartment tower is the ultimate surf retreat. There are budget dorms, apartments and a hip penthouse begging for a party. A different take on the hostel concept.

Nirvana Apartment $$$
(☑07-5506 5555; www.nirvanabythesea.com.au; 1 Douglas St; 2-/3-bedroom apt from $205/365) Attaining some sort of salty nirvana across from Kirra beach, this sleek new apartment tower comes with all the whistles and bells: two pools, gym, cinema room, ocean views and sundry salons. (Hey, wasn't that Kurt Cobain in the cafe downstairs?)

Eating & Drinking

Burger Lounge Burgers $
(☑07-5599 5762; www.burgerlounge.com.au; cnr Musgrave & Douglas Sts; mains $10-17; ⊗10am-9pm Thu-Tue, 11am-9pm Wed) Awesome bun-fest in a triangular-shaped room at the base of the Nirvana apartment tower (fast-food nirvana?). The chicken and mango chilli burger is a winner! Lots of good beers, cocktails and wines too, and sangria by the jug.

Bread 'n' butter Tapas, Bar $$
(☑07-5599 4666; www.breadnbutter.com.au; 76 Musgrave St; tapas $13-22; pizzas $19-25; ⊗5.30-late) 🍴 Head upstairs to the

137

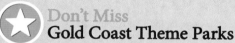

⭐ Don't Miss
Gold Coast Theme Parks

The gravity-defying rollercoasters and waterslides at these American-style parks offer some seriously dizzy action – keeping your lunch down is a constant battle. Discount tickets are sold in most of the tourist offices on the Gold Coast; the VIP Pass (per person $110) grants unlimited entry to Sea World, Warner Bros Movie World and Wet'n'Wild.

Dreamworld (☎1800 073 300, 07-5588 1111; www.dreamworld.com.au; Dreamworld Pkwy, Coomera; adult/child $95/75, online $90/70; ⏰10am-5pm) Home to the 'Big 8 Thrill Rides', including the Claw (pictured above), Giant Drop and Tower of Terror II. Lots of kid-centric rides too. Get your photo taken with Aussie animals or a Bengal tiger at Tiger Island. Access to WhiteWater World included in ticket price.

Sea World (☎13 33 86, 07-5588 2222; www.seaworld.com.au; Seaworld Dr, The Spit, Main Beach; adult/child $83/50; ⏰9.30am-5.30pm) See polar bears, sharks, seals, penguins and performing dolphins at this aquatic park, which also has the mandatory rollercoasters and waterslides. Animal shows throughout the day.

Warner Bros Movie World (☎13 33 86, 07-5573 3999; www.movieworld.com.au; Pacific Hwy, Oxenford; adult/child $83/50; ⏰9.30am-5pm) Movie-themed shows, rides and attractions, including the Batwing Spaceshot, Justice League 3D Ride and Scooby-Doo Spooky Rollercoaster. Batman, Austin Powers, Porky Pig et al roam through the crowds.

Wet'n'Wild (☎13 33 86, 07-5556 1660; www.wetnwild.com.au; Pacific Hwy, Oxenford; adult/child $60/35; ⏰10am-5pm) The ultimate waterslide here is the Kamikaze, where you plunge down an 11m drop in a two-person tube at 50km/h. This vast water park also has pitch-black slides, white-water rapids and wave pools.

WhiteWater World (☎1800 073 300, 07-5588 1111; www.whitewaterworld.com.au; Dreamworld Parkway, Coomera; adult/child $95/75, online $90/70; ⏰10am-4pm) Connected to Dreamworld; features nautical waterslide rides such as the Temple of Huey, the Green Room and the Cave of Waves. You can learn to surf here too! Ticket price includes entry to Dreamworld.

Bread 'n' Butter balcony, where moody lighting and chilled tunes make this tapas bar perfect for a drink, some pizza or some tapas (or all three). Uses local and home-grown produce and recycles precisely 78% of waste. DJs spin on Friday and Saturday nights.

BRISBANE

Australia's most underrated city? Booming Brisbane is an energetic river town on the way up, with an edgy arts scene, pumping nightlife and great coffee and restaurants. Plush parks and historic buildings complete the picture, all folded into the elbows of the meandering Brisbane River.

Sights

City Centre

Commissariat Store Museum   Museum
(www.queenslandhistory.org; 115 William St; adult/child/family $5/3/10; ☺10am-4pm Tue-Fri) Built by convicts in 1829, this former government storehouse is the oldest occupied building in Brisbane. Inside is an immaculate little museum devoted to convict and colonial history.

City Botanic Gardens   Park
(www.brisbane.qld.gov.au; Alice St; ☺24hr; 📶) FREE On the river, Brisbane's favourite green space is a mass of lawns, tangled Moreton Bay figs, bunya pines and macadamia trees descending gently from the Queensland University of Technology campus. Free guided tours leave the rotunda at 11am and 1pm Monday to Saturday.

City Hall   Historic Building
(www.brisbane.qld.gov.au; btwn Ann & Adelaide Sts) Overlooking King George Sq, this fine 1930s sandstone edifice is fronted by a row of sequoia-sized corinthian columns and has an 85m-high clocktower. By the time you read this a three-year renovation should be complete: see if the observation platform and Museum of Brisbane (www.museumofbrisbane.com.au) are open yet.

South Bank

Gallery of Modern Art   Art Gallery
(GOMA; www.qagoma.qld.gov.au; Stanley Pl; ☺10am-5pm Mon-Fri, 9am-5pm Sat & Sun; 📶) FREE All angular glass, concrete and black metal, must-see GOMA focuses on Australian art from the 1970s to today. Continually changing and often confronting, exhibits range from painting, sculpture and photography to video, installation and film. There's also an arty bookshop here, kids' activity rooms, a cafe and free guided tours at 11am and 1pm.

South Bank Parklands   Park
(www.visitsouthbank.com.au; Russell St; ☺dawn-dusk) FREE This beautiful smear of green – technically on the western side of the Brisbane River – is home to performance spaces, sculptures, buskers, eateries, bars, pockets of rainforest, BBQ areas, bougainvillea-draped pergolas and hidden lawns. The big-ticket attractions here are Streets Beach (p143), a kitsch artificial swimming beach resembling a tropical lagoon; and the London Eye–style **Wheel of Brisbane** (www.thewheelofbrisbane.com. au; Russel St; adult/child/family $15/10/42; ☺11am-9.30pm Mon-Thu, 10am-11pm Fri & Sat, 10am-10pm Sun), which offers 360-degree views from its 60m heights. Rides last around 10 minutes and include audio commentary (and air-con!).

Queensland Museum & Sciencentre   Museum
(www.southbank.qm.qld.gov.au; cnr Grey & Melbourne Sts; ☺9.30am-5pm) FREE Queensland's history is given the once-over here, with interesting exhibits including a skeleton of the state's own dinosaur *Muttaburrasaurus* (aka 'Mutt'), and the *Avian Cirrus*, the tiny plane in which Queenslander Bert Hinkler made the first England-to-Australia solo flight in 1928.

Also here is the **Sciencentre** (Sciencentre adult/child/family $13/10/40), an educational fun house with over 100

A **B** **C** **D**

Roma St

Pacific Mwy

Roma Street Parkland

Go Between Bridge

Roma St

18

SPRING HILL

Brisbane Transit Centre

Wickham Tce

Makerston St

Wickham Park

14

Kurilpa Bridge

Herschel St

King Edward Park

Upper Edward St

M3

Tank St

Roma St

Montague Rd

10 4

CityCat Ferry

Pacific Mwy

George St

Turbot St

Central Station

Peel St

6 5

Victoria Bridge

North Quay

King George Square

King George Sq Bus Station

2

Ann St

Adelaide St

Anzac Square

Post Office Square 9

SOUTH BRISBANE

Melbourne St

Melbourne St

Brisbane River

26 23

Burnett La

19

Queen Street Mall

Myer Centre

Queen St Bus Station

Brisbane Visitor Information Centre

Elizabeth St

Edward St

Market St

10

Russell St

Merivale St

South Brisbane

25

North Quay

8

10

Pacific Mwy

17

3

Stephens La

Charlotte St

Mary St

Margaret St

Albert St

George St

William St

7

South Bank 1&2

M3

Glenelg St

Stanley Street Plaza

QUT

Alice St

City Botanic Gardens

1

Cordelia St

Merivale St

Colchester St

Ernest St

Grey St

Little Stanley St

27 13

SOUTH BANK

CityHopper Ferry

Queensland University of Technology (QUT)

41

22

Tribune St

South Bank

South Bank 3

CityCat Ferry

CityHopper Ferry

Stephens Rd

Sidon St

Goodwill Bridge

M3

Vulture St

Maritime Museum

Captain Cook Bridge

River Tce

Stephens Rd

CT White Park

Kangaroo Point Cliffs

Stanley St

Vulture St

Pacific Mwy

Llewellyn St

Main St

10

WOOLOONGABBA

River Tce

Gabba (400m)

15

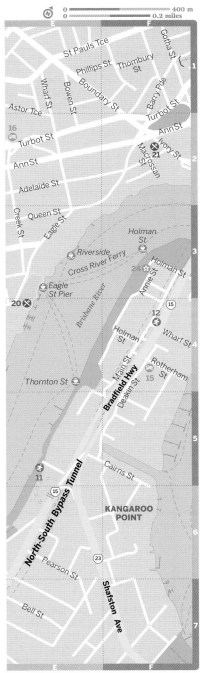

Central Brisbane

hands-on, interactive exhibits that delve
into life science and technology.

Queensland Art Gallery Art Gallery
(QAG; www.qagoma.qld.gov.au; Melbourne St;
◎10am-5pm Mon-Fri, 9am-5pm Sat & Sun)
FREE Duck into the QAG to see the fine
permanent collection. Australian art
dates from the 1840s to the 1970s: check
out works by celebrated masters including Sir Sidney Nolan, Arthur Boyd, William

Brisbane for Children

Start with the city's leafy inner-city parks: **South Bank Parklands** (p139) has lawns, BBQs, playgrounds and the slow-spinning **Wheel of Brisbane** (p139) – a real mind-blower for anyone under 15. The lifeguard-patrolled **Streets Beach** (p143) is here too, with a shallow section for really small swimmers. **New Farm Park** is a beaut spot by the river, with a series of treehouse-like platforms interlinking huge (and shady) Moreton Bay fig trees.

Too humid for the park? Head for the air-con at the **Queensland Cultural Centre** on South Bank. Here the **Queensland Museum** (p139) runs some fab, hands-on programs for little tackers during school holidays. The incorporated **Sciencentre** has plenty of push-this-button-and-see-what-happens action. The **Queensland Art Gallery** (p141) has a Children's Art Centre that runs regular programs throughout the year, as does the **State Library of Queensland** and the **Gallery of Modern Art** (p139).

The river is a big plus. Take a ferry ride around the bends of central Brisbane, or chug further afield to the **Lone Pine Koala Sanctuary**, where they can cuddle up to a critter.

Dobell and George Lambert. Free guided tours start at 1pm.

Fortitude Valley & New Farm

Brisbane Powerhouse   Arts Centre
(www.brisbanepowerhouse.org; 119 Lamington St; ☉9am-5pm Mon-Fri, 10am-4pm Sat & Sun) On the eastern flank of New Farm Park stands the Powerhouse, a once-derelict power station that's been superbly transformed into a contemporary arts centre. The Powerhouse hosts a range of visual arts, comedy and music performances (many free), and has two restaurants with killer river views.

Institute of Modern Art   Art Gallery
(IMA; www.ima.org.au; 420 Brunswick St, Fortitude Valley; ☉11am-5pm Tue-Sat, to 8pm Thu) FREE With risqué, emerging and experimental art for grown-ups, it's GOMA's naughty little cousin.

Chinatown   Neighbourhood
(Duncan St) Brisbane's Chinatown occupies only one street, but is just as flamboyant and flavour-filled as its Sydney and Mel-

bourne counterparts. Glazed flat ducks hang behind steamy windows; aromas of Thai, Chinese, Vietnamese, Laotian and Japanese cooking fill the air.

Greater Brisbane

Mt Coot-tha Reserve   Nature Reserve
(www.brisbane.qld.gov.au; Mt Coot-tha Rd, Mt Coot-tha; ☉24hr) FREE A 15-minute drive or bus ride from the city, this huge bush reserve is topped by 287m Mt Coot-tha (more of a hill, really). On the hillsides you'll find a botanic garden, planetarium and the eye-popping **Mt Coot-tha Lookout** (www.brisbanelookout.com; 1012 Sir Samuel Griffith Dr; ☉24hr) FREE.

To get here via public transport, take bus 471 from Adelaide St in the city, opposite King George Sq ($4.80, 25 minutes).

Lone Pine Koala Sanctuary   Nature Reserve
(☏07-3378 1366; www.koala.net; 708 Jesmond Rd, Fig Tree Pocket; adult/child/family $33/22/80; ☉9am-5pm) About 12km south of the city centre, Lone Pine Koala Sanctuary occupies a patch of parkland beside

the river. It's home to 130 or so koalas, plus kangaroos, possums, wombats, birds and other Aussie critters.

To get here catch bus 430 ($6.70, 45 minutes) from the Queen St bus station. Alternatively, **Mirimar II** (☎0412 749 426; www.mirimar.com; incl park entry per adult/child/family $65/38/190) cruises to the sanctuary along the Brisbane River, departing from the Cultural Centre Pontoon on South Bank next to Victoria Bridge. It departs daily at 10am, returning from Lone Pine at 1.45pm.

 Activities

SWIMMING

Streets Beach   Swimming
(www.visitsouthbank.com.au; South Bank; ⊙daylight hours) FREE A central spot for a quick (and free) dip is the man-made, riverside Streets Beach at South Bank. Lifeguards, hollering kids, beach babes, strutting gym-junkies, ice-cream carts – it's all here.

CYCLING

Bicycle Revolution   Bicycle Rental
(www.bicyclerevolution.org.au; 294 Montague Rd, West End; per day/week $35/100; ⊙9am-5pm

Streets Beach, South Bank Parklands

Mon, 9am-6pm Tue-Fri, 8am-2pm Sat) Friendly community shop with a great range of re-cycled city bikes with reconditioned parts.

CLIMBING & ABSEILING

Riverlife Adventure
Centre   Rock Climbing
(☎07-3891 5766; www.riverlife.com.au; Naval Stores, Kangaroo Point Bikeway, Kangaroo Point; ⊙9am-5pm) Near the 20m Kangaroo Point cliffs, Riverlife runs rock climbing sessions (from $49) and abseiling exploits ($39). They also offer kayaking river trips (from $39) and hire out bikes (per four hours $30), kayaks (per two hours $33) and in-line skates (per four hours $40).

Tours

CityCat   Boat Tour
(☎13 12 30; www.translink.com.au; one-way $5.60; ⊙5.25am-11.50pm) Stand on an open-air deck and glide under the Story Bridge to South Bank and the city centre. Ferries run every 15 to 30 minutes between the University of Queensland in the south-west to Apollo Road terminal north of the city, stopping at 14 terminals in between,

LINDSAY BROWN/GETTY IMAGES ©

including New Farm Park, North Quay (for the CBD), South Bank and West End.

XXXX Brewery Tour
Tour

(📞07-3361 7597; www.xxxxbrewerytour.com.au; cnr Black & Paten Sts, Milton; adult/child $25/16; 🕐hourly 11am-4pm Mon-Fri, 12.30pm, 1pm & 1.30pm Sat, 11am, noon & 12.30pm Sun) Grown-up entry to this brewery tour includes a few humidity beating ales, so leave the car at home. Also on offer are beer-and-barbecue tours on Wednesday nights and Saturday during the day (adult/child $38/29), which include lunch. Book all tours in advance, online or by phone. Wear enclosed shoes.

CitySights
Guided Tour

(www.citysights.com.au; day tickets per adult/child/family $35/20/80; 🕐9am-3.45pm) This hop-on-hop-off shuttle bus wheels past 19 of Brisbane's major landmarks, including the CBD, Mt Coot-tha, Chinatown, South Bank and Story Bridge. Tours depart every 45 minutes from Post Office Sq on Queen St. The same ticket covers you for unlimited use of CityCat ferry services.

River City Cruises
Cruise

(📞0428 278 473; www.rivercitycruises.com.au; South Bank Parklands Jetty A; adult/child/family $25/15/60) River City runs 1½-hour cruises with commentary from South Bank to New Farm and back. They depart from South Bank at 10.30am and 12.30pm (plus 2.30pm during summer).

 Sleeping

City Centre

Diamant Hotel
Boutique Hotel $$

(📞07-3009 3400; www.8hotels.com; 52 Astor Tce; d from $139; 🅿❄🛜) Behind an ultra-mod black-and-white facade, seven-storey Diamant has compact, contemporary rooms with natty wallpaper and thoughtful touches (original artwork, iPod docks, free wi-fi). The bigger suites have kitchenettes and lounge areas, and there's a bar-restaurant on the ground floor.

Urban Brisbane
Hotel $$

(📞07-3831 6177; www.hotelurban.com.au; 345 Wickham Tce; d from $150; ❄@🛜🏊) Still looking sexy after a $10-million makeover in 2008, the Urban has stylish rooms with masculine hues, balconies and high-end fittings (super-comfy beds, big TVs, fuzzy bathrobes). There's also a heated outdoor pool, a bar, and lots of uniformed flight attendants checking in and out.

Inchcolm Hotel
Heritage Hotel $$

(📞07-3226 8888; www.theinchcolm.com.au; 73 Wickham Tce; r $160-250; 🅿❄🛜🏊) Built in the 1930s as doctors' suites, the heritage-listed Inchcolm (pronounced as per 'Malcolm') retains elements of its past (love the old elevator!), but the rooms have been overhauled. Those in the newer wing have more space and light; in the older wing there's more character.

Treasury
Luxury Hotel $$$

(📞07-3306 8888; www.treasurybrisbane.com.au; 130 William St; r from $230; 🅿❄@🛜) Brisbane's most lavish hotel is behind the equally lavish exterior of the former Land Administration Building. Each room is unique and awash with heritage features, with high ceilings, framed artwork, polished wood furniture and elegant furnishings. The best rooms have river views.

Fortitude Valley

Limes
Boutique Hotel $$$

(📞07-3852 9000; www.limeshotel.com.au; 142 Constance St; d from $230; ❄🛜) A slick slice of style in the Valley, Limes has 21 handsome rooms that make good use of tight space – each has plush furniture, kitchenettes and thoughtful extras (iPod docks, free wi-fi, free gym pass). The rooftop bar and cinema (!) are magic.

New Farm

Bowen Terrace
Guesthouse $

(📞07-3254 0458; www.bowenterrace.com.au; 365 Bowen Tce; dm/s/d without bathroom $35/60/85, d/f with bathroom $99/145; 🅿@🏊) A beautifully restored, 100-year-old

ANDREW WATSON/GETTY IMAGES ©

 Don't Miss
Story Bridge Adventure Climb

A Brisbane must-do, the bridge climb offers unbeatable views of the city – either dawn, day, twilight or night. The 2½-hour climb scales the southern half of the bridge, taking you 80m above the twisting, muddy Brisbane River below. Minimum age is 10. Bridge abseiling expeditions are also available.

NEED TO KNOW

✆1300 254 627; www.sbac.net.au; 170 Main St, Kangaroo Point; adult/child from $99/85

Queenslander, this guesthouse is in a quiet part of New Farm. There are TVs, bar fridges, quality bed linens and lofty ceilings with fans in every room. Out the back there's a deck overlooking the enticing pool. No air-con but real value for money, with far more class than your average hostel.

Kangaroo Point

Il Mondo   Hotel $$
(✆07-3392 0111, 1300 665 526; www.ilmondo.com.au; 25 Rotherham St; r $160, 1-/3-bedroom apt $250/500; P ✳ @ ⚹ ⚊) In a beaut location near the Story Bridge, this

postmodern-looking, seven-storey hotel has handsome rooms and apartments with minimalist design, high-end fixtures and plenty of space.

Paddington & Around

Casabella
Apartment   Apartment $$
(✆07-3217 6507; www.casabella-apartment.com; 211 Latrobe Tce, Paddington; apt $185; P ⚹)
The understorey of this fuschia-coloured house at the quiet end of Paddo's main drag has been converted into a very comfortable self-contained unit. There are two bedrooms (sleeps three), warm

145

Mediterranean colour schemes, recycled timber floors and lots of louvres to let the cross-breeze through (no air-con). Lovely!

Latrobe Apartment
Apartment $$$

(☎0448 944 026; www.stayz.com.au/77109; 183a Latrobe Tce, Paddington; apt $200; P✳🖨) Underneath a chiropractor in affluent Paddington is this excellent two-bedroom apartment, sleeping four, with two bathrooms, polished floorboards, sexy lighting and a fabulous BBQ deck. It's a sleek, contemporary design, with quality everything: linen, toiletries, kitchenware, TV, iPod dock, leather lounge...

 ## Eating

City Centre

Brew
Cafe, Wine Bar $

(☎07-3211 4242; www.brewgroup.com.au; Lower Burnett La; mains $6-12; ⏱7am-5pm Mon, to 10pm Tue & Wed, to 11.30pm Thu & Fri, 9am-11.30pm Sat, to 3pm Sun) You'd expect to find this kind of subcultural underground cafe in Seattle or Berlin...but Brisbane? Breaking new coffee-cultural ground in Queensland, Brew takes the caffeine into the alleyways, serving simple food (tapas, pastas, sandwiches) to go with the black stuff.

E'cco
Modern Australian $$$

(☎07-3831 8344; www.eccobistro.com; 100 Boundary St; mains $43; ⏱noon-3pm Tue-Fri, 6-10pm Tue-Sat) One of the finest restaurants in the state, award-winning E'cco is a culinary must! Menu masterpieces from chef Philip Johnson include liquorice-spiced pork belly with caramelised peach, onion jam and kipfler potatoes. The interior is suitably swish: all black, white and stainless steel.

Cha Cha Char
Steakhouse $$$

(☎07-3211 9944; www.chachachar.com.au; Shop 5, 1 Eagle St Pier; mains $38-95; ⏱noon-11pm Mon-Fri, 6pm-11pm Sat & Sun) Wallowing in awards, this long-running favourite serves Brisbane's best steaks, along with first-rate seafood and roast game meats. The classy semicircular dining room in the Eagle St Pier complex has floor-to-ceiling windows and river views.

 ## South Bank & Kangaroo Point

Piaf
French $$

(☎07-3846 5026; www.piafbistro.com.au; 5/182 Grey St, South Bank; breakfast mains $6-18, lunch & dinner $24-28; ⏱7am-late) A chilled-out but still intimate bistro with a loyal following, Piaf serves a small selection (generally just five mains and a few salads and other light options) of good-value, contemporary French-inspired food. French wines by the glass. No sign of Edith...

CityCat ferry ride (p143)

Fortitude Valley & Chinatown

The Vietnamese
Vietnamese $

(☎07-3252 4112; www.thevietnameserestaurant.com.au; 194 Wickham St; mains $10-20; ⊗11am-3pm & 5pm-10pm) Aptly if unimaginatively named, this is indeed *the* place in town to eat Vietnamese, with exquisitely prepared dishes served to an always crowded house.

Ortiga
Spanish $$

(☎07-3852 1155; www.ortiga.com.au; 446 Brunswick St; tapas $6-50, mains $18-32; ⊗12.30-3pm Fri, 6pm-late Tue-Sun) One of Brisbane's best restaurants, Ortiga offers a stylish upstairs tapas bar (heavy on the meats) with a pressed-tin ceiling and window bench, and an elegant subterranean dining room with an open kitchen. Top picks include Basque pork sausage, *pulpo a gallega* (Galician-braised octopus) and whole slow-cooked lamb shoulder.

New Farm

Himalayan Cafe
Nepalese $

(☎07-3358 4015; 640 Brunswick St; mains $15-25; ⊗5.30-10pm Tue-Sun; ♪) Awash with prayer flags and colourful cushions, this karmically positive, unfussy restaurant serves authentic Tibetan and Nepalese fare such as tender *fhaiya darkau* (lamb with vegies, coconut milk and spices).

West End

Gunshop Café
Cafe, Modern Australian $$

(☎07-3844 2241; www.thegunshopcafe.com; 53 Mollison St; mains $17-33; ⊗6.30am-2pm Mon, to late Tue-Sat, to 2.30pm Sun) With cool tunes, interesting art and happy staff, this peaceably repurposed gun shop has exposed-brick walls, sculptural ceiling lamps and an inviting back garden. The locally sourced menu changes daily, but regulars include smoked chicken lasagne, a pulled pork baguette and wild-mushroom risotto.

Mondo Organics
Modern Australian $$

(☎07-3844 1132; www.mondo-organics.com.au; 166 Hardgrave Rd; mains $25-36; ⊗8.30-11.30am Sat & Sun, noon-2.30pm Fri-Sun, 6pm-late Wed-Sat) ♪ Using the highest-quality organic and sustainable produce, Mondo Organics earns top marks for its delicious seasonal menu. Recent hits include duck breast with fig, sage and strawberry; and potato and parmesan gnocchi with golden shallots, zucchini and salsa verde.

Little Greek Taverna
Greek $$

(☎07-3255 2215; www.littlegreektaverna.com.au; Shop 5, 1 Browning St; mains $15-30, banquets per person $35-42; ⊗11am-9pm) Up-tempo, eternally busy and in a prime West End location, the LGT is perfect for a big Greek feast and some people-watching. Kid-friendly, too.

Drinking & Nightlife

City Centre

Super Whatnot
Bar

(www.superwhatnot.com; 48 Burnett La; ⊗3pm-late Tue-Sat) Trailblazing Super Whatnot is a funky, industrial laneway space, with a mezzanine floor and sunken lounge. Drinks: bottled boutique Australian beers and cocktails (try the cure-all Penicillin). Food: American-inspired bar snacks (hotdogs, mini burritos, nachos). Tunes: vinyl DJs Thursday to Saturday spinning funk, soul and hip-hop; live acoustic acts Wednesday. Winning combo!

Fortitude Valley

Alfred & Constance
Bar

(www.alfredandconstance.com.au; 130 Constance St; ⊗10am-3am) Wow! Fabulously eccentric A&C occupies two old weatherboard houses. Inside, fluoro-clad ditch diggers, tattooed lesbians, suits and surfies roam between the tiki bar, rooftop terrace, cafe area and lounge rooms checking out the interiors: chandeliers,

Below: The Gabba, Brisbane Cricket Ground (p150); **Right:** Queensland Performing Arts Centre (p150)

(BELOW) PETER HARRISON/GETTY IMAGES ©; (RIGHT) RICHARD I'ANSON/GETTY IMAGES ©

skeletons, surfboards, old hi-fi equipment... It's weird, and very wonderful.

Bowery
Cocktail Bar

(www.thebowery.com.au; 676 Ann St; ⏰5pm-late Tue-Sun) The exposed-brick walls, gilded mirrors, booths and foot-worn floorboards at this long, narrow bar bring a touch of substance to the valley fray. The cocktails and wine list are top-notch (and priced accordingly), and there's live jazz/dub Tuesday to Thursday. DJs spin on weekends.

Birdees
Club

(www.birdees.com.au; 608 Ann St; ⏰4pm-late Mon-Thu, noon-5am Fri & Sat, noon-late Sun) Part of the sprawling Bunk Backpackers complex, Birdees fills, predictably, with backpackers going berserk. Big fun.

Cloudland
Club

(www.katarzyna.com.au/venues/cloudland; 641 Ann St; ⏰5pm-late Thu & Fri, noon-late Sat & Sun) Like stepping into a surreal cloud forest, this multi-level club has a huge plant-filled lobby with a retractable glass roof, a wall of water and wrought-iron birdcage-like nooks. Even if you're not a clubber, peek through the windows during the day: the interior design is astonishing!

West End

Archive Beer Boutique
Bar

(www.archivebeerboutique.com.au; 100 Boundary St; ⏰11am-late) Interesting beer, interesting place: welcome to Archive, a temple of beer with many a fine frothy on tap (try the Evil Twin West Coast Red Ale). Check the bar made of books! Oh, and the food's good, too (steaks, mussels, pasta).

The End
Bar

(www.73vulture.com; 1/73 Vulture St; ⏰3pm-midnight) This mod-industrial shopfront conversion is a real locals' hangout, with hipsters, cheese boards, Morrisey on the turntable, DJs and live acoustic

troubadours. The Blackstar mocha stout (caffeine courtesy of the local roaster) will cheer up your rainy river afternoon.

New Farm & Around

Breakfast Creek Hotel   Pub
(www.breakfastcreekhotel.com; 2 Kingsford Smith Dr, Albion; ⊙10am-late) This historic 1889 pub is a Brisbane classic. Built in lavish French Renaissance style, it has various bars and dining areas (including a beer garden and an art-deco 'private bar' where you can drink beer tapped from a wooden keg).

Paddington & Petrie Terrace

Cabiria   Bar
(www.cabiria.com.au; 6 The Barracks, 61 Petrie Tce, Petrie Terrace; ⊙7-10.30am Mon, 7am-late Tue-Sat) Brisbane's old police barracks have been converted into a complex of quality bars and eateries, the pick of which is cool Cabiria. It's a skinny, dim-lit, moody room with big mirrors and shimmering racks of booze (35 different tequilas!).

Normanby Hotel   Pub
(www.thenormanby.com.au; 1 Musgrave Rd, Brisbane; ⊙10am-3pm) A handsome 1889 red-brick pub on the end of Petrie Tce, with a beer garden under a vast fig tree. Goes nuts during 'Sunday Sessions' (boozy wakes for the weekend).

Entertainment

LIVE MUSIC

Lock 'n' Load   Live Music
(www.locknloadbistro.com.au; 142 Boundary St, West End; ⊙10am-late Mon-Fri, 7am-late Sat & Sun) This ebullient, woody, two-storey gastro-pub lures an upbeat crowd of music fans. Bands play the small front stage (jazz and originals).

Market-Lovers Guide to Brisbane

Jan Power's Farmers Market (www.janpowersfarmersmarkets.com.au; Brisbane Powerhouse, 119 Lamington St, New Farm; ◷6am-noon 2nd & 4th Sat of month) Fancy some purple heirloom carrots or blue bananas? This fab farmers market, with more than 120 stalls, coughs up some unusual produce. Also great for more predictably coloured flowers, cheeses, coffees and fish.

Davies Park Market (www.daviesparkmarket.com.au; Davies Park, West End; ◷6am-2pm Sat) Under a grove of huge Moreton Bay fig trees in the West End, this hippie riverside market features organic foods, gourmet breakfasts, herbs and flowers, bric-a-brac and buskers.

South Bank Lifestyle Markets (www.southbankmarket.com.au; Stanley St Plaza, South Bank; ◷5-10pm Fri, 10am-5pm Sat, 9am-5pm Sun) It's a bit touristy, but this riverside market has a great range of clothing, craft, art, handmade goods and souvenirs (just ignore the lacquered boomerangs).

Hi-Fi
Live Music

(www.thehifi.com.au; 125 Boundary St, West End) This mod, minimalist rock room has unobstructed sight lines and a great line-up of local and international talent (from the Gin Blossoms to Suicidal Tendencies).

Brisbane Jazz Club
Jazz

(☎07-3391 2006; www.brisbanejazzclub.com.au; 1 Annie St, Kangaroo Point; ◷6.30-11pm Thu-Sat, 5.30-9.30pm Sun) Straight out of the bayou, this tiny riverside jazz shack has been Brisbane's jazz beacon since 1972. Anyone who's anyone in the scene plays here when they're in town.

CINEMAS
Moonlight Cinema
Cinema

(www.moonlight.com.au; Brisbane Powerhouse, 119 Lamington Rd, New Farm; adult/child $16/12; ◷7pm Wed-Sun) New Farm Park behind the Powerhouse hosts alfresco flicks between December and February. Arrive early to get a good spot.

Palace Barracks
Cinema

(www.palacecinemas.com.au; 61 Petrie Tce, Petrie Terrace; adult/child $17.50/13; ◷10am-late) Near Roma St Station, plush, six-screen Palace Barracks shows Hollywood and alternative fare. And there's a bar!

PERFORMING ARTS
Brisbane Powerhouse
Performing Arts

(www.brisbanepowerhouse.org; 119 Lamington St, New Farm) Nationally and internationally acclaimed theatre, music, comedy, dance... There are loads of happenings at the Powerhouse – many free – and the venue, with its cool bar-restaurants, enjoys a gorgeous setting overlooking the Brisbane River.

Queensland Performing Arts Centre
Performing Arts

(QPAC; www.qpac.com.au; Queensland Cultural Centre, cnr Grey & Melbourne Sts, South Bank; ◷box office 9am-8.30pm Mon-Sat) Brisbane's main high-arts performance centre comprises three venues and features concerts, plays, dance and performances of all genres: anything from flamenco to the Australian Ballet and *West Side Story* revivals.

SPORT

Catch some interstate or international cricket at the **Gabba** (Brisbane Cricket Ground; www.thegabba.org.au; 411 Vulture St, Woolloongabba), south of Kangaroo Point. The cricket season runs from October to March.

The Gabba is also a home ground for the Brisbane Lions, an **Australian Football League** (AFL; www.afl.com.au) team. Watch them in action, often at night under lights, between March and September.

The Brisbane Broncos, part of the **National Rugby League** (NRL; www.nrl.com.au) competition, play home games over winter at **Suncorp Stadium** (www.suncorpstadium.com.au; 40 Castlemaine St, Milton).

Also calling Suncorp home are the Queensland Roar football (soccer) team, part of the **A-League** (www.footballaustralia.com.au/aleague), attracting massive crowds in recent years. The domestic football season lasts from August to February.

🔒 Shopping

Queen St Mall and the **Myer Centre** in the CBD have big chain stores, upmarket outlets and the obligatory touristy trash.

Title Books
(www.titlespace.com; 1/133 Grey St, South Bank; ⏱10am-6pm Mon-Sat, to 4pm Sun) Offbeat and alternative art, music, photography and cinema books, plus vinyl, CDs and DVDs – a quality dose of subversive, lefty rebelliousness (just what South Bank needs!).

Record Exchange Music
(www.recordexchange.com.au; L1, 65 Adelaide St, Brisbane; ⏱9am-5pm) Home to an astounding collection of vinyl, plus CDs, DVDs, posters and other rock memorabilia. 'Brisbane's most interesting shop' (self-professed).

Blonde Venus Clothing
(www.blondevenus.com.au; 707 Ann St, Fortitude Valley; ⏱10am-6pm Mon-Sat, 11am-4.30pm) One of the top boutiques in Brisbane, Blonde Venus has been around for 20-plus years, stocking a well-curated selection of both indie and couture labels. One of a string of great boutiques along this slice of Ann St.

ℹ️ Information

Medical Services

Royal Brisbane & Women's Hospital (📞07-3636 8111; www.health.qld.gov.au/rbwh; cnr Butterfield St & Bowen Bridge Rd, Herston) Has a 24-hour casualty ward.

Tourist Information

Brisbane Visitor Information Centre (📞07-3006 6290; www.visitbrisbane.com.au; Queen St Mall, Brisbane; ⏱9am-5.30pm Mon-Thu, to 7pm Fri, to 5pm Sat, 10am-5pm Sun) Located between Edward and Albert Sts. Great one-stop info counter for all things Brisbane.

ℹ️ Getting There & Away

Air

Brisbane Airport (www.bne.com.au) is about 16km northeast of the city centre at Eagle Farm, and has separate international and domestic

Davies Park Market
PHILIP QUIRK/GETTY IMAGES ©

terminals about 2km apart. These are linked by the **Airtrain** (📞07-3215 5000; www.airtrain. com.au), which runs every 15 to 30 minutes from 5.45am to 10pm (per person $5).

Bus

Brisbane's main terminus and booking office for all long-distance buses and trains is the **Brisbane Transit Centre** (Roma St Station; www.brisbanetransitcentre.com.au; Roma St, Brisbane), about 500m west of the city centre. Booking desks for **Greyhound** (www.greyhound. com.au) and **Premier Motor Service** (www. premierms.com.au) are here.

Car & Motorcycle

Brisbane has five major motorways (M1 to M5) run by **Queensland Motorways** (📞13 33 31; www.qldmotorways.com.au). If you're just passing through north–south/south–north, take the Gateway Motorway (M1), which bypasses the city centre ($4.05 toll; see the website for payment options, in advance or retrospectively).

Train

Brisbane's main station for long-distance trains is Roma St Station (aka Brisbane Transit Centre). For reservations and information contact the **Queensland Rail Travel Centre** (📞13 16 17, 07-3235 1323; www.queenslandrail.com.au; 305 Edward St, Central Station) at Central Station.

ⓘ Getting Around

Brisbane's excellent public-transport network – bus, train and ferry – is run by **TransLink** (📞13 12 30; www.translink.com.au).

Fares Buses, trains and ferries operate on a zone system: most of the inner-city suburbs are in Zone 1, which translates into a single fare of $4.80/2.40 per adult/child.

Go Card To save around 30% on individual fares, buy a *Go Card* ($5 starting balance), which is sold (and recharged) at transit stations and newsagents, or by phone or online.

To/From the Airport

Airtrain (adult/child $15/7.50) runs every 15 to 30 minutes from 5.45am to 10pm from the airport to Fortitude Valley, Central Station, Roma St Station (Brisbane Transit Centre) and other key destinations.

If you prefer door-to-door service, **Coachtrans** (📞07-5556 9888; www.coachtrans.com.au) runs regular shuttle buses between the airport and CBD hotels (adult/child $20/10); it also connects Brisbane Airport to Gold Coast hotels (adult/child $46/23).

A taxi into the centre from the airport will cost $35 to $45.

Cylinder Beach, North Stradbroke Island

Boat

In addition to the fast CityCat (p143) services, Translink runs Cross River Ferries, connecting Kangaroo Point with the CBD, and New Farm Park with Norman Park on the adjacent shore (and also Teneriffe and Bulimba further north). The fares/zones apply as per all other Brisbane transport.

Free (yes, free!) CityHopper Ferries zigzag back and forth across the water between North Quay, South Bank, the CBD, Kangaroo Point and Sydney St in New Farm.

Bus

Translink runs free City Loop and Spring Hill Loop bus services that circle the CBD and Spring Hill, stopping at key spots like the Queensland University of Technology (QUT), Queen Street Mall, City Botanic Gardens, Central Station and Roma Street Parkland. It runs every 10 minutes on weekdays between 7am and 6pm.

The main stops for local buses are the underground Queen St Bus Station and King George Sq Bus Station.

Taxi

Black & White (☎13 32 22; www.blackandwhitecabs.com.au)

Yellow Cab Co (☎13 19 24; www.yellowcab.com.au)

Train

The fast Citytrain network has six main lines, which run as far north as Gympie on the Sunshine Coast and as far south as Varsity Lakes on the Gold Coast. All trains go through Roma St, Central and Fortitude Valley Stations; there's also a handy South Bank Station.

MORETON BAY

Lapping at Brisbane's urban verges, shallow Moreton Bay is packed full of marine life, including whales, dolphins, dugongs and eponymous Moreton Bay bugs (crayfish-like crustaceans). The bay also has some startlingly beautiful islands, easily accessible from the mainland.

North Stradbroke Island

An easy 30-minute ferry chug from Cleveland, this unpretentious holiday isle is like Noosa and Byron Bay rolled into one.

There's a string of glorious powdery white beaches, great surf and some quality places to stay and eat. It's also a hot-spot for spying dolphins, turtles, manta rays and, between June and November, hundreds of humpback whales.

 ## Sights

At Point Lookout, the eye-popping **North Gorge Headlands Walk** is an absolute highlight. It's an easy 20-minute loop around the headland along boardwalks, with the thrum of cicadas as your soundtrack. Keep an eye out for turtles, dolphins and manta rays offshore. The view from the headland down Main Beach is a showstopper.

There are several gorgeous **beaches** around Point Lookout. A patrolled swimming area, **Cylinder Beach** is popular with families and is flanked by Home Beach and Deadman's Beach.

 ## Activities

North Stradbroke Island
Surf School   Surfing
(☎0407 642 616; www.northstradbrokeislandsurfschool.com.au; lessons from $50; ⏱daily) Small-group, 90-minute surf lessons in the warm Straddie waves.

 ## Tours

North Stradbroke
Island 4WD Tours &
Camping Holidays   Driving Tour
(☎07-3409 8051; www.stradbroketourism.com; adult/child half-day $35/20, full day $85/55) Offers 4WD tours around the Point Lookout area, with lots of bush, beaches and wildlife. Beach fishing is $45/30 per adult/child.

Straddie Kingfisher
Tours   Driving Tour
(☎07-3409 9502; www.straddiekingfishertours.com.au; adult/child island pick-up $80/40, from Brisbane or Gold Coast $195/145) Operates six-hour 4WD and fishing tours; also has whale-watching tours in season. Ask about kayaking and sandboarding options.

 Sleeping

Straddie Views   B&B $$

(☑07-3409 8875; www.northstradbrokeisland.
com/straddiebb; 26 Cumming Pde, Point Lookout;
r from $150) There are two spacious down-
stairs suites in this B&B, run by a friendly
Straddie couple. Cooked breakfast is
served on the upstairs deck with fab sea
views.

Stradbroke Island
Beach Hotel   Hotel $$$

(☑07-3409 8188; www.stradbrokehotel.
com.au; East Coast Rd, Point Lookout; d from
$235; ❄❄) Straddie's only pub has 12
cool, inviting rooms with shell-coloured
tiles, blonde timbers, high-end gadgets
and balconies. Walk to the beach, or
get distracted by the open-walled bar
downstairs en route (serving breakfast,
lunch and dinner; mains $15 to $36).
Flashy three- and four-bed apartments
also available.

Getting There & Away

The gateway to North Stradbroke Island is the
seaside suburb of Cleveland. Regular Citytrain
(www.translink.com.au) services run from
Brisbane's Central and Roma St stations to
Cleveland station ($9.50, one hour); buses to the
ferry terminal meet the trains at Cleveland station
($4.80, 10 minutes).

Big Red Cat (☑1800 733 228, 07-3488 9777;
www.bigredcat.com.au; return per vehicle incl
passengers $146, walk-on adult/child $20/10;
⏰5.15am-6pm Mon-Sat, 7am-7pm Sun) In a
tandem operation with Stradbroke Ferries, the
feline-looking Big Red Cat vehicle/passenger
ferry does the Cleveland–Dunwich run around
eight times daily (45 minutes).

Stradbroke Ferries (☑07-3488 5300; www.
stradbrokeferries.com.au; return per vehicle incl
passengers $146, walk-on adult/child $20/10;
⏰5.15am-6pm Mon-Sat, 7am-7pm Sun) Teaming
up with Big Red Cat, Stradbroke Ferries'
passenger and passenger/vehicle services runs
to Dunwich and back around 12 times daily
(passenger ferries 25 minutes, vehicle ferries
45 minutes).

Moreton Island

You'll be reassured to learn that Moreton
Island's cache of sandy shores, bushland,
bird life, dunes and glorious lagoons are
well protected – 95% of the isle is designated national park (see www.nprsr.qld.
gov.au/parks/moreton-island).

◉ Sights & Activities

Dolphin feeding happens each evening
around sunset at Tangalooma, halfway
down the western side of the island.
Around half-a-dozen dolphins swim in
from the ocean and take fish from the
hands of volunteer feeders. You have
to be a guest of the Tangalooma Island
Resort to participate, but onlookers are
welcome. The resort organises whale-
watching cruises (June to October).

Just north of the resort, off the coast,
are the rusty Tangalooma Wrecks – 15
sunken ships forming a sheltered boat
mooring (and a brilliant snorkelling
spot!). You can hire snorkelling gear from
the resort, or Tangatours (☑07-3410
6927; www.tangatours.com.au; Tangalooma
Island Resort) offers guided snorkelling
trips around the wrecks ($45) as well as
guided paddleboarding ($59) and dusk
kayaking tours ($49).

Tours

Dolphin Wild   Adventure Tour

(☑07-3880 4444; www.dolphinwild.com.au;
Newport Marina, Scarborough; per adult/child/
family incl lunch $125/75/325) These full-day
ecotours head out to Moreton Island with
commentary from a marine naturalist and
guided snorkel tours ($20/10 per adult/
child) around the Tangalooma wrecks.
Transfers from Brisbane and the Gold
Coast available.

Adventure
Moreton Island   Adventure Tour

(☑1300 022 878; www.adventuremoretonisland
.com; 1-day tours from $129) Operated in
cahoots with Tangatours at Tangalooma
Island Resort, these tours offer a range
of activities (paddleboarding, snorkelling,

sailing, kayaking, fishing etc), from Brisbane. Overnight resort accommodation packages also available (including tour from $288).

Sleeping

Tangalooma Island Resort
Hotel, Apartments $$$
(07-3637 2000, 1300 652 250; www.tangalooma.com; 1-night packages from $370; ✳ @ 🛜 ⛴) This beautifully sited place has the island resort market cornered. There are abundant sleeping options, starting with simple hotel rooms. A step up are the units and suites, where you'll get beachside access and more contemporary decor. The apartments range from two- to four-bedroom configurations. The resort has several eating options; accommodation prices generally include return ferry fares and transfers.

ⓘ Getting There & Around
Several ferries operate from the mainland. To explore once you get to the island, bring a 4WD on one of the ferries or take a tour (most tours are from Brisbane, and include ferry transfers).

Tangalooma Flyer (07-3268 6333, shuttle bus 07-3637 2000; www.tangalooma.com; adult/child return $45/25) Fast passenger catamaran operated by Tangalooma Island Resort. It makes the 75-minute trip to the resort three times daily from Holt St Wharf in Brisbane (see the website for directions). A shuttle bus (adult/child one way $20/10) scoots to the wharf from the CBD or airport; bookings essential.

NOOSA & THE SUNSHINE COAST

From the tip of Bribie Island, the 'Sunny Coast' stretches north for 100 golden kilometres to the Cooloola Coast, just beyond the exclusive, leafy resort town of Noosa.

Forming a stunning backdrop to this spectacular coastline are the ethereal Glass House Mountains.

ⓘ Getting There & Away

Air
The Sunshine Coast Airport is at Mudjimba, 10km north of Maroochydore and 26km south of Noosa. Jetstar (☎ 13 15 38; www.jetstar.com.au)

White-bellied sea eagle, Moreton Island

MARK A. JOHNSON/ALAMY©

DARRELL GULIN/GETTY IMAGES ©

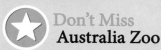

Don't Miss
Australia Zoo

Just north of Beerwah is one of Queensland's, if not Australia's, most famous tourist attractions. Australia Zoo is a fitting homage to its founder, zany celebrity wildlife enthusiast Steve Irwin. In addition to all things slimy and scaly, the zoo has an amazing wildlife menagerie and features a Cambodian-style Tiger Temple, the Asian-themed Elephantasia, as well as the famous Crocoseum. There are macaws, birds of prey, giant tortoises, snakes, otters, camels, and more crocs and critters than you can poke a stick at.

Various companies offer tours from Brisbane and the Sunshine Coast. The zoo operates a free courtesy bus from towns along the coast, as well as from the Beerwah train station (bookings essential).

NEED TO KNOW

☏07-5494 1134; www.australiazoo.com.au; Steve Irwin Way, Beerwah; adult/child/family $59/35/172; ☉9am-5pm

and Virgin Australia (☏13 67 89; www. virginaustralia.com) have daily flights from Sydney and Melbourne.

Bus

Greyhound Australia (☏1300 473 946; www.greyhound.com.au) has daily services from Brisbane to Caloundra ($25, two hours), Maroochydore ($25, two hours) and Noosa ($29, 2½ hours). Premier Motor Service (☏13 34

10; www.premierms.com.au) also services Maroochydore and Noosa from Brisbane.

ⓘ Getting Around

Several companies offer transfers from the Sunshine Coast Airport and Brisbane to points along the coast.

Col's Airport Shuttle (☏07-5450 5933; www. airshuttle.com.au)

Noosa Transfers & Charters (07-5450 5933; www.noosatransfers.com.au)

Train

Citytrain has services from Nambour to Brisbane ($22, two hours). Trains also go to Beerwah ($12, 1½ hours), near Australia Zoo.

....

Noosa

Once a little-known surfer hang-out, Noosa is now a stylish resort town and one of Queensland's star attractions. Noosa's stunning natural landscape of crystalline beaches and tropical rainforests blends seamlessly with its fashionable boulevard, Hastings St, and the sophisticated beach elite who flock here.

◎ Sights

One of Noosa's best features, the lovely **Noosa National Park** (07-5447 3243; Hastings St; 9am-3pm) covers the headland and offers fine walks, great coastal scenery and a string of bays with waves that draw surfers from all over the country.

Pick up a walking-track map from the **Queensland Parks & Wildlife Service (QPWS) centre** (9am-3pm), at the entrance to the park.

Activities

Noosa River is excellent for canoeing and kayaking. It's possible to follow it north past beautiful homes through to Lakes Cooroibah and Cootharaba, and the Cooloola section of the Great Sandy National Park, just south of Rainbow Beach Rd. **Noosa Ocean Kayak Tours** (0418 787 577; www.noosakayaktours.com; 2hr tours $66, kayak hire per day $55) hires out kayaks and offers sea-kayaking tours around Noosa National Park and Noosa River.

Numerous companies offer surf lessons and board hire, including **Merrick's Learn to Surf** (0418 787 577; www.learntosurf.com.au; 2hr lessons $60; 9am & 1.30pm), **Go Ride A Wave** (1300 132 441; www.gorideawave.com.au; 2hr lessons $65, 2hr surfboard hire $25, 1hr stand-up paddleboard hire $30) and **Noosa Kite Surfing** (0458 909 012; www.noosakitesurfing.com.au; 2hr lessons $95).

Noosa Heads

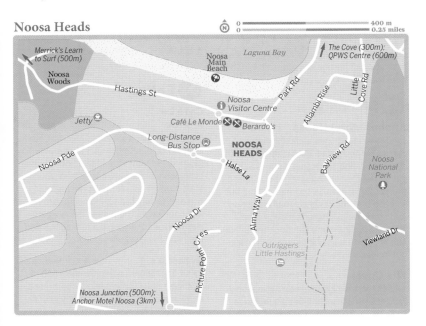

N

0   400 m
0   0.25 miles

Merrick's Learn to Surf (500m)

Noosa Woods

Hastings St

Laguna Bay

Noosa Main Beach

The Cove (300m); QPWS Centre (600m)

Park Rd

Allambi Rise

Little Cove Rd

Noosa Visitor Centre

Jetty

Café Le Monde

Berardo's

Long-Distance Bus Stop

NOOSA HEADS

Noosa Pde

Halse La

Bay View Rd

Noosa National Park

Noosa Dr

Alma Way

Picture Point Cres

Outriggers Little Hastings

Viewland Dr

Noosa Junction (500m); Anchor Motel Noosa (3km)

Detour:
Eumundi

Sweet little Eumundi is a quaint highland village with a quirky New-Age vibe greatly amplified during its famous market days.

The **Eumundi markets** (🕐6.30am-2pm Sat, 8am-1pm Wed) attract thousands of visitors to their 300-plus stalls and have everything from hand-crafted furniture and jewellery to homemade clothes and alternative-healing booths, plus food and live music.

Sunbus runs hourly from Noosa Heads ($4.20, 40 minutes) and Nambour ($5.10, 30 minutes). A number of Noosa tour operators visit the Eumundi markets.

 Tours

Fraser Island Adventure Tours
Adventure Tour

(☏07-5444 6957; www.fraserislandadventure tours.com.au; day tours $165) The very popular day tour to Eli Creek and Lake McKenzie packs as much punch as a two-day tour.

Offbeat Ecotours
Ecotour

(☏1300 023 835; www.offbeattours.com.au; Full-day tours adult/child $155/110) These spirited day trips into the Noosa Hinterland – the 'oxygen tank' of Noosa – feature waterfall swimming, intimate encounters with ancient flora and a gourmet lunch to rival the Hastings St massive.

 **Sleeping**

Anchor Motel Noosa
Motel $$

(☏07-5449 8055; www.anchormotelnoosa. com.au; cnr Anchor St & Weyba Rd; r from $110; ❄🔊🏊) Ships ahoy, this place is a bargain! There's nothing pretentious about the spotless, marine-themed rooms but all have bathrooms and small balconies, and some have king-sized beds. The shared space around the pool and barbecue are good launching pads for a night out in Noosaville.

The Cove
Apartment $$

(☏5447 4111; www.thecovenoosa.com.au; cnr Park Rd & Little Cove Rd; 2-bedroom apt from $200; 🅿❄🏊) Opposite charming Little Cove Beach, this well-managed, low-key resort has spacious, bright apartments that suit longer stays. There's an excellent pool in the internal courtyard and the popular penthouse suites have outdoor spas.

Outriggers Little Hastings
Resort $$$

(☏07-5449 2277; www.outrigger.com; Viewland Dr, access via Little Cove Rd after 7pm; 1-/2-bedroom apt $269/339) The Noosa Outriggers is typically stylish with clean lines and soft colours throughout. The balconies and windows all look out on thick greenery and there is ample space for a post-hillclimb cocktail party.

 Eating

Café Le Monde
Modern Australian $$

(Hastings St; mains $15-28; 🕐breakfast, lunch & dinner) Opposite the surf club, but with plum street views, Le Monde offers classic Noosa dining: attractive and attentive staff, huge menu running throughout the day, family friendly yet still somehow hip. Food-wise, the pick is the burgers. Happy-hour drinks are a real scene and live music is a regular feature.

Berardo's
Modern Australian $$$

(☏07-5447 5666; Hastings St; mains $30-42; 🕐dinner) Still Noosa's most celebrated restaurant, Berardo's is a study in contemporary cuisine inspired by the decor of yesteryear. With its classically trained musicians and impeccable waitstaff, this is the place for intimate celebration.

❶ Information

Noosa Visitor Centre (📞07-5430 5020; www.visitnoosa.com.au; Hastings St, Noosa Heads; ⏰9am-5pm)

❶ Getting There & Around

Long-distance buses stop at the bus stop near the corner of Noosa Dr and Noosa Pde. The state-of-the-art Noosa Junction station opened in 2012 and now acts as the bus hub for the region.

Sunbus has frequent services to Maroochydore ($5, one hour) and the Nambour train station ($5, one hour).

Glass House Mountains

Rising high above the green subtropical hinterland are the 16 volcanic crags known as the Glass House Mountains. Mt Beerwah (556m), the highest of these ethereal cornices, is the mother according to Dreaming mythology.

Hikers are spoilt for choice here. If you're in a hurry, the **Glass House Mountains lookout** provides a fine view of the peaks and the distant beaches. The **lookout circuit** (800m) is a short and steep walking track that leads through open scribbly-gum forest and down a wet gully before circling back.

If you're looking for something more intense, you should check out the 1.4km (return) hike to the summit of **Mt Ngungun** (253m).

FRASER ISLAND & THE FRASER COAST

Fraser Island

Fraser Island is the largest sand island in the world (measuring 120km by 15km) and the only place where rainforest grows on sand.

The island is home to a profusion of bird life and wildlife, including the purest strain of dingo in Australia, while offshore waters teem with dugong, dolphins, sharks and migrating humpback whales.

Eumundi markets

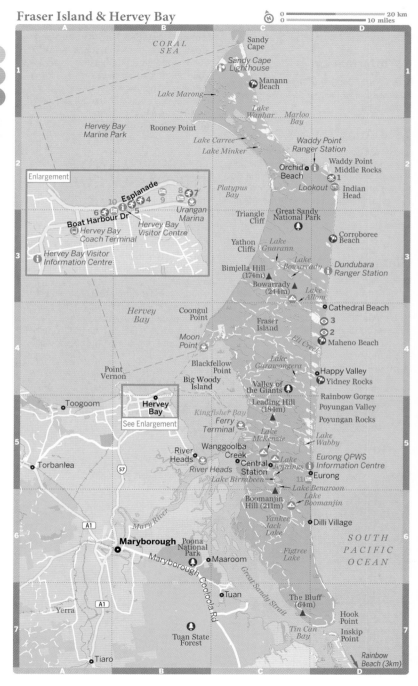

N

0 — 20 km
0 — 10 miles

CORAL SEA

Sandy Cape

Sandy Cape Lighthouse

Manann Beach

Lake Marong

Lake Wanhar

Marloo Bay

Hervey Bay Marine Park

Rooney Point

Lake Carree

Lake Minker

Waddy Point Ranger Station

Waddy Point Middle Rocks

Orchid Beach

Platypus Bay

Lookout

Indian Head

Enlargement

Esplanade

8 7

10 4

6

5

Urangan Marina

Boat Harbour Dr

Hervey Bay Coach Terminal

Hervey Bay Visitor Centre

Hervey Bay Visitor Information Centre

Triangle Cliff

Great Sandy National Park

Corroboree Beach

Yathon Cliffs

Lake Gnarann

Dundubara Ranger Station

Bimjella Hill (174m)

Lake Bowarrady

Bowarrady (244m)

Lake Allom

Hervey Bay

Coongul Point

Fraser Island

Cathedral Beach

3

Moon Point

Eli Creek

2

Maheno Beach

Blackfellow Point

Lake Garawongera

Happy Valley

Point Vernon

Big Woody Island

Valley of the Giants

Yidney Rocks

Hervey Bay

See Enlargement

Leading Hill (184m)

Rainbow Gorge

Poyungan Valley

Poyungan Rocks

Toogoom

Kingfisher Bay Ferry Terminal

Lake McKenzie

Lake Wabby

Torbanlea

River Heads

Wanggoolba Creek

Eurong QPWS Information Centre

River Heads

Central Station

Lake Jennings

Eurong

57

Lake Birrabeen

11

Lake Benaroon

Boomanjin Hill (211m)

Lake Boomanjin

A1

Mary River

Maryborough

Poona National Park

Yankee Jack Lake

Dilli Village

SOUTH PACIFIC OCEAN

Maryborough Cooloola Rd

Maaroom

Figtree Lake

Great Sandy Strait

A1

Yerra

Tuan

The Bluff (64m)

Hook Point

Tuan State Forest

Tin Can Bay

Inskip Point

Tiaro

Rainbow Beach (3km)

⊙ Sights & Activities

Seventy-Five Mile Beach runs the length of the island's east coast and offers some captivating scenery along the way. From Fraser's southern tip, use the high-tide access track between Hook Point and **Dilli Village**, rather than the beach. From here on, the eastern beach is the main thoroughfare. Stock up at nearby **Eurong**, the start of the inland track, across to Central Station and Wanggoolba Creek (for the ferry to River Heads).

In the middle of the island is **Central Station**, the starting point for numerous walking trails.

About 4km north of Eurong along the beach is a signposted walking trail to **Lake Wabby**. Wabby is edged on three sides by eucalypt forest, while the fourth side is a massive sandblow, which is encroaching on the lake at a rate of about 3m a year.

Driving north along the beach you'll pass **Happy Valley**, with many places to stay, and **Eli Creek**. About 2km from Eli Creek is the wreck of the **Maheno**, a passenger liner that was blown ashore by a cyclone in 1935 while being towed to a Japanese scrapyard.

Roughly 5km north of the *Maheno* you'll find the **Pinnacles** (a section of coloured sand cliffs) and, about 10km beyond, **Dundubara**. Then there's a 20km stretch of beach before you come to the rocky outcrop of **Indian Head**, which is the best vantage point on the island. Sharks, manta rays, dolphins and (during the migration season) whales can often be spotted from the top of the headland.

From Indian Head the trail branches inland, passing the **Champagne Pools**, the only safe spot on the island for saltwater swimming. This inland road leads back to **Waddy Point** and **Orchid Beach**, the last settlement on the island.

On the island you can take a scenic flight with **MI Helicopters** (☎07-4125 1599, 1800 600 345; www.mihelicopters.com.au; 25min flights $230) or with **Air Fraser** (☎1800 600 345, 07-4125 3600; www.airfraserisland.com.au; same day return flight from Hervey Bay $125).

Sleeping & Eating

Fraser Island Retreat
Cabin $$

(☎07-4127 9144; www.fraserisretreat.com.au; Happy Valley; cabins per 2 nights $330; @ 🛜 ⊠) The nine timber cabins here are some of the best-value accommodation on the island. While lacking self-catering facilities, the cabins are airy, bright and sleep up to four. There's a restaurant and shop on-site.

Fraser Island Beachhouses
Cabin $$

(☎07-4127 9205, 1800 626 230; www.fraserislandbeachhouses.com.au; Eurong Second Valley; per 2 nights studio $300, 2-bedroom house from $700; ⊠) These are loads of fun for small groups who want an element of privacy. The sunny, self-contained units are kitted out with polished wood, cable TVs and ocean views.

ⓘ Information

The main ranger station, Eurong QPWS Information Centre (☎4127 9128) is at Eurong. Others can be found at Dundubara (☎07-4127 9138) and Waddy Point (☎07-4127 9190).

⭐ Don't Miss
Sand Safaris: Exploring Fraser Island

The only way to explore Fraser Island is with a 4WD vehicle. For most travellers there are three transport options: tag-along tours, organised tours or 4WD hire.

Popular with backpackers, **tag-along tours** feature a group of travellers that pile into a 4WD convoy and follow a lead vehicle with an experienced guide and driver. Rates hover around $300 to $320 for three-day/two-night packages, and exclude food, fuel and alcohol.

Package tours leave from Hervey Bay, Rainbow Beach and Noosa and typically cover rainforests, Eli Creek, Lakes McKenzie and Wabby, the coloured Pinnacles and the *Maheno* shipwreck. There are also tour companies based in Hervey Bay:

Fraser Explorer Tours (☎ 1800 249 122, 07-4194 9222; www.fraserexplorertours.com.au; 1-/2-day tours $175/319) Popular budget option.

Fraser Experience (☎ 1800 689 819, 07-4124 4244; www.fraserexperience.com; 1-/2-day tours $180/327) Small groups and more freedom about the itinerary.

Hire companies lease out 4WD vehicles in Hervey Bay, Rainbow Beach and on the island itself. Most companies will help arrange ferries and permits and hire camping gear. Rates for multiday rentals start at $185 per day depending on the vehicle. On the island, **Aussie Trax 4WD** (☎ 07-4124 4433, 1800 062 275; www.fraser island4wd.com.au; Kingfisher Bay Resort; per day $227) hires out 4WDs from $227 per day.

Permits

You will need permits for vehicles (per month/year $42.15/211.30) and camping (per person/family $5.85/21.80), and these must be purchased before you arrive. It's best to purchase the permits online at www.derm.qld.gov.au or contact QPWS (☎ 13 74 68). Permits aren't required for private camping grounds or resorts. Permit-issuing offices include the following:

Great Sandy Information Centre (☎07-5449 7792; 240 Moorinidil St; ⊙8am-4pm) Near Noosa.

Rainbow Beach QPWS (☎07-5486 3160; Rainbow Beach Rd)

River Heads Information kiosk (☎07-4125 8485; ⊙6.15-11.15am & 2-3.30pm) Ferry departure point at River Heads, south of Hervey Bay.

Getting There & Away

Vehicle ferries connect Fraser Island with River Heads, about 10km south of Hervey Bay, or further south at Inskip Point, near Rainbow Beach.

Fraser Island Barges (☎1800 227 437; www.fraserislandferry.com.au) makes the crossing (vehicle and four passengers $155 return, 30 minutes) from River Heads to Wanggoolba Creek on the western coast of Fraser Island. It departs daily from River Heads at 8.30am, 10.15am and 4pm, and returns from the island at 9am, 3pm and 5pm.

Kingfisher Vehicular Ferry (☎1800 072 555; www.fraserislandferry.com) operates a daily vehicle and passenger ferry (pedestrian adult/child $50/25 return, and four passengers $155 return, 50 minutes) from River Heads to Kingfisher Bay, departing at 6.45am, 9am, 12.30pm, 3.30pm, 6.45pm and 9.30pm and returning at 7.50am, 10.30am, 2pm, 5pm, 8.30pm and 11pm.

Coming from Rainbow Beach, the operators **Rainbow Venture & Fraser Explorer** (☎07-4194 9300; pedestrian/vehicle return $10/80) and **Manta Ray** (☎07-5486 8888; vehicle return $90) both make the 15-minute crossing from Inskip Point to Hook Point on Fraser Island continuously from about 7am to 5.30pm daily.

Air Fraser Island (☎07-4125 3600; www.airfraserisland.com.au) charges from $125 for a return flight (20 minutes each way) to the island's eastern beach, departing from Hervey Bay airport.

Rainbow Beach

Gorgeous Rainbow Beach is a tiny town at the base of the Inskip Peninsula with spectacular multicoloured sand cliffs overlooking its rolling surf and white

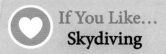

If You Like...
Skydiving

1 **SKYDIVE RAINBOW BEACH**
(☎0418 218 358; www.skydiverainbowbeach.com; 2400/4200m dives $299/369) Lands on the beach.

2 **SKYDIVE HERVEY BAY**
(☎0458 064 703; www.skydiveherveybay.com.au) Tandem skydives for $250 from 3000m and $270 from 4200m. Add an extra $30 for skydives over the beach.

3 **SKYDIVE BYRON BAY**
(☎1800 800 840, 02-6684 1323; www.skydivebyronbay.com; Tyagarah Airport; tandem flights $264-504) Tandem dives ($249 to $334) are priced depending on altitude and time of freefall (20 to 70 seconds).

4 **JUMP THE BEACH BRISBANE**
(☎1800 800 840; www.jumpthebeach brisbane.com.au; skydives from $344) Picks up from the CBD and offers tandem skydives over Brisbane, landing on the sand in Redcliffe.

sandy beach. Convenient access to Fraser Island (only 15 minutes by barge) and the Cooloola section of the Great Sandy National Park has made it one of Queensland's real coastal beauty spots.

The town is named for the **coloured sand cliffs**, a 2km walk along the beach.

Activities

Rainbow Beach Dolphin View Sea Kayaking Kayaking
(☎0408 738 192; Shop 1, 6 Rainbow Beach Rd; 3hr tours per person $65) Leaves from the Rainbow Beach Surf Centre.

Rainbow Beach Surf School Surfing
(☎0408738192; www.rainbowbeachsurfschool.com; 3hr session $55) Same mob that runs the kayaking hangs ten on a long, safe beach break.

163

Giants of the Sea: Whale Watching in Hervey Bay

Every year, from August to early November, thousands of humpback whales (*Megaptera novaeangliae*) cruise into Hervey Bay's sheltered waters for a few days before continuing their arduous migration south to the Antarctic.

Cruises go from the Urangan Marina out to Platypus Bay and then zip around from pod to pod to find the most active whales. In a very competitive market, vessels offer half-day (four-hour) tours that include breakfast or lunch and cost around $115 for adults and $60 for children. Some recommended operators include the following:

Spirit of Hervey Bay (☎1800 642 544; www.spiritofherveybay.com; ⏰8.30am & 1.30pm) The largest vessel with the greatest number of passengers. Has an underwater hydrophone and underwater viewing window.

That's Awesome (☎1800 653 775; www.awesomeadventure.com.au; ⏰7am, 10.30am & 2.30pm) This rigid inflatable boat speeds out to the whales faster than any other vessel. The low deck level means you're nearly eyeball-to-eyeball with the big mammals.

MV Tasman Venture (☎1800 620 322; www.tasmanventure.com.au; ⏰8.30am & 1.30pm) Maximum of 80 passengers; underwater microphones and viewing windows.

Blue Dolphin Marine Tours (☎07-4124 9600; www.bluedolphintours.com.au; adult/child $120/90; ⏰7.30am) Maximum 20 passengers on a 10m catamaran.

Wolf Rock Dive Centre Diving
(☎0438 740 811, 07-5486 8004; www.wolfrock dive.com.au; double dive charters from $210) Grey nurse sharks and plenty of spooky ledges in one of Australia's premier dive spots.

Sleeping

Debbie's Place B&B $$
(☎07-5486 3506; www.rainbowbeachaccommo dation.com.au; 30 Kurana St; d/ste from $99/109, 3-bedroom apt from $260; ❄) Pet- and people-friendly, Debbie's is an institution in Rainbow Beach for its terrific-value, self-contained rooms in a timber Queens-lander. The namesake owner works hard to ensure guests are at ease. The outdoor areas have shared cooking facilities.

Plantation Resort Apartment $$$
(☎07-5486 9000; www.plantationresortat rainbow.com.au; 1 Rainbow Beach Rd; 1-bed-room apt from $199; ❄ @ ☲) These swish apartments have perfect ocean views, and the outdoor cane settings and white plantation-themed rooms will have you reaching for the nearest gin and tonic.

Getting There & Around

Greyhound Australia (☎1300 473 946; www. greyhound.com.au) and **Premier Motor Service** (☎13 34 10; www.premierms.com.au) have daily services from Brisbane ($46, five hours), Noosa ($30, 3 hours) and Hervey Bay ($26, 2 hours).

Hervey Bay

As the main gateway to Fraser Island, Hervey Bay has matured from a welfare-by-the-sea escape into a low-key tourist destination thanks to its lovely sandy bay (and soothing sea breezes), steady resort development and huge pods of hump-back whales.

Activities

FRASER ISLAND TRIPS

Hervey Bay is great for arranging a 4WD adventure on Fraser Island. Some hostels put groups together in tag-along tours. A maximum of five vehicles follow a lead vehicle with an experienced guide and driver. Rates hover around $300 to $320 for a three-day/two-night camping trip, and exclude food, fuel and alcohol. Places that offer trips include **Colonial Village YHA** (☏1800 818 280; www.cvyha.com), **Fraser Roving** (☏1800 989 811, 07-4125 6386; www.fraserroving.com.au), **Nomads** (☏1800 354 535, 07-4125 3601; www.nomadshostels. com), **Next Backpackers** (☏07-4125 6600; www.nextbackpackers.com.au) and **Palace Adventures** (☏1800 063 168; www.palace adventures.com.au).

If you prefer to go on your own (not recommended for inexperienced off-road drivers), consider hiring a car.

Sleeping

Flashpackers
Hostel $

(☏07-4124 1366; www.flashpackersherveybay. com; 195 Torquay Tce, Torquay; dm $25-30, d $70; ❄️🛜🏊) Here's a hostel worth exporting, with a comfortable, spacious dorm and rooms with bathrooms. Reading lights, numerous power sockets, walk-in communal fridge, spotless (albeit brand new) communal areas and showers with power. Set a street back from the beach and now the new standard for backpacker accommodation in Hervey Bay.

Akama
Apartment $$

(☏07-4197 0777, 1800 770 661; www.akama resort.com.au; 625 Charlton; 1-/2-bedroom apt from $175/220; 🅿️❄️🏊) A tall, modern complex overlooking a fairly busy road near the marina, Akama excels on the inside. The apartments are enormous, with white interiors, slick bathrooms and open-plan living straight from a design catalogue. Staff are exceptional.

Bay B&B
B&B $$

(☏07-4125 6919; www.baybedandbreakfast.com. au; 180 Cypress St; s $100, d $125-140; ❄️@🏊) An honest B&B with enough charm to compete with the spread of resorts in the area. It's run by a friendly, well-travelled Frenchman, his wife (and their dog). Guest rooms are in a comfy annexe out the back, while the famed breakfasts are served in a tropical garden. Excellent value.

ℹ️ Information

Hervey Bay Visitor Centre (☏1800 649 926; 401 The Esplanade; internet per hr $4) Friendly, privately run booking office with internet access.

Hervey Bay Visitor Information Centre (☏1800 811 728; www.herveybaytourism.com. au; cnr Urraween & Maryborough Rds) Helpful tourist office on outskirts of town.

ℹ️ Getting There & Away

Boat

Boats to Fraser Island leave from River Heads, about 10km south of town, and Urangan Marina. Most tours leave from Urangan Harbour.

Bus

Long-distance buses depart from **Hervey Bay Coach Terminal** (☏07-4124 4000; Central Ave, Pialba).

ℹ️ Getting Around

Plenty of rental companies make Hervey Bay the best place to hire a 4WD for Fraser Island:

Fraser Island 4WD Hire (☏07-4125 6612; www. fraser4wdhire.com.au; 5 Kruger Crt, Urangan)

Safari 4WD Hire (☏1800 689 819; www. safari4wdhire.com.au; 102 Boat Harbour Dr, Pialba)

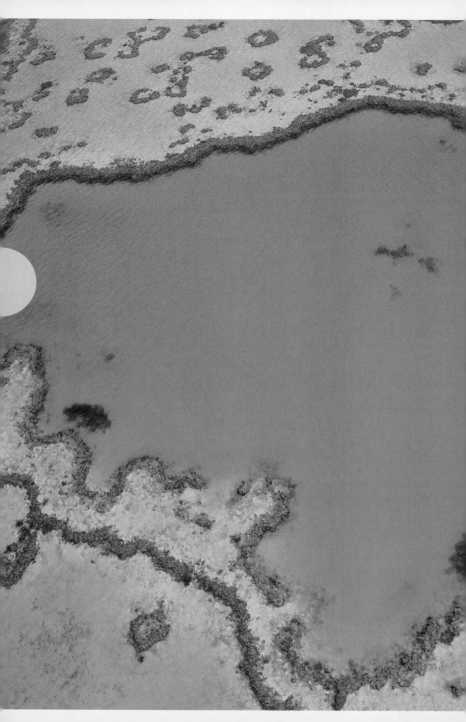

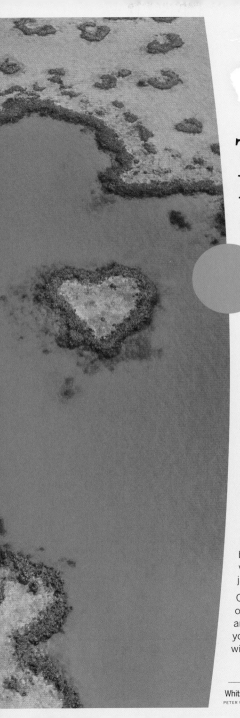

Tropical North Queensland

Awash with picture-perfect landscapes and vibrant towns, Queensland's tropical north is intriguing. Three unmissable highlights provide a backdrop of natural splendour: the Whitsunday Islands archipelago, the luminous green Daintree Rainforest, and the Great Barrier Reef, with its hyper-coloured coral and clear blue waters.

Also here are some of the country's lesser-known treasures, delivering wow-factor with gusto. You only have to peel back the postcard to find corners seemingly untouched by other visitors – spectacular national parks with tumbling waterfalls, hippie villages and foodie towns, white-sand beaches fringed by kaleidoscopic coral, vibrant and unique Indigenous festivals and jaw-dropping sunsets.

Cairns is a travellers' mecca, a far-flung town on the way up that's surprisingly worldly and cosmopolitan. From here you can launch yourself into the jungle or out onto the reef with ease.

Whitsunday Islands (p179), Great Barrier Reef

Tropical North Queensland

PAPUA NEW GUINEA

CORAL SEA

Great Barrier Reef

Cape York

Bamaga

Jardine River National Park

Shelburne Bay

Iron Range National Park

Lockhart River

Wepa

Mungkan Kandju National Park

Aurukun

Coen

Pormpuraaw

Kowanyama

Cape York Peninsula

Mitchell River

Staaten River National Park

Cape Melville National Park

Barrow Point

Princess Charlotte Bay

Lakefield National Park

Laura

Lizard Island

Hope Vale

Cooktown

Wujal Wujal

Cape Tribulation

Daintree National Park

Mossman

Port Douglas

Kuranda

Mareeba

Atherton Tableland

Atherton

Cairns

Fitzroy Island

Frankland Islands

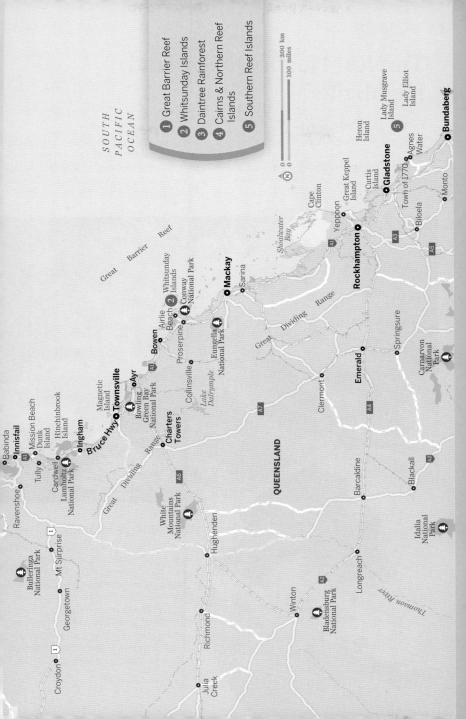

Tropical North Queensland Highlights

Great Barrier Reef

Queensland's Great Barrier Reef (p176) is amazing: battered by natural and human impacts, which are causing a continuing decline, the reef is remarkably resilient and always seems to offer something new. Operators in Airlie Beach, Cairns and Port Douglas arrange reef visits, or head for reef resorts in places like Heron Island, Lizard Island and Green Island. Feather-duster worm

Whitsunday Islands

There's no better way to experience the hedonistic Whitsunday Islands (p179) than on an overnight sailing adventure. Make the most of your time by exploring the best of the 74 Whitsunday Islands. Don your snorkel and check out the crystal-clear waters and amazing marine life around Hook and Whitsunday Islands; or take to the air for a fabulous angle on Whitehaven Beach. Whitsunday Island (p184)

Daintree Rainforest

Everyone in Australia knows its name, but the Daintree (p197) still suffers from an identity crisis: is it a village? Is it a national park? A river? A World Heritage area? It's actually all four, but mostly it's a rainforest – an amazing, remote tropical wilderness with incredible biodiversity and more precious jungle-meets-sea beaches than you have lazy afternoons to spare.
Mossman Gorge (p203)

Cairns & Northern Reef Islands

Cairns (p188) is the kind of regional outpost where, 30 years ago, tourists might have feared to tread. But these days it's a lively tourist hotspot with multicultural eateries, great places to stay and easy access to the Daintree Rainforest, Great Barrier Reef and northern reef islands (p196) such as Green Island, Fitzroy Island and Lizard Island – perfect for castaway fantasies-come-true. Green Island (p196)

Southern Reef Islands

The photogenic Whitsunday Islands get all the good press, but along the Great Barrier Reef's southern reaches off the Capricorn Coast there are some other fabulous isles (p176) that have all the hallmarks without the hype. Check out Lady Elliot Island and Lady Musgrave Island for some magical dive sites, and secluded Heron Island for a pristine coral encounter. Lady Elliot Island (p176)

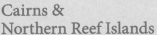

Tropical North Queensland's Best...

Island Escapes

○ **Whitsunday Island** Lovely enough to lend its name to the surrounding archipelago. (p184)

○ **Green Island** Day trippers from Cairns come for the beaches and snorkelling (or stay overnight in luxury). (p196)

○ **Hamilton Island** Not for Robinson Crusoes: luxury resort with abundant activities and entertainment options. (p185)

○ **Lizard Island** Bask like a lizard on this remote and un-touristed isle. (p204)

Diving & Snorkelling

○ **Green Island** Quick and easy access from Cairns with super offshore snorkelling. (p196)

○ **Hook Island** Superb access to coral coupled with fabulous camping or simple budget digs. (p184)

○ **Frankland Islands National Park** Fabulous coral reef surrounds these uninhabited national park islands off Cairns. (p178)

○ **Reef day trips** Get amongst the real reef on a day trip from Cairns of Port Douglas. (p197)

Tropical Wilds

○ **Daintree Rainforest** Crocodiles, rivers, swamps, palm-fringed beaches...it's all here. (p197)

○ **Great Barrier Reef** OK, so it's underwater, but what a wild place! (p176)

○ **Cape Tribulation** Jungle-meets-sea photogenics north of Port Douglas. (p205)

○ **Kuranda Scenic Railway** Take a rail ride through the rainforest wilds behind Cairns. (p199)

Need to Know

Urban Delights

○ **Port Douglas** Cool in the tropical heat: a classy town with superior restaurants, cafes and bars. (p200)

○ **Cairns** Big-smoke Cairns delivers plenty of city-size comforts. (p188)

○ **Mission Beach** Low-key in the best possible way, Mission Beach is the perfect little tropical town. (p185)

○ **Airlie Beach** Party hard in Airlie, then recover on the Whitsunday Islands. (p179)

ADVANCE PLANNING

○ **One month before** Organise internal flights, train trips and resort accommodation.

○ **Two weeks before** Book a seat on a Great Barrier Reef tour from Cairns or Port Douglas.

○ **One week before** Book a table at a top Port Douglas or Cairns eatery: try Ochre (p193) in Cairns and Harrisons Restaurant (p203) in Port Douglas.

RESOURCES

○ **Queensland Holidays** (www.queenslandholidays.com.au) Great resource for planning your trip.

○ **Tourism Queensland** (www.tq.com.au) Government-run body promoting Queensland.

○ **Tourism Tropical North Queensland** (www.ttnq.org.au) Helpful resources for TNQ.

○ **Cairns & Tropical North Visitor Information Centre** (www.cairns-great barrierreef.org.au) Cairns-based info and bookings for TNQ.

○ **Royal Automobile Club of Queensland** (RACQ; www.racq.com.au) Driving info and roadside assistance.

GETTING AROUND

○ **Walk** Around the Cairns, Port Douglas and Airlie Beach waterfronts.

○ **Train** Ride the *Tilt Train* to Cairns and the scenic railway to Kuranda.

○ **Cableway** Dangle in a cable-car gondola above the slopes between Kuranada and Cairns.

○ **Catamaran** To the reef and islands on superfast catamarans.

○ **Drive** Through the Atherton Tableland.

BE FOREWARNED

○ **Box jellyfish** In coastal waters north of Agnes Water from October to April (potentially deadly).

○ **Saltwater crocodiles** A real danger this far north: found in estuaries, creeks and rivers. Observe the signs.

Left: Butterflyfish, Great Barrier Reef; **Above:** Hamilton Island (p185)

(LEFT) JEFF HUNTER/GETTY IMAGES ©;
(ABOVE) PETER HARRISON/GETTY IMAGES ©

Tropical North Queensland Itineraries

Queensland's far north is a remarkable place with a tropical vibe. Change down a gear or two, slip into beach (or reef) mode and enjoy the good life under the sun.

PORT DOUGLAS TO CAIRNS

Leisure Stations

An hour or so north of Cairns is a tropical gem worth discovering: ❶ **Port Douglas** (p200) is the kind of town where you plan to spend the night but end up staying a week. The lure here is quality accommodation, great restaurants, relaxed but still-stylish bars and pubs (a rarity in these latitudes); plus access to both the Daintree Rainforest and Great Barrier Reef. Spend a day unwinding, then sign up for a reef snorkelling trip or a Daintree excursion (look for cassowaries!).

The next day, travel south along the scenic inland road (Hwy 1), through the ❷ **Atherton Tablelands** (p197) – check out the coffee, tea and sugarcane plantations – to ❸ **Mission Beach** (p185). This quiet little seaside town has instant appeal, with just enough cafes and restaurants to keep your pulse ticking over.

After a night in Mission Beach, track north again to ❹ **Cairns** (p188), where you could easily blow your budget on fine food, shopping or daiquiris by the pool. There are some great galleries here too, plus the educational Indigenous-owned Tjapukai Cultural Park, and day trips and activities aplenty.

Top Left: Salsa Bar & Grill (p202), Port Douglas; **Top Right:** Kuranda Scenic Railway (p199)

5 DAYS

CAIRNS TO HAMILTON ISLAND

Reef Madness

Kick off this coral-coloured escapade in the tropical hub of ❶**Cairns** (p188). Spend a day splashing around in the lagoon and mooching between restaurants. No visit to Cairns is complete without a boat ride to the nearby coral-fringed islands – ❷**Green Island** (p196) is our pick – or a snorkelling day-trip to the pristine outer Great Barrier Reef. Didn't pack your sea legs? Take the scenic railway or cableway to explore the hippie markets and Australian Butterfly Sanctuary at nearby ❸**Kuranda** (p198).

From Cairns, head down to ❹**Airlie Beach** (p179): plenty of accommodation, water-based activities and excuses to drink beer. It's the logical base for exploring the sandy ❺**Whitsunday Islands** (p184) archipelago. From here, ferry or fly directly to ❻**Hamilton Island** (p185), where the resort lifestyle grips you as soon as you step off the plane. Spend a day fooling around with watercraft or lazing by the pool, then explore some other islands: Whitsunday Island, with dazzling Whitehaven Beach, or the laid-back and naturally beautiful Hook and South Molle Islands.

Discover Tropical North Queensland

GREAT BARRIER REEF

Southern Reef Islands

More and more savvy travellers are doing their Great Barrier Reef thing here – and for good reason. There's the diving wilderness of Lady Elliot and Lady Musgrave, while at secluded Heron Island you can literally wade into an underwater paradise.

The Town of 1770 is the most common stepping-off point; otherwise, use Hervey Bay or Bundaberg. Tours to the islands (from $175) stop at a number of beaches and snorkelling spots and include lunch.

LADY ELLIOT ISLAND

On the southern frontier of the Great Barrier Reef, Lady Elliot is a 40-hectare vegetated coral cay popular with divers, snorkellers and nesting sea turtles. Divers can walk straight off the beach to explore an ocean bed of shipwrecks, coral gardens, bommies (coral pinnacles or outcroppings) and blowholes, and abundant marine life including barracuda, giant manta rays and harmless leopard sharks.

Lady Elliot Island Resort (☏1800 072 200; www.ladyelliot. com.au; per person $147-350) may have a monopoly on the island's accommodation, but it's still great value for a bed on the edge of heaven. Accommodation is in tent cabins, simple motel-style units, or more expensive two-bedroom self-contained suites with the sand at stretching distance. Rates include breakfast and dinner, snorkelling gear and some tours.

Green turtle hatchling, Lady Elliot Island
AUSCAPE/GETTY IMAGES ©

LADY MUSGRAVE ISLAND

Wannabe castaways, look no further. This tiny 15-hectare cay, 100km northeast of Bundaberg, sits on the western rim of a stunning, turquoise-blue reef lagoon renowned for its safe swimming, snorkelling and diving. Birds nest from October to April, green turtles from November to February.

Day trips to Lady Musgrave depart from the Town of 1770 marina.

HERON & WILSON ISLANDS

With the underwater reef world accessible directly from the beach, Heron Island is famed for scuba diving and snorkelling, although you'll need a fair amount of cash to visit.

The former five-star **Heron Island Resort** (07-4972 9055, 1800 737 678; www.heronisland.com; s/d incl buffet breakfast from $398/499) has seen better days but it is certainly not reason to stay away from the island. The Point Suites still have the best views and the family rooms are comfortable enough not to detract from the island experience. Guests will pay $200/100 per adult/child for launch transfer, or $790/430 for helicopter transfer. Both are from Gladstone.

Wilson Island (www.wilsonisland.com; s/d from $853/1100), also part of a national park, is an exclusive wilderness retreat with six permanent tents and solar-heated showers. The inclusive menu is superb, as are the beaches, especially for snorkelling. The only access is from Heron Island and you'll need to buy a combined Wilson-Heron package and spend at least two nights on Wilson Island.

Agnes Water & Town of 1770

Surrounded by national parks, sandy beaches and the blue Pacific, the twin coastal towns of Agnes Water and Town of 1770 are among Queensland's most appealing seaside destinations. The tiny settlement of Agnes Water has a lovely white-sand beach, the east coast's most northerly surf beach, while the even tinier Town of 1770 (little more than a marina!) marks Captain Cook's first landing in Queensland.

 ## Activities

Reef 2 Beach Surf School Surfing
(07-4974 9072; www.reef2beachsurf.com; 1/10 Round Hill Rd, Agnes Water) Learn to surf on the gentle breaks of the main beach with this highly acclaimed surf school. A three-hour group surfing lesson is $17, and surfboard hire is $20 for four hours.

1770 Liquid Adventures Kayaking
(0428 956 630; www.1770liquidadventures. com.au; 2hr kayak rental $40) Liquid runs a spectacular twilight kayak tour ($55).

 ## Tours

Lady Musgrave Cruises Cruise
(07-4974 9077; www.1770reefcruises.com; Captain Cook Dr; adult/child $175/85) Has excellent day trips to Lady Musgrave Island aboard the *Spirit of 1770*. Trips include snorkelling, fishing gear, coral viewing in a semisubmersible, lunch and snacks.

ThunderCat 1770 Adventure Tour
(0427 177 000; adult/child $85/65) Ride in a 4m inflatable surf-racing craft across the waves or visit secluded beaches, learn some local history and explore 1770's pristine waterways and national-park coastline.

 ## Sleeping

LaLaLand Retreat Retreat **$$**
(4974 9554; www.lalaland1770aw.com.au; 61 Bicentennial Dve, Agnes Water; cabin from $170; P ❄ ⬈) The four colourful cabins at this new guesthouse on the road into town are set in attractive bushland scrub and each sleeps four people easily. There is an excellent lagoon-style pool, wheelchair access and, aside from potential nosy neighbours, a sense of remove from civilisation.

If you like venturing into the wilds, take some time to explore these fab Queensland national parks:

1 CONWAY NATIONAL PARK

The mountains of Conway and the semi-submerged peaks that form the Whitsunday Islands are part of the same coastal mountain range. Expect waterfalls, lookouts, walking trails and beaches. Access is via Shute Harbour Rd, a short hop south of Airlie Beach.

2 EUNGELLA NATIONAL PARK

Eungella (young-gulla) is the oldest and longest stretch of subtropical rainforest in Australia, cut off from other rainforest areas for roughly 30,000 years. Platypuses are the stars of the show. Buses don't cover Eungella, so you'll need a car or an organised tour from Mackay.

3 CARNARVON NATIONAL PARK

Inland from Rockhampton, Carnarvon Gorge is a 30km-long, 200m-high gorge carved out over millions of years by Carnarvon Creek. What's left behind is a lush, otherworldly oasis containing giant cycads, king ferns, river oaks, flooded gums, cabbage palms, deep pools and platypuses in the creek. Allow at least a whole day for a visit.

4 FRANKLAND GROUP NATIONAL PARK

If the idea of hanging out on one of five uninhabited coral-fringed islands with excellent snorkelling and stunning white-sand beaches appeals (and if not, why not?), cruise out to the Frankland Group National Park near Cairns. **Frankland Islands Cruise & Dive** (07-4031 6300; www.franklandislands.com.au; adult/child from $149/79) runs excellent day trips.

Beach Shacks Apartment **$$**
(07-4974 9463; www.1770beachshacks.com; 578 Captain Cook Dr; d from $190) The best accommodation in the Town of 1770 proper is run by a charming Canadian lady. These 'shacks' are more than humble beach dwellings, with cane, bamboo and timber on the outside, and contemporary decor on the inside. Ask for the Light House.

Agnes Water Beach Club Apartment **$$**
(07-4974 7355; www.agneswaterbeachclub.com.au; 3 Agnes St; 1-/2-bedroom apt from $145/190; [❄][@][🏊]) Brand-new luxury apartments with excellent facilities in a great location.

Eating

1770 Beach Hotel Modern Australian **$$**
(07-4974 7446; 576 Captain Cook Dr; mains $14-38; ⏱breakfast, lunch & dinner) Immaculate service, high quality seafood and a location to warrant making a sea change for make this one of the finest restaurants on the Capricorn Coast. The front bar is a salty gem while the more refined indoor stand-up is perfect for a post-sunset pick-me-up. Take away booze available.

Bustards Cafe **$$**
(7 Agnes St; mains $12-25; ⏱breakfast, lunch & dinner) The hottest breakfast spot in Agnes Water is close to the main beach and rightfully popular for its locally sourced seafood and light lunches. Service comes in buckets and spades.

Information

Agnes Water Visitor Information Centre
(07-4902 1533; 71 Springs Rd; ⏱9am-4.30pm Mon-Fri) Very friendly and helpful staff at this brand-new $1-million community centre about 700m from the main intersection.

Getting There & Away

Only one of several daily **Greyhound** (13 20 30; www.greyhound.com.au) buses detours off the Bruce Hwy to Agnes Water; the direct bus from Bundaberg ($25, 1½ hours) arrives opposite Cool Bananas at 6.10pm. Others, including **Premier Motor Service** (13 34 10; www.premierms.com.au), drop passengers at Fingerboard Rd.

Whitsunday Islands

Opal-jade waters and white sandy beaches fringe the forested domes of these 'drowned' mountains where you can camp in secluded bays as a modern-day castaway, laze in a tropical island resort, snorkel, dive or set sail through this stunning archipelago. The gateway to the islands, Airlie Beach, is a vibrant backpacker hub with a throbbing nightlife.

Only seven of the islands have tourist resorts – catering to every budget and whim, from the basic accommodation at Hook Island to the exclusive luxury of Hayman Island.

AIRLIE BEACH

Airlie is the kind of town where humanity celebrates its close proximity to natural beauty by partying very hard. A relatively tiny town that can at times feel as busy as Brisbane, Airlie draws a stream of budget travellers, the sailing fraternity (who converge here for the mainland conveniences), families (who flock to the fine restaurants and boutique hotels) and shrewd, often short-sighted developers.

 **Activities**

Air Whitsunday Seaplanes   Scenic Flights
(☏07-4946 9111; www.airwhitsunday.com.au) This outfit offers three-hour Reef Adventures (adult/child $360/280), a Whitehaven experience ($240/210) and the signature four-hour Panorama Tour ($475/390) where you fly to Hardy Lagoon to snorkel or ride a semi-submersible, then fly to Whitehaven Beach for a picnic lunch. It

also runs day trips to exclusive Hayman Island ($245).

Whitsunday Escape   Sailing
(☏1800 075 145; www.whitsundayescape.com; Abel Point Marina) Specialises in bareboat charters – charter boats that come without a skipper or crew, where you skipper the boat yourself. The outfit can provide a sail guide, provisions and a cook if requested.

Salty Dog Sea Kayaking   Kayaking
(☏07-4946 1388; www.saltydog.com.au; half-/full-day trips $80/130) Offers guided full-day tours and kayak rental ($50/70 per half-/full day), plus longer kayak/camping missions (the six-day challenge costs $1490). It's a charming and healthy way to see the islands.

HeliReef   Scenic Flights
(☏07-4946 9102; www.helireef.com.au) Offers helicopter flights to the reef and a picnic lunch on Whitehaven Beach ($349).

Whitsunday Island (p184)
ANDREW BAIN/GETTY IMAGES ©

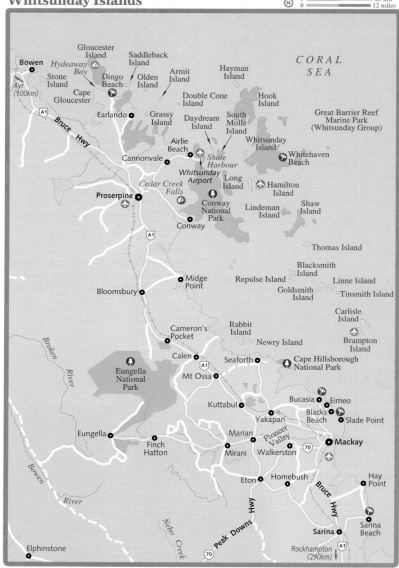

Tours

Voyager 4 Island Cruise Boat Tour
(📞07-4946 5255; www.wiac.com.au; adult/child $140/80) A good-value day cruise, with snorkelling at Hook Island, swimming at White-haven Beach, and checking out Daydream Island. Add a scenic flight for $60.

Cruise Whitsundays Boat Tour
(📞07-4946 4662; www.cruisewhitsundays.com) The biggest operator in town runs speed-

boat trips to the Barrier Reef Marine Base ($210), a pontoon located in Knuckle Reef Lagoon, where you can snorkel, dive or just cruise at sea.

Ocean Rafting
Boat Tour

(📞07-4946 6848; www.oceanrafting.com.au; adult/child/family $124/81/374) Fast-paced day tours let you swim at Whitehaven Beach, view Aboriginal cave paintings at Nara Inlet and snorkel the reef at Mantaray Bay or Border Island.

Big Fury
Boat Tour

(📞07-4948 2201; adult/child/family $130/70/350) Speeds out to Whitehaven Beach on an open-air sports boat followed by lunch and then snorkelling at a secluded reef nearby.

 ## Sleeping

Whitsundays Central Reservation Centre
Accommodation Services

(📞1800 677 119; www.airliebeach.com; 259 Shute Harbour Rd) To take the hassle out of finding the right accommodation, Whitsundays Central Reservation Centre can be of enormous assistance.

The Summit
Apartment $$

(📞1800 463 417; www.summitairliebeach.com. au; 15 Flame Tree Court; 1-/2-bedroom apt from $160/190; 🅿 ❄ 🛜 🏊) Nestled high above Airlie Beach are these exceptional apartments with some of the best views of the Whitsundays and hinterland. Try to nab one in the 600s. The fittings and furnishings are equally top notch and the shaded recreation area by the pool has free wi-fi and a spacious outlook.

Waterview
Apartment $$

(📞07-4948 1748; www.waterviewairliebeach. com.au; 42 Airlie Cres; studios/1-bedroom units from $135/149; ❄ 🛜) An excellent choice for both location and comfort, this boutique accommodation overlooks the main street and has gorgeous views of the bay. The rooms are modern, airy and spacious and have kitchenettes for self-caterers.

Whitsunday Islands

BY TINA COOK, WHITSUNDAY BOOKINGS OWNER/MANAGER & FREQUENT SKYDIVER

1 **THE WHITSUNDAY NGARO SEA TRAIL**
Blending seaways with kayaking and a range of walks, the Whitsunday Ngaro Sea Trail highlights the iconic features that have made the area famous: pure white sands, turquoise waters, ancient rock art, rugged headlands, dry rainforest, rolling grasslands and breathtaking views.

2 **BAIT REEF**
Bait Reef is a sensational spot for either snorkelling or scuba diving: it's one of the most pristine sites on the Great Barrier Reef and is classed as a Special Management Area. The best dive sites are Manta Ray Drop Off, The Stepping Stones and Paradise Lagoon.

3 **CRAYFISH BEACH, HOOK ISLAND**
Crayfish is my favourite camping getaway in the Whitsundays. It is at the top of Hook Island (p184) and offers fantastic snorkelling, a beautiful beach and a secluded camp site that takes a maximum of 13 people. Perfect for anyone wanting the absolute getaway.

4 **BALI HAI REEF & LANGFORD REEF**
Bali Hai and Langford Reefs are special spots around the Whitsunday Islands: very protected from weather, and at most times of the year there's great coral viewing and turtle spotting.

5 **THE ESPLANADE, AIRLIE BEACH**
The Esplanade at Airlie Beach (p179) is a great spot to just relax and watch people pass by while enjoying great food and drinks at one of the many restaurants. The Airlie Beach markets are at the end of the Esplanade every Saturday morning.

Don't Miss
Sailing the Whitsundays

Aside from day trips, most overnight sailing packages are for three days and two nights or two days and two nights.

Most vessels offer snorkelling on the fringing reefs (the reefs around the islands). Check if snorkel equipment, stinger suits and reef taxes are included in the package. Diving usually costs extra.

Once you've decided what suits, book at one of the many booking agencies in town such as **Whitsundays Central Reservation Centre** (☎1800 677 119; www.airliebeach. com; 259 Shute Harbour Rd; ☺7am-7pm), or a management company such as **Whitsunday Sailing Adventures** (☎07-4940 2000; www.whitsundaysailing.com; Shute Harbour Rd) or **Explore Whitsundays** (☎07-4946 5782; www.explorewhitsundays.com; 4 The Esplanade).

Some of the recommended sailing trips are the following:

Camira (day trips $175) Run by Cruise Whitsundays, one of the world's fastest commercial sailing catamarans is now a lilac-coloured Whitsunday icon. This good-value day trip includes Whitehaven Beach, snorkelling, morning and afternoon tea, a barbecue lunch and all refreshments (including wine and beer).

SV Domino (day trip $150) A co-op of local operators takes a maximum of eight guests to Bali Hai island, a little-visited 'secret' of the Whitsundays. Includes lunch and a good two-hour snorkel.

Whitehaven Xpress (day trip $160) Locally owned and operated for over a decade, the Xpress rivals the bigger operators for its Hill Inlet and Whitehaven tours.

Wings 2 (two-day-and-two-night trips from $475) Comfortable, well-maintained fast cat for those wanting to sail, dive and make new friends.

Club Crocodile
Hotel $$

(☏ 07-4946 7155; www.clubcroc.com.au; d from $119; P ✱ ⛱) On the road between Cannovale and Airlie Beach is this excellent budget option that is really popular with domestic tourists and young families. The Olympic-sized swimming pool is the hub of the action and even features a waterfall. How lovely!

Sunlit Waters
Apartment $$

(☏ 07-4946 6352; www.sunlitwaters.com; 20 Airlie Cres; studios from $92, 1-bedroom apt $115; ✱ ⛱) One of the best-value accommodation options in Airlie Beach, these large studios have everything you could want, including a self-contained kitchenette and some stunning views from the long balconies.

Airlie Beach Hotel
Hotel $$

(☏ 1800 466 233; www.airliebeachhotel.com. au; cnr The Esplanade & Coconut Grove; s/d $135/145, hotel $179-289; ✱ 🛜 ⛱) The spacious hotel rooms with sea views are much better value than the drab motel unit. Note also that the reception closes at 9pm.

Water's Edge Resort
Apartment $$$

(☏ 07-4948 4300; www.watersedgewhitsundays .com.au; 4 Golden Orchid Dr; 1-bedroom apt $210-260, 2-bedroom apt $275-345; ✱ ⛱) It's easy walking distance to town for such an elegant retreat. The languid heat subsides upon entering reception and the rooms don't disappoint: pastels and creamy hues, cane headboards and cooling use of shutters maximise the tropical experience. The staggered pool area will subdue the most restless soul.

Airlie Waterfront B&B
B&B $$$

(☏ 07-4946 7631; www.airliewaterfrontbnb.com. au; cnr Broadwater Ave & Mazlin St; d $259-285; ✱ @) Offering absolutely gorgeous views and immaculately presented from top to toe, this sumptuously furnished B&B oozes class and is a leisurely five-minute walk into town along the boardwalk.

Eating

Marino's Deli
Deli $

(Whitsunday Shopping Centre, Cannonvale; dishes $7-16; ⏱ 11am-8pm Mon-Sat) In a new premises in Cannonvale, Marino's is still the first choice for locals looking for delicious homemade pasta and huge salads. Affordable, high quality Italian food is available for takeaway.

Mr Bones
Pizza, Tapas $$

(☏ 0416 011 615; Shop 8, Lagoon Plaza, 263 Shute Harbour Rd; shared plates $12-17, pizza $15-23; ⏱ 9am-9pm Tue-Sat) Mr Bones is the new standard bearer in Airlie Beach for hip, affordable dining. The location opposite the lagoon is a gastronomic thoroughfare and diners here relish the prompt service and inventive cooking. The thin-based pizzas are tremendous – try the prawn and harissa – while the eggplant chips ($15) and spicy sardines ($17) suggest a playfulness that suits the holiday vibe.

Fish D'vine
Seafood $$

(☏ 07-4948 0088; 303 Shute Harbour Rd; mains $14-28; ⏱ lunch & dinner) The mixture of sugary liquor and seafood is strangely palatable at this popular Airlie institution. A selection of over 200 different rums somehow complements big plates of barbecued tiger prawns ($26) and yummy four-fish tasting plates ($27).

Waterline
Modern Australian $$

(☏ 07-4948 1023; 1 Shingley Dr; mains $20-30; ⏱ lunch & dinner Wed-Sun, breakfast Sun) With stunning views over the marina, this restaurant at Shingley Beach Resort has one of the best locations for waterfront dining.

The decor is tropical beach-chic. Recommended by the locals for its good service, great food and consistent quality.

ⓘ Getting There & Around

The closest major airports are at Proserpine and on Hamilton Island. The small Whitsunday Airport (☏ 07-4946 9180, 07-4946 9933) is about 6km southeast of town.

Greyhound (☏ 13 20 30; www.greyhound. com.au) and Premier Motor Service (☏ 13 34 10; www.premierms.com.au) have bus connections

Tully River Rafting

The Tully River provides thrilling white water year-round thanks to all that rain and the river's hydroelectric floodgates. Rafting trips are timed to coincide with the daily release of the floodgates, resulting in grade-four rapids, with stunning rainforest scenery as a backdrop.

Day trips with **Raging Thunder Adventures** (☎07-4030 7990; www.ragingthunder. com.au/rafting.asp; standard/'xtreme' trips $185/215) or **R'n'R White Water Rafting** (☎07-4041 9444; www.raft.com.au; trips $185) include a barbecue lunch and transport from Tully or nearby Mission Beach. The cost is between $215 and $230, which includes transfers from as far north as Palm Cove.

to Brisbane ($230, 19 hours), Mackay ($38, two hours), Townsville ($58, 4½ hours) and Cairns ($140, 11 hours). Long-distance buses stop on The Esplanade, between the sailing club and Airlie Beach Hotel.

Whitsunday Transit (☎07-4946 1800) connects Proserpine (Proserpine Airport), Cannonvale, Abel Point, Airlie Beach and Shute Harbour. Buses operate from 6am to 10.30pm.

LONG ISLAND

Underrated Long Island has the best of everything. The island is about 9km long but not much more than 1.5km wide, and a channel only 500m wide separates it from the mainland. Day trippers can use the facilities at **Long Island Resort** (☎1800 075 125; www.oceanhotels.com.au/longisland; d incl all meals $260-380; ❄@☀).

SOUTH MOLLE ISLAND

Lovers of birds and long, sandy beaches will enjoy the largest island of the Molle archipelago. Nearly 15km of splendid walking tracks traverse this mountainous 4-sq-km island; the highest point is Mt Jeffreys (198m), but the climb up Spion Kop is also worthwhile.

DAYDREAM ISLAND

Recently purchased by Chinese investors, Daydream Island feels more like a pontoon than a natural wonder. It's only a 15-minute ferry ride from the mainland so most appeals to families with kids, or day trippers.

The **Daydream Island Resort & Spa** (☎1800 075 040; www.daydreamisland. com; d from $328; ❄🛜☀) feels a bit like an island theme park but it still prides itself on excellent service as well as remarkable building and grounds maintenance.

HOOK ISLAND

The second largest of the Whitsundays, the 53-sq-km Hook Island is predominantly national park and rises to 450m at Hook Peak. Hook boasts some of the best diving and snorkelling locations in the Whitsundays.

Those who don't mind roughing it book in at the **Hook Island Wilderness Resort** (☎07-4946 9380; www.hookislandresort. com; camp sites per person $20, d with/without bathroom $120/100; ❄☀), a battered place with basic quarters and a licensed restaurant (mains $16-27).

WHITSUNDAY ISLAND

Whitehaven Beach, on Whitsunday Island, is a much-fabled, pristine 7km-long stretch of dazzling white sand bounded by lush tropical vegetation and a brilliant blue sea. From Hill Inlet, at the northern end of the beach, the swirling pattern of pure white sand through the turquoise and aquamarine water paints a magical picture. There's excellent snorkelling from its southern end.

HAMILTON ISLAND

Hamilton Island is the most 'liveable' island in the Whitsundays. There's a school, a new marina, a golf course, a busy domestic airport and, despite the crowds, a sense of in-the-know exclusivity.

Hamilton Island Resort (☎07-4946 9999; www.hamiltonisland.com.au; d from $370; ✱@☎☎) has extensive options, including bungalows, luxury villas, plush hotel rooms and self-contained apartments. At the high-end, **Qualia** (☎07-4948 9222, 1300 780 959; www.qualia.com.au; d from $1510) regularly scoops international awards.

Hamilton is a ready-made day trip from Shute Harbour, and you can use some of the resort's facilities.

HAYMAN ISLAND

The most northern of the Whitsunday group, Hayman is just 4 sq km in area and rises to 250m above sea level. It has forested hills, valleys and beaches, and a five-star resort.

An avenue of huge date palms leads to **Hayman Island Resort** (☎07-4940 1234, 1800 075 175; www.hayman.com.au; r incl breakfast $466-8000; ✱@☎), one of the most luxurious on the Great Barrier Reef.

Mission Beach

Less than 30km east of the Bruce Hwy's rolling sugar-cane and banana plantations, the hamlets that make up greater Mission Beach are hidden amongst World Heritage rainforest. The rainforest extends right to the Coral Sea, giving this 14km-long palm-fringed stretch of secluded inlets and wide, empty beaches the castaway feel of a tropical island.

Fanning out around Mission are picturesque walking tracks, which are fine places to see wildlife, including cassowaries – in fact, Australia's highest density of cassowaries (around 40) roam the surrounding rainforests.

◉ Sights & Activities

Adrenalin junkies flock to Mission Beach for extreme and water-based sports, including white-water rafting on the nearby Tully River.

The **walking** in the area is superb. The visitor centre stocks walking guides detailing trails.

Babinda Kayak Hire   Kayaking
(☎07-4067 2678; www.babindakayakhire.com.au; 330 Stager Rd, Babinda; half-day/full day $42/75) Easy yet breathtakingly beautiful

---

The Cassowary

The flightless cassowary is as tall as a grown man, has three toes, a blue-and-purple head, red wattles (fleshy lobes hanging from its neck), a helmet-like horn and unusual black feathers, which look more like ratty hair. It could certainly be confused with an ageing rocker.

The cassowary is an endangered species; there are less than 1000 left. Its biggest threat is loss of habitat, and eggs and chicks are vulnerable to dogs and wild pigs. A number of birds are also hit by cars: heed road signs warning drivers to be cassowary-aware. You're most likely to see cassowaries around Mission Beach and the Cape Tribulation section of the Daintree National Park.

Next to the Mission Beach visitor centre, there are cassowary-conservation displays at the **Wet Tropics Environment Centre** (☎07-4068 7197; www.wettropics.gov.au; Porter Promenade; ☺10am-4pm), which is staffed by volunteers from the **Community for Cassowary & Coastal Conservation** (C4; www.cassowaryconservation.asn.au).

If You Like...
Diving & Snorkelling

If you like splashing around in the deep blue sea, check out these dive operators around Queensland:

1 1770 UNDERWATER SEA ADVENTURES (☎1300 553 889; www.1770underseaadventures.com.au) Check availability prior to landing in town. Courses, reef trips and wreck dives all doable. At Town of 1770.

2 WHITSUNDAY DIVE ADVENTURES (☎07-4948 1239; www.whitsundaydivecentre.com; 303 Shute Harbour Rd) Offers a range of instruction, including open-water PADI-certified dive courses ($660). Half-day dive trips cost $175. Many boat cruises. At Airlie Beach.

3 CALYPSO DIVE (☎07-4068 8432; www.calypsodive.com.au; per person from $245) Experienced divers can join trips to the *Lady Bowen* wreck. Calypso also offers reef dives and PADI open-water courses ($625). Alternatively, you can snorkel the reef ($169). At Mission Beach.

4 HABA (☎07-4098 5000; www.habadive.com.au; Marina Mirage; adult/child $175/99) Long-standing local dive company; 25-minute glass-bottom-boat tours ($16/8 per adult/child) available. At Port Douglas.

kayaking tours through permanently flowing mountain streams in Wooroonooran National Park. A bit of a must-do if you're in the area.

Ingan Tours   Cultural Tour
(☎1300 728 067; www.ingan.com.au; adult/child $120/60) An Indigenous operator with impeccable credentials is causing a stir for its 'Spirit of the Rainforest' tour (adult/child $120/60, Tuesday, Thursday and Saturday).

Jump the Beach   Skydiving
(☎1800 444 568; www.jumpthebeach.com.au; 2700/3300/4200m tandem dives $284/345/369) Mission Beach is one of the most popular spots in Queensland to skydive. Jump the Beach claims to offer 'Australia's highest dive'.

Fishin' Mission   Fishing
(☎07-4088 6121; www.fishinmission.com.au; half/full day $130/190) Relaxed yet thoroughly professional fishing charters to either Dunk Island or a handful of 'secret' reefs.

Mission Beach Charters   Boat Tour
(☎07-4068 7009; www.missionbeachcharters.com.au; 1349c El Arish-Mission Beach Road) Astute operator with a whole raft of flexible products including Dunk Island drop-offs (and all-important camping permits) and whale-watching tours in season.

Sleeping

Scotty's Mission Beach House   Hostel $
(☎1800 665 567; www.scottysbeachhouse.com.au; 167 Reid Rd; dm $24-29, d $61-71; ❄@🛜🏊) Scotty's is run by the kind of crowd who legitimately love what they do and share that passion with their guests. Includes impeccable dorms and a lush pool area. A happening bar and restaurant, Scotty's Bar & Grill (mains $10-30, open dinner), welcomes the outside world.

Hibiscus Lodge B&B   B&B $$
(☎07-4068 9096; www.hibiscuslodge.com.au; 5 Kurrajong Cl; r $105-120) Only three rooms but an abundance of grace from the hosts and a luxurious setting above a bird-filled garden remind you why you came to Mission in the first place. The only requirement is to rise for sunset drinks, and maybe the breakfast, which is one of the best in town.

Mission Beach Ecovillage   Cabin $$
(☎07-4068 7534; www.ecovillage.com.au; Clump Point Rd; d $135-220; ❄🛜🏊) Nestled on a

0.8-hectare patch of banana tree–filled rainforest running to the beach, this quiet, family-friendly resort is a seductive introduction to Mission Beach. The restaurant (mains $19, open dinner Tuesday to Saturday) is deservedly popular. Some bungalows have spas.

Rainforest Motel
Motel **$$**

(☑ 07-4068 7556; www.missionbeachrainforest motel.com; 9 Endeavour Ave; s/d $98/119; ✴@ 🛜 ⌁) Terrific-value motel just a short walk from the Mission Beach shops, yet secreted away in rainforest foliage. The friendly owners take great pride in presenting the cool, tiled rooms. Free bikes available.

Sejala on the Beach
Cabin **$$$**

(☑ 07-4088 6699; http://missionbeachholidays. com.au/sejala; 26 Pacific Pde; d $260; ✴⌁) Intimate rainforest chic in these three huts (go for one of the two facing the beach) that are perfect for couples. All have decks with private barbecues.

Eating

Early Birds Cafe
Cafe **$**

(Shop 2, 46 Porter Promenade; mains $6-15; 🕓6am-3pm, closed Wed; 🍴) The pick of the breakfast joints and always busy.

Cafe Rustica
Italian **$$**

(☑ 07-4068 9111; Wongaling Beach Rd; mains $18-25; 🕓5pm-late Wed-Sat, 10am-late Sun; 🍴) We loved the homemade pasta and traditional crispy-crust pizzas prepared by this friendly couple at the Wongaling beach shack.

The Garage
Australian **$$**

(☑ 07-4088 6280; Donkin Lane; mezze plate $17; 🕓7am-late; 🍴) The hottest new spot in the Village Green serves delicious 'sliders' (mini burgers), free-pour cocktails ($14), good coffee, cakes and tapas. Diners congregate around dark wooden tables in the courtyard. Live music rolls through the busy periods.

Na Na Thai
Thai **$$**

(☑ 07-4068 9101; 165 Reid St; mains $16-26; 🕓5pm-8.30pm Tue-Sun) Na Na serves exquisite northern Thai food in a laid-back setting. It's run by a friendly Aussie bloke who graciously does the rounds and knows his menu intimately.

ℹ Information

The efficient **Mission Beach visitor centre** (☑ 07-4068 7099; www.missionbeachtourism. com; Porters Promenade; 🕓9am-4.45pm Mon-Sat, 10am-4pm Sun) has reams of info in multiple languages.

ℹ Getting There & Around

Greyhound Australia (☑ 1300 473 946; www. greyhound.com.au) and **Premier Motor Service** (☑ 13 34 10; www.premierms.com.au) buses stop in Wongaling Beach next to the giant 'big

Green Island (p196)
DAVID WALL PHOTO/GETTY IMAGES ©

TROPICAL NORTH QUEENSLAND CAIRNS

cassowary'; fares with Greyhound/Premier are $26 to Cairns, $40 to Townsville.

Mission Beach Adventure Centre rents out bikes (per half-day/day $10/20).

Cairns

Cairns has come a long way from struggling cane town to international resort city.

For many visitors this is the end of the line on the east-coast jaunt (or the start for those flying into Cairns' international airport), and the city is awash with bars and nightclubs, as well as accommodation and eateries in all price ranges.

◉ Sights

Cairns Foreshore & Lagoon

Waterfront

(☺Lagoon 6am-10pm Thu-Tue, noon-10pm Wed)
FREE In the absence of a beach, sunbathers flock around Cairns' shallow but spectacular saltwater swimming **lagoon** on the city's reclaimed foreshore. The artificial 4800-sq-metre lagoon is patrolled by lifeguards and illuminated at night.

Flecker Botanic Gardens   Gardens

(www.cairns.qld.gov.au; Collins Ave; ☺7.30am-5.30pm Mon-Fri, 8.30am-5.30pm Sat & Sun, information centre 9am-4.30pm Mon-Fri, 10am-2.30pm Sat & Sun; 🚌131) These beautiful tropical gardens are an explosion of greenery and rainforest plants. Sections include an area for bush-tucker plants and the Gondwanan Evolutionary Garden, which traces the 415-million-year heritage of tropical plants. Free guided walks depart from Tuesday to Friday at 10am from the **information centre**.

Tanks Arts Centre   Gallery, Theatre

(www.tanksartscentre.com; 46 Collins Ave; ☺gallery 10am-4pm Mon-Fri, market day last Sun of month Apr-Nov) Three gigantic WWII fuel-storage tanks have been transformed into studios, galleries showcasing Australian

artists' work and an inspired performing-arts venue (with some great bands), plus a lively **market day**.

Cairns Regional Gallery   Gallery
(www.cairnsregionalgallery.com.au; cnr Abbott & Shields Sts; adult/child under 16 5/free; ⏱9am-5pm Mon-Fri, 10am-5pm Sat, to 2pm Sun) In a colonnaded 1936 heritage building, Cairns' acclaimed regional gallery hosts exhibitions reflecting the consciousness of the tropical north region, with an emphasis on local and Indigenous works and top-notch visiting exhibitions such as Goya's etchings.

Tjapukai Cultural Park   Cultural Centre
(☎07-4042 9999; www.tjapukai.com.au; Kamerunga Rd; adult/child $36/18, Tjapukai by Night adult/child $99/49.50; ⏱9am-5pm, Tjapukai by Night 7-9.30pm) This Indigenous-owned cultural extravaganza features the Creation Theatre, which tells the story of creation using giant holograms and actors, a dance theatre and a gallery, as well as boomerang- and spear-throwing demonstrations and didgeridoo lessons. A fireside corroboree is the centrepiece of the **Tjapukai by Night** dinner-and-show deal.

Centre of Contemporary Arts   Gallery, Theatre
(www.coca.org.au; 96 Abbott St; ⏱10am-5pm Mon-Sat) FREE CoCA houses the **KickArts** (www.kickarts.org.au) galleries of local contemporary visual art, as well as the **Jute Theatre** (☎07-4050 9444; www.jute.com.au; CoCA, 96 Abbott St; tickets from $20) and the **End Credits Film Club** (www.endcredits.org.au).

Reef Teach   Interpretive Centre
(☎07-4031 7794; http://reefteach.wordpress.com; 2nd fl, Main Street Arcade, 85 Lake St; adult/child $18/9; ⏱lectures 5.30-8.30pm Tue-Sat) 🌿 Before heading out to the reef, take your knowledge to greater depths at this excellent and informative centre, where marine experts explain how to identify

189

specific types of coral and fish and how to treat the reef with respect.

Sleeping

Dreamtime Travellers Rest
Hostel $

(☎07-40316753, 1800 058 440; www.dreamtimehostel.com; cnr Bunda & Terminus Sts; d, $24-26, tw without bathroom $59, d without bathroom $58-62; @ 🛜 ⛲) This chilled-out hostel at the edge of the city combines friendly staff with cozy rooms in an old Queenslander. The charming compound offers pockets of space to curl up with a book. Cheap pizza and barbecue nights round off the package.

Floriana Guesthouse
Guesthouse $$

(☎07-4051 7886; www.florianaguesthouse.com; 183 The Esplanade; s $75, d $89 & $140; ❄ @ 🛜 ⛲) Run by charismatic jazz musician Maggie, Cairns-of-old still exists at this old-fashioned guesthouse, which retains its original polished floorboards and art deco fittings. The swirling staircase leads to 10 individually decorated rooms, some with bay windows and window seats, others with balconies.

Inn Cairns
Apartment $$

(☎07-4041 2350; www.inncairns.com.au; 71 Lake St; apt $125-188; P ❄ @ 🛜 ⛲) Behind the unassuming facade, this is true inner-city apartment living. Take the lift up to the 1st-floor pool or to the rooftop garden for a sundowner. The elegant self-contained apartments have separate bedroom and living areas and friendly staff will make you feel at home 'Inn' Cairns.

Balinese
Motel $$

(☎07-4051 9922, 1800 023 331; www.balinese.com.au; 215 Lake St; d from $110; ❄ @ 🛜 ⛲) Bali comes to Cairns at this small low-rise complex: waking up among the authentic wood furnishings and ceramic pieces, you may be taken with the sudden urge to have your hair beaded.

Bay Village
Resort $$

(☎07-4051 4622; www.bayvillage.com.au; cnr Lake & Gatton Sts; d $150-330; ❄ @ ⛲) Smart units encircle a central pool at this sprawling resort. It's popular with package tours but no worse for that. Pricier rooms are self-contained, with kitchens and lounges; Balinese chefs cook up aromatic cuisine at the on-site **Bay Leaf Restaurant** (mains $16 to $31, lunch Monday to Friday, dinner daily). It offers free airport transfers.

Mid City
Apartment $$

(☎07-4051 5050; www.midcity.com.au; 6 McLeod St; 1-/2-bedroom apt $175/225; ❄ @ 🛜 ⛲) The immaculate, terracotta-tiled apartments in this arctic-white building are self-contained, with good kitchens, washing machines and dryers, and a balcony to enjoy balmy nights outside.

Inn Cairns apartments
PAUL DYMOND/GETTY IMAGES ©

Villa Vaucluse
Apartment $$

(☎07-4051 8566; www.villavaucluse.com.
au; 141-143 Grafton St; 1-bedroom apt $258;
❄🛜⊠) Mediterranean decor meets
tropical influences, with central atrium,
secluded saltwater swimming pool and
sumptuous self-contained apartments.
Online rates knock about 50% off rack
rates.

201 Lake Street
Hotel $$$

(☎07-4053 0100, 1800 628 929;
www.201lakestreet.com.au; 201 Lake St; r $120-
260, apt $215-260) Lifted from the pages of
a trendy magazine, this apartment complex has a lemongrass-scented reception
area, stellar pool and a touch of exclusivity. Grecian white predominates and
guests can choose from a smooth hotel
room or contemporary apartments with
an entertainment area, a plasma-screen
TV and balcony.

 Eating

Meldrum's Pies in Paradise
Bakery $

(97 Grafton St; pies $4.70-5.90; ⏲7am-5pm
Mon-Fri, to 2.30pm Sat; 🖉) A Cairns institution, Meldrum's bakes some 40 inventive
varieties of the humble Aussie pie – from
chicken and avocado to pumpkin gnocchi
or tuna mornay. Great for lunch on the
(budget) run.

Fusion Organics
Cafe $

(www.fusionorganics.com.au; cnr Aplin & Grafton
Sts; dishes $4-19.50; ⏲7am-3pm Mon-Fri, to 2pm
Sat; 🖉) In the wicker-chair-strewn corner
courtyard of an historic 1921 red-brick
former ambulance station, hard-working
chefs whip up Fusion's organic, allergy-
free fare like quiches, frittatas, corn
fritters and filled breads you can finish off
with fresh juice.

Fetta's Greek Taverna
Greek $$

(☎07-4051 6966; www.fettasgreektaverna.com.
au; 99 Grafton St; dishes $13-25; ⏲11.30am-3pm
Mon-Fri, 5.30pm-late daily) The white walls
and blue-accented windows do a great
job evoking Santorini. But it's the food
that's the star of the show here, with clas-
sic Greek dishes. For the indecisive, the

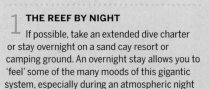

Local Knowledge

Great Barrier Reef

BY LEN ZELL, GREAT BARRIER
REEF GUIDE & AUTHOR (WWW.
LENZELL.COM)

1 THE REEF BY NIGHT
If possible, take an extended dive charter
or stay overnight on a sand cay resort or
camping ground. An overnight stay allows you to
'feel' some of the many moods of this gigantic
system, especially during an atmospheric night
dive.

2 GETTING WET
Staff at all snorkelling and diving
destinations will help you get wet in the best
way for your ability or, best of all, take you way
beyond your imagined ability – safely. Seeing
an 80-year-old Scottish woman who had never
gone beyond knee-deep be led into the water and
stay there for more than an hour shows anyone
can do it.

3 WATERY WILDLIFE ENCOUNTERS
Don't miss the magnificent manta rays at
Lady Elliot Island (p176), the most southerly of
the reef's islands. Tranquil Heron Island (p177)
is a nesting ground for birds, and green and
loggerhead turtles, and features the 'bommie', a
fish-filled mini-reef or coral head. Snorkel with
minke whales mid-year between Cairns and
Lizard Island, eyeball massive cod at the Cod
Hole on No 10 Ribbon Reef, and dive with sea
snakes in the Swain Reefs.

4 THE CHANCE TO EXPLORE
Seek out the remote and the less-visited
reefs to witness the unexpected, which may
include reefs recently smashed by cyclones,
devoured by crown-of-thorns sea stars,
or reefs in recovery mode. Check out the
fascinating wreck of the *Yongala*, between
Bowen and Townsville, the outer reefs far off
Cairns, and the rarely visited islands and
reefs north of Lizard Island (p204), towards
Torres Strait.

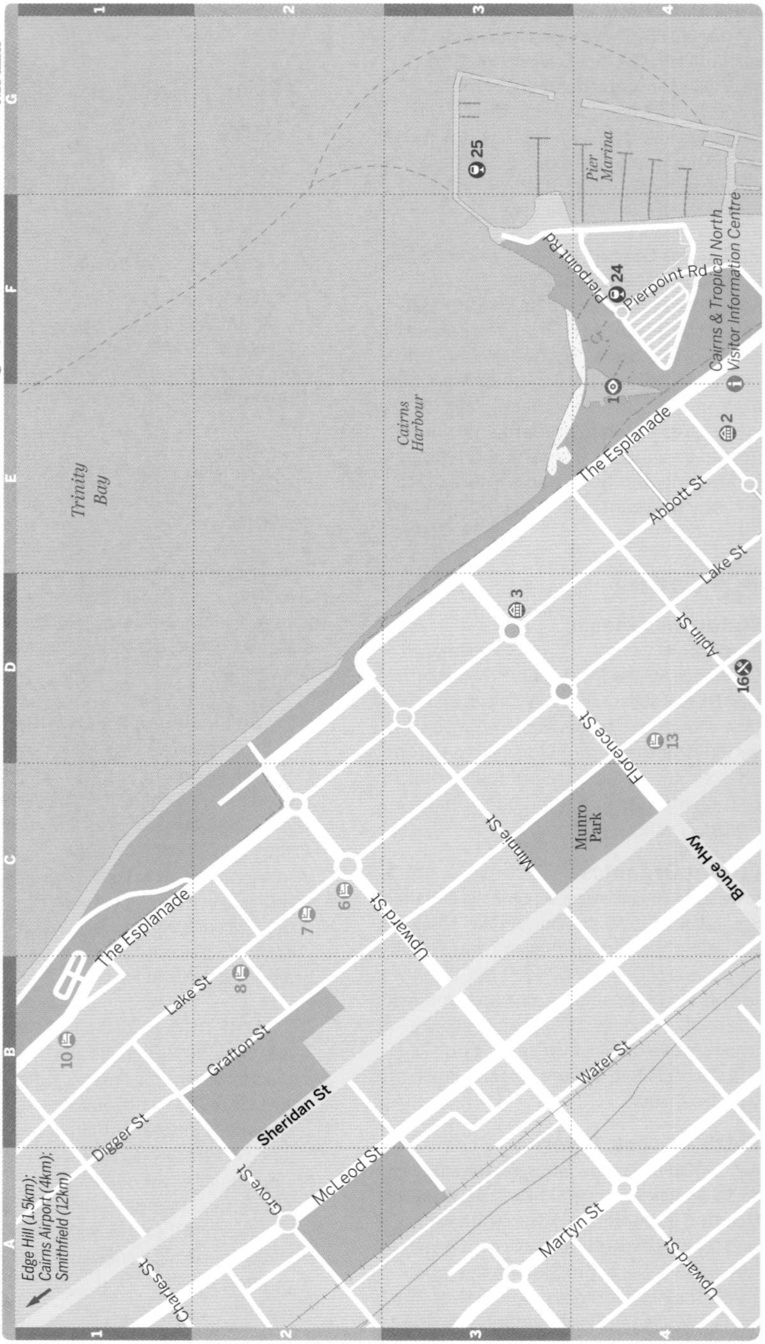

Cairns

0 0.25 miles
0 500 m

Edge Hill (1.5km);
Cairns Airport (4km);
Smithfield (12km)

Trinity
Bay

Cairns
Harbour

Cairns & Tropical North
Visitor Information Centre

Pier
Marina

Pierpoint Rd

The Esplanade

Abbott St

Lake St

Aplin St

Florence St

Minnie St

Munro
Park

The Esplanade

Lake St

Grafton St

Sheridan St

Digger St

McLeod St

Grove St

Charles St

Upward St

Water St

Bruce Hwy

Martyn St

Upward St

25

24

10

2

3

16

13

7

6

8

10

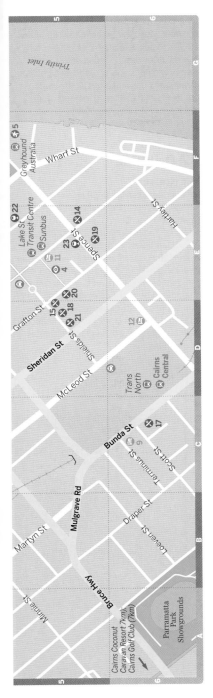

Cairns

$35 set menu goes the whole hog – dip, saganaki, mousakka, salad, grilled meats, calamari, baklava *and* coffee.

Ochre Modern Australian **$$**
(☎07-4051 0100; www.ochrerestaurant.com. au; 43 Shields St; mains $23-37; ⏱11am-3pm Mon-Fri, 6-10.30pm daily; ☝) In an ochre- and plum-toned dining room, the changing menu at this innovative restaurant utilises native Aussie fauna (such as croc with native pepper, or roo with quandong-chilli glaze) and flora (wattle-seed damper loaf with peanut oil and native dukka; lemon-myrtle panacotta). Croc burgers and

193

wallaby topside round off the menu. Can't decide? Try a tasting plate.

Green Ant Cantina — Mexican $$

(☎07-4041 5061; www.greenantcantina.com; 183 Bunda St; mains $15-40; ☺6pm-late daily; 🎵) This funky little slice of Mexico behind the railway station is worth seeking out for its homemade quesadillas, enchiladas and Corona-battered barramundi. Great cocktail list, cool tunes and the occasional live band.

Marinades — Indian $$

(☎07-4041 1422; 43 Spence St; mains $14-30; ☺11am-2.30pm, 6-10pm Tue-Sun; 🎵) A long, *long* menu of aromatic dishes like lobster marinated in cashew paste, or Goan prawn curry, along with restrained decor in its dining room, make Marinades the pick of Cairns' Indian restaurants.

La Fettuccina — Italian $$

(☎07-4031 5959; www.lafettuccina.com; 41 Shields St; mains $26-31; ☺6-10.30pm daily) Homemade sauces and pasta are a speciality at this small, atmospheric Italian restaurant. Try for a seat on the tiny, internal wrought-iron mezzanine balcony. Licensed and BYO.

Cherry Blossom — Japanese $$$

(☎07-4052 1050; cnr Spence & Lake Sts; mains $29-53; ☺noon-2pm Tue-Fri, 5-11pm Mon-Sat) This 1st-floor restaurant is reminiscent of an *Iron Chef* cook-off, with two chefs working at opposite ends of the restaurant floor. Despite being in need of an interior update, the restaurant is popular for sushi, teppanyaki and plenty of theatre.

🍷 Drinking

Salt House — Bar

(www.salthouse.com.au; 6/2 Pierpoint Rd; ☺9am-2am Fri-Sun, 11am-2am Mon-Thu) Located next to Cairns' yacht club, Salt House has a sleek nautical design that has seen it become the city's most sought-after bar since it opened a couple of years ago. Killer cocktails are paired with occasional live music, or DJs hitting the decks. The restaurant serves up excellent modern Australian dishes including line-caught fish and succulent steaks, and it's definitely is worth migrating to after sundowners.

Salt House

Court House Hotel
Pub

(38 Abbott St; ⊙9am-late) Situated in Cairns' gleaming-white former courthouse building, dating from 1921, the Court House pub is replete with a polished timber island bar and Scales of Justice statue – and cane-toad races on Wednesday night. DJs spin on Fridays. On any other day, park yourself in the quiet beer garden outside.

Pier Bar & Grill
Bar

(www.pierbar.com.au; Pierpoint Rd; ⊙11.30am-late) A local stalwart for its waterfront location and well-priced meals. The Pier's Sunday session are packed to the gills and *the* place to be.

Heritage Nightclub
Club

(☑07-4031 8070; www.theheritagecairns.com; cnr Spence & Lake Sts; ⊙9pm-3am Thu, 10pm-5am Sat & Sun) When the DJ starts revving, a high-energy crowd downs cocktails and shots and spills out onto the enormous 1st-floor balcony. It can get messy but you can't go wrong if you're looking for a party.

ℹ Information

Medical Services

Cairns Base Hospital (☑07-4050 6333; The Esplanade) Has a 24-hour emergency service.

Cairns City 24 Hour Medical Centre (☑07-4052 1119; cnr Florence & Grafton Sts) General practice and dive medicals.

Tourist information

Cairns & Tropical North Visitor Information Centre (☑1800 093 300; www.cairns-great barrierreef.org.au; 51 The Esplanade; ⊙8.30am-6.30pm daily) Government-run centre that doles out impartial advice and can book accommodation and tours.

ℹ Getting There & Away

Air

Qantas (☑13 13 13; www.qantas.com.au), Virgin Australia (☑13 67 89; www.virginaustralia.com.au) and Jetstar (☑13 15 38; www.jetstar.com.au) all service Cairns, with flights to/from Brisbane, Sydney, Melbourne, Darwin (including via Alice Springs) and Townsville. There are international flights to/from places including China and Singapore.

Bus

Greyhound Australia (☑1300 473 946; www.greyhound.com.au) Has four daily services down the coast to Brisbane ($295, 29 hours) via Townsville ($59, six hours), Airlie Beach ($130, 11 hours) and Rockhampton ($190, 18 hours).

John's Kuranda Bus (☑0418 772 953) Runs a service between Cairns and Kuranda two to five times daily ($5, 30 minutes).

Premier Motor Service (☑13 34 10; www.premierms.com.au) Runs one daily service to Brisbane ($205, 29 hours) via Innisfail ($19, 1½ hours), Mission Beach ($19, two hours), Tully ($26, 2½ hours), Cardwell ($30, three hours), Townsville ($55, 5½ hours) and Airlie Beach ($90, 10 hours).

Sun Palm (☑07-4087 2900; www.sunpalmtransport.com) Runs northern services from Cairns to Port Douglas ($40, 1½ hours) via Palm Cove and the northern beaches (from $20) and Mossman ($45, 1¾ hours).

Trans North (☑07-4095 8644; www.transnorthbus.com; Cairns Central Rail Station) Has five daily bus services connecting Cairns with the tableland, serving Kuranda ($8, 30 minutes, five daily), Mareeba ($18, one hour, one to three daily), Atherton ($23.40, 1¾ hours, one to three daily).

Car & Motorcycle

All major car-rental companies have branches in Cairns and at the airport, with discount car- and campervan-rental companies proliferating throughout town.

Train

The *Sunlander* departs from Cairns' train station (Bunda St) on Tuesday, Thursday and Saturday for Brisbane (one way from $200, 31½ hours); the Scenic Railway runs daily to/from Kuranda. Contact Queensland Rail (☑131 617; www.traveltrain.com.au).

ℹ Getting Around

To/From the Airport

The airport is located about 7km north of central Cairns; many accommodation places offer courtesy pick-ups. Sun Palm (p195) meets all incoming flights and runs a shuttle bus (adult/

195

child $12/6) to the CBD. You can also book airport transfers to/from Cairns' northern beaches ($20), Palm Cove ($20), Port Douglas ($40), and Mossman ($45). **Black & White Taxis** (☎13 10 08) charges around $30.

Bicycle

Bike Man (☎07-4041 5566; www.bikeman.com.au; 99 Sheridan St; per day/week $15/60) Hire, sales and repairs.

Bus

Sunbus (☎07-4057 7411; www.sunbus.com.au; Lake St Transit Centre) runs regular services in and around Cairns from the Lake Street Transit Centre, where schedules are posted.

Taxi

Black & White Taxis has a rank near the corner of Lake and Shields Sts, and one on McLeod St, outside Cairns Central Shopping Centre.

Islands off Cairns

GREEN ISLAND

Green Island's long, dog-legged jetty heaves under the weight of boatloads of day trippers who depart by mid-afternoon, leaving the island a picture-postcard ghost town for resort guests. This beautiful coral cay is only 45 minutes from Cairns and has a rainforest interior with interpretive walks, a fringing white-sand beach and snorkelling just offshore. You can walk around the island in about 30 minutes.

Luxurious **Green Island Resort** (☎07-4031 3300, 1800 673 366; www.greenislandresort.com.au; ste $570-670; ✲@⛱) has large, tasteful timber-clad rooms, and bookings include breakfast, sunset drinks, guided walks and free snorkle equipment and kayak hire.

Great Adventures (☎07-4044 9944; www.greatadventures.com.au; 1 Spence St, Cairns; adult/child $79/37.50) and **Big Cat** (☎07-4051 0444; www.greenisland.com.au; adult/child from $79/37.50) run day trips, with optional glass-bottomed boat and semisubmersible tours.

FITZROY ISLAND

A steep mountaintop rising from the sea, Fitzroy Island has coral-strewn beaches, woodlands and walking tracks, and Australia's last staffed lighthouse. The most popular snorkelling spot is around the rocks at **Nudey Beach** (1.2km from the resort), which, despite its name, is not clothing-optional, so bring your togs.

Refurbished accommodation at the **Fitzroy Island Resort** (☎07-4044 6700; www.fitzroyisland.com; studios $195, cabins $369, 1 & 2 bedroom ste $350-515; ✲⛱) ranges from studios and beachfront cabins through to two-bedroom apartments. Raging Thunder (www.ragingthunder.com.au) runs one trip a day from Cairns (departing 8.30am, adult/child $60/30).

Nudey Beach
WAYNE WALTON/GETTY IMAGES ©

Day Trips from Cairns

GREAT BARRIER REEF

Reef operators generally include transport, lunch and snorkelling gear in their tour prices. Many have diving options, including introductory dives requiring no prior experience. The outer reefs are more pristine; inner-reef areas can be patchy, showing signs of damage from humans, coral bleaching and crown-of-thorns starfish.

Great Adventures (☏07-4044 9944; www.greatadventures.com.au; Reef Fleet Terminal, 1 Spence St; adult/child from $201/101) Fast catamaran day trips to a floating pontoon for snorkelling, with an optional stopover on Green Island (from $222/111), as well as semisubmersibles and a glass-bottomed boat. Diving add-on available.

Passions of Paradise (☏1800 111 346, 07-4041 1600; www.passions.com.au; adult/child $139/89) Sexy sailing catamaran taking you to Michaelmas Cay and Paradise Reef for snorkelling or diving.

Sunlover (☏07-4050 1333; www.sunlover.com.au; adult/child/family $180/65/425) Fast family-friendly catamaran rides to a snorkelling pontoon on the outer Moore Reef. Options include semisubmersible trips and helmet diving.

Great Barrier Reef Helicopters (☏07-4081 8888; www.gbrhelicopters.com.au; 20/60min flight per person from $260/559) Helicopter flights departing from Green Island (10 minutes $148) to an hour-long reef and rainforest trip ($529).

CAPE TRIBULATION & THE DAINTREE

Billy Tea Bush Safaris (☏07-4032 0077; www.billytea.com.au; day trips adult/child $185/135) Exciting eco day tours to Cape Trib and along the 4WD Bloomfield Track to Emmagen Creek. Also offers tours to Chillagoe, Cooktown and Cape York.

BTS Tours (☏07-4099 5665; www.btstours.com.au; day trips adult/child $165/120) Small-group tours, including swimming and canoeing to the Daintree River and Mossman Gorge.

Cape Trib Connections (☏07-4032 0500; www.capetribconnections.com; day trips adult/child $119/99) Includes Mossman Gorge and Cape Tribulation Beach. Also overnight tours (from $135).

Tropical Horizons Tours (☏07-4035 6445; www.tropicalhorizonstours.com.au; day tours from $117) Day trips to Cape Trib and the Daintree; overnight tours available.

DAINTREE RAINFOREST

Atherton Tableland

Waterfalls, lush green pastures complete with well-fed dairy cows and patches of remnant rainforest make up the table-lands, though the bordering areas are dramatically different; expect dry, harsh outback and much thinner cattle.

🛈 Getting There & Around

Trans North (p199) has regular bus services connecting Cairns with the tableland, departing from Cairns Central Rail Station and running to Kuranda ($8, 30 minutes), Mareeba ($16.80, one hour), Atherton ($22, 1¾ hours) and Herberton ($28, two hours).

Below: Heritage Markets; Right: Australian Butterfly Sanctuary

John's Kuranda Bus (📞 0418 772 953) runs a service between Cairns and Kuranda two to five times daily ($5, 30 minutes).

KURANDA

Kuranda is a hop, skip and jump – or make that a historic train journey, sky-rail adventure or winding bus trip – from Cairns. The village itself is a sprawling set of markets nestled in a spectacular tropical-rainforest setting where you'll find everything from made-in-China Aboriginal art to emu oil. There's little reason to stay overnight, as this is really a day trippers' domain.

◉ Sights & Activities

Kuranda Original Rainforest Markets   Market

(www.kurandaoriginalrainforestmarket.com.au; Therwine St; ⏰ 9am-3pm) With revamped boardwalks terraced in the rainforest and wafting incense, the original markets first opened in 1978 and are still the best place to pick up hemp products, handicraft, and sample local produce such as honey and fruit wines.

Heritage Markets   Market

(www.kurandamarkets.com.au; Rob Veivers Dr; ⏰ 9am-3pm) Across the road from the original markets, the heritage markets overflow with souvenirs and crafts such as ceramics, emu oil, jewellery, clothing, secondhand books and that kangaroo scrotum bottle opener you've always wanted.

Rainforestation   Zoo

(📞 07-4085 5008; www.rainforest.com.au; Kennedy Hwy; adult/child $40/21; ⏰ 9am-4pm) An enormous tourist park east of town with a wildlife section, river cruises and an Indigenous cultural show.

Kuranda Koala Gardens   Wildlife Reserve

(📞 07-4093 9953; www.koalagardens.com; Heritage Markets, Rob Veivers Dr; adult/child

$16.50/8.25; ⊘9.45am-4pm daily) Check out native Aussie animals such as koalas, wallabies, wombats and reptiles galore.

Australian Butterfly Sanctuary
Wildlife Reserve

(☑07-4093 7575; www.australianbutterflies.com; 8 Rob Veivers Dr; adult/child $18/9; ⊘9.45am-4pm daily) Flighty, pretty things. Half-hour tours available.

ⓘ Information

The Kuranda visitor centre (☑07-4093 9311; www.kuranda.org; ⊘10am-4pm) is centrally located in Centenary Park.

ⓘ Getting There & Away

Trans North (☑07-4095 8644; www.transnorthbus.com) has five daily bus services from Cairns Central Rail Station to Kuranda ($8, 30 minutes). This is the cheapest way, though the other options are more spectacular.

Winding 34km from Cairns to Kuranda through picturesque mountains and 15 tunnels, the Kuranda Scenic Railway (☑07-4036 9333; www.ksr.com.au) line took five years to build and opened in 1891. The 1¾-hour trip costs $48/24 per adult/child one way, and $72/36 return. Trains depart from Cairns at 8.30am and 9.30am daily, returning from pretty Kuranda station on Arara St at 2pm and 3.30pm.

At 7.5km, Skyrail Rainforest Cableway (☑07-4038 1555; www.skyrail.com.au; adult/child one way $45/22.50, return $68/34; ⊘9am-5.15pm) is one of the world's longest gondola cableways. The Skyrail runs from the corner of Kemerunga Rd and the Cook Hwy in the northern Cairns suburb of Smithfield (15 minutes' drive north of Cairns) to Kuranda (Arara St), taking 90 minutes. The last departure from Cairns and Kuranda is at 3.30pm; transfers are available to/from the Cairns departure terminal. Combination Scenic Railway and Skyrail deals are available.

MAREEBA

At the centre of industrious cattle, coffee and sugar enterprises, Mareeba is essentially an administrative and supply town for the northern tableland and parts of Cape York Peninsula.

199

Detour:
Chillagoe

Even on a day trip from Cairns, the charismatic former gold-rush town of Chillagoe, about 140km west of Mareeba, can fulfil any romantic notion you may have of the outback – but owing to the distance involved in travelling here, an overnight stay is preferable.

Chillagoe's excellent visitor centre, the **Hub** (📞07-4094 7111; www.chillagoehub.com. au; Queen St; ⏰8.30am-5pm Mon-Fri, 8am-3.30pm Sat & Sun), has interesting historical displays. Knowledgeable staff can direct you to **Aboriginal rock-art sites**, the local **swimming hole**, the old **smelter site**, a hodge-podge little **history museum** with a piano played during silent movies, and an eccentric local with a cool old **Ford collection**. It also books ranger-guided tours of Chillagoe's amazing, must-see **limestone caves** (adult/child $31/16.50).

Billy Tea Bush Safaris (www.billytea.com.au; tours adult/child $195/140) runs day tours from Cairns.

◎ Sights & Activities

First stop is the **Mareeba Heritage Museum & Tourist Information Centre** (📞07-4092 5674; www.mareebaheritagecentre.com. au; Centenary Park, 345 Byrnes St; ⏰8am-4pm) **FREE**, which has helpful staff and a huge room filled with displays on the area's past and present commercial industries, as well as its natural surrounds.

Mareeba Wetlands   Park
(📞07-4093 2514; www.mareebawetlands.org; adult/child $15/7.50; ⏰9am-4.30pm Apr-Jan) This is a 20-sq-km reserve of woodlands, grasslands, swamps and the expansive Clancy's Lagoon, a birdwatchers' nirvana. A huge range of bird species flock here, and you might see other animals such as kangaroos and freshwater crocs. Over 12km of walking trails criss-cross the wetlands. Various safari tours (from $38) depart during the week, or you can take a 30-minute ecocruise (adult/child $15/7.50) or paddle in a canoe ($15 per hour). The on-site **Jabiru Safari Lodge** (📞07-4093 2514; ww.jabirusafarilodge.com. au; cabins per person incl breakfast $128-150, all inclusive $198-229) has solar-powered tented cabins and a spa. Take the Pickford Rd turn-off from Biboohra, 7km north of Mareeba.

Port Douglas

Port Douglas (or just 'Port') is the flashy playground of tropical northern Queensland. For those looking to escape Cairns' bustling traveller scene, Port Douglas is more sophisticated and intimate. It also has a beautiful white-sand beach right on its doorstep, and the Great Barrier Reef is less than an hour offshore.

◎ Sights & Activities

On a sunny, calm day, Four Mile Beach will take your breath away. It is sand and palm trees for as far as you can see – head up to **Flagstaff Hill** (Island Point Rd) lookout for a great view.

At the Cooktown Hwy turn-off, **Wildlife Habitat Port Douglas** (📞07-4099 3235; www.wildlifehabitat.com.au; Port Douglas Rd; adult/child $32/16; ⏰8am-5pm) endeavours to keep and showcase native animals, such as tree kangaroos, in enclosures that closely mimic their natural environment.

On Sunday the grassy foreshore of Anzac Park spills over with the excellent **Port Douglas Markets** (end of Macrossan St; ⏰8am-1.30pm Sun). You'll find stalls selling arts, crafts and jewellery, local tropical fruits, food stalls and even massage tents.

Tours

BTS Tours
Guided Tour
(☎ 07-4099 5665; www.btstours.com.au; 49 Macrossan St; Daintree adult/child $150/115, Mossman Gorge $48/26) Tours to the Daintree Rainforest and Cape Trib, including canoeing. Also to Mossman Gorge.

Poseidon
Snorkelling
(☎ 07-4099 4772; www.poseidon-cruises.com.au; adult/child $210/145) Friendly family-owned and -operated luxury catamaran with trips to Agincourt Reef.

Quicksilver
Cruise
(☎ 07-4087 2100; www.quicksilver-cruises.com; adult/child $212/106) Major operator with fast cruises to Agincourt Reef. Offers helmet dives ($142), plus scenic helicopter flights from the pontoon on the reef ($148, minimum two passengers).

Reef & Rainforest Connections
Ecotour
(☎ 07-4035 5566; www.reefandrainforest.com.au; adult/child from $163/105) A range of day-long ecotours, including Cape Trib and Bloomfield Falls, Kuranda and Mossman Gorge.

Sailaway
Sailing, Snorkelling
(☎ 07-4099 4772; www.sailawayportdouglas.com; adult/child $205/125) Popular sailing and snorkelling trip to the Low Isles that's great for families. Also offers 90-minute twilight sails ($50) off the Port Douglas coast.

 Sleeping

Pink Flamingo
Boutique Hotel $$
(☎ 07-4099 6622; www.pinkflamingo.com.au; 115 Davidson St; r $125 & 185; ❄@🖥🏊) Flamboyant fuchsia-, purple- and orange-painted rooms opening to private walled courtyards (with hammocks, outdoor baths and outdoor showers) and a groovy mirror-balled alfresco bar make the Pink Flamingo a fun place. Outdoor movie nights, a gym and bike rental are also offered. Gay-owned, gay-friendly and all-welcoming (except for kids).

By the Sea Port Douglas
Apartment $$
(☎ 07-4099 5387; www.bytheseaportdouglas.com.au; 72 Macrossan St; d from $185; ❄@🖥🏊) Close to the beach and town centre, the 12 self-contained rooms here are spread over three levels – the upper rooms have 'filtered' views through the palm trees to the beach. Rooms are self-contained and renovated in neutral hues. Cheap online rates.

QT Resort
Resort $$$
(☎ 07-4099 8900; www.qtportdouglas.com.au; 87-109 Port Douglas Rd; d $240-260, villa $290-410; ❄@🖥🏊) Port's newest resort is also its hippest with its cool mod decor and DJ-spinning lounge beats in the cocktail bar. The in-house restaurant, Bazaar,

Limestone caves near Chillagoe
ANDREW WATSON/GETTY IMAGES ©

serves up a quality buffet spread and staff are all smiles as they lead you to your stylish rooms complete with flat-screen TVs and plush beds. QT also hosts Moonlight Cinema. Competitive online packages.

Sea Temple Resort & Spa
Resort **$$$**

(☎07-4084 3500, 1800 833 762; www.mirvachotels.com.au; Mitre St; d from $300; ❄@🛜🏊) Port Douglas' most luxurious five-star resort and its championship links golf course are set in lush tropical gardens near the southern end of Four Mile Beach. Rooms range from slick spa studios to the opulent 'swim out' penthouse with direct access to the enormous lagoon pool.

Hibiscus Gardens
Resort **$$$**

(☎1800 995 995; www.hibiscusportdouglas.com.au; 22 Owen St; d $145-385; ❄@🏊) Balinese influences of teak furnishings and fixtures, bi-fold doors and plantation shutters – as well as the occasional Buddha – give this stylish resort an exotic ambience. The in-house day spa, specialising in Indigenous healing techniques and products, is a great place to be pampered.

Eating

Original Mocka's Pies
Takeaway **$**

(☎07-4099 5295; 9 Grant St; pies $4.50-6; ⏰8am-4pm) An institution serving amazing Aussie pies filled with exotic ingredients such as crocodile and kangaroo. The steak pie is oozing with chunks of tender, slow-cooked Black Angus.

Salsa Bar & Grill
Modern Australian **$$**

(☎07-4099 4922; www.salsaportdouglas.au; 26 Wharf St; mains $20-37; ⏰11.30am-3pm & 5.30-10.30pm; 🍴) In a white Queenslander, Salsa is a stayer on Port's often fickle scene. Try the Cajun jambalaya (rice with prawns, yabbies, squid, crocodile sausage and smoked chicken) or the kangaroo loin with sweet potato pie.

On the Inlet
Seafood **$$**

(☎07-4099 5255; www.portdouglasseafood.com; 3 Inlet St; mains $24-40; ⏰11.30am-10pm) At this restaurant jutting out over Dickson Inlet, tables are spread out along an atmospheric deck where you can await the daily 5pm arrival of George the 250kg

Daintree National Park: Then & Now

The greater Daintree rainforest is protected as part of Daintree National Park. The area has a controversial history: despite conservationist blockades, in 1983 the Bloomfield Track was bulldozed through lowland rainforest from Cape Tribulation to the Bloomfield River, and the ensuing international publicity indirectly led the federal government to nominate Queensland's wet tropical rainforests for World Heritage listing. The move drew objections from the Queensland timber industry and the state government, but in 1988 the area was inscribed on the World Heritage list, resulting in a total ban on commercial logging within its boundaries.

World Heritage listing doesn't affect land ownership rights or control, and since the 1990s efforts have been made by the Queensland government and conservation agencies to buy back and rehabilitate freehold properties, add them to the Daintree National Park and install visitor-interpretation facilities. Sealing the road to Cape Tribulation in 2002 opened the area to rapid settlement, triggering the buy-back of hundreds more properties. Coupled with development controls, these efforts are now bearing fruit in the form of forest regeneration. Check out **Rainforest Rescue** (www.rainforestrescue.org.au) for more information.

Detour:
Mossman

Mossman is an unassuming town criss-crossed with cane-train tracks and featuring the wonderful **Mossman Gorge** (☎07-4099 7000; www.mossmangorge.com.au; Mossman Gorge Centre; shuttle bus adult/child $5/2.50; ⏱8am-6.30pm), which draws in tourists by the van-load. There's a great 2.4km walk here, and swimming is possible, but be aware of the danger of swimming after heavy rain.

To truly appreciate the gorge's cultural significance, book one of the 1½-hour Indigenous-guided **Kuku-Yalanji Dreamtime Walks** (www.yalanji.com.au; adult/child $50/25; ⏱9am, 11am, & 3pm) through the **Mossman Gorge Centre**. This is the slick new gateway to the gorge, complete with an art gallery, retail section and an in-house restaurant that serves bush tucker.

BTS (☎07-4099 5665; www.portdouglasbus.com; 49 Macrossan St, Port Douglas) has return shuttles from Port Douglas to Mossman Gorge (adult/child $22/15, 8.15am and 12.15pm) and also runs day trips to the gorge. **Coral Reef Coaches** (☎07-4098 2800; www.coralreefcoaches.com.au) runs coaches from Cairns (adult/child $40/20). Book ahead.

grouper, who comes to feed. Take up the bucket-of-prawns-and-a-drink deal for $18 from 3.30pm to 5.30pm, or choose your own crayfish and mud crabs from the live tank.

Beach Shack Modern Australian **$$**
(☎07-4099 1100; www.the-beach-shack.com.au; 29 Barrier St, Four Mile Beach; mains $23-34; ⏱11.30am-3pm & 5.30-10pm; 🅿) There'd be an outcry if this locals' favourite took its macadamia-crumbed eggplant (with grilled and roast vegies, goat's cheese and wild rocket) off the menu. The unique setting, a lantern-lit garden with sand underfoot, lures diners to the southern end of Four Mile Beach. Good reef fish, pizzas and blackboard specials, too.

Harrisons Restaurant Modern Australian **$$$**
(☎07-4099 4011; www.harrisonsrestaurant.com.au; 22 Wharf St; mains $38-56, 4-/6-course $75/100) Marco-Pierre-White-trained chef/owner Spencer Patrick whips up culinary gems that stand toe-to-toe with Australia's best. Fresh locally sourced produce is turned into dishes such as rabbit croquettes with goats curd fondant and Angus rib eye *steak frites* served with melt-in-your-mouth bone marrow. The degustation menu is a bargain. Possibly the only place in Port where diners bother swapping their thongs for shoes.

🍷 Drinking & Nightlife

Tin Shed Club
(www.thetinshed-portdouglas.com.au; 7 Ashford Ave; drinks from $4; ⏱10am-10pm) Port Douglas' Combined Services Club is a locals' secret. This is a rare find: bargain dining on the waterfront, and even the drinks are cheap. Sign in, line up and grab a table on the river- or shore-fronting deck.

Iron Bar Pub
(☎07-4099 4776; www.ironbarportdouglas.com.au; 5 Macrossan St; mains $15-30; ⏱11am-3am) A bit of wacky outback-shearing-shed decor never goes astray in Queensland. It's well done – all rustic iron and distressed timber. After polishing off your aged steaks, grab a beer and head upstairs for a flutter on the cane-toad races ($5).

Court House Hotel Pub
(☎07-4099 5181; www.courthouseportdouglas.com.au; cnr Macrossan & Wharf Sts; mains $20-30; ⏱11am-late) Commanding a prime corner location, the 'Courty' is a lively local, with cover bands on weekends.

Detour:
Lizard Island

The spectacular islands of the Lizard group are clustered just 27km off the coast about 100km from Cooktown. Jigurru (Lizard Island), a sacred place for the Dingaal Aboriginal people, has dry, rocky and mountainous terrain for bushwalking, glistening white swimming beaches, and a relatively untouched fringing reef for snorkelling and diving. Apart from the ground where the luxury resort stands, the entire island is a national park, so it's open to anyone who makes the effort to get here.

There are good dives right off the island, and the outer Barrier Reef is less than 20km away, including two of Australia's best-known dive sites – Cod Hole and Pixie Bommie. Lizard Island Resort offers a full range of diving facilities to its guests.

There are great walks through country that switches from mangrove to rainforest to dry and rocky in mere minutes, including a superb hike up to **Cook's Look** (368m); allow three hours return.

Lizard Island Resort (☑1300 863 248; www.lizardisland.com.au; Anchor Bay; d from $1444; ❄@ 🛜 ❋) has luxurious villas, spa treatments and a top restaurant. Kids aren't allowed.

Book through the resort for all air transfers to/from Cairns (return $590). Flight time is one hour. **Daintree Air Services** (☑1800 246 206, 07-4034 9400; www. daintreeair.com.au) has full-day tours from Cairns at 8am (from $750). The trip includes lunch, snorkelling gear, transfers and a local guide.

⭐ Entertainment

Moonlight Cinema   Cinema
(www.moonlight.com.au; 87-109 Port Douglas Rd, QT Resort, Port Douglas; tickets adult/child $16/12; ☺Jun-Oct) Bring a picnic or hire a bean bag for twilight outdoor movie screenings.

ℹ Information

The **Port Douglas Tourist Information Centre** (☑07-4099 4540; www.tourismportdouglas. com.au; 50 Macrossan St; ☺8am-6.30pm) has maps and makes tour bookings.

ℹ Getting There & Away

Sun Palm (☑07-4087 2900; www.sunpalm transport.com) has frequent daily services between Port Douglas and Cairns ($35, 1½ hours) via the northern beaches and the airport, and up the coast to Mossman ($10, 20 minutes), Daintree Village and the ferry ($20, one hour), and Cape Tribulation ($48, three hours).

Airport Connections (☑07-4099 5950; www.tnqshuttle.com; adult/child $36/18; ☺btwn 3am & 5pm) runs a shuttle-bus service ($36, four daily) between Port Douglas, Cairns' northern beaches and Cairns Airport, continuing on to Cairns CBD.

Daintree Village

Surprisingly, given its tropical-rainforest surrounds, Daintree Village itself is not tree-covered; cattle farms operate in large clearings next to the Daintree River. Most folk come here to see crocodiles, and there are several small operators who will take you on croc-spotting boat tours.

🚢 Tours

Bruce Belcher's Daintree   Cruise
(☑07-4098 7717; www.daintreerivercruises.com; 1hr cruises adult/child $25/10) One-hour river cruises on a covered boat.

Daintree Argo Rainforest Tours
Tour

(☎0409 627 434; www.daintreeadventuretours.com.au; Upper Daintree Rd; 1hr tours $45) Rainforest and cattle-country tours aboard an open-topped amphibious vehicle.

 ## Sleeping & Eating

Red Mill House
B&B $$$

(☎07-4098 6233; www.redmillhouse.com.au; 11 Stewart St; s/d $160/220; ❄ @ ≋) The large verandah overlooking the rainforest garden is a prime spot to observe the resident bird life. There are four well-appointed rooms, a large communal lounge and library, and a two-bedroom family unit (from $270). Guided birding walks are available on request.

Croc Eye Cafe
Cafe $$

(☎07-4098 6229; www.croceyecafe.com; 3 Stewart St; mains $17-40; ❀8am-3pm) Serves fish and chips, burgers and, of course, crocodile dishes such as spaghetti and san choi bao.

Cape Tribulation

This little piece of paradise retains a frontier quality, with low-key development, road signs alerting drivers to cassowary crossings, and crocodile warnings that make beach strolls that little bit less relaxing.

The rainforest tumbles right down to two magnificent, white-sand beaches – Myall and Cape Trib – separated by a knobby cape.

 ## Sights & Activities

Jungle Surfing
Tour, Hiking

(☎07-4098 0043; www.junglesurfing.com.au; zipline $90, night walks $40; ❀night walks 7.30pm) Jungle Surfing is an exhilarating zipline (flying fox) through the rainforest canopy, stopping at five tree platforms. It also runs guided **forest night walks**. Rates include pick-ups throughout Cape Trib.

Ocean Safari
Snorkelling

(☎07-4098 0006; www.oceansafari.com.au; adult/child $119/76; ❀9am & 1pm) Ocean Safari leads small groups (25 people maximum) on snorkelling cruises to the Great Barrier Reef, just half an hour offshore. Free pick-up from your Cape Trib accommodation.

 ## Tours

Cape Trib Horse Rides
Horse Riding

(☎07-4098 0030; www.capetribhorserides.com.au; per person $89; ❀8am & 2.30pm) Leisurely rides along the beach. Free pick-up from your accommodation.

Paddle Trek Kayak Tours
Kayaking

(☎07-4098 0043; www.capetribpaddletrek.com.au; kayak hire per hour $16-55, trips from $69) Guided kayaking trips and kayak hire. Free pick-up from your accommodation.

D'Arcy of the Daintree
Driving Tour

(☎07-4098 9180; www.darcyofdaintree.com.au; tours adult/child from $119/80) Entertaining 4WD trips up the Bloomfield Track to Wujal Wujal Waterfalls and as far as Cooktown and down Cape Tribulation Rd. Free pick-ups from Cape Trib and Cow Bay.

 ## Sleeping

Cape Trib Exotic Fruit Farm Cabins
Cabin $$

(☎07-4098 0057; www.capetrib.com.au; Lot 5, Nicole Dr; d $185) Amid the orchards of Cape Trib Exotic Fruit Farm, this pair of timber pole cabins have exposed timber floors, ceilings and huge decks, and are equipped with electric Eskies. Rates include breakfast hampers filled with tropical fruit from the farm. Minimum stay is two nights. Book in advance!

❶ Getting There & Away

Country Road Coach Lines (☎07-4045 2794; www.countryroadcoachlines.com.au) travels the coastal route from Cairns to Cooktown via Cape Tribulation (adult/child $49/24.50) on Monday, Wednesday and Friday (departing from Cairns at 7am) and departs from Cape Tribulation for Cairns at 10.10am on Tuesday, Thursday and Saturday.

Melbourne & the Great Ocean Road

Melbourne, Australia's second-largest city and Victoria's urban epicentre, is the nation's artistic heartland. A truly global melting pot, it's a place where culture junkies and culinary perfectionists can feast on art, music, theatre, cinema and cuisine. Australia's best baristas compete for your morning trade, and you're never far from a live-music gig, a gallery opening or a quirky street-art installation. It's a big town, but Melbourne retains a vibrant neighbourhood spirit, embodied in the fierce rivalries between local Australian Rules football teams (Carlton vs Collingwood at the MCG is a quasi-religious experience).

Further south, scalloping its way around coves, beaches and cliffs, the Great Ocean Road is one of the world's great road trips. Wild surf pounds the shoreline and enigmatic coastal towns mingle with lush national parks. Also down south is the Australian mainland's southernmost tip – the spiritually reviving Wilsons Promontory National Park.

View of Melbourne (p216) along the Yarra River
GLENN VAN DER KNIJFF/GETTY IMAGES ©

Modern city tram, Melbourne
DAVID HILL/GETTY IMAGES ©

Melbourne & the Great Ocean Road

Legend

1. Federation Square
2. Queen Victoria Market
3. Great Ocean Road
4. Melbourne Street Art
5. Eating & Drinking in Melbourne

50 km
25 miles

VICTORIA

MELBOURNE

Werribee
Geelong
Queenscliff
Torquay
Anglesea
Aireys Inlet
Lorne
Apollo Bay
Cape Otway

Great Otway National Park

Great Ocean Rd

Winchelsea
Colac
Lake Corangamite
Mortlake
Hamilton
Portland
Warrnambool
Port Fairy
Griffiths Island
Moyne River
Peterborough
Port Campbell National Park
Bay of Islands
Twelve Apostles

Midland Hwy
Hamilton Hwy
Princes Hwy
Henty Hwy

Bellarine Peninsula
Corio Bay
Port Phillip
Portsea
Mornington Peninsula
Cape Schanck
Hastings
Flinders
Phillip Island
French Island
Western Port
San Remo
Cape Paterson
Wonthaggi
Inverloch
Cape Liptrap
Yanakie

Nepean Hwy
Bass Hwy

Melbourne Airport
Dandenong
Cranbourne
Pakenham
Warragul
Korumburra
Leongatha
Foster
Yarram
Wilsons Promontory National Park
Tidal River
Wilsons Promontory
Snake Island

Princes Fwy
La Trobe River
Moe
Morwell
Traralgon
Gippsland

Yarra Glen
Healesville
Yarra River Yarra Valley
Melba Hwy
Maroondah Hwy

Ferry to Tasmania

BASS STRAIT

King Island

TASMANIA

Hogan Group

Melbourne & the Great Ocean Road Highlights

Federation Square

'Fed Square' raised plenty of eyebrows when it was being built, but this eccentric, angular congregation of spaces and places is now close to the hearts of Melburnians. It's home to the Australian Centre for the Moving Image (p216) and the Ian Potter Centre: NGV Australia (p216)...but mostly it's a place to meet, eat, drink and watch massive sports events on massive screens.

Queen Victoria Market

The largest open-air market in the southern hemisphere, Queen Victoria Market (p220) hosts more than 600 traders and has a history dating back over 130 years. Saturdays are hectic, with thousands of Melburnians stocking up on fresh fruit, veg, meat and fish. On Sundays clothing stalls proliferate: you mightn't be looking for a VB beer singlet or an Kanye T-shirt, but the prices might tempt you.

Great Ocean Road

3

The wild ocean beaches and bushland along the Great Ocean Road (p249) are enduring holiday hot-spots for Melburnians. Torquay is Victoria's 'surf city' and the gateway to this spectacular coast: an inspirational combination of beach and bush awaits as you travel west towards the famous Twelve Apostles.

4

Melbourne Street Art

Melbourne is rated in the top five street-art cities of the world. Hosier La and Union La in the city feature colourful council-sanctioned stencil art and graffiti...and there are myriad other quirky spaces down alleys or in anonymous buildings where artists can interpret, exploit and explain the city. Look for work by artists such as Miso, Ghostpatrol, Rhone and the Ever-fresh Group. ACDC Lane

5

Eating & Drinking in Melbourne

Melbourne's inner neighbourhoods each have a multicultural main street. Favourites include Brunswick St, Fitzroy (cafes, bars and pubs); Smith St, Collingwood (everything from Greek patisseries to Balinese); and Victoria St, Richmond (Vietnamese). Booze-wise, Melbourne's old pubs and new small bars make for an eclectic night's imbibing and live-music appreciation. Brunswick St, Fitzroy

Melbourne & the Great Ocean Road's Best..

Arts & Culture

○ **Arts Centre Melbourne** Under Melbourne's Southbank spire: concert halls, theatres and Victoria's premier art gallery. (p217)

○ **Melbourne Museum** Broad natural and cultural-heritage collection. (p221)

○ **Ian Potter Centre: NGV Australia** Amazing Australian art: colonial, contemporary and Indigenous. (p216)

○ **Federation Square** Melbourne's favourite meeting hosts galleries and cultural events. (p229)

Places with a View

○ **Twelve Apostles** Rocky stacks battling the wild ocean. (p257)

○ **Eureka Skydeck** Big Melbourne building, big Melbourne views. (p220)

○ **Seal Rocks** Ogle magical views of the ocean and the Nobbies rock formation. (p248)

○ **Great Ocean Road** Super-scenic road between waves and wilderness. (p249)

Nature Escapes

○ **Wilsons Promontory National Park** Silvery beaches, verdant gullies and inquisitive wombats. (p258)

○ **The Otways** Cycle or hike through these bushy Great Ocean Road wilds. (p256)

○ **Phillip Island** Cavorting fur seals and the famous Penguin Parade. (p247)

○ **Melbourne's parks** Formal Victorian parks and gardens. (p216)

Need to Know

Places for Lunch

- **Chinatown** Garish scarlet-and-gold restaurants. (p217)

- **Melbourne's pubs** It's not just about beer: Melbourne's pubs do hefty meals (...and beer). (p238)

- **Queen Victoria Market** Fill your picnic hamper. (p220)

- **Melbourne Cricket Ground** Bite into a pie while barracking for your team. (p221)

Left: Arts Centre Melbourne (p217); **Above:** Little penguins, Phillip Island

ADVANCE PLANNING

- **One month before** Reserve Melbourne theatre seats and check live-music listings.

- **Two weeks before** Plan your Great Ocean Road journey: book accommodation, a surfing lesson and a hire car.

- **One week before** Book a table at a top-notch restaurant (we love MoVida, p232) or a seat at the football at the MCG.

RESOURCES

- **Visit Victoria** (www.visitvictoria.com) Information, ideas and events.

- **Melbourne Visitor Centre** (www.visitmelbourne.com) At Federation Square in the central city.

- **Half Tix** (www.halftixmelbourne.com) Cheap theatre tickets and day trips.

- **That's Melbourne** (www.thatsmelbourne.com.au) Downloadable maps, info and podcasts.

- **Parks Victoria** (www.parkweb.vic.gov.au) Oversees Victoria's fab national parks.

- **Royal Automobile Club of Victoria** (RACV; www.racv.com.au) Touring info plus emergency roadside assistance.

GETTING AROUND

- **Walk** Through the caffeine-infused laneways of central Melbourne.

- **Tram** Between Melbourne's inner neighbourhoods.

- **Drive** Along the curves and bends of the Great Ocean Road.

- **Train** To Melbourne's outer suburbs.

- **Bus** To the Phillip Island Penguin Parade and to/from Melbourne Airport on the Skybus.

BE FOREWARNED

- **Driving in Melbourne** Watch out for passengers stepping down from trams, and for the peculiar 'hook turn' at many downtown intersections – to turn right, pull into the *left* lane, wait until the *other* light turns green, then complete the turn.

- **Phillip Island's Penguin Parade** It kicks off *after* sunset.

Melbourne & the Great Ocean Road Itineraries

From Australia's hippest city (arts, eating, drinking, football – take your pick) to sleepy surf towns along the Great Ocean Road, Victoria punches well above its relatively modest acreage.

MELBOURNE
GEELONG
Port Phillip
TORQUAY
ANGLESEA
PORT CAMPBELL
NATIONAL PARK
LORNE
PHILLIP
ISLAND
CAPE OTWAY
BASS STRAIT
WILSONS
PROMONTORY

MELBOURNE TO WILSONS PROMONTORY RETURN
Nightlife & Wildlife

3 DAYS

Start your trip in Victoria's cool capital ❶**Melbourne** (p216): indulge in global cuisines, catch a live band, ride around on the trams and check out eclectic theatre. Once you've had your fill of bar-hopping, overdosed on lattes, seen a show or yelled yourself hoarse at the football, leave the city lights behind and dip into Victoria's wild side.

It's easy to organise a day tour or hire a car to visit ❷**Phillip Island** (p247), 140km south of the city. The island is home to the famous Penguin Parade, where cute little penguins march up the beach in a quirky floodlit spectacle. There's more to see here,

too, including a colony of Australian fur seals and some excellent beaches (bring your airport novel).

From Phillip Island truck over to ❸**Wilsons Promontory** (p258), a couple of hours further east. 'The Prom' offers abundant wildlife, pristine beaches and excellent bushwalking tracks. Go barefoot on the white sand at Squeaky Beach (find out where the name comes from!), then loop back to Melbourne.

5 DAYS

MELBOURNE TO PORT CAMPBELL NATIONAL PARK

Along the Great Ocean Road

Pick up a set of wheels in ❶ **Melbourne** (p216) and head west. The regional hub of ❷ **Geelong** has come a long way in recent years: check out the waterfront and grab a bite to eat.

The Great Ocean Road officially starts at ❸ **Torquay** (p250), the bubbly hub of Victoria's surfing scene. Visit the surf museum or hire a board and hurl yourself into the waves. There are gentle breaks and surf schools here; nearby is the famous Bells Beach (not for beginners).

Next up is ❹ **Anglesea** (p253), home to a more relaxed surf culture, while ❺ **Lorne** (p253) offers superb bushwalks,

waterfalls and beaches, plus quality places to eat and stay. Quiet towns, secluded beaches, spectacular views and the ever-winding road continue to ❻ **Cape Otway** (p256), along the rugged 'Shipwreck Coast'. Beyond the cape is the eye-popping ❼ **Port Campbell National Park** (p256), where crumbling limestone cliffs retreat from the pounding surf, leaving natural arches, blowholes and the eerie Twelve Apostles rock stacks.

Torquay (p250)
RODNEY HYETT/GETTY IMAGES ©

Discover Melbourne & the Great Ocean Road

At a Glance

● **Melbourne** (p216) Multifaceted and artistic with global pizzazz.

● **Great Ocean Road** (p250) A classic road trip along photogenic coastline.

● **Wilsons Promontory** (p259) Mainland Australia's southern-most tip: beaches, rocky outcrops, forests and bushwalking.

● **Phillip Island** (p247) Low-key holiday escape with quirky wildlife.

Birrarung Marr
TOM PUTT/GETTY IMAGES ©

MELBOURNE

There's a lot of fun packed into this city of some four million people. Coffee, food, art and fashion are taken mighty seriously, but that doesn't mean they're only for those in the know; all you need to eat well, go bar-hopping or shopping is a bit of cash and a deft ability to find hidden stairways down graffiti-covered laneways.

◎ Sights

Central Melbourne

Ian Potter Centre: NGV Australia Gallery
(Map p230; ☎03-8662 1555; www.ngv.vic. gov.au; Federation Sq; exhibition costs vary; ⏱10am-5pm Tue-Sun; ☒1, 3, 5, 6, 8, 16, 64, 67, 72, ☒Flinders St) **FREE** Houses a collection of Australian paintings, decorative arts, photography, prints, drawings, sculpture, fashion, textiles and jewellery. The gallery's Indigenous collection dominates the ground floor and seeks to challenge ideas of the 'authentic'. The contemporary exhibits upstairs are well-worth checking out.

Australian Centre for the Moving Image Museum
(ACMI; Map p230; ☎03-8663 2200; www. acmi.net.au; Federation Sq; ⏱10am-6pm; ☒1, 3, 5, 6, 8, 16, 64, 67, 72, ☒Flinders St) **FREE** ACMI educates, enthrals and entertains in equal parts, and has enough games and movies on call for days, or even months of screen time. 'Screenworld' is an exhibition that celebrates the work of mostly Australian cinema and TV and, upstairs, the Australian Mediatheque is set aside for the

viewing of programs from the National Film and Sound Archive and ACMI.

Birrarung Marr
Park

(Map p230; http://federationbells.com.au; btwn Federation Sq & the Yarra River; 🚊1, 3, 5, 6, 8, 16, 64, 67, 72, 🚉Flinders St) **FREE** Featuring grassy knolls, river promenades and a thoughtful planting of indigenous flora, Birrarung Marr also houses the sculptural and musical **Federation Bells**, which ring according to a varying schedule.

Hosier Lane
Street

(Map p230; Hosier Ln; 🚊75, 70) **FREE** This lane is Melbourne's best-known canvas for street art; its cobbled length draws camera-wielding crowds. Pieces change almost daily, and reach for the sky. Keep an eye down low, too, you might even find oddities like a cement gun.

Young & Jackson's
Historic Building

(Map p230; www.youngandjacksons.com.au; cnr Flinders & Swanston Sts; 🚉Tourist Shuttle, 🚊City Circle, 1, 3, 5, 6, 8, 16, 64, 67, 72, 🚉Flinders St) This pub is known more for its painting of pre-pubescent *Chloe* than beer. Painted by Jules Joseph Lefebvre, naked Chloe was a hit at the Paris Salon of 1875. It caused an outcry in pursed-lipped provincial Melbourne, and was removed from the National Gallery of Victoria. Bought by a publican, *Chloe* continues to enthral at Young & Jackson's.

Melbourne Aquarium
Aquarium

(Map p230; 🕿03-9923 5925; www.melbourne aquarium.com.au; cnr Flinders & King Sts; adult/child/family $35/22/92; ⏰9.30am-6pm, last entry 5pm; 🚊70, 75) This aquarium is home to rays, groupers and sharks, all of which cruise around a 2.2-million-litre tank, watched closely by visitors through a see-through tunnel. Talks and feedings are included in the admission fee.

Immigration Museum
Museum

(Map p230; 🕿13 11 02; www.museumvictoria. com.au/immigrationmuseum; 400 Flinders St; adult/child $10/free; ⏰10am-5pm; 🚊70, 75) The Immigration Museum uses personal and community voices, images and memorabilia to tell the many stories of

immigration. The changing exhibitions are often poignant. It's symbolically located in the old Customs House (1858–70).

Chinatown
Neighbourhood

(Map p230; Little Bourke St, btwn Spring & Swanston Sts; 🚊1, 3, 5, 6, 8, 16, 64, 67, 72) **FREE** Chinese miners arrived in search of the 'new gold mountain' in the 1850s and settled in this strip of Little Bourke St, now flanked by red archways. Here you'll find an interesting mix of bars and restaurants, including one of Melbourne's best, Flower Drum (p234). Come here for yum cha, or explore its attendant laneways for late-night dumplings or cocktails.

Koorie Heritage Trust
Cultural Centre

(Map p230; www.koorieheritagetrust.com; 295 King St; gold-coin donation; ⏰9am-5pm Mon-Fri; 🚉Flagstaff) 🖉 This centre is devoted to southeastern Aboriginal culture, and cares for artefacts and oral history. Its gallery shows a variety of contemporary and traditional work. There's a model scar tree at the centre's heart, as well as a permanent chronological display of Victorian Koorie history. There's also a shop with books, CDs, crafts and bush-food supplies.

Southbank & Docklands

Arts Centre Melbourne
Arts Centre

(Map p230; www.theartscentre.com.au; 100 St Kilda Rd; 🚉Tourist Shuttle, 🚊1, 3, 5, 6, 8, 16, 64, 67, 72, 🚉Flinders St) Arts Centre Melbourne is made up of two separate buildings: **Hamer Hall** (Melbourne Concert Hall; Map p230; www.theartscentre.net.au; 100 St Kilda Rd, Arts Centre Melbourne) and the **theatres building** (under the spire). The **Famous Spiegeltent**, (a Belgian mirror tent) stages cabaret, music and comedy from February to April. Explore the free galleries **Gallery 1** and **St Kilda Road Foyer Gallery** and the weekly **makers market** (Sundays from 10am to 4pm).

NGV International
Gallery

(Map p218; 🕿03-8662 1555; www.ngv.vic.gov.au; 180 St Kilda Rd; exhibition costs vary; ⏰10am-5pm

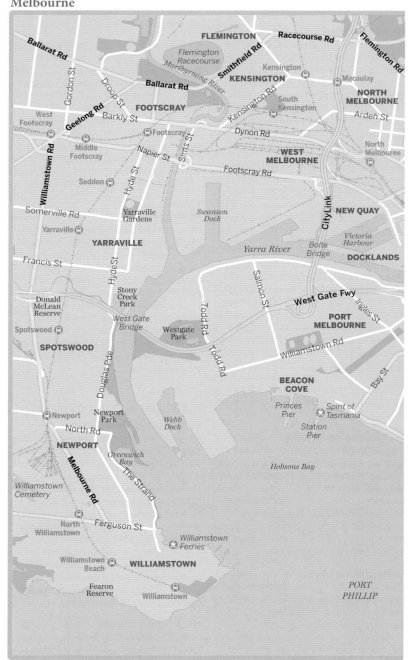

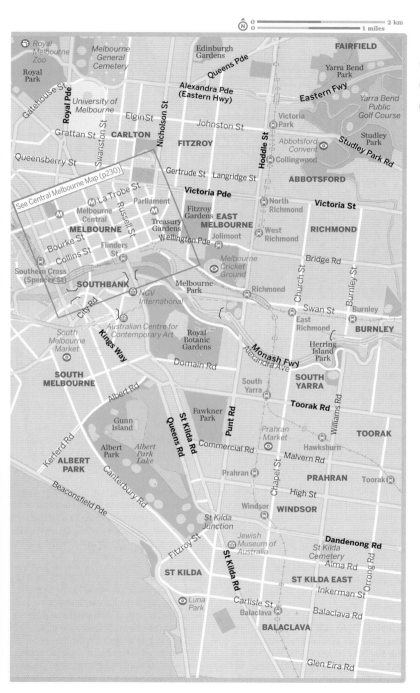

Royal Melbourne Zoo
Melbourne General Cemetery
Edinburgh Gardens
FAIRFIELD
Royal Park
Yarra Bend Park
Gatehouse St
Royal Pde
University of Melbourne
Elgin St
Alexandra Pde (Eastern Hwy)
Queens Pde
Eastern Fwy
Yarra Bend Public Golf Course
Grattan St
CARLTON
Nicholson St
Johnston St
Victoria Park
Studley Park
Queensberry St
Swanston St
FITZROY
Hoddle St
Abbotsford Convent
Studley Park Rd
See Central Melbourne Map (p230)
Gertrude St
Langridge St
Collingwood
ABBOTSFORD
La Trobe St
Victoria Pde
North Richmond
Victoria St
Melbourne Central
Parliament
Russell St
Fitzroy Gardens
EAST MELBOURNE
RICHMOND
MELBOURNE
Treasury Gardens
Jolimont
West Richmond
Bourke St
Collins St
Flinders St
Wellington Pde
Church St
Bridge Rd
Burnley St
Southern Cross (Spencer St)
SOUTHBANK
Melbourne Cricket Ground
Richmond
Swan St
Burnley
City Rd
NGV International
Melbourne Park
East Richmond
BURNLEY
South Melbourne Market
Australian Centre for Contemporary Art
Royal Botanic Gardens
Herring Island Park
Kings Way
Monash Fwy
Alexandra Ave
SOUTH MELBOURNE
Domain Rd
SOUTH YARRA
Albert Rd
South Yarra
Toorak Rd
Williams Rd
Kerferd Rd
Gunn Island
Fawkner Park
Punt Rd
Prahran Market
TOORAK
St Kilda Rd
Queens Rd
Commercial Rd
Hawksburn
Albert Park
Albert Park Lake
Malvern Rd
ALBERT PARK
Canterbury Rd
Prahran
PRAHRAN
Toorak
Beaconsfield Pde
Chapel St
High St
Windsor
WINDSOR
Fitzroy St
St Kilda Junction
Jewish Museum of Australia
Dandenong Rd
St Kilda Cemetery
Alma Rd
Orrong Rd
ST KILDA
St Kilda Rd
ST KILDA EAST
Inkerman St
Luna Park
Carlisle St
Balaclava
Balaclava Rd
BALACLAVA
Glen Eira Rd

0 2 km
0 1 miles

GLENN BEANLAND/GETTY IMAGES ©

 Don't Miss
Queen Victoria Market

This site has been a market since 1878, prior to which it was a burial ground, and it is where Melburnians shop for fresh produce. There's a deli, meat and fish hall as well as a restaurant zone. From mid-November to February a lively night market with food stalls, bars and music takes over.

NEED TO KNOW

Map p230; www.qvm.com.au; 513 Elizabeth St; ⏱6am-2pm Tue & Thu, to 5pm Fri, to 3pm Sat, 9am-4pm Sun; 🚌 Tourist Shuttle, 🚊19, 55, 57, 59

Wed-Mon; 🚌Tourist Shuttle, 🚊1, 3, 5, 6, 8, 16, 64, 67, 72) **FREE** Beyond the water wall you'll find international art that runs from the ancient to the contemporary. Completed in 1967, the original NGV building – Roy Grounds' 'cranky icon' – was one of Australia's most controversial but ultimately respected Modernist masterpieces. Don't miss gazing up at the Great Hall's stained-glass ceiling.

Eureka Skydeck   Lookout
(Map p230; www.eurekaskydeck.com.au; 7 Riverside Quay; adult/child/family $19/10/42, The Edge extra $12/8/29; ⏱10am-10pm, last entry 9.30pm; 🚌Tourist Shuttle) Eureka

Tower, built in 2006, has 92 storeys. Take a wild elevator ride to almost the top and you'll do 88 floors in 38 seconds. 'The Edge' – not a member of U2, but a slightly sadistic glass cube – propels you out of the building.

Docklands   Neighbourhood
(www.docklands.vic.gov.au; 🚌Tourist Shuttle, 🚊70, 86, City Circle) This waterfront area was the city's main industrial and docking area until the mid-1960s. In the mid-1990s a purpose-built studio complex and residential, retail and entertainment area was built. Of most interest to travellers is **New Quay**, with its public art and

promenades. **Waterfront City** has restaurants, bars, shops and an observation wheel that is yet to turn successfully.

Australian Centre for Contemporary Art
Gallery

(ACCA; Map p218; ☑03-9697 9999; www.acca online.org.au; 111 Sturt St; ☺10am-5pm Tue-Fri, 11am-6pm Sat & Sun; ☒1) FREE ACCA is one of Australia's most exciting and challenging contemporary galleries. It shows a range of local and international artists in a building that is fittingly sculptural, with a deeply rusted exterior evoking the factories that once stood on the site, and a slick, soaring, ever-adapting interior.

East Melbourne & Richmond

Melbourne Cricket Ground
Sport Stadium

(MCG; Map p218; ☑03-9657 8888; www.mcg. org.au; Brunton Ave; tour adult/child/family $20/10/50; ☺10am-3pm; ☒Tourist Shuttle, ☒48, 75, ☒Jolimont) For many Australians the 'G' is considered hallowed ground. In 1858 the first game of Aussie Rules football was played here, and in 1877 it was the venue for the first Test cricket match between Australia and England. Tours get you right out onto the ground. Pedestrian access from the CBD is via William Barak bridge.

The MCG was the central stadium for the 1956 Melbourne Olympics and the 2006 Commonwealth Games.

National Sports Museum
Museum

(NSM; ☑03-9657 8879; www.nsm.org.au; Brunton Ave; adult/child/family $20/10/50; ☺10am-5pm) See Cathy Freeman's famous Sydney Olympics running suit and more of Australia's sporting memorabilia. The interactive gallery is a hit with kids, as they get to handball a footy and shoot hoops. There's a discount if you buy an MCG tour and NSM entry together.

Fitzroy Gardens
Park

(Wellington Pde, btwn Lansdowne & Albert Sts; ☒Tourist Shuttle, ☒75, ☒Jolimont) The city

drops away suddenly just east of Spring St, giving way to Melbourne's beautiful backyard, the Treasury and Fitzroy Gardens, whose stately avenues are lined with English elms, flowerbeds, expansive lawns, strange fountains, a photogenic observatory and a creek.

Fitzroy & Around

Centre for Contemporary Photography
Gallery

(CCP; ☑03-9417 1549; www.ccp.org.au; 404 George St; ☺11am-6pm Wed-Fri, noon-5pm Sat & Sun; ☒86) FREE This not-for-profit centre has a changing schedule of modern photographic exhibitions across four galleries. It's worth passing by after dark to see the night projection window.

Abbotsford Convent
Historic Site

(Map p218; ☑03-9415 3600; www.abbotsford convent.com.au; 1 St Heliers St; ☺7.30am-10pm; ☒200, 201, 207, ☒Collingwood) FREE The convent, which dates back to 1861, is spread over 7 hectares of riverside land 4km from the CBD. The nuns have been replaced with a rambling collection of creative studios and community offices. The **Convent Bakery** supplies impromptu picnic provisions, and **Shadow Electric** (http://shadowelectric.com.au; Abbotsford Convent, 1 St Heliers St; movies $20; ☒200, 201, 207, ☒Collingwood) provides beverages and open-air cinema over summer. Most weekends see market action, too.

Carlton & Around

Melbourne Museum
Museum

(Map p230; ☑13 11 02; www.museumvictoria.com. au; 11 Nicholson St; adult/child & student $10/ free, exhibitions extra; ☺10am-5pm; ☒Tourist Shuttle, ☒City Circle, 86, 96, ☒Parliament) This modern museum mixes old-style object displays with themed interactive areas. It provides a grand sweep of Victoria's natural and cultural histories: walk through the reconstructed laneway lives of the 1800s or become immersed in the legend of champion racehorse Phar Lap. Bunjilaka,

on the ground floor, presents indigenous stories and history told through objects and Aboriginal voices.

Royal Exhibition Building
Historic Building

(Map p230; ☏ 13 11 02; http://museumvictoria.com.au/reb; Nicholson St; tours adult/child $5/3.50; 🚌 Tourist Shuttle, 🚋 City Circle, 86, 96, 🚉 Parliament) Built for the International Exhibition in 1880, and winning Unesco World Heritage status in 2004, this Victorian edifice symbolises the glory days of the Industrial Revolution, Empire and 19th-century Melbourne's economic supremacy. Australia's first parliament was held here in 1901; these days it's often home to food, hot-rod and design shows. Tours depart Melbourne Museum most days at 2pm.

Royal Melbourne Zoo
Zoo

(Map p218; ☏ 03-9285 9300; www.zoo.org.au; Elliott Ave; adult/child $26.10/13 (free on weekends); ⏰ 9am-5pm; 🚌 505, 🚋 55, 🚉 Royal Park) This large zoo's theme is 'fighting extinction', and there are plenty of conservation messages on the lush grounds. The elephant enclosure is a standout, as is the hothouse full of butterflies. Native animals are in natural bush settings, and there's a platypus aquarium. Zoo Twilights bring live music to the zoo as the sun goes down from late Jan–Mar.

South Yarra, Prahran & Windsor

Royal Botanic Gardens
Gardens

(www.rbg.vic.gov.au; ⏰ 7.30am-sunset. Children's Garden open Wed-Sun, closed school term 3; 🚌 Tourist Shuttle, 🚋 8) FREE These beautiful gardens feature a global selection of plants and a surprising amount of wildlife, including waterfowl, ducks, swans, child-scaring eels, cockatoos and possums. Kids love the nature-based **Ian Potter Children's Garden**. Around the gardens is the **Tan**, a 4km-long former horse-exercising track, now used to exercise joggers. Summer sees the gardens play host

to the Moonlight Cinema (p241).

Prahran Market   Market

(Map p218; www.prahranmarket.com.au; 163 Commercial Rd; ⊙7am-5pm Tue, Thu & Sat, to 7pm Fri, 10am-3pm Sun; 🚊72, 78, 🚉Prahran) The Prahran Market has been an institution since it opened in 1864 and is one of the finest produce markets in the city. As well as fresh offerings, an upmarket selection of stalls serve coffee, chocolates and fine food.

St Kilda & Around

Luna Park   Amusement Park

(Map p218; 🕿03-9525 5033; www.lunapark.com.au; 18 Lower Esplanade; adult/child single-ride ticket $10/8, unlimited-ride ticket $46/36; 🚊16, 96) It opened a century ago and still retains the feel of an old-style amusement park with creepy Mr Moon's gaping mouth swallowing you up whole on entering. There's a heritage-listed scenic railway and the full complement of gut-

churning modern rides. For grown-ups, the noise and lack of greenery or shade can pall all too quickly. Check the website for opening hours.

St Kilda Foreshore   Beach

(Jacka Blvd; 🚊16, 96) Despite palm-fringed promenades, a parkland strand and a long stretch of sand, don't expect Bondi or Noosa. St Kilda's seaside appeal is more Brighton, England than *Baywatch,* despite 30-odd years of glitzy development. And that's the way Melburnians like it; a certain depth of character and an all-weather charm, with wild days on the bay providing for spectacular cloudscapes and terse little waves, as well as the more predictable sparkling blue of summer.

Jewish Museum of
Australia   Museum

(Map p218; 🕿03-9834 3600; www.jewish museum.com.au; 26 Alma Rd; adult/child/family $10/5/20; ⊙10am-4pm Tue-Thu, to 5pm

223

Melbourne for Children

Ian Potter Children's Garden (www.rbg.vic.gov.au; Observatory Precinct, Royal Botanic Gardens, Birdwood Ave, South Yarra; ⊙10am-4pm Wed-Sun, daily during Victorian school holidays; 🚌8) Has natural tunnels in the rainforest, a kitchen garden and water-play areas.

Australian Centre for the Moving Image (p216) Free access to computer games and movies may encourage square eyes, but it's a great spot for a rainy day.

Royal Melbourne Zoo (p222) A broad range of animals are housed in nature-like enclosures.

National Sports Museum (p221) Just walking in will get your junior champion's heart rate up.

Melbourne Museum (p221) The Children's Museum has hands-on exhibits that make kids squeal.

Sun; 🚌3, 67) Interactive displays tell the history of Australia's Jewish community from the earliest days of European settlement, while permanent exhibitions celebrate Judaism's rich cycle of festivals and holy days. To get there, follow St Kilda Rd from St Kilda Junction then turn left at Alma Rd.

South Melbourne, Port Melbourne & Albert Park

South Melbourne Market   Market
(Map p218; www.southmelbournemarket.com. au; cnr Coventry & Cecil Sts; ⊙8am-4pm Wed, Sat & Sun, to 5pm Fri; 🚌96) The market's labyrinthine interior is packed to overflowing with an eccentric collection of stalls selling everything from carpets to bok choy (Chinese greens). Its hangover-relieving dim sims are famous and sold at various cafes around Melbourne (as 'South Melbourne Market Dim Sims' no less!). Don't miss a coffee from **Clement** (http://clementcoffee.com; Stall 89, 116-136 Cecil St; ⊙7.30am-4.30pm).

Albert Park Lake   Lake
(btwn Queens Rd, Fitzroy St, Aughtie Dr & Albert Rd; 🚌96) Elegant black swans give their inimitable bottoms-up salute as you circumnavigate the 5km perimeter of this artificial lake. Jogging, cycling, walking or clamouring over play equipment is the appropriate human equivalent. Lakeside Dr was an international motor-racing circuit in the 1950s, and since 1996 the revamped track has been the venue for the **Australian Formula One Grand Prix** (☎1800 100 030; www.grandprix.com.au; Albert Park; tickets from $55; ⊙Mar), which is held each March.

⚙ Activities

Studley Park Boathouse   Canoeing
(☎03-9853 1828; www.studleyparkboathouse. com.au; 1 Boathouse Rd, Kew) Pack a picnic then hire a two-person canoe or kayak from the boathouse ($36 for the first hour).

Humble Vintage   Bicycle Rental
(☎0432 032 450; www.thehumblevintage.com) 🌿 Get yourself a set of special wheels from this collection of retro racers, city bikes and women's bikes. Rates are $30 per day, or $80 per week, and include lock, helmet and a terrific map. Bikes can be picked up from St Kilda, Fitzroy and the CBD.

Rentabike @ Federation Square
Bicycle Rental, Bike Tour

(Map p230; ☑ 0417 339 203; www.rentabike. net.au; Federation Sq; bike hire 1hr/day/week $15/35/100; ☒Flinders St) ✎ Rents out bikes including child seats and 'tagalongs'. Also runs bike tours.

North Fitzroy Bowls
Lawn Bowls

(☑ 03-9481 3137; www.barefootbowling.com.au; 578 Brunswick St; ☒112) There's maximum hipster enjoyment to be had here, with lights for night bowls, green-side bar-becues and cheap beer. Phone to make a booking and for opening times. From Fitzroy, continue north along Brunswick St and cross Alexander Pde – it's on your right.

Stand Up Paddle Boarding
Paddleboarding

(☑ 0416 184 994; www.supb.com.au; St Kilda Seabaths, 10-18 Jacka Blvd; per hour $25; ☒96) Hire SUP equipment and explore the bay off St Kilda Beach.

Melbourne City Baths
Swimming

(Map p230; ☑ 03-9663 5888; 420 Swanston St; adult/child $6/3; ☺6am-10pm Mon-Thu, to 8pm Fri, 8am-6pm Sat & Sun; ☒Melbourne Central) The City Baths first opened in 1860 and were intended to stop people bathing in the seriously polluted Yarra River. Enjoy a swim in the beautiful 1903 heritage-listed building.

Tours

Aboriginal Heritage Walk
Cultural Tour

(☑ 03-9252 2300; www.rbg.vic.gov.au; Royal Bo-tanic Gardens, Birdwood Ave, South Yarra; adult/child $25/10; ☺11am Tue-Fri and 1st Sun of the month; ☒Tourist Shuttle, ☒8) ✎ The Royal Botanic Gardens are on a traditional camping and meeting place of the area's original owners, and this tour takes you through their story – from songlines to plant lore, all in 90 minutes.

City Circle Trams
Tram Tour

(☑ 1800 800 007; http://ptv.vic.gov.au; ☒35) Free W-class trams that trundle around the city perimeter (and into the depths of Docklands) from 9am to 6pm daily.

Freddy's Bike Tours
Bike Tour

(Map p230; ☑ 0431 610 431; http://freddys-biketours.com.au; Federation Sq; $39; ☺tour departs 10.30am) ✎ Explore Melbourne's highlights in small groups on fire-engine-red bicycles. It's a blister-free way to get orientated.

Greeter Service
Walking Tour

(Map p230; ☑ 03-9658 9658; Melbourne Visitor Centre, Federation Sq) ✎ **FREE** This free two-hour 'orientation tour' departs Fed Square daily at 9.30am (bookings required) and is run by volunteer 'greeters' who are keen to share their knowledge. It's aimed at giving visitors to Melbourne a good understanding of the layout and sights of Melbourne.

Hidden Secrets Tours
Laneways

(☑ 03-9663 3358; www.hiddensecretstours. com; tours $70-195) ✎ Offers a variety of walking tours covering lanes and arcades, wine, architecture, coffee and cafes, and vintage Melbourne.

Kayak Melbourne
Kayak Tour

(☑ 0418 106 427; www.kayakmelbourne.com. au; tours $99; ☒11, 31, 48) ✎ **FREE** Takes you past Melbourne city's newest develop-ments and you'll get explanations about the older ones, too. Moonlight tours are most evocative and include a fish 'n' chips dinner; they depart from North Wharf Rd, Shed 2, Victoria Harbour.

Melbourne By Foot
Walking Tour

(☑ 0418 394 000; www.melbournebyfoot.com; tours $35) ✎ Take a couple of hours out with Dave and experience a mellow, in-formative walking tour that covers street-art, politics, and gives great insights into Melbourne's history and diversity. Dave also runs evening beer tours ($80). Highly recommended.

Melbourne City Tourist Shuttle
Bus Tour

(Tourist Shuttle; www.thatsmelbourne.com. au; adult/child under 10yr $5/free; ☺9.30am-4.30pm) **FREE** This free hop-on/hop-off tourist shuttle takes about 90 minutes to make its 13 stops around Melbourne and its inner suburbs. Stops include Lygon St, Queen Victoria Market, Docklands, Melbourne Museum, the MCG and the Shrine.

Sleeping

Central Melbourne

Melbourne Central YHA Hostel $
(Map p230; ☎03-9621 2523; www.yha.com.au; 562 Flinders St; dm/d $34/100; @ 🛜; 🚊70) This heritage building has been totally transformed by the YHA gang. Expect handsome rooms, two compact kitchens, a great rooftop area and, for something unique, choose one of the two rooftop doubles.

Ovolo Boutique Hotel $$
(Map p230; ☎03-8692 0777; www.ovologroup. com; 19 Little Bourke St; r incl breakfast $195; P @ 🛜; 🚊96, 🚊Parliament) Shh, don't tell everyone, but there's a free minibar in each room, and a free daily happy hour. Wait, tell everyone, because this new

boutique hotel is friendly, fun and one of Melbourne's best. Rooms are light-filled and edgy, with interesting views.

Econolodge City Square Hotel $$
(Map p230; ☎03-9654 7011; www.citysquare motel.com.au; 67 Swanston St; incl breakfast s $90-100 d $125-145; P ❄ 🛜; 🚊Flinders St) The foyer is not much, but the rooms are dirt cheap and the staff charming. Windows are double-glazed to dull the sound of tram bells, and there's bread, butter and Vegemite in the room for breakfast.

Pensione Hotel Hotel $$
(Map p230; ☎03-9621 3333; www.pensione.com. au; 16 Spencer St; r $125; P ❄ @ 🛜; 🚊96, 109, 112) The Pensione isn't being cute christening some rooms 'petit double' – they're squeezy – but what you don't get in size is more than made up for in spot-on style and super-reasonable rates. Rooms close to the neighbouring back-packers get a 'sweet dreams' pack.

Alto Hotel on Bourke Hotel $$
(Map p230; ☎03-8608 5500; www.alto hotel.com.au; 636 Bourke St; r from $140; P ❄ @ 🛜; 🚊86, 96) 🌿 This environ-ment-minded hotel runs on 100% green

Albert Park Lake (p224)

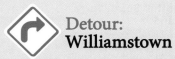

Detour:
Williamstown

Williamstown is a yacht-filled gem just a short boat ride (or drive or train ride) from Melbourne's CBD. It has stunning views of Melbourne, and a bunch of touristy shops along its esplanade. The park by the marina is made for picnics or takeaway fish 'n' chips.

Gem Pier is where passenger ferries dock to drop off and collect those who visit Williamstown by boat. It's a fitting way to arrive, given the area's maritime ambience. **Williamstown Ferries** (Map p218; ☏03-9517 9444; www.williamstownferries. com.au; one way Williamstown-CBD adult/child $15/7.50) plies Hobsons Bay daily, stopping at Southgate and visiting a number of sites along the way, including Docklands. **Melbourne River Cruises** (Map p230; ☏03-8610 2600; www.melbcruises. com.au; one way Williamstown-CBD adult/child $22/11) also docks at Gem Pier, travelling up the Yarra River to Southgate. Pick up a timetable from the very useful visitors centre in Williamstown or at Federation Sq, or contact the companies directly; bookings are advised.

power and has water-saving showers, double-glazed windows that open, its own beehive and in-room recycling. Rooms are also well equipped, light and neutrally decorated.

Adina Apartment Hotel
Serviced Apartments $$
(Map p230; ☏03-8663 0000; www.adinahotels. com.au; 88 Flinders St; apt from $165; P❉☇; ☐City Circle, 70, 75) These cool monochromatic apartments are extra large and luxurious. Ask for one at the front for amazing parkland views or get glimpses into Melbourne's lanes from the giant timber-floored studios. All have full kitchens.

Robinsons in the City
Boutique Hotel $$
(Map p230; ☏03-9329 2552; www.ritc.com. au; 405 Spencer St; r incl breakfast from $165; P❉☇; ☐75, 96) Robinsons is a gem with six large rooms and warm service. The building is a former bakery, dating from 1850, but it's been given a modern, eclectic look. Most rooms have their own bathroom in the hall.

Causeway Inn on the Mall
Hotel $$
(Map p230; ☏03-9650 0688; www.causeway. com.au; 327 Bourke St Mall; r incl breakfast $153; ❉@☇; ☐86, 96) The Causeway Inn is always busy and often full. Bonuses include helpful staff and daily paper, and a location bang in the middle of the city. The hotel entrance is actually in the Causeway.

Hotel Lindrum
Boutique Hotel $$$
(MGallery Accor; Map p230; ☏03-9668 1111; www.hotellindrum.com.au; 26 Flinders St; r from $245; P❉☇; ☐70, 75) This attractive hotel was once the pool hall of the legendary and literally unbeatable Walter Lindrum. It's one of Melbourne's most interesting boutique hotels, but spring for a deluxe room so you will snare either arch or bay windows and marvellous views of Melbourne. And, yes, there's a pool table.

Fitzroy & Around

Nunnery
Hostel $$
(☏03-9419 8637; www.nunnery.com.au; 116 Nicholson St, Fitzroy; dm incl breakfast $32, s/d $90/120; @☇; ☐96) The Nunnery oozes atmosphere, with sweeping staircases and many original features; the walls are dripping with religious works of art and ornate stained-glass windows. You'll be giving thanks for the big comfortable lounges and communal areas.

Brooklyn Arts Hotel
B&B $$

(☎03-9419 9328; www.brooklynartshotel.com. au; 50 George St, Fitzroy; s/d incl breakfast $95/135; 🛜; 🚌86) There are seven very different rooms in this rustic B&B. Owner Maggie has put the call out for artistic people and they've responded by staying, so expect lively conversation over the Continental breakfast. Rooms are clean (but certainly not sterile!), colourful and beautifully decorated; one even houses a piano.

Carlton

Downtowner on Lygon
Hotel $$

(Map p230; ☎03-9663 5555; www.downtowner. com.au; 66 Lygon St; r from $174; P❄@🛜❄; 🚌1, 8) The Downtowner is a surprising complex of different-sized rooms, including joining rooms perfect for families and other groups. Ask for a light-bathed room if you can. It's perfectly placed between the CBD and Lygon St restaurants.

169 Drummond
B&B $$

(☎03-9663 3081; www.169drummond.com. au; 169 Drummond St; d $135-145; 🚌1, 8) A privately owned and very friendly guest-house with ensuite rooms in a renovated, 19th-century terrace. It's located in the inner north, just one block from vibrant Lygon St.

South Yarra, Prahran & Windsor

Art Series (Cullen)
Boutique Hotel $$

(☎03-9098 1555; www.artserieshotels.com.au/ cullen; 164 Commercial Rd, Prahran; r from $189; ❄@🛜; 🚌72, 78, 79, 🚉Prahran) Expect visions of Ned Kelly shooting you from the glam opaque room/bathroom dividers in this lively hotel resplendent in the works of recently departed Sydney artist Adam Cullen. Borrow the 'Cullen Car' ($55 per day) or Kronan bike ($5 per hour) and let the whole of Melbourne know where you're staying.

Punthill South Yarra Grand
Apartments $$

(☎1300 731 299; www.punthill.com.au; 7 Yarra St, South Yarra; r from $180; P❄🛜; 🚌8,78, 🚉South Yarra) It's the little things, like a blackboard and chalk in the kitchen for messages, and chocolates by the bed, that make this modern apartment hotel ooze friendliness. All rooms have a laundry, balcony and a tin dog chilling out on fake grass. Right in the hub of the Claremont district.

The Como Melbourne
Hotel $$$

(MGallery Collection; ☎03-9825 2222; www. mirvachotels.com; 630 Chapel St, South Yarra; r from $275; P❄@🛜❄; 🚌8, 78, 🚉South Yarra) From its pink foyer with water features, to rooms with almost floor-to-ceiling mirrors and grand bathrooms, MGallery screams five star. It's certainly got great service, and plenty of style.

St Kilda & Around

Base
Hostel $$

(☎03-8598 6200; www.stayatbase.com; 17 Carlisle St; dm/r $30/115; P❄@🛜; 🚌3a, 16, 79, 96) Fun-filled Base has stream-lined dorms, each with en suite, or slick doubles. There's a 'sanctuary' for female travellers, where tea and coffee is delivered free on weekend mornings, maybe to make up for the weekly free champagne 'for ladies'. Live-music nights keep the good-time vibe happening.

Hotel Tolarno
Hotel $$

(☎03-9537 0200; www.hoteltolarno.com.au; 42 Fitzroy St; r from $155; ❄@🛜; 🚌3a, 16, 96, 112) This is an art hotel, pure and simple. The owner acquires new paintings annually, and even the location was once Georges Mora's seminal gallery Tolarno. The restaurant downstairs bears the name of his artist wife, Mirka. Every room is different, expect bright colours and eclectic furniture.

Prince
Hotel $$

(☎03-9536 1111; www.theprince.com.au; 2 Acland St; r incl breakfast from $169; P❄@

RODNEY HYETT/GETTY IMAGES ©

⭐ Don't Miss
Federation Square

Striking Fed Square is the place to celebrate, protest, relax or party. Occupying a prominent city block, the 'square' is far from square. Its undulating forecourt of Kimberley stone echoes the town squares of Europe. Free tours of the square depart Monday to Saturday at 11am. There's also free wi-fi.

NEED TO KNOW

Map p230; www.fedsquare.com.au; cnr Flinders & Swanston Sts; 🛜; 🚋1, 3, 5, 6, 8, 16, 64, 67, 72, 🚉Flinders St

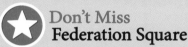 🛜 ♿; 🚋3a, 16, 96, 112) The Prince has a suitably dramatic lobby and the rooms are an interesting mix of the original pub's proportions, natural materials and a pared-back aesthetic. Larger rooms and suites feature some key pieces of vintage modernist furniture.

Middle Park Hotel   Pub $$
(☏ 03-9690 1958; www.middleparkhotel.com.au; 102 Canterbury Rd; r incl breakfast from $160; ❄@🛜; 🚋96) When you're given an x-rated 'intimacy' pack ($70), you might be wondering what kind of hotel you've booked yourself into, but relax. Rooms

are luxurious and modern – expect iPod docks and rain showerheads at the top of the wooden staircase. There's a modern pub and restaurant downstairs, and the cooked gourmet breakfast is a treat.

Eating

Central Melbourne

Camy Shanghai Dumpling Restaurant   Chinese $
(Map p230; 23-25 Tattersalls Lane; dishes $6.50; ⏲11.30am-10pm) There's nothing fancy

229

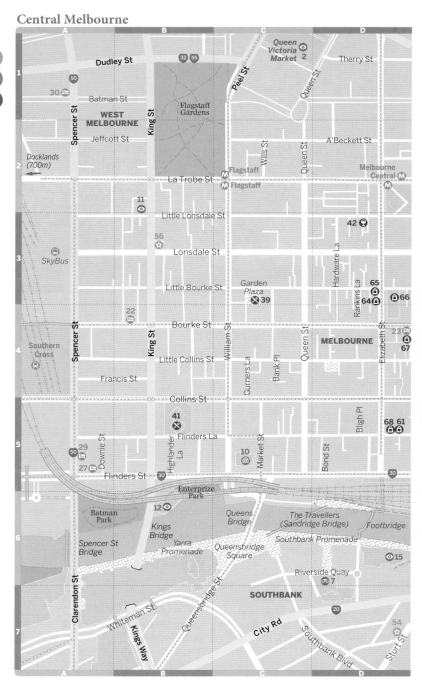

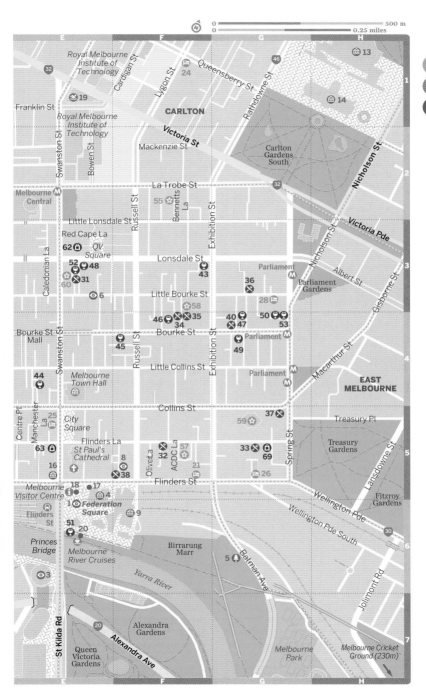

Central Melbourne

here: pour your own plastic cup of over-boiled tea from the urn, then try a variety of dumplings with some greens. Put up with the dismal service and you've found one of the last places in town you can fill up for under $10.

MoVida
Spanish $$

(Map p230; ☎03-9663 3038; http://movida.com.au; 1 Hosier Lane; tapas $4-6, raciones $10-24; ⊙noon-late; 🚋70, 75, 🚆Flinders St) Finished looking at the surrounding street art? Now line up along the bar, cluster around little window tables or, if you've

booked, take a table in the dining area.
Movida Next Door (Map p230; cnr Flinders St
& Hosier Lane; ◷5pm-late Tue-Thu, noon-midnight Fri & Sat, 2-9pm Sun) is the perfect place
for tapas, while in the lawyer end of town
is the larger **Movida Aqui** (Map p230; ☎03-
9663 3038; 500 Bourke St, 1st fl; ◷noon-late
Mon-Fri, 6pm-late Sat), also home to a lovely
terrace that houses lively Paco's Tacos
($6 tacos).

Mamasita   Mexican $$
(Map p230; ☎03-9650 3821; www.mamasita.
com.au; Level 1, 11 Collins St; mains $15-28;
◷noon-12pm Mon-Thu, to 2am Fri & Sat, to 10pm
Sun; ﹅City Circle, 11, 31, 48, 109, 112) You see
a line snaking along Collins St at 7pm and
wonder if it's worth it. Mamasita has been
making Melburnians wait for years now,
and the lines only get longer so, in short,
yes! There are 180 types of tequila, and
the two-bite *tostaditas* are piled high with
delicious ingredients like prawn or pork
shoulder. Don't miss the chargrilled corn.

Cumulus Inc   Modern Australian $$
(Map p230; www.cumulusinc.com.au; 45 Flinders
Lane; mains $21-38; ◷7am-11pm Mon-Fri,
8am-11pm Sat & Sun; ﹅City Circle) Watch Melburnians mope into their smartphones
at this reasonably priced and very cool
restaurant. The focus is on beautiful produce and simple but artful
cooking, and its $16 breakfast
(including sublime coffee) is
better than anything a hotel
can muster up.

Chin Chin   Thai $$
(Map p230; ☎03-8663
2000; www.chinchinrestaurant.com.au; 125 Flinders
Lane; mains $19-33;
◷11am-late) Spunky
Thai dining thrives in
this busied-up shell
of an old building on
Flinders Lane. The
menu is long, curries
are madly tasty and
everything on the plates

is bright and fresh, with ribbons of flavour
ticking the right palate boxes. No bookings, but Go Go Bar downstairs will have
you till there's space.

HuTong Dumpling Bar   Chinese $$
(Map p230; www.hutong.com.au; 14-16 Market
Lane; mains $15-22; ◷11.30am-3pm & 5.30pm-
10.30pm) HuTong's windows face out on
famed Flower Drum, and its reputation for
divine *xiao long bao* (soupy dumplings)
means getting a lunchtime seat anywhere in this three-level building is just as
hard. Downstairs, watch chefs make the
delicate dumplings, then hope they don't
watch you making a mess eating them.

Pellegrini's
Espresso Bar   Italian, Cafe $$
(Map p230; ☎03-9662 1885; 66 Bourke St; mains
$16-18; ◷8am-11.30pm Mon-Sat, noon-8pm Sun)
The iconic Italian equivalent of a classic
1950s diner, Pellegrini's has remained
genuinely unchanged for decades. Pick
and mix from the variety of pastas and
sauces and enjoy the jovial atmosphere.

MoVida, Hosier Lane
WAYNE FOGDEN/GETTY IMAGES ©

In summer, finish with a ladle of $3 watermelon granita.

Longrain
Thai $$

(Map p230; ☎03-9671 3151; www.longrain.com; 44 Little Bourke St; mains $25-40; ⊗noon-3pm Fri & dinner 6pm-late Mon-Thu, from 5.30pm Fri-Sun; ☒Parliament) Perfectly balanced Thai food served in a dining hall and adjacent noisy bar. No bookings, so you'll be encouraged to have a drink to stop your mouth watering while you wait.

Flower Drum
Chinese $$$

(Map p230; ☎03-9662 3655; www.flower-drum. com; 17 Market Lane; mains $35-55; ⊗noon-3pm & 6-11pm Mon-Sat, 6-10.30pm Sun) The Flower Drum continues to be Melbourne's most celebrated Chinese restaurant. The finest, freshest produce prepared with absolute attention to detail keeps this Chinatown institution booked out for weeks in advance. The sumptuous but ostensibly simple Cantonese food is delivered with the slick service you'd expect in such elegant surrounds.

Vue de Monde
French $$$

(Map p230; ☎03-9691 3888; www.vuedemonde. com.au; Rialto, 525 Collins St; degustation $200-250; ⊗reservations from noon-2pm Tue-Fri & Sun, 6-9.15pm Mon-Sat; ☒11, 31, 48, 109, 112, ☒Southern Cross) Melbourne's favoured spot for occasion dining has extraordinary views from the 55th floor of the Rialto. Expect fantastic French cuisine thanks to visionary Shannon Bennett and, design-wise, there's plenty of kangaroo fur and locally made bespoke furniture. Book ahead. If you can't get in, at least venture up for a fabulous cocktail from the Lui Bar (p238).

North Melbourne

Courthouse Hotel
Pub Fare $$

(☎03-9329 5394; www.thecourthouse.net. au; 86 Errol St; mains $22-37; ⊗noon-3pm & 6-10pm Mon-Sat ; ☒57) This corner pub has managed to retain the comfort and familiarity of a local while taking food, both in its public bar and its more formal dining spaces, very seriously. Enjoy mains like rare roasted and cured kangaroo or choose from its simpler (and cheaper) bar menu.

Richmond

Richmond Hill Cafe & Larder
Cafe $$

(☎03-9421 2808; www.rhcl. com.au; 48-50 Bridge Rd; lunch $12-26; ⊗8.30am-5pm; ☒75, ☒West Richmond) Once the domain of well-known cook Stephanie Alexander, it still boasts its lovely cheese room and simple, comforting food like cheesy toast. There are breakfast cocktails for the brave and it is quite un-hipsterfied. Wellington Pde in the CBD becomes Bridge Rd.

Richmond Hill Cafe & Larder
LONELY PLANET/GETTY IMAGES ©

Baby
Pizza **$$**

(☎ 03-9421 4599; www.babypizza.com.au; 631-633 Church St, Richmond; mains $17; ⏱ 7am-11pm; ☒ 70, 78, ☒ East Richmond) Ignore the porno light feature (you won't notice it if you dine by day) and get into the food and vibe. Delicious pizza, the occasional Aussie TV star and many, many trendy folk. It's busy, bold and run by restaurant king Christopher Lucas (Chin Chin), so it's quite brilliant. Even for a pizza joint.

Fitzroy & Around

Vegie Bar
Vegetarian **$**

(www.vegiebar.com.au; 380 Brunswick St; mains $14-16; ⏱ 11am-late Mon-Fri, from 9am Sat & Sun; ☒; ☒ 112) Tasty vegetarian curries, burgers, raw foods and seasonal broths can be eaten outside along fab Brunswick St itself, or in the cavernous, shared-table space inside.

Babka Bakery Cafe
Bakery, Cafe **$**

(358 Brunswick St; mains $10-16; ⏱ 7am-7pm Tue-Sun; ☒ 112) Russian flavours infuse the lovingly prepared breakfast and lunch dishes, and the heady aroma of cinnamon and freshly baked bread makes even just a coffee worth queuing for. Cakes are notable and can be taken away whole.

Moroccan Soup Bar
North African, Vegetarian **$$**

(☎ 03-9482 4240; 183 St Georges Rd; banquet $20; ⏱ 6pm-10pm Tue-Sun; ☒; ☒ 112) Prepare to queue before being seated by Hana, who'll recite the menu. Best bet is the banquet, which, for three courses, is great value. The sublime chickpea bake has locals queuing with their own pots and containers to nab some take away. From Fitzroy, continue north along Brunswick St and cross Alexander Pde.

Marios
Cafe **$$**

(303 Brunswick St; mains $17-30; ⏱ 7am-9.30pm; ☒ 112) Mooching at Marios is on the Melbourne 101 curriculum. Breakfasts are big and served all day, the service is swift and the coffee is old-school strong.

Commoner
Modern British **$$**

(☎ 03-9415 6876; www.thecommoner.com.au; 122 Johnston St; mains $13-30; ⏱ noon-3pm Fri-Sun, 6pm-late Wed-Sun ; ☒ 112) If you need to be convinced of this off-strip restaurant's serious intent, the Sunday wood-grilled meats should do it. There's the brilliant five-course 'feed me' menu too. Take a breather in its upstairs bar.

Cutler & Co
Modern Australian **$$$**

(☎ 03-9419 4888; www.cutlerandco.com.au; 55 Gertrude St; mains $39-47; ⏱ noon-late Fri & Sun, 6pm-late Mon-Thu; ☒ 86) This is Andrew McConnell's fine dining restaurant, and though its decor might be a little over the top, its attentive, informed staff and joy-inducing meals have quickly made this one of Melbourne's best.

Carlton & Around

Tiamo
Italian **$**

(303 Lygon St; mains $9-24; ⏱ 7am-10.30pm Mon-Sat, to 10pm Sun; ☒ Tourist Shuttle) When you've had enough of pressed, siphoned, slayered, pour-over filtered and plunged coffee, head here to one of Lygon St's original Italian cafe-restaurants. There's laughter and the relaxed joie de vivre only a time-worn restaurant can have.

Abla's
Lebanese **$$**

(☎ 03-9347 0006; www.ablas.com.au; 109 Elgin St; mains $27; ⏱ noon-3pm Thu & Fri, 6-11pm Mon-Sat; ☒ 205, ☒ 1, 8, 96) The kitchen is steered by Abla Amad, whose authentic, flavour-packed food has been feeding customers since 1979. Bring a bottle of your favourite plonk and enjoy the $60 compulsory banquet on Friday and Saturday nights.

Rumi
Middle Eastern **$$**

(☎ 03-9388 8255; 116 Lygon St; mains $17-23; ⏱ 6-10pm; ☒ 1, 8) A fabulously well-considered place that serves up a mix of traditional Lebanese cooking and contemporary interpretations of old Persian dishes. The *sigara boregi* (cheese and pine-nut pastries) are a local institution and tasty mains like slow-cooked lamb are balanced with an interesting selection of vegetable dishes. From Carlton, continue north along Lygon St into East Brunswick.

Hellenic Republic   Greek $$

(☎ 03-9381 1222; www.hellenicrepublic.com.au; 434 Lygon St; mains $16-30; ⏰ noon-4pm Fri, 11am-4pm Sat & Sun, 5.30pm-late Mon-Sun; 🚌 1, 8) The Iron Bark grill at George Calombaris' restaurant works overtime grilling up pitta, tiger prawns, local snapper and luscious lamb. Follow Lygon St north from Carlton – it's in East Brunswick.

....

South Yarra, Prahran & Windsor

Lucky Coq   Pizza $

(www.luckycoq.com.au; 179 Chapel St , Windsor; mains $4; ⏰ noon-3am; 🚌 6, 78, 🚋 Prahran) Bargain pizzas and plenty of late-night DJ action make this a good start or end to a Chapel St eve. Dress code is no suits or jackets (yay!).

Two Birds One Stone   Cafe $$

(☎ 03-9827 1228; http://twobirdsonestonecafe. com.au; 12 Claremont St, South Yarra; mains

$15-19; ⏰ 7am-4pm Mon-Fri, from 8am Sat & Sun; 🚌 8, 78, 🚋 South Yarra) This nouveau industrial cafe in buzzing Claremont St serves almost perfect coffee and unusual cafe fare including king whiting pide and twice-cooked marmalade French toast.

Colonel Tan's   Thai $$

(www.coloneltans.com.au; 229 Chapel St, Prahran; mains $16; ⏰ 5-11pm Tue-Thu & Sat, noon-11pm Fri; 🚌 78, 🚋 Prahran) Lamps hang upside down alongside chandeliers in this share-house-style restaurant, yet you'll still barely be able to see the one-page menu or your food. It morphs into a disco come weekends, but get in while the food's hot; this is Thai done beautifully.

....

St Kilda & Around

Lentil as Anything   Vegetarian $

(www.lentilasanything.com; 41 Blessington St, St Kilda; prices at customers' discretion; ⏰ 11am-9pm; 🍴 ; 🚌 16, 96) Choose from the always-organic, no-meat menu and pay what you can afford. This unique not-for-profit operation provides training and educational opportunities for marginalised people.

Lentil as Anything, St Kilda

Food Trucks

Perhaps appealing to our love of 'pop-up' shops and bars (outlets that 'pop up' in a space, then disappear once the hype has died), fabulous food trucks have begun plying the streets of Melbourne. Each day the different trucks use Twitter and Facebook to let their followers and friends know where they will be, and dutiful, hungry folk respond by turning up street-side for a meal. Favourite Melbourne food trucks to chase down include Taco Truck (@tacotruckmelb); Gumbo Kitchen (@GumboKitchen, serving New Orleans–style food) and Beatbox Kitchen (@beatboxkitchen, serving gourmet burgers and fries to beat).

There's another branch at the **Abbotsford Convent** (1 St Heliers St).

Galleon Cafe
Cafe $
(9 Carlisle St, St Kilda; mains $10; ⏰7am-5pm; 🚊3a, 16, 79) Friendly folk, a decent amount of elbow room and low-key music make this a cheery place to down a coffee and lunch in busy St Kilda. At night, hit **Radio Mexico** (📞03-9534 9990; www.radiomexico.com.au; 11-13 Carlisle St) next door.

Cicciolina
Mediterranean $$
(www.cicciolinastkilda.com.au; 130 Acland St, St Kilda; mains $19-40; ⏰lunch & dinner; 🚊16, 96) This warm room of dark wood, subdued lighting and pencil sketches is a St Kilda institution. The inspired mod-Med menu is smart and generous, and the service warm. It doesn't take bookings; eat early or while away your wait in the moody little back bar. The sister restaurant, **Ilona Staller** (📞03-9534 0488; www.ilonastaller.com.au; 282 Carlisle St; mains $38-41; ⏰noon-late; 🚊3, 16, 🚉Balaclava), is nearby.

Stokehouse Cafe
Italian $$
(📞03-9525 5445; www.stokehouse.com.au; 30 Jacka Blvd, St Kilda; shared plates $6-25; ⏰noon-late Tue-Fri, 7.30am-late Sat-Mon; 🚊3a, 16, 96) It's hard to beat this iconic Melbourne restaurant's beachfront position, and renovations have turned the cafe downstairs into a modern share-plate style cafe. Upstairs is dedicated to fine diners, with mains around $36.

Claypots
Seafood $$
(📞03-9534 1282; 213 Barkly St, St Kilda; mains $25-35; ⏰noon-3pm & 6pm-1am; 🚊96) A local favourite, Claypots serves up seafood in its namesake. You should get in early, not just to get a seat but also to ensure the good stuff is still available, as hot items go fast.

I Carusi II
Pizza $$
(📞03-9593 6033; 231 Barkly St, St Kilda; pizza $16-21; ⏰6-11pm; 🚊16, 96) Located beyond the Acland St chaos in this nostalgic corner shop, I Carusi pizzas have a particularly tasty dough and follow the less-is-more tenet, with top-quality mozza, pecorino and a small range of other toppings. Bookings are recommended, and don't miss the upstairs bar.

Attica
Modern $$$
(📞03-9530 0111; www.attica.com.au; 74 Glen Eira Rd, Ripponlea; 8-course tasting menu $175; ⏰6.30pm-late Tue-Sat; 🚊67, 🚉Ripponlea) Staking its claim to fame by being the only Melbourne restaurant to regularly make it onto San Pellegrino's Best Restaurant list, Attica is a suburban restaurant that serves Ben Shewry's creative dishes degustation-style. You can expect small portions of texture-oriented delight, such as potatoes cooked in earth. To get here, follow Brighton Rd south to Glen Eira Rd.

Gay & Lesbian Melbourne

These days, Melbourne's gay and lesbian community is well and truly integrated into the general populace. Here are some highlights:

● Midsumma Festival (www.midsumma.org.au) has a diverse program with around 150 cultural, community and sporting events.

● *MCV* (http://gaynewsnetwork.com.au) is a free weekly newspaper, and is online.

● Gay and lesbian community radio station JOY 94.9 FM (www.joy.org.au) is another important resource for visitors and locals.

● Gay men are particularly welcomed at the **Peel Hotel** (🖉03-9419 4762; www.thepeel.com.au; 113 Wellington St; ⏱9pm-dawn Thu-Sat; 🚌86) nightclub, and 169 Drummond (p228) has been offering gay-friendly accommodation for two decades.

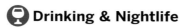

🍷 Drinking & Nightlife

Central Melbourne

Bar Americano   Cocktail Bar
(Map p230; www.baramericano.com; 20 Pesgrave Pl, off Howey Pl; ⏱8.30am-1am) Bring your cash and throw it away on some of the most bespoke cocktails around. This is a petite hideaway with authentic class.

Lui Bar   Cocktail Bar
(Map p230; www.vuedemonde.com.au; Level 55, 525 Collins Street, Rialto ; ⏱5.30pm-midnight Mon, noon-midnight Tue-Fri, 5.30pm-late Sat, noon-evening Sun) Set high on level 55 of the Rialto is this *tres* fancy bar with a very sophisticated air. Cocktails come from 'yesterday' or 'tomorrow' and snacks include chickpea fries and apple and cinnamon donuts. An experience (dress nicely). Live music Sundays.

1000£Bend   Bar
(Map p230; www.thousandpoundbend.com.au; 361 Little Lonsdale St; ⏱8.30am-11.30pm Mon-Wed, to 1am Thu-Sat; 📶) Breakfast, lunch, dinner and cruisy folk using the free wi-fi – that's not all at this mega warehouse of entertainment. It's also a whopping great venue for art shows and plays.

Riverland   Bar
(Map p230; 🖉03-9662 1771; www.riverlandbar.com; Vaults 1-9 Federation Wharf, under Princes Bridge; ⏱10am-late; 🚆Flinders St) This bluestone beauty sits by the water below Princes Bridge and keeps things simple with good wine, four beers on tap and bar snacks.

Section 8   Bar
(Map p230; www.section8.com.au; 27-29 Tattersalls Lane; ⏱10am-late Mon-Fri, noon-late Sat & Sun) The latest in bar-in-a-carpark entertainment. Come and sink a local Mountain Goat beer with the after-work crowd, who make do with shipping pallets for decor. **Ferdydurke** (Map p230; 🖉03-9639 3750; www.ferdydurke.com.au; 31 Tattersalls Lane, levels 1 & 2, corner Lonsdale St; ⏱noon – 1am) is a neighbouring rooftop bar run by the same wacky folk.

Double Happiness   Bar
(Map p230; 🖉03-9650 4488; http://double-happiness.org; 21 Liverpool St; ⏱4pm-1am Mon-Wed, to 3am Thu & Fri, 6pm-3am Sat, to 1am Sun; 🚌86, 96, 🚆Parliament) This stylish hole in the wall doesn't just do Chinese-themed decor, it also offers Chinese and Vietnamese beers. You should try a Beer Hanoi (rice lager) or Great Leap Forward cocktail.

Melbourne Supper Club   Bar

(Map p230; 🕿03-9654 6300; 161 Spring St, 1st fl; ⏱5pm-4am Sun-Thu, to 6am Fri & Sat; 🚊95, 96, 🚉Parliament) The gorgeous, oh-so-sophisticated Supper Club is open very late and is a favoured after-work spot for performers and hospitality types. Cosy into a Chesterfield, browse the encyclopaedic wine menu and relax; the sommeliers will cater to any liquid desire. Upstairs rooftop bar **Siglo** (Map p230; 🕿03-9654 6300; 161 Spring St, Level 2; ⏱5pm-3am) is stunning.

Croft Institute   Bar

(Map p230; 🕿03-9671 4399; www.thecroft institute.com; 21-25 Croft Alley; ⏱5pm-1am Mon-Thu, 8pm-3am Fri & Sat) Located in a laneway off a laneway, the lab-themed Croft is a test of drinkers' determination. Prescribe yourself a beaker of house-distilled vodka in the downstairs laboratory (some come complete with fat plastic syringes). There's a $10 cover charge on Friday and Saturday nights.

Alumbra   Club

(www.alumbra.com.au; 161 Harbour Esplanade, Shed 9, Central Pier; ⏱6pm-late Thu, 4pm-3am

Fri & Sat, to 1am Sun; 🚉Tourist Shuttle, 🚊70, City Circle) Great music and a stunning location will impress – even if the Bali-meets-Morocco follies of the decorator don't.

Brown Alley   Club

(Colonial Hotel; Map p230; 🕿03-9670 8599; www.brownalley.com; 585 Lonsdale St; ⏱9pm-late Thu-Sun; 🚉Flagstaff) This historic pub hides away four fully fledged nightclubs with a 24-hour licence. It's enormous, with distinct rooms that can fit up to 1000 people.

Richmond, Prahran & Windsor

Windsor Castle Hotel   Pub

(89 Albert St; 🚊5, 64, 🚉Windsor) Cosy nooks, sunken pits, fireplaces (or, in summer, a very popular beer garden) and yummo pub meals make this off-the-main-drag pub an attractive option.

Mountain Goat Brewery   Brewery

(www.goatbeer.com.au; cnr North & Clark Sts; ⏱from 5pm Wed & Fri only; 🚊48, 75,

Alumbra

(🚇Burnley) This local microbrewery is set in a massive beer-producing warehouse. Enjoy its range of beers while nibbling on pizza, or join a free brewery tour on Wednesday night. To find it head down Richmond's Bridge Rd, turn left at Burnley St and right at North St.

Revolver Upstairs   Club
(www.revolverupstairs.com.au; 229 Chapel St; ⏲noon-4am Mon-Fri, 24hr Sat-Mon; 🚊6, 🚇Prahran) Rowdy Revolver can feel like an enormous version of your own lounge room, but with 54 hours of nonstop music starting late Saturday night and ending Monday morning, you're probably glad it's not.

Fitzroy & Around

Naked for Satan   Bar
(☎03-9416 2238; www.nakedforsatan.com.au; 285 Brunswick St; ⏲noon-12am Sun-Thu, to 1am Fri & Sat; 🚊112) Vibrant, loud and reviving an apparent Brunswick St legend (a man nicknamed Satan who would get down and dirty, naked because of the heat, in an illegal vodka distillery under the shop), this place packs a punch both with its popular *pintxos* (bite-sized sandwiches; $1–2) and cleverly named beverages. Its stunning, sprawling rooftop bar is outstanding.

Napier Hotel   Pub
(☎03-9419 4240; www.thenapierhotel.com; 210 Napier St; ⏲3-11pm Mon-Thu, 1pm-1am Fri & Sat, to 11pm Sun; 🚊112, 86) The Napier has stood on this corner for over a century and many pots have been pulled as the face of the neighbourhood changed. It's still a great spot for pub grub.

Little Creatures
Dining Hall   Beer Hall
(www.littlecreatures.com.au; 222 Brunswick St; ⏲8am-late; 📶; 🚊112) With free community bikes for customers, complimentary wi-fi and a daytime kid-friendly groove, this vast drinking hall is the perfect place to spend up big on pizzas ($18) and enjoy local wine and beer.

Carlton & Around

Gerald's Bar   Wine Bar
(386 Rathdowne St, North Carlton; ⏲5-11pm Mon-Sat; 🚊253, 🚊1, 8) Wine by the glass is democratically selected at Gerald's and they spin some fine vintage vinyl from behind the curved wooden bar. If you get hungry, there are delightfully fresh morsels to sink your teeth into (it owns the neighbouring butcher and fruit and veg shop too).

Temple Brewery   Brewery
(☎03-9380 8999; www.templebrewing.com.au; 122 Weston St, East Brunswick; ⏲5.30-11pm Wed & Thu, noon-11pm Fri & Sat, to 9pm Sun; 🚊1, 8) Try a seasonal craft brew (there are eight on tap) at this very classy brewery with a brasserie, or try five for $19. Don't miss a taste of Saison.

St Kilda & Around

Carlisle Wine Bar   Wine Bar
(☎03-9531 3222; www.carlislewinebar.com.au; 137 Carlisle St, Balaclava; ⏲Mon-Fri 3pm-1am, Sat & Sun 11am-1am; 🚊3, 16, 🚇Balaclava) Locals love this often-rowdy, wine-worshipping former butcher's shop. The staff will treat you like a regular and find you a glass of something special, or effortlessly throw together a cocktail amid the weekend rush.

George Public Bar   Bar
(www.georgepublicbar.com.au; Basement, 127 Fitzroy St; 🚊96, 16) There are five bars within this building; behind the Edwardian arched windows of the George Hotel is the Melbourne Wine Room and a large front bar that keeps the after-work crowd happy. In the bowels of the building is the George Public Bar, once referred to as the Snakepit but it's wearing a classier skin now.

Veludo   Bar
(www.veludo.com.au; 175 Acland St; ⏲4pm-2am Wed & Thu, noon-3am Fri-Sun. ; 🚊96) It's big, it's brassy and it's got a rooftop bar. Veludo's relatively late closing means that most St Kilda-ites have ducked in here after everything else has shut. Upstairs has live music most nights.

⭐ Entertainment

CINEMAS

Astor   Cinema

(☎03-9510 1414; www.astortheatre.net.au; cnr
Chapel St & Dandenong Rd; adult/child $15/13;
🚃5, 64, 78, 🚉Windsor) This place holds
not-to-be-missed art deco nostalgia,
with double features every night of old
and recent classics. Wicked Wednesday
tickets are $10.

Cinema Nova   Cinema

(www.cinemanova.com.au; 380 Lygon St; adult/
child $18/11; 🚌Tourist Shuttle, 🚃1, 8) Nova
has great current film releases. On Mondays, tickets are a measly $6 before 4pm,
$9 after.

Kino Cinemas   Cinema

(Map p230; ☎03-9650 2100; www.palacecin-
emas.com.au; Collins Pl, 45 Collins St; adult/
child $19.50/14.50; 🚃11, 31, 48, 109, 112) This
licensed cinema specialises in quality art-
house releases. It's close to great bars,
too, for after-flick drinks.

OUTDOOR CINEMAS

St Kilda Open Air Cinema   Cinema

(http://openaircinemas.com.au; South Beach
Reserve, Jacka Blvd; 🚃79, 96) There's often
live pre-movie music and, of course, salty
sea air to inhale.

Rooftop Cinema   Cinema

(Map p230; www.rooftopcinema.com.au; Level 6,
Curtin House, 252 Swanston St) Has amazing
city views, an ABD (all day burger) stall
to keep you fed and a bar to keep you
watered.

Moonlight Cinema   Cinema

(www.moonlight.com.au; Gate D, Royal Botanic
Gardens, Birdwood Ave) Bring along a rug,
pillow and moonlight supper, and set up
an outdoor living room in the middle of
the gardens.

THEATRE

Malthouse Theatre   Theatre

(☎03-9685 5111; www.malthousetheatre.
com.au; 113 Sturt St; 🚃1) The Malthouse
Theatre Company produces theatre that

♥ If You Like...
Rooftop Drinking

If you like your brew with a view, swing up
to these excellent Melbourne rooftop bars:

1 **MADAME BRUSSELS**
(Map p230; www.madamebrussels.com; 59-63
Bourke St, level 3; ⊘noon-1am) Head here if you've
had it with Melbourne's 'black is the uniform' and
all that dark wood. Although named for a famous
19th-century madam, it feels as though you've
fallen into a camp '60s rabbit hole, with much
Astroturfery and staff dressed à la the country club.
The decor might veer towards the hysterical, but
it's just the tonic on a chilly winter's day; they even
provide lap rugs for the terrace.

2 **CARLTON HOTEL**
(Map p230; www.thecarlton.com.au; 193 Bourke
St; ⊘4pm-late) Over-the-top Melbourne rococo
gets another workout here and never fails to raise a
smile. Check the rooftop **Palmz**, if you're looking for
some Miami-flavoured vice or just a great view.

3 **AYLESBURY**
(Map p230; ☎03-9077 0451; 103 Lonsdale
St; ⊘noon-late) Stylish newcomer Aylesbury
is accessed by a lift to a sophisticated terrace
with a stunning vista of the spires of St Patrick's
Cathedral.

4 **ROOFTOP CINEMA**
(Map p230; www.rooftopcinema.com.au;
Level 6, Curtin House, 252 Swanston St) This
rooftop is a bar, loved 'beatbox' kitchen and, in
summer, a cinema.

makes you sit on the edge of your seat.
From Flinders St Station walk across
Princes Bridge and along St Kilda Rd. Turn
right at Grant St then left into Sturt St.

**Melbourne Theatre
Company**   Theatre

(MTC; ☎03-8688 0800; www.mtc.com.au; 140
Southbank Blvd; 🚃1) Melbourne's oldest
theatrical company creates around 15
productions annually, ranging from
contemporary and modern (including

many new Australian works) to Shake-speare and other classics.

LIVE MUSIC

Northcote Social Club   Live Music
(☏03-9489 3917; www.northcotesocialclub.com; 301 High St; ⏰4pm-late Mon, noon-late Tue-Thu & Sun, to 3am Fri & Sat; 🚌86, 🚆Northcote) This awesome live-music venue sees plenty of big and little stars from abroad and home. If you're just after a drink, the front bar buzzes, or there's a large deck out the back for lazy afternoons. A perfect and well-loved local. Head north along Hoddle St to reach High St.

Corner Hotel   Live Music
(☏03-9427 9198; www.cornerhotel.com; 57 Swan St; ⏰4pm-late Tue & Wed, noon-late Thur-Sun; 🚌70, 🚆Richmond) This midsized venue has seen plenty of loud and live action over the years. If your ears need a break, check out the huge rooftop bar with city skyline glimpses. The crowd upstairs is often more suburban than the music fans below. Wednesday night trivia (from 7.30pm, bookings ☏03-9427 7300) has a cult following.

Bennetts Lane   Live Music
(Map p230; www.bennettslane.com; 25 Bennetts Lane; tickets from $15; ⏰9pm-late) Bennetts Lane has long been the boiler room of Melbourne jazz. It attracts the cream of local and international talent and an audience that knows when it's time to applaud a solo. Beyond the cosy front bar, there's another space reserved for big gigs.

Ding Dong Lounge   Live Music
(Map p230; www.dingdonglounge.com.au; 18 Market Lane; ⏰7pm-late Wed-Sat) Ding Dong walks the live-music walk and is a great place to see a smaller touring act or catch local bands. There's indie music on Friday nights and a disco till dawn on Saturday nights.

Esplanade Hotel   Live Music
(☏03-9534 0211; http://espy.com.au; 11 The Esplanade; ⏰noon-1am Mon-Wed & Sun, to 3am Thu & Fri, 8am-3am Sat; 🚌96, 16) Rock pigs rejoice. The Espy remains gloriously shabby and welcoming to all. Bands play most nights in a variety of rooms, including the front bar, and there's a spruced-up diner-like kitchen along the side. And for

Esplanade Market

the price of a pot you get front row seats for the pink-stained St Kilda sunset.

Tote
Live Music

(www.thetotehotel.com; cnr Johnston & Wellington Sts; ⊙4pm-late Tue-Sun; 🚊86) The Tote's closure in 2010 brought Melbourne to a stop. People protested on the CBD streets against the liquor-licensing laws that were blamed for the closure, and there were howls of displeasure on the radio waves. The punters won, laws changed and the Tote reopened to continue its tradition of live bands playing dirty rock.

Cherry
Live Music

(Map p230; http://cherrybar.com.au; AC/DC Lane; ⊙6-12pm Mon & Tue, 5pm-3am Wed, to 5am Thu-Sat, 1pm-midnight Sun) This rock 'n' roll refuge has local acts till 11.30pm, when a DJ takes over. Secret performances are popular, especially when well-known bands are in town. There's often a queue, but once inside, a relaxed, slightly anarchic spirit prevails.

DANCE

Australian Ballet
Ballet

(Map p230; ☎1300 369 741; www.australianballet.com.au; 2 Kavanagh St) Based in Melbourne and now over 40 years old, the Australian Ballet performs traditional and new works at the Arts Centre Melbourne (p217).

Chunky Move
Dance

(www.chunkymove.com; 111 Sturt St) Melbourne-based Chunky Move perform 'genre-defying' dance around the world and, when at home, at the CUB Malthouse.

🛍 Shopping

Central Melbourne

Captains of Industry
Clothing

(Map p230; ☎03-9670 4405; www.captainsofindustry.com.au; Level 1, 2 Somerset Pl; ⊙8am-9pm Mon-Thu, 8am-11pm Fri; 🚊19, 57, 59) Where can you get a haircut, and a bespoke suit and pair of shoes made in the one place? Here. The hard-working folk at Captains also offer homey breakfasts,

❤ If You Like...
Markets

If you like Melbourne's amazing Queen Victoria Market, we think you'll enjoy these other city markets:

1 ROSE STREET ARTISTS' MARKET
(www.rosestmarket.com.au; 60 Rose St; ⊙11am-5pm Sat; 🚊112) One of Melbourne's most popular art-and-craft markets, just a short stroll from Brunswick St. It's firmly of the new-gen variety (if you find dolly toilet-roll covers, it's because they're the newest thing) – here you'll find up to 70 stalls selling jewellery, clothing, furniture, paintings, screen prints and ugly-cute toys.

2 CAMBERWELL SUNDAY MARKET
(www.sundaymarket.com.au; Station St, behind cnr of Burke & Riversdale Rds; gold-coin donation; ⊙7am-12.30pm Sun; 🚊70, 75, 🚉Camberwell) Filled with secondhand and handcrafted goods, this is where Melburnians come to offload their unwanted items and antique hunters come to find them.

3 ESPLANADE MARKET
(www.esplanademarket.com; St Kilda, btwn Cavell & Fitzroy Sts; ⊙10am-5pm Sun; 🚊96) Fancy shopping with a seaside backdrop? A kilometre of trestle tables joined end-to-end carry individually crafted products from toys to organic soaps to large metal sculptures of fishy creatures.

4 CHAPEL STREET BAZAAR
(☎03-9521 3174; 217-223 Chapel St; ⊙10am-6pm; 🚊78, 🚉Prahran) Calling this a 'permanent undercover collection of market stalls' won't give you any clue to what's tucked away here. This old arcade is a retro-obsessive riot. It doesn't matter if Italian art glass or Noddy egg cups are your thing, you'll find it here.

thoughtful lunches and beery dinners. To work!

Shop
Craft, Design

(Craft Victoria; Map p230; www.craft.org.au; 31 Flinders Lane; ⊙10am-5pm Mon-Sat; 🚊70, 75,

City Circle) The retail arm of Craft Victoria, Shop showcases the handmade. Its range of jewellery, textiles, accessories, glass and ceramics bridges the art/craft divide and makes for some wonderful mementos of Melbourne. It has three vibrant gallery spaces.

Alice Euphemia Fashion, Jewellery
(Map p230; Shop 6, Cathedral Arcade, 37 Swanston St, Nicholas Building; ⏱10am-6pm Mon-Sat & noon-5pm Sun; 🚉Flinders St) Art-school cheek abounds in the labels sold here and the jewellery similarly sways between the shocking and exquisitely pretty. Everything here is Australian made.

Aesop Beauty
This home-grown skincare company specialises in products made from simple ingredients in simple packaging. The range is wide and based on botanical extracts. With branches in **QV** (Map p230; QV, 35 Albert Coates Lane), **Flinders Lane** (Map p230; 268 Flinders Lane), **Fitzroy** (242 Gertrude St) and **Prahran** (143 Greville St).

Fitzroy

Third Drawer Down Design
(www.thirddrawerdown.com; 93 George St; ⏱11am-5pm Mon-Sat; 🚉86) This seller-of-great-things makes life beautifully unusual by stocking everything from sesame-seed grinders to beer o'clock beach towels and 'come in, we're closed' signs.

Crumpler Accessories
(📞03-9417 5338; www.crumpler.com.au; 87 Smith St, cnr Gertrude St; ⏱10am-6pm; 🚉86) Crumpler's bike-courier bags started it all and its durable, practical designs can now be found all over the world. It makes bags for cameras, laptops and iPods as well as its original messenger-style ones. There are also branches in the **CBD** (Map p230; 📞03-9600 3799; 355 Little Bourke St, Melbourne; ⏱10am-6pm, until 8pm Fri) and **Prahran** (📞03-9529 7837; 182 Chapel St; ⏱10am-6pm, until 8pm Fri).

Polyester Records Music
(387 Brunswick St; ⏱10am-9pm; 🚉112) This great record store has been selling Melburnians independent music from around the world for decades, and also sells tickets for gigs. There's also a CBD **branch** (Map p230; 288 Flinders Lane).

Carlton

Readings Books
(www.readings.com.au; 309 Lygon St; 🚉Tourist Shuttle, 🚉16) A potter around this defiantly prospering indie bookshop can occupy an entire afternoon if you're so inclined. There's a dangerously loaded (and good-value) specials table, switched-on staff and everyone from Lacan to *Charlie and Lola* on the shelves. Also in **St Kilda** (📞03-9525 3852; www.readings.com.au; 112 Acland St; 🚉96) and elsewhere.

South Yarra, Prahran & Windsor

Fat Fashion, Accessories
(www.fat4.com; 272 Chapel St; 🚉78, 🚉Prahran) The Fat girls' empire has changed the way Melbourne dresses, catapulting a fresh generation of designers into the city's consciousness, including locals P.A.M and Kloke. Other branches are in the **city centre** (Map p230; GPO, 350 Bourke St) and **Fitzroy** (209 Brunswick St).

St Kilda & Around

Hunter Gatherer Fashion
(82a Acland St; 🚉96) This op shop features the most retro of welfare organisation Brotherhood of St Laurence's 26-odd op shops. Branches include **Fitzroy** (274 Brunswick St; ⏱10.15am-5.45pm, until 8pm Fri) and **Melbourne** (Map p230; Royal Arcade).

ⓘ Information

Medical Services

The **Travel Doctor** (TVMC; 📞03-9935 8100; www.traveldoctor.com.au; Level 2, 393 Little

Bourke St, City Centre), in the city centre, specialises in vaccinations.

The Royal Melbourne Hospital (☎03-9342 7000; www.rmh.mh.org.au; cnr Grattan St & Royal Pde; 🚋19, 59) is the most central public hospital with an emergency department.

Tourist Information

Melbourne Visitor Centre (MVC; Map p230; ☎03-9658 9658; Federation Sq; ⏰9am-6pm daily; 📶) Comprehensive tourist information including excellent resources for mobility-impaired travellers.

Getting There & Away

Air

Two airports serve Melbourne: Avalon (☎1800 282 566, 5227 9100; www.avalonairport.com.au) and Tullamarine (www.melbourneairport.com.au), though at present only Jetstar (☎13 15 38; www.jetstar.com) operates from Avalon. Tullamarine Airport also has some Jetstar flights, in addition to domestic and international flights offered by Tiger (☎03-9034 3733; www.tigerairways.com), Qantas (☎13 13 13; www.qantas.com), Virgin Australia (☎13 67 89; www.virginaustralia.com) and other carriers.

Boat

Spirit of Tasmania (Map p218; ☎1800 634 906; www.spiritoftasmania.com.au) Spirit of Tasmania crosses Bass Strait from Melbourne to Devonport, Tasmania, at least nightly; there are also day sailings during peak season. It takes 11 hours and departs from Station Pier, Port Melbourne.

Bus & Train

Southern Cross Station (www.southerncrossstation.net.au) Interstate trains arrive and depart from here. It is also the main terminal for interstate bus services.

Getting Around

To/From the Airport

Tullamarine Airport

There are no trains or trams to Tullamarine Airport. Taxis charge from $45 for the trip to Melbourne's CBD, or you can catch SkyBus (Map p230; ☎03-9335 2811; www.skybus.com.au; adult/child one-way $17/7; 🚌Southern Cross Station) a 20-minute express bus service to/from Southern Cross Station; allow for more time during peak hour.

Readings, Carlton

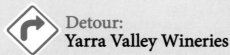

Detour:
Yarra Valley Wineries

The Yarra Valley, about an hour northeast of Melbourne, has more than 80 wineries and 50 cellar doors scattered around its rolling hills – the first vines were planted at Yering Station in 1838. The region produces cool-climate, food-friendly drops such as chardonnay and pinot noir.

Some top Yarra Valley wineries with cellar-door sales and tastings include:

Domain Chandon (⏰03-9738 9200; www.chandon.com.au; 727 Maroondah Hwy; 🕐10.30am-4.30pm) This slick operation is worth a visit for the free guided tours (11am, 1pm and 3pm). Tastings $5.

Sticks (⏰03-9730 1022; www.sticks.com.au; 179 Glenview Rd; 🕐10am-5pm) Small, energetic winery with Sunday Sessions rocking the vines with live music.

TarraWarra Estate (⏰03-5957 3510; www.tarrawarra.com.au; 311 Healesville–Yarra Glen Rd; art gallery admission $5; 🕐11am-5pm) TarraWarra has a striking and modern art gallery showing wonderful exhibitions. Refuel at the neighbouring bistro and cellar door. Tastings $4.

Yering Farm Wines (⏰03-9739 0461; www.yeringfarmwines.com; St Huberts Rd; 🕐10am-5pm) A rustic and friendly little cellar door in an old hay shed with lovely views.

Yering Station (⏰03-9730 0100; www.yering.com; 38 Melba Hwy; 🕐10am-5pm Mon-Fri, to 6pm Sat & Sun) Taste wines in the original 1859 winery and walk through the lovely grounds to the modern fine-dining restaurant.

Avalon Airport

Avalon Airport Transfers (⏰03-9689 7999; www.sitacoaches.com.au; Southern Cross Station; one-way $22; 🕐50 min) Avalon Airport Transfers meet Jetstar flights into and out of Avalon. It departs from Southern Cross Station; check website for times. No booking required.

Bicycle

Melbourne Bike Share (⏰1300 711 590; www.melbournebikeshare.com.au) Melbourne Bike Share began in 2010 and has had a slow start, mainly blamed on Victoria's compulsory helmet laws. Subsidised safety helmets are now available at 7Eleven stores around the CBD ($5 with a $3 refund on return). Daily ($2.70) and weekly ($8) subscriptions require a credit card and $50 security deposit. Each first half-hour of hire is free.

Car & Motorcycle

Car Hire

Avis (⏰13 63 33; www.avis.com.au)

Budget (⏰13 27 27; www.budget.com.au)

Europcar (⏰1300 131 390; www.europcar.com.au)

Hertz (⏰13 30 39; www.hertz.com.au)

Rent a Bomb (⏰13 15 53; www.rentabomb.com.au)

Thrifty (⏰1300 367 227; www.thrifty.com.au)

Car Sharing

Car-sharing companies that operate in Melbourne include **Green Share Car** (⏰1300 575 878; http://greensharecar.com.au), **Go Get** (⏰1300 769 389; www.goget.com.au) and **Flexi Car** (⏰1300 363 780; www.flexicar.com.au). You rent the cars by the hour or the day, and the price includes petrol. They vary on joining fees (between $25 and $40) and how they charge (per hour and per kilometre). The cars are parked in and around the CBD in designated 'car share' car parks. Car sharing costs around $15 per hour depending on the plan you choose.

Toll Roads

Motorcycles travel free on CityLink; car drivers will need to purchase a pass if they are planning on using one of the two toll roads (CityLink or

EastLink, which runs from Ringwood to near Frankston).

Public Transport

Flinders St Station is the main metro train station connecting the city and suburbs. The City Loop runs under the city, linking the four corners of town.

An extensive network of tram lines covers every corner of the city, running north–south and east–west along most major roads. Trams run roughly every 10 minutes Monday to Friday, every 10 to 15 minutes on Saturday, and every 20 minutes on Sunday. Check **Public Transport Victoria** (PTV; 📞1800 800 007; http://ptv.vic. gov.au; Southern Cross Station; 🚉Southern Cross) for more information. Also worth considering is the free City Circle (p225) tram, which loops around town, and the Melbourne City Tourist Shuttle (p225) bus.

Melbourne's buses, trams and trains use **myki** (www.myki.com.au), which is a 'touch on, touch off' card. You must purchase a plastic myki card ($6) and put credit on it before you travel, which can be problematic for travellers. Some hostels are collecting myki cards from travellers who leave Melbourne, but it's best to buy a myki Visitor Pack ($14) at the airport, Skybus terminal or the PTV Hub at Southern Cross Station on arrival.

The myki card can be topped up at 7Eleven stores, machines at most train stations and at some CBD tram stops (online top-ups can take 24 hours to process). Fines for not travelling with a valid myki are $207 and ticket inspectors are vigilant and unforgiving.

Costs for zone 1, which is all that most travellers will need: Myki Money two-hour $3.50, daily $7.

Taxi

Melbourne's taxis are metered and require an estimated prepaid fare when hailed between 10pm and 5am. You may need to pay more or get a refund depending on the final fare. Toll charges are added to fares. A small tip is usual but not compulsory.

PHILLIP ISLAND

Famous for the Penguin Parade and Grand Prix racing circuit, Phillip Island is a spectacular natural environment, attracting a curious mix of surfers, petrolheads and international tourists making a beeline for those little penguins.

👁 Sights & Activities

PHILLIP ISLAND NATURE PARKS

The nature parks comprise three of the island's biggest attractions: the **Penguin Parade** (📞03-5951 2800; www.penguins. org.au; Summerland Beach; adult/child/family $22/11/55; ⊙10am-dusk, penguins arrive at sunset); **Koala Conservation Centre** (📞03-5951 2800; www.penguins.org.au; adult/child/family $11/5.50/27.50; ⊙10am-5pm, extended hrs in summer), with elevated boardwalks; and **Churchill Island** (📞03-5956 7214; www.penguins.org.au; Phillip Island Rd, Newhaven; adult/child/family $11/5.50/27.50; ⊙10am-5pm), a working farm, where Victoria's first crops were planted. Today it features

Yarra Valley vineyard
PETER WALTON/GETTY IMAGES ©

historic displays, including butter churning and blacksmithing.

Most people come for the little penguins, the smallest of their kind in the world. The penguin complex includes two concrete amphitheatres that hold up to 3800 spectators, who visit to see the little fellas waddle from the sea to their land-based nests just after sunset. There are a variety of specialised tours, which offer ranger accompaniment or seeing the penguins from the vantage of a Skybox (an elevated platform).

SEAL ROCKS & THE NOBBIES

The extreme southwestern tip of Phillip Island leads to the Nobbies. Beyond them is Seal Rocks, inhabited by Australia's largest colony of Australian fur seals. The **Nobbies Centre** (☏03-5951 2852; www. penguins.org.au; ☉11am-one hour before sunset) **FREE** houses an interesting interpretive display with interactive panels and games. You can see the 10,000 to 20,000 Australian fur seals if you pay $5 (for four minutes) to remotely control a video camera that watches over Seal Rocks. The best way to see them is on a Wildlife Coast Cruise (p249).

MOTOR RACING CIRCUIT

Even when the motorbikes aren't racing, petrolheads love the **Grand Prix Motor Racing Circuit** (☏03-5952 9400), which holds the Australian Motorcycle Grand Prix each October. The **visitor centre** (☏03-5952 9400; www.phillipislandcircuit.com. au; Back Beach Rd; ☉9.30am-5pm) **FREE** runs 45-minute **guided circuit tours** (adult/ child/family $19/10/44; ☉tours 11am & 2pm), which include access to the History of Motorsport Display. You can also cut laps of the track in hotted-up V8s ($195, booking essential).

Tours

Go West Day Tour
(☏1300 736 551; www.gowest.com.au; 1-day tour $130) Tour from Melbourne that includes food tastings, entry fees and iPod commentary in several languages. It visits several island attractions, including the Penguin Parade.

Wildlife Coast Cruises Boat Tour
(☏03-5952 3501; www.wildlifecoastcruises.com. au; Rotunda Bldg, Cowes Jetty; seal-watching adult/child $70/48) A variety of cruises from

The Nobbies, Phillip Island

RICHARD I'ANSON/GETTY IMAGES ©

Cowes including a daily two-hour seal-watching cruise.

 Sleeping

Surf & Circuit Accommodation
Apartments **$$**

(📞03-5952 1300; www.surfandcircuit.com; 113 Justice Rd; apt $135-380; ❄️🏊) Ideal for families or groups, these eight spacious, modern and comfortable two- and three-bedroom units accommodate up to six and 10 people. They have kitchens and lounges with plasma TVs and patios, and some have spas.

Waves Apartments
Apartments **$$**

(📞03-5952 1351; www.thewaves.com.au; 1 Esplanade, Cowes; d/tr/q from $180/220/240; ❄️📶) Some of these slick apartments overlook Cowes main beach so you can't beat the balcony views if you go for a beachfront unit. The modern self-contained apartments come with spa and balcony or patio.

 Eating

Madcowes
Cafe, Deli **$**

(📞03-5952 2560; 17 The Esplanade; mains $9-19; 🕖7am-4pm) This excellent cafe looks out to the main beach. Try the hotcakes or the grazing platter and enjoy one of the most popular cafes in town.

Infused
Modern Australian **$$**

(📞03-5952 2655; www.infused.com.au; 115 Thompson Ave; mains $28-42; 🕘9am-late Wed-Mon) Infused's groovy mix of timber, stone and lime-green decor makes a relaxed place to enjoy a beautifully presented lunch or dinner, or just a late-night cocktail. The eclectic Mod Oz menu is strong on seafood and moves from freshly shucked oysters to grain-fed Scotch fillet.

 Information

Phillip Island Visitor Centre (📞1300 366 422; www.visitphillipisland.com; 🕘9am-5pm, till 6pm school holidays) The main visitor centre for the island is located on the main road in Newhaven (895 Phillip Island Tourist Rd), and there's a

---

smaller centre at Cowes (cnr Thompson & Church Sts).

 **Getting There & Away**

By car, Phillip Island is accessed from the mainland across the bridge at San Remo. From Melbourne take the Monash Fwy (M1) and exit at Pakenham, joining the South Gippsland Hwy at Koo Wee Rup.

V/Line (📞1800 800 007; www.vline.com.au) V/Line has train services from Melbourne's Southern Cross Station to Dandenong Station or Koo Wee Rup connecting to a bus to Cowes ($12.40, 2½–3½ hours). There are no direct services.

Getting Around

Island E-bike Hire (📞0457 281 965; 142 Thompson Ave, Cowes, Caltex; per hr/per day $20/50) Hire an electric bike and zoom around the whole island. Includes helmets.

Oz Bikes (📞0401 863 622; 1 The Esplanade, Cowes; per hr/day $25/35) Plenty of bikes for hire here.

GREAT OCEAN ROAD

The Great Ocean Road (B100) is one of Australia's most famous road-touring routes. It takes travellers past world-class surfing breaks, through pockets of rainforest and calm seaside towns, and under koala-filled tree canopies. It shows off heathlands, dairy farms and sheer limestone cliffs and gets you up close and personal with the dangerous crashing surf of the Southern Ocean. Walk it, drive it, enjoy it.

Tours

Port Campbell Touring Company
Tours

(☎03-5598 6424; www.portcampbelltouring.com.au; half-day tours $85) Runs evening and day tours from Port Campbell and two to three day tours from Melbourne.

Adventure Tours
Tour

(☎1800 068 886; www.adventuretours.com.au; $130) Day trips from Melbourne along the Great Ocean Road to Twelve Apostles (and back).

Go West Tours
Tour

(☎1300 736 551; www.gowest.com.au; tour $120) Full-day tour exploring the Great Ocean Road with lunch and wi-fi included.

Otway Discovery Tour
Tour

(☎03-9629 5844; www.greatoceanroadtour.com.au; tours $95) A cheap Great Ocean Road tour that includes Bells Beach and the Twelve Apostles.

Ride Tours
Tour

(☎1800 605 120; www.ridetours.com.au; tours $195) Two-day, one-night trips along the Great Ocean Road. Includes breakfast, dinner and accommodation.

ℹ Getting Around
GREAT OCEAN ROAD DISTANCES & TIMES

Melbourne-Geelong	75km	1hr
Geelong-Torquay	21km	15min
Torquay-Anglesea	21km	15min
Anglesea-Aireys Inlet	10km	10min
Aireys Inlet-Lorne	22km	15min
Lorne-Apollo Bay	45km	1hr
Apollo Bay-Port Campbell	88km	70min
Port Campbell-Warrnambool	66km	1hr
Warrnambool-Port Fairy	28km	20min
Port Fairy-Portland	72km	1hr
Portland-Melbourne	440km	6½hr

Torquay

In the 1960s and '70s, Torquay was just another sleepy seaside town. Back then surfing in Australia was a decidedly

Twelve Apostles (p257)

counter-cultural pursuit, and its devotees were crusty hippy drop-outs living in clapped-out Kombis, smoking pot and making off with your daughters. Since then surfing has become unabashedly mainstream, a huge transglobal business. The town's proximity to world-famous Bells Beach and status as home of two iconic surf brands – Ripcurl and Quiksilver, both initially wetsuit makers – ensures Torquay is the undisputed capital of Australian surfing.

Sights & Activities

Surf World Museum
Museum

(www.surfworld.com.au; Surf City Plaza, Beach Rd; adult/child/family $10/6/20; ⊙9am-5pm) Embedded at the rear of the Surf City Plaza is this homage to Australian surfing, with shifting exhibits, a theatre and displays of old photos and rare and unique surfboards.

Go Ride a Wave
Surfing

(☏1300 132 441; www.gorideawave.com.au; 1/15 Bell St; 2hr lessons incl hire $65; ⊙9am-5pm summer) Hires surfing gear, sells secondhand equipment and offers lessons (cheaper when booked in advance).

Torquay Surfing Academy
Surfing

(☏03-5261 2022; www.torquaysurf.com.au; 34a Bell St; 2hr lesson $60; ⊙9am-5pm) Surf school offering travellers' surf passes for $99 (includes two-hour surf lesson and four-hour board hire) and return packages from Melbourne for $149.

Sleeping

Beachside Accommodation Torquay
Apartments $$

(☏03-5261 5258; www.beachsideaccommoda tiontorquay.com.au; 24 Felix Cres; d $100; ❄ 🛜) Clean, compact and just two minutes from Fishermans Beach, the two units are great value and ideal for a few days' stay.

Bellbrae Harvest
Apartments $$$

(☏0438 662 090; www.bellbraeharvest.com. au; 45 Portreath Rd; d $200; ❄) Far from the madding crowd, here are three separate

1 **TORQUAY**
Immerse yourself in surf culture. The Surf World Museum (p251) is recognised as the world's largest, and is dedicated to telling the story of Australian surfing. Local surfing schools offer the chance to learn how to get on a board, and there are funky galleries encapsulating surfing cool.

2 **BELLS BEACH**
Bells (p252) is a spectacular surf beach with a rich history and is home to the world's longest running surfing competition, the Rip Curl Pro. It's worth a detour as cliff-top platforms provide great views of the waves and surfers.

3 **LORNE**
There are a number of waterfalls and bushwalks around Lorne (p253) that can give you a chance to unwind and plug back into nature. If you can tug yourself away from Lorne's pretty bay, head to Qdos Art Gallery (p253), among the trees just out of Lorne, which features some great contemporary art.

4 **THE RIDE**
There is a beautiful rhythm to the Great Ocean Road. At a number of spots you are only metres from the water and there are some great sandy beaches and secluded little coves that can be accessed by simply parking and walking to them.

5 **PORT CAMPBELL NATIONAL PARK**
At Port Campbell National Park (p257), sheer 70m cliffs confront relentless seas, which have carved out spectacular arches, blowholes and stacks, such as the (most famous) Twelve Apostles, from the soft limestone.

Beach at Loch Ard Gorge (p257)

GLENN VAN DER KNIJFF/GETTY IMAGES ©

(and stunning) split-level apartments looking onto a dam. Expect rainwater shower heads, kitchenettes, huge flat-screen TVs and lots and lots of peace.

✖ Eating

Scorched Modern Australian **$$**
(🕿 03-5261 6142; www.scorched.com.au; 17 The Esplanade; mains $26-36; ⊙3-9pm Mon-Thu, 10.30am-9pm Fri-Sun Dec & Jan; 3-9pm Wed-Thu, 10.30am-9pm Fri & Sat, to 3pm Sun Feb-Nov) This restaurant overlooks the waterfront and has windows that open right up to let the sea breeze in. It's about seasonal food served tapas-style here, so make a reservation and try the grazing plate.

ℹ Information

Torquay Visitor Information Centre (www. greatoceanroad.org; Surf City Plaza, Beach Rd; ⊙9am-5pm) Torquay has a well-resourced tourist office next to the Surfworld Museum.

ℹ Getting There & Away

McHarry's Buslines (🕿 03-5223 2111; www. mcharrys.com.au) runs buses almost hourly between 7am and 9pm from Geelong Station to Torquay ($3.60, 30 minutes). **V/Line** (🕿 1800 800 007; www.vline.com.au) has four buses daily from Geelong to Torquay (two on weekends).

If you're driving, Torquay is 15 minutes south of Geelong on the B100.

Torquay to Anglesea

About 7km from Torquay is **Bells Beach** (Great Ocean Rd; car). The powerful point break at Bells is part of international surfing folklore (it's here, in name only, that Keanu Reeves and Patrick Swayze had their ultimate showdown in the film *Point Break*). It's notoriously inconsistent, but when the long right-hander is working it's one of the longest rides in the country. Since 1973, Bells has hosted the **Rip Curl Pro** (www.aspworldtour.com) every Easter – *the* glamour event on the world-championship ASP World Tour.

Nine kilometres southwest of Torquay is the turn-off to spectacular **Point Addis** (3km after the turn-off). It's a vast sweep of pristine 'clothing optional' beach that attracts surfers, hang-gliders and swimmers. At Point Addis there's a signposted **Koorie Cultural Walk**, a 1km circuit trail to the beach through the **Ironbark Basin** nature reserve.

Anglesea

Anglesea's **Main Beach** is the ideal spot to learn to surf, while sheltered **Point Roadknight Beach** is good for kiddies.

Activities

Go Ride A Wave   Surfing

(☎1300 132 441; www.gorideawave.com.au; 143b Great Ocean Rd; ⏰9am-5pm) Rents out kayaks and surfboards and runs two-hour surfing lessons (from $65).

 Information

Anglesea Visitor Information Centre
(Anglesea River Bank, Great Ocean Rd; ⏰9am-5pm) Get your information then cook up some sausages in the adjacent BBQ area.

ⓘ Getting There & Away

V/Line (p252) has services linking Anglesea with Geelong and the Great Ocean Road.

The Geelong bypass has reduced the time it takes to drive from Melbourne to Anglesea to around 75 minutes.

Lorne

Lorne has an incredible natural beauty; tall gum trees line its hilly streets and Loutit Bay gleams irresistibly. Lorne gets busy; in summer you'll be competing with day-trippers for restaurant seats and boutique bargains but, thronged with tourists or not, Lorne is a lovely place to hang out.

◉ Sights & Activities

Qdos Art Gallery   Gallery

(☎03-5289 1989; www.qdosarts.com; 35 Allenvale Rd; ⏰8.30am-6pm daily Dec & Jan, 9am-5.30pm Thu-Mon Feb-Nov) Qdos, tucked in the hills behind Lorne, always has something arty in its galleries, and sculptures dot its Aussie bush landscape. Its cafe fare is nothing but delicious, and you can stay the night in one of the luxury Zen treehouses ($225 per night, two-night minimum, no kids).

Erskine Falls   Waterfall

Head out of town to see this lovely waterfall. It's an easy walk to the viewing platform or 250 (often slippery) steps down to its base, from which you can explore further or head back on up.

How Many Apostles?

The Twelve Apostles are not 12 in number, and, from all records, never have been. From the viewing platform you can clearly count seven Apostles, though are there some obscure others over there? We consulted widely with Parks Victoria officers, tourist office staff and the cleaner at the lookout, but it's still not clear. Locals tend to say 'It depends where you look from', which, really, is true.

The Apostles are called 'stacks' in geologic lingo, and the rock formations were originally called the Sow and Piglets. Someone in the '60s (nobody can recall who) thought they might attract some tourists with a more venerable name, so they were renamed 'the Apostles'. Since apostles tend to come by the dozen, the number 12 was added sometime later.

So there aren't 12 stacks; in a boat or helicopter you might count 11. If you look carefully at how the waves lick around the pointy part of the cliff base, you can see a new Apostle being born.

The Wreck of the Loch Ard

The Victorian coastline between Cape Otway and Port Fairy was a notoriously treacherous stretch of water in the days of sailing ships, due to hidden reefs and frequent heavy fog. Over 40 years more than 80 vessels came to grief on this 120km stretch.

The most famous wreck was that of the iron-hulled clipper *Loch Ard,* which foundered off Mutton Bird Island at 4am on the final night of its long voyage from England in 1878. Of 37 crew and 19 passengers on board, only two survived. Eva Carmichael, a nonswimmer, clung to wreckage and was washed into a gorge, where apprentice officer Tom Pearce rescued her. Tom heroically climbed the sheer cliff and raised the alarm but no other survivors were found. Eva and Tom were both 19 years old, leading to speculation in the press about a romance, but nothing actually happened – they never saw each other again and Eva soon returned to Ireland (this time, perhaps not surprisingly) via steamship.

Sleeping

Great Ocean Road Backpackers
Hostel $

(☏ 03-5289 1070; 10 Erskine Ave; dm/d $35/90; ❄ 🛜) Tucked away in the bush among the cockatoos and koalas is this two-storey timber lodge with simple dorms and doubles. There's a pleasant deck and small kitchen.

Chapel
Cottages $$$

(☏ 03-5289 2622; thechapellorne@bigpond.com; 45 Richardson Blvd; d $200; ❄) Outstanding – this contemporary two-level bungalow has tasteful Asian furnishings, splashes of colour and bay windows (without curtains) that open into the forest. It's secluded and romantic.

Allenvale Cottages
Cottages $$$

(☏ 03-5289 1450; www.allenvale.com.au; 150 Allenvale Rd; d from $215) These four self-contained early-1900s timber cottages each sleep four (or more), and have been luxuriously restored. They're 2km northwest of Lorne, arrayed among shady trees and green lawns, complete with bridge, babbling brook and clucking chickens. Ideal for families.

Eating

Bottle of Milk
Burgers $

(www.thebottleofmilk.com; 52 Mountjoy Pde; burgers from $8.50; ⊙ 6.30am-9pm daily high season, 8am-3pm Mon-Fri, to 8pm Sat & Sun low season) Sit back on one of the old-school chairs at this cool version of a diner, and tuck into a classic burger stacked with fresh ingredients. Check out Pizza Pizza by the river (it's run by the same clever folk).

Mexican Republic
Mexican $

(☏ 03-5289 1686; 1a Grove Rd; large plates $12-14; ⊙ noon-9pm high season, call for low season hours) Mexican isn't only a Melbourne phenomenon; Lorne welcomed a brand new Mexican restaurant in 2012. *Tostaditas* come with pork shoulder or pumpkin; large plates offer marinated chicken burritos or black bean quesadillas. Wine here is served in a latte glass.

Information

Lorne Visitor Centre (☏ 1300 891 152; www.visitsurfcoast.com.au; 15 Mountjoy Pde; ⊙ 9am-5pm) Stacks of information, helpful staff and an accommodation booking service.

Apollo Bay

Apollo Bay is synonymous with music festivals, the Otways and some lovely beaches. Majestic rolling hills provide a postcard backdrop to the town, while broad white-sand beaches dominate the foreground. It's an ideal base for exploring magical Cape Otway and Otway National Park.

 Sights & Activities

Community Market — Market
(www.apollobay.com/market_place; ☼9am-1pm Sat) This market is held along the main strip and is the perfect spot for picking up local apples, locally made souvenirs and just-what-you've-always-wanted table lamps made from tree stumps.

Apollo Bay Sea Kayaking — Kayaking
(☎0405 495 909; www.apollobaysurfkayak.com.au; 2hr tours $65) Head out from Marengo beach to an Australian fur seal colony on a two-seated kayak. Not recommended for under 12-year-olds.

Sleeping

YHA Eco Beach — Hostel $
(☎03-5237 7899; 5 Pascoe St; dm $35-42, d $85-102, f $100-122; @ 🗢) 🍃 Even if you're not on a budget this three-million-dollar, architect-designed hostel is an outstanding place to stay. Its eco-credentials are too many to list here, but it's a wonderful piece of architecture with great lounge areas, kitchens, TV rooms, internet lounge and a rooftop terrace.

Nelson's Perch B&B — B&B $$
(☎03-5237 7176; www.nelsonsperch.com; 54 Nelson St; d $185; ❄@🗢) Nelson's looks fresher than some of the town's weary B&Bs, though it's not close to the bay. There are three smart rooms, each with a courtyard.

Eating

Apollo Bay Fishermen's Co-op — Seafood $
(Breakwater Rd; ☼11am-7pm) Sells fresh fish and seafood from the wharf as well as uber-fresh fish and chips.

Great Otway National Park, Great Ocean Road

GRANT DIXON/GETTY IMAGES ©

Detour:
Port Fairy

This seaside township at the mouth of the Moyne River was settled in 1835, and the first arrivals were whalers and sealers. Port Fairy still has a large fishing fleet and a relaxed, salty feel, with its old bluestone and sandstone buildings, whitewashed cottages, colourful fishing boats and tree-lined streets. The town is very much a luxury tourist destination and is home to art galleries, antique shops and boutiques.

The visitor centre has brochures and maps that show the popular **Shipwreck Walk** and **History Walk**. On **Battery Hill** there's a lookout point, and cannons and fortifications that were positioned here in the 1860s. Below there's a lovely one-hour walk around **Griffiths Island**, where the Moyne River empties into the sea.

Australia's premier folk-music festival, **Port Fairy Folk Festival** (www. portfairyfolkfestival.com; adult/child 13-17 $235/80; ☉Mar) is held on the Labour Day long weekend in early March. Book accommodation early.

Port Fairy Visitor Centre (☏03-5568 2682; www.visitportfairy-moyneshire.com.au; Bank St; ☉9am-5pm) can recharge your mobile phone's battery while providing spot-on information. Port Fairy is 20 minutes west of Warrnambool on the A1.

La Bimba   Modern Australian **$$$**
(☏03-5237 7411; 125 Great Ocean Rd; mains $36-42; ☉8am-3.30pm & 6-10pm) This upstairs Mod Oz restaurant is outstanding – definitely worth the splurge. It's a warm, relaxed smart-casual place with views, friendly service and a good wine list.

ℹ️ Information

Great Ocean Road Visitor Centre (☏1300 689 297; 100 Great Ocean Rd; ☉9am-5pm) Sells discount tickets and pins up accommodation vacancy sheets for those who arrive after hours.

Cape Otway

Cape Otway is the second-most southerly point of mainland Australia (after Wilsons Promontory) and one of the wettest parts of the state. This coastline is particularly beautiful, rugged and dangerous. More than 200 ships came to grief between Cape Otway and Port Fairy between the 1830s and 1930s, which led to its 'Shipwreck Coast' moniker. At the end of Lighthouse Rd is Australia's oldest lighthouse, **Cape Otway Lightstation** (☏03-5237 9240;

www.lightstation.com; Lighthouse Rd; adult/child/family $19/8/47; ☉9am-5pm), dating back to 1848. You can't see anything from the car park, and an entry fee is required to view the lighthouse. Inside you'll find a cafe, art gallery, roaming actors and haunted lightkeeper's house.

Port Campbell National Park

The road levels out after leaving the Otways and enters narrow, relatively flat scrubby escarpment lands that fall away to sheer, 70m cliffs along the coast between Princetown and Peterborough – a distinct change of scene. This is Port Campbell National Park, home to the Twelve Apostles – the most famous and photographed stretch of the Great Ocean Road.

The **Gibson Steps**, hacked by hand into the cliffs in the 19th century by local landowner Hugh Gibson (and more recently replaced by concrete steps), lead down to feral **Gibson Beach**, an essential stop. This beach, and others along this stretch of coast, is not suitable for swimming because of strong currents and undertows – you can walk along the beach, but be careful not to be stranded by high tides or nasty waves.

The lonely **Twelve Apostles** are rocky stacks that have been abandoned in the ocean by retreating headland. Today, only seven Apostles can be seen from the viewing platforms. The understated roadside **lookout** (Great Ocean Rd; ☺9am-5pm), 6km past Princetown, has public toilets and a cafe. Helicopters zoom around the Twelve Apostles, giving passengers an amazing view of the rocks. **12 Apostles Helicopters** (☎03-5598 8283; www.12apostleshelicopters.com.au) is just behind the car park at the lookout and offers a 10-minute tour covering the Twelve Apostles, Loch Ard Gorge, Sential Rock and Port Campbell for $145 per person (including a DVD).

Nearby **Loch Ard Gorge** is where the Shipwreck Coast's most famous and haunting tale, in which two young survivors of the wrecked iron clipper *Loch Ard* made it to shore, unfolded.

··

Port Campbell

This small, windswept town is poised on a dramatic, natural bay, eroded from the surrounding limestone cliffs, and almost perfectly rectangular in shape. It's a friendly place with some great bargain accommodation options, and makes an ideal spot for debriefing after the Twelve Apostles.

Sights & Activities

A 4.7km **Discovery Walk**, with signage, gives an introduction to the area's natural and historical features. It's just out of town on the way to Warrnambool.

 ## Sleeping & Eating

Port Campbell Guesthouse
Guesthouse **$**
(☎0407 696 559; www.portcampbellguesthouse.com.au; 54 Lord St; s/d $40/70 incl breakfast; ❄@) It's great to find a home away from home, and this property close to town has a cosy house with four bedrooms out back and a separate motel-style 'flashpackers' section up front. Clean and friendly.

12 Rocks Cafe Bar
Cafe **$$**
(19 Lord St; mains $20-30; ☺8.30am-11pm) Watch flotsam wash up on the beach from this busy place, which has the best beachfront views. Try a local Otways beer with a pasta or seafood main, or just duck in for a coffee.

ⓘ Information

Port Campbell Visitor Centre (☎1300 137 255; www.visit12apostles.com.au; 26 Morris St; ☺9am-5pm) Stacks of regional and accommodation information and interesting

Moyne River, Port Fairy
GLENN BEANLAND/GETTY IMAGES ©

Top Prom Short Walks

Lilly Pilly Gully Nature Walk An easy 5km (two-hour) walk through heathland and eucalypt forests, with lots of wildlife. Start at the car park or from Tidal River.

Mt Oberon Summit This moderate-to-hard 7km (2½-hour) walk is an ideal introduction to the Prom, with panoramic views from the summit. The free Mt Oberon shuttle bus can take you to the Telegraph Saddle car park and back.

Squeaky Beach Nature Walk Another easy 5km return stroll from Tidal River through coastal tea trees and banksias to a sensational white-sand beach.

shipwreck displays – the anchor from the *Loch Ard*, salvaged in 1978, is out the front.

ℹ Getting There & Away

V/Line (☎1800 800 007; www.vline.com.au; **Merri St**) train departs Southern Cross Station in Melbourne 9am Monday, Wednesday and Friday; change to a bus in Geelong for Port Campbell ($33, 6½ hours).

Port Campbell to Warrnambool

The Great Ocean Road continues west of Port Campbell passing more rock stacks. The next one is the **Arch**, offshore from Point Hesse.

Nearby is **London Bridge**...fallen down! Now sometimes called London Arch, it was once a double-arched rock platform linked to the mainland. Visitors could walk out across a narrow natural bridge to the huge rock formation. In January 1990 the bridge collapsed, leaving two terrified tourists marooned on the world's newest island – they were eventually rescued by helicopter. Nearby is the **Grotto**.

The **Bay of Islands** is 8km west of tiny **Peterborough**, where a short walk from the car park takes you to magnificent lookout points.

The Great Ocean Road ends near here where it meets the Princess Hwy, which continues through the traditional lands

of the Gunditjmara people into South Australia.

GIPPSLAND

It might not be as well known as the Great Ocean Road to the west, but Victoria's southeast coast easily boasts the state's best beaches, along with impossibly pretty lakeside villages and Victoria's finest coastal national parks, typified by the glorious Wilsons Promontory.

Wilsons Promontory National Park

'The Prom', as it's affectionately known, is one of the most popular national parks in Australia and our favourite coastal park. The bushland and coastal scenery here is out of this world and the hiking and camping opportunities are exceptional.

The southern-most part of mainland Australia, the Prom once formed a land bridge that allowed people to walk to Tasmania.

Tidal River, 30km from the park entry, is the hub, and home to the Parks Victoria office, a general store, cafe and accommodation. The wildlife around Tidal River is remarkably tame: kookaburras and rosellas lurk expectantly (resist the urge to feed them), and wombats nonchalantly waddle out of the undergrowth.

Although there's a staffed **entry station** (☉9am-sunset), where you receive a ticket, entry is free. There's no fuel available at Tidal River.

Activities

There are more than 80km of marked **walking trails** here, taking you through forests, marshes, valleys of tree ferns, low granite mountains and along beaches backed by sand dunes. Even nonwalkers can enjoy much of the park's beauty, with car park access off the Tidal River road leading to gorgeous beaches and lookouts.

Swimming is safe from the beautiful beaches at **Norman Bay** (Tidal River) and around the headland at **Squeaky Beach** – the ultra-fine quartz sand here really does sing beneath your feet!

Tours

Bunyip Tours   Bus Tour
(☎1300 286 947; www.bunyiptours.com; from $120; ☉Wed & Sun) One-day guided tour to the Prom from Melbourne, with several hours of bushwalking and the option of staying on another two days to explore by yourself.

Sleeping

TIDAL RIVER

Situated on Norman Bay, and a short walk to a stunning beach, Tidal River is justifiably popular. Book ahead through Parks Victoria for weekends and holidays. For the Christmas school-holiday period there's a ballot for sites (apply online by 31 July).

Accommodation includes **camp sites** (unpowered sites per car and three people $33, powered sites per vehicle and up to eight people $55); **huts** (4-/6-bed $80/121); **cabins** (d $207, extra adult $28); luxury **safari tents** (d $302, extra person $22); and the isolated **Lighthouse Keepers' Cottage** (8-bed cottage $90-100, 20-bed $120-134) at the southern tip of the Prom.

YANAKIE

Black Cockatoo Cottages   Cottages $$
(☎03-5687 1306; www.blackcockatoo.com; 60 Foley Rd; d $160, six-person house $180) You can take in glorious views of the national park without leaving your very comfortable bed in these stylish, black-timber cottages. There are three modern cottages and a three-bedroom house.

Eating

Tidal River General Store & Café   Cafe $
(mains $5-22; ☉9am-5pm Sun-Fri, to 6pm Sat) The store stocks grocery items and some camping equipment, but if you're hiking or staying a while it's cheaper to stock up in Foster. The attached cafe serves take-away food such as pies and sandwiches, as well as breakfast, light lunches and bistro-style meals on weekends and holidays.

Information

Parks Victoria (☎13 19 63; www.parkweb.vic. gov.au; ☉8.30am-4.30pm) The helpful visitor centre books all park accommodation, including permits for camping away from Tidal River.

❶ Getting There & Away

The Prom is best reached with your own wheels or on a tour.

Darwin, Uluru & the Red Centre

From Australia's youngest city, the lively Top End capital of Darwin, the Stuart Hwy tracks southeast to incredible Kakadu National Park. This park is a tropical wonderland full of Aboriginal rock-art galleries, crocodiles, waterfalls and raucous birdlife. The famous *Ghan* train carries you further south, passing through ancient, little-populated desert lands. In this vast and apparently empty country, locals' wits are as dry as dusty boots, and ancient spirituality rubs up against Western ways.

Darwin looks towards Asia and, at the same time, celebrates the region's Indigenous culture and amazing natural splendour. Kakadu offers an unsurpassed education in both. The Red Centre of Australia – the sand really is red – offers a different story. Here the harsh climate has shaped a bare beauty and deep spirituality that is lost on few who visit Uluru (Ayers Rock). The nearby formations of Kata Tjuta (the Olgas) are just as mesmerising.

Nitmiluk (Katherine Gorge) National Park (p284)

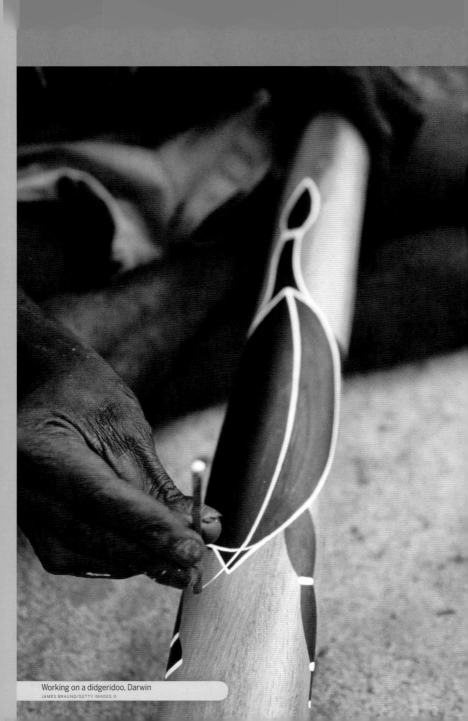

Working on a didgeridoo, Darwin

Darwin, Uluru & the Red Centre

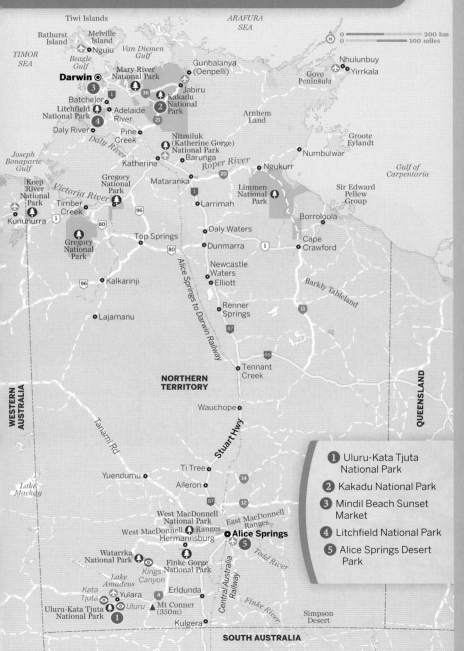

Tiwi Islands

ARAFURA SEA

Bathurst Island
Melville Island
Nguiu

TIMOR SEA

Beagle Gulf

Van Diemen Gulf

Gunbalanya (Oenpelli)

Nhulunbuy
Yirrkala

Gove Peninsula

Darwin

❸ Batchelor
Litchfield National Park ❹
Daly River

Mary River National Park ❷ 36
Jabiru
❷ Kakadu National Park 21
Adelaide River

Arnhem Land

Pine Creek
Nitmiluk (Katherine Gorge) National Park
Barunga

Groote Eylandt

Numbulwar

Joseph Bonaparte Gulf

Keep River National Park
Kununurra

Victoria River
Timber Creek

Gregory National Park
Katherine
Mataranka
Roper River
Ngukurr
20
Larrimah
Limmen National Park

Gulf of Carpentaria

Sir Edward Pellew Group

Borroloola

96
80

Gregory National Park
96 Kalkarinji

Top Springs
80
Daly Waters
Dunmarra
1
Cape Crawford

Barkly Tableland

Lajamanu

Newcastle Waters
Elliott

Renner Springs
87
11

Tanami Rd

NORTHERN TERRITORY

Tennant Creek
66

Wauchope

Alice Springs to Darwin Railway

Stuart Hwy

WESTERN AUSTRALIA

QUEENSLAND

Yuendumu

Ti Tree
Aileron
14
12
87

West MacDonnell National Park
West MacDonnell ❷ Ranges
Hermannsburg
East MacDonnell Ranges
Alice Springs ❺

Lake Mackay

Watarrka National Park ❷
Kings Canyon
Finke Gorge National Park

Lake Amadeus
Kata Tjuta
Yulara
Uluru-Kata Tjuta National Park ❷ Uluru ❶
❹ Mt Conner (350m)
Erldunda
Central Australia Railway
Todd River
Finke River

Kulgera

Simpson Desert

SOUTH AUSTRALIA

0   200 km
0   100 miles

❶ Uluru-Kata Tjuta National Park
❷ Kakadu National Park
❸ Mindil Beach Sunset Market
❹ Litchfield National Park
❺ Alice Springs Desert Park

Darwin, Uluru & the Red Centre Highlights

Uluru-Kata Tjuta National Park

Come and see the sun rise over an ancient and spectacular rock in the middle of the continent, just as it has done every day for more than 3000 million years. The astonishing Uluru (Ayers Rock; p292) has provided water to resourceful local Indigenous people for tens of thousands of years. Nearby, walk through the Valley of the Winds or check out Walpa Gorge at the amazing Kata Tjuta (the Olgas; p291). Kata Tjuta

1

Kakadu National Park

2

There's an incredibly broad range of things to see and do in Kakadu (p281): flora, fauna, waterfalls, Indigenous culture, lookouts, walks... The distinct shifts between the Wet and the Dry seasons alter the landscape dramatically – enough to warrant two visits! Early in the Dry season (May or June) is our favourite time in Kakadu – when the waterfalls are flowing and things are still green. Aboriginal rock art

MINT IMAGES/ART WOLFE/GETTY IMAGES ©

Mindil Beach Sunset Market

The essence of tropical boomtown Darwin, magical Mindil Beach Sunset Market (p275) happens behind the dunes north of the city at Mindil Beach. Every Thursday and Sunday from May to October, the market plays host to didgeridoo players, cavorting dance troupes, pan-Asian food stalls, souvenir stalls, masseurs, tarot readers, henna tattooists and more dreadlocks than Barbados.

HOLGER LEUE/GETTY IMAGES ©

MARTIN HARVEY/GETTY IMAGES ©

Litchfield National Park

Just 115km south of Darwin via the Stuart Hwy, impressive Litchfield National Park (p280) makes a brilliant, compact alternative to Kakadu if you're short on time. The park's waterfalls and swimming holes are as accessible as they are photogenic – and best of all you can take a swim! Crocodiles are less of an issue here than in Kakadu, and sealed roads make for a smooth-riding day trip.  Wangi Falls

Alice Springs Desert Park

Take a trip beyond the outskirts of Alice to discover this wonderful wildlife park (p288), where Australia's desert's creatures shed just enough shyness for you to get a good look at them. Make sure you catch the acrobatic birds-of-prey show, or come for breakfast or dinner to see either dawn-lit birdlife or spot-lit nocturnal beasties scratching through the sand. Black-breasted buzzard

Darwin, Uluru & the Red Centre's Best...

Indigenous Cultural Experiences

○ **Kakadu National Park** Amazing rock art, ranger talks and tours. (p281)

○ **Uluru-Kata Tjuta Cultural Centre** A window into local Aboriginal culture. (p290)

○ **Museum & Art Gallery of the Northern Territory** Don't miss these Indigenous art exhibits. (p271)

○ **Alice Springs** Explore 'the Alice' with a local Warlpiri guide. (p286)

Wildlife Encounters

○ **Kakadu National Park** Crocodiles, brolgas, lizards, snakes, sea eagles, butterflies, barramundi... (p281)

○ **Alice Springs Desert Park** Meet Australia's mostly nocturnal and shy desert wildlife. (p288)

○ **Territory Wildlife Park** A showcase of Top End animals and birds. (p281)

○ **Crocosaurus Cove** Crocs in downtown Darwin! (p270)

Outdoor Activities

○ **Hiking at Kata Tjuta** The Valley of the Winds is a timeless trip. (p291)

○ **Canoeing at Nitmiluk (Katherine Gorge) National Park** Paddle below Nitmiluk's massive walls. (p284)

○ **Swimming at Litchfield National Park** Rock pools and cascading waterfalls. (p280)

○ **Cycling in Darwin** A flat city with good bike tracks. (p270)

Need to Know

Shopping Opportunities

○ **Mindil Beach Sunset Market** Multicultural food, crafts and buskers. (p275)

○ **Darwin's Indigenous Galleries** Everything from dot paintings to craft from the Tiwi Islands. (p279)

○ **Alice Springs Galleries** Close to the wellspring of Central Desert art. (p289)

○ **Maruku Arts** Carvings and boomerangs at Uluru. (p290)

ADVANCE PLANNING

○ **One month before** In peak times (winter: June to August), book your accommodation at Yulara (near Uluru) at least a month before you visit.

○ **Two weeks before** Reserve a seat on the *Ghan* railway plus accommodation and a hire car in Darwin.

○ **One week before** Book a guided overnight tour of Kakadu National Park or a day-trip to Litchfield National Park from Darwin.

RESOURCES

○ **Tourism Top End** (www.tourismtopend.com.au) Darwin-based tourism body.

○ **Travel NT** (www.travelnt.com) Official tourism site.

○ **Parks & Wildlife Service** (www.parksandwildlife.nt.gov.au) Details on Northern Territory parks and reserves.

○ **Automobile Association of the Northern Territory** (AANT; www.aant.com.au) Driving information and emergency roadside assistance.

○ **Road Report** (www.ntlis.nt.gov.au/roadreport) NT road-conditions report.

GETTING AROUND

○ **Fly** To Alice Springs or Darwin from Adelaide or the big east-coast cities.

○ **Drive** Around Kakadu and Litchfield National Parks.

○ **Walk** Around the base of Uluru and through Kata Tjuta's gorges.

○ **Train** Between Darwin and Alice Springs (or further south to Adelaide) on the legendary *Ghan*.

BE FOREWARNED

○ **Crocodiles** Crocs move a long way inland – believe the warning signs.

○ **Box jellyfish** Yes, we know, it's hot and sticky, but swimming in the tropical sea between October and May is a bad idea.

○ **Yulara** Accommodation here gets mightily stretched in the peak season, so book well in advance.

Left: Didgeridoo player, Alice Springs; **Above:** Museum & Art Gallery of the Northern Territory (p271)

Darwin, Uluru & the Red Centre Itineraries

There's an ethereal feel to Australia's red centre and Top End: blue skies collide with the flat desert expanse around Uluru, while Darwin and the tropical north burst with birdlife, wild rivers and untamed wilderness.

3 DAYS

DARWIN TO KAKADU NATIONAL PARK

Top End Taster

Start your tour at the Top End capital of ❶ **Darwin** (p270), savouring the delights of Asia and other cuisines amidst the smoky aisles of Mindil Beach Sunset Market. You'll also see crocodile, emu, kangaroo and barramundi on the menus at many of the city's relaxed restaurants. Celebrate your culinary bravery over a beer on Mitchell St afterwards.

Head south down the Stuart Hwy and follow the signs to ❷ **Litchfield National Park** (p280), which boasts some of the best natural swimming holes (some beneath tumbling waterfalls) in the entire Top End. Nearby Batchelor has a slew of good accommodation options and a busy pub.

Next stop is ❸ **Kakadu National Park** (p281), via the croc-spotting boat tours at Adelaide River Crossing. You can catch your own barramundi at Kakadu, or join a bush-tucker Indigenous tour: learn about the hunt, the seasonal migrations of animals and vegetation changes. Watch bush food being prepared, join in and taste the results. Don't miss a hike up Nourlangie or Ubirr to check out ancient Aboriginal rock-art.

Top Left: Florence Falls, Litchfield National Park (p280); **Top Right:** Frill-necked lizard, Kakadu National Park
(TOP LEFT) DANITA DELIMONT/GETTY IMAGES ©; (TOP RIGHT) NATPHOTOS/GETTY IMAGES ©

5 DAYS

KAKADU NATIONAL PARK TO ULURU-KATA TJUTA NATIONAL PARK

Journey to the Red Centre

Begin this journey in the tropical Top End at ❶**Kakadu National Park** (p281) where, as the many rock-art galleries attest, Aboriginal people have lived for millennia. There are few places in Australia with such a rich wild-food bounty.

For a different national park perspective, canoe through the gorgeous gorges of ❷**Nitmiluk (Katherine Gorge) National Park** (p284) near Katherine, or jump on the famous *Ghan* train and head south to ❸**Alice Springs** (p286). Don't miss a visit to the excellent Alice Springs Desert Park to see how the local wildlife survives the desert heat.

The many colours and moods of ❹**Uluru** (p292) change with the hours of the day, and a full appreciation of this amazing region requires a couple of days. The excellent Uluru-Kata Tjuta Cultural Centre is a good place to start. Take some time to converse with the country by yourself – by walking around Uluru and the eerie rust-red domes of ❺**Kata Tjuta** (p291).

Discover Darwin, Uluru & the Red Centre

Wave Lagoon, Darwin Waterfront Precinct
DANITA DELIMONT/GETTY IMAGES ©

DARWIN

Australia's only tropical capital, Darwin gazes out confidently across the Timor Sea. It's closer to Bali than Bondi, and many from the southern states still see it as some frontier outpost or jumping-off point for Kakadu National Park.

But Darwin is a surprisingly affluent, cosmopolitan, youthful and multicultural city, thanks in part to an economic boom fuelled by the mining industry and tourism. It's a city on the move but there's a small-town feel and a laconic, relaxed vibe that fits easily with the tropical climate.

◎ Sights

Central Darwin

Crocosaurus Cove　Zoo
(www.croccove.com.au; 58 Mitchell St; adult/child $30/18; ⊘8am-6pm, last admission 5pm) If the tourists won't go out to see the crocs, then bring the crocs to the tourists. Right in the middle of Mitchell St, Crocosaurus Cove is as close as you'll ever want to get to these amazing creatures. Six of the largest crocs in captivity can be seen in state-of-the-art aquariums and pools. You can be lowered right into a pool with them in the transparent **Cage of Death** (one/two people $150/220).

Darwin Waterfront Precinct

The bold redevelopment of the old Darwin Waterfront Precinct (www.waterfront. nt.gov.au) has transformed the city. The multimillion-dollar redevelopment features a cruise-ship terminal, luxury hotels, boutique restaurants and shopping, the Sky Bridge, an elevated walkway and elevator at the south end of Smith St, and a Wave Lagoon.

The old Stokes Hill Wharf (p277) is well worth an afternoon promenade. At the end of the wharf an old warehouse houses a food centre that's ideal for an alfresco lunch, cool afternoon beer or a seafood dinner as the sun sets over the harbour.

Wave & Recreation Lagoons
Water Park

(www.waterfront.nt.gov.au; Wave Lagoon adult/child half-day $5/3.50, full day $8/5; ⊙Wave Lagoon 10am-6pm) The hugely popular **Wave Lagoon** is a hit with locals and travellers alike. There are 10 different wave patterns produced (20 minutes on with a 10-minute rest in between) and there are lifeguards, a kiosk and a strip of lawn to bask on. Adjacent is the **Recreation Lagoon** with a sandy beach, lifeguards and stinger-filtered seawater (although the nets and filters are not guaranteed to be 100% effective).

Fannie Bay

Museum & Art Gallery of the Northern Territory
Museum

(MAGNT; www.magnt.nt.gov.au; Conacher St, Fannie Bay; ⊙9am-5pm Mon-Fri, 10am-5pm Sat & Sun) **FREE** This superb museum and gallery boasts beautifully presented galleries of Top End–centric exhibits. The **Indigenous art collection** is a highlight, with carvings from the Tiwi Islands, bark paintings from Arnhem Land and dot paintings from the desert.

An entire room is devoted to **Cyclone Tracy**, in a display that graphically illustrates life before and after the disaster. You can stand in a darkened room and listen to the whirring sound of Tracy at full throttle – a sound you won't forget in a hurry.

Pride of place among the stuffed animals undoubtedly goes to **Sweetheart**: a 5m-long, 780kg saltwater crocodile. It became a Top End personality after attacking several fishing

dinghies on the Finniss River south of Darwin.

 Activities

Darwin Holiday Shop
Bicycle Rental

(☏08-89810277; www.darwinholidayshop.com.au; 88 The Esplanade, Shop 2, Mantra on the Esplanade; ⊙9am-5pm Mon-Fri, to 1pm Sat) Mountain bikes per half-/full day $20/25.

Oz Jet
Jetboating

(☏1300 135 595; www.ozjetboating.com/darwin; 30min rides adult/child $55/30) If a harbour cruise is too tame, jump on Oz Jet for a white-knuckle ride around the harbour that'll test how long it's been since you had lunch. Departs from Stokes Hill Wharf.

Tours

CITY TOURS

Darwin Walking & Bicycle Tours
Walking Tour, Cycling

(☏08-8981 0227; www.darwinwalkingtours.com.au) 🚶 Two-hour guided history walks around the city for $25 (children free), plus three-hour bike tours (adult/child $55/40) that take you out to Fannie Bay and East Point.

Tour Tub
Bus Tour

(☏08-8985 6322; www.tourtub.com.au; adult/child $45/20; ⊙9am-4pm Apr-Sep) This open-sided hop-on/hop-off minibus tours around Darwin's big-ticket sights throughout the day. Call for bookings, pick-up times and locations. Pay the driver onboard – cash only.

HARBOUR CRUISES

Anniki Pearl Lugger Cruises
Sailing

(☏0428 414 000; www.australianharbourcruises.com.au; tours adult/child $70/50) Three-hour sunset cruises on this historical pearl lugger depart at 4.45pm from Cullen Bay Marina and include sparkling wine and nibbles. You might recognise the ship from the film *Australia*.

Sunset Sail
Sailing

(☏0408 795 567; www.sailnt.com.au; tours adult/child $70/45) This three-hour

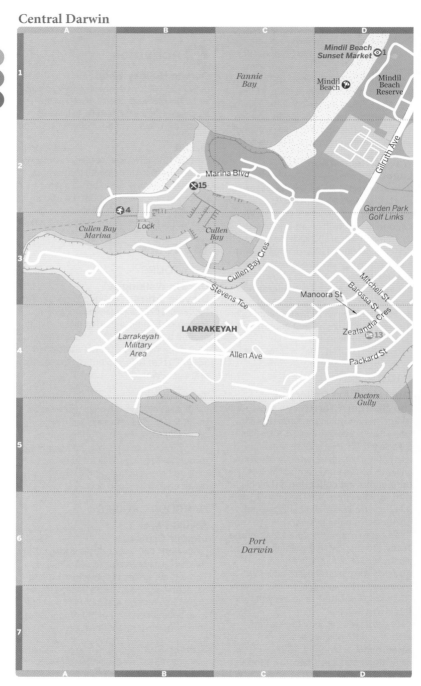

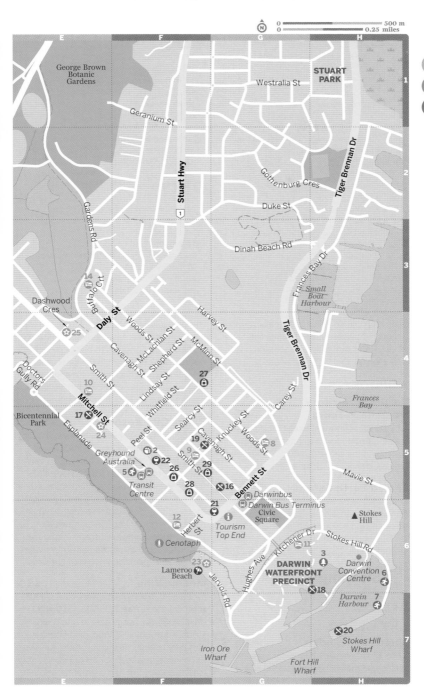

George Brown
Botanic
Gardens

STUART
PARK

Westralia St

Geranium St

Stuart Hwy

Gothenburg Cres

Tiger Brennan Dr

Duke St

Dinah Beach Rd

Frances Bay Dr

Small
Boat
Harbour

Gardens Rd

Buffalo Crt

14

Dashwood
Cres

25

Daly St

Woods St

McLachlan St

Cavenagh St

Shepherd St

McMinn St

Harvey St

Tiger Brennan Dr

27

Smith St

Mitchell St

10

17

Lindsay St

Whitfield St

Searcy St

Knuckey St

Woods St

Carey St

Frances
Bay

Doctors
Gully Rd

Bicentennial
Park

Esplanade

24

Peel St

Cavenagh St

19

8

Greyhound
Australia

2

9

Smith St

29

22

Mavie St

5

26

28

16

Bennett St

Transit
Centre

21

Darwinbus

Darwin Bus Terminus
Civic
Square

Stokes
Hill

12

Herbert St

Tourism
Top End

11

Stokes Hill Rd

Cenotaph

23

Kitchener Dr

DARWIN
WATERFRONT
PRECINCT

3

Darwin
Convention
Centre

6

Lameroo
Beach

Hughes Ave

Jervois Rd

18

Darwin
Harbour

7

20

Stokes Hill
Wharf

Iron Ore
Wharf

Fort Hill
Wharf

0   500 m
0   0.25 miles

273

Central Darwin

afternoon cruise aboard the catamaran *Daymirri 2* departs from Stokes Hill Wharf. Refreshments are included but BYO alcohol.

TERRITORY TRIPS

Northern Territory Indigenous Tours *Cultural Tour*
(☏ 1300 921 188; www.ntitours.com.au) Upmarket Indigenous tours to Litchfield National Park stopping off at Territory Wildlife Park (adult/child $249/124).

Sacred Earth Safaris *Outdoors*
(☏ 08-8981 8420; www.sacredearthsafaris.com.au) Multiday, small-group 4WD camping tours around Kakadu, Katherine and the Kimberley. Two-day Kakadu tour starts at $850; the five-day Top End tour is $2250.

 Sleeping

City Centre

Dingo Moon Lodge *Hostel* $
(☏ 08-8941 3444; www.dingomoonlodge.com; 88 Mitchell St; dm $31-36, d & tw $100, all incl breakfast; ❄@🛜🏊) Howl at the moon at the Dingo, a great addition to the Darwin hostel scene. It's a two-building affair with 65 beds – big enough to be sociable but not rowdy. A highlight is the pool, sparkling underneath a massive frangipani tree, and a great outdoor kitchen. No TV room – have a conversation instead.

Palms City Resort *Resort* $$
(☏ 1800 829 211, 08-8982 9200; www.citypalms.com; 64 The Esplanade; motel d $195, villas d $285; P❄🛜🏊) True to name, this centrally located resort is fringed by palm-filled gardens. If you covet a microwave and have space cravings, the superior motel rooms are worth a bit extra, while the Asian-influenced, hexagonal villas with outdoor spas are utterly indulgent. Butterflies and dragonflies drift between bougainvilleas in the knockout gardens.

Medina Vibe *Hotel* $$$
(☏ 08-8941 0755; www.medina.com.au; 7 Kitchener Dr; d/studio from $215/235, apt from $335; P❄@🛜🏊) Two hotels in one building: standard doubles at Vibe, and studios and apartments next door at the Medina. Either way, you're in for an upmarket stay with friendly staff and a great location in

Don't Miss
Mindil Beach Sunset Market

As the sun heads towards the horizon on Thursday and Sunday, half of Darwin descends on Mindil Beach, with tables, chairs, rugs, grog and kids in tow. Food is the main attraction – Thai, Sri Lankan, Indian, Chinese and Malaysian to Brazilian, Greek, Portuguese and more – all at around $5 to $10 a serve. Don't miss a flaming satay stick from Bobby's brazier. Top it off with fresh fruit salad, decadent cakes or luscious crepes. But that's only half the fun – arts and crafts stalls bulge with handmade jewellery, fabulous rainbow tie-died clothes, Aboriginal artefacts, and wares from Indonesia and Thailand. Peruse and promenade, stop for a pummelling massage or to listen to rhythmic live music. Mindil Beach is about 2km from the city centre; an easy walk or hop on buses 4 or 6 which go past the market area.

NEED TO KNOW
www.mindil.com.au; off Gilruth Ave; ⊙5-10pm Thu, 4-9pm Sun May-Oct

the Darwin Waterfront Precinct. The Wave Lagoon is right next door if the shady swimming pool is too placid for you.

Darwin Central Hotel   Hotel $$$
(☑08-8944 9000, 1300 364 263; www.darwin central.com.au; 21 Knuckey St; d from $180; P✳@⧈⧈; ☐4, 5, 8, 10) Right in the centre of town, this plush independent oozes contemporary style and impecca-ble facilities, including an award-winning restaurant. There are a range of stylish

rooms with excellent accessibility for disabled travellers.

Argus   Apartments $$$
(☑08-8925 5000; www.argusdarwin.com. au; 6 Cardona Ct; 1-/2-/3-bedroom apt from $280/360/590; P✳@⧈) In a corner of town awash with apartment towers, this quality option stands out. Apartments are *very* spacious, with lovely bathrooms, gen-erous expanses of cool floor tiles, simple balcony living/dining spaces and snazzy kitchens with all the requisite appliances.

Below: Nightcliff Market (p278); **Right:** Stokes Hill Wharf

(RIGHT) ANDREW WATSON/GETTY IMAGES ©; (BELOW) JAMES BRAUND/GETTY IMAGES ©

private entrances. Breakfast happens in the tropical garden.

City Fringe & Suburbs

Vitina Studio Motel Motel **$$**
(☎ 08-8981 1544; www.vitinastudiomotel.com.
au; 38 Gardens Rd; d $149, ste $199; P ❄ @
🛜 ≋) Vitina is a convenient option
providing bright, stylish accommodation
in contemporary motel rooms as well as
larger studios with kitchenettes. It's right
on the city fringe convenient to the Gar-
dens Park golf course, Botanic Gardens
and Mindil Beach. Ask about discounts.

Steeles at Larrakeyah B&B **$$**
(Darwin City B&B; ☎ 08-8941 3636; www.
darwinbnb.com.au; 4 Zealandia Cres, Larrakeyah;
d from $175, 1-/2-bedroom apt $250/270; ❄ ≋)
With a quiet residential location midway
between the city centre, Cullen Bay and
Mindil Beach, the three rooms in this
pleasant Spanish Mission–style home are
equipped with fridges, flat-screen TVs and

Feathers Sanctuary Boutique Hotel **$$$**
(☎ 08-8985 2144; www.featherssanctuary.com;
49a Freshwater Rd, Jingili; d incl breakfast $330;
❄ ≋) A sublime retreat for twitchers and
nature lovers, Feathers has beautifully de-
signed 'Bali-meets-bush' timber-and-iron
cottages with semi-open-air bathrooms
and luxurious interiors. The lush gardens
have a private aviary breeding some rare
birds, and a waterhole – more tropical
birds than you're ever likely to see in one
place again!

Eating

City Centre

Four Birds Cafe **$**
(32 Smith St Mall, Shop 2, Star Village; items
$4-8; ⏰ breakfast & lunch Mon-Fri, plus Sat

Jun-Aug) Nooked into the arcade on the site of the old Star Cinema (a '74 cyclone victim), this hole-in-the-wall does simple things very well: bagels, toasted sandwiches, muffins, paninis and coffee (we reckon it's the best in Darwin). Book-reading office types and travellers sit on stools scattered under a burgeoning frangipani tree.

Stokes Hill Wharf   Seafood, Fast Food $

(www.darwinhub.com/stokes-hill-wharf; Stokes Hill Wharf; mains $8-16; ⊙lunch & dinner) Squatting on the end of Stokes Hill Wharf is a hectic food centre with half-a-dozen food counters and outdoor tables lined up along the pier. It's a pumping place for some fish and chips, oysters, a stir-fry, a laksa or just a cold sunset beer.

Hanuman   Indian, Thai $$

(☑08-8941 3500; www.hanuman.com.au; 28 Mitchell St; mains $16-38; ⊙lunch Mon-Fri, dinner daily; ☑) Ask most locals about

fine dining in Darwin and they'll usually mention Hanuman. Sophisticated but not stuffy, enticing aromas of innovative Indian and Thai Nonya dishes waft from the kitchen to the stylish open dining room and deck. The signature dish is oysters bathed in lemon grass, chilli and coriander, but the menu is broad, with exotic vegetarian choices and banquets also available.

Moorish Café   Middle Eastern $$

(☑08-8991 0010; www.moorishcafe.com.au; 37 Knuckey St; tapas $4-12, mains $20-40; ⊙lunch & dinner Mon-Sat) Seductive aromas emanate from this divine terracotta-tiled cafe fusing North African, Mediterranean and Middle Eastern delights. The lunchtime crowd arrives for tantalising tapas and lunch specials, but it's an atmospheric place for dinner too – order a tagine of NT prawns, apple cider, local jewfish, coconut and lime, or the four-course banquet ($38 per person with a minimum of six diners; booking essential).

277

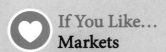

If You Like...
Markets

If you like Darwin's magical Mindil Beach Sunset Market, check out these other excellent city markets:

1 **PARAP VILLAGE MARKET**
(www.parapvillage.com.au; Parap Shopping Village, Parap Rd, Parap; ⊙8am-2pm Sat) This compact, crowded food-focused market is a local favourite, with the full gamut of Southeast Asian cuisine, as well as plenty of ingredients to cook up your own tropical storm.

2 **HAPPY YESS MARKET**
(http://happyyess.tumblr.com; 56 Woods St; ⊙2-6pm 1st Sun each month) Associated with the Darwin Visual Arts Association, this popular market is a great way to laze away a Sunday afternoon. The stalls are filled with secondhand treasures, tasty treats and whimsical stalls.

3 **RAPID CREEK MARKET**
(www.rapidcreekshoppingcentre.com.au; 48 Trower Rd, Rapid Creek; ⊙6.30am-1.30pm Sun) Darwin's oldest market is another Asian marketplace, with a tremendous range of tropical fruit and vegetables mingled with a heady mixture of spices and swirling satay smoke.

4 **NIGHTCLIFF MARKET**
(www.nightcliffmarkets.com; Pavonia Way, Nightcliff; ⊙8am-2pm Sun) Another popular community market, north of the city in the Nightcliff Shopping Centre, where you will find lots of secondhand goods and designer clothing.

Il Lido Italian $$$
(☎08-8941 0900; www.illidodarwin.com.au; Wharf One, 3/19 Kitchener Dr, Waterfront Precinct; tapas $8-18, pizzas $17-27, mains $28-44) Taking pride of place in the Waterfront Precinct is this modern Italian restaurant developed by the folks that introduced Hanuman restaurant to Darwin two decades ago. Delightful breakfasts and a stunning balcony for sunset drinks and tapas.

City Fringe & Suburbs

Saffrron Indian $$
(☎08-8981 2383; www.saffrron.com; 34 Parap Rd, Shop 14, Parap; mains $14-26; ⊙lunch Tue-Fri, dinner Tue-Sun, brunch Sun;) Saffrron is Darwin's best Indian restaurant, a contemporary but intimate dining experience. The menu spans the subcontinent, from rich butter chicken masala to barramundi *mooli*. There are plenty of vegetarian choices, traditional Indian sweets, and takeaways available.

Buzz Café Modern Australian $$
(☎08-8941 1141; www.darwinhub.com/buzz-cafe; 48 Marina Blv, Cullen Bay; mains $18-40; ⊙lunch & dinner daily, breakfast Sun) This chic bar-restaurant furnished in Indonesian teak and Mt Bromo lava has a super multilevel deck overlooking the marina and makes a seductively sunny spot for a lazy lunch and a few drinks. Meals are Mod Oz, with some zingy salads and dishes to share. Aim for a deck table cantilevering out over the water.

🍷 Drinking

Tap on Mitchell Bar
(www.thetap.com.au; 51 Mitchell St) One of the busiest of the Mitchell St terrace bars, the Tap is always buzzing and there are inexpensive meals (nachos, burgers, calamari) to complement a great range of beer and wine.

Darwin Ski Club Sports Club
(www.darwinskiclub.com.au; Conacher St, Fannie Bay) Leave Mitchell St behind and head for a sublime sunset at this laid-back (and refreshingly run-down) water-ski club on Vesteys Beach. The view through the palm trees from the beer garden is a winner, and there are often live bands.

Deck Bar Bar
(www.thedeckbar.com.au; 22 Mitchell St) At the nonpartying parliamentary end of Mitchell St, the Deck Bar still manages to get lively with happy hours, pub trivia and regular live music. Blurring the line

between indoors and outdoors brilliantly, the namesake deck is perfect for people-watching.

Entertainment

LIVE MUSIC

Nirvana   Jazz, Blues

(📞08-8981 2025; www.nirvanarestaurantdarwin. com; 6 Dashwood Cres) Behind an imposing dungeon-like doorway, this cosy restaurant-bar has live jazz/blues every Thursday, Friday and Saturday night and an open-mic jam session every Tuesday. And the Thai/Indian/Malaysian food here is magic.

CLUBS

Discovery & Lost Arc   Nightclub

(www.discoverydarwin.com.au; 89 Mitchell St; ⏲9pm-4am Fri & Sat) Discovery is Darwin's biggest, tackiest nightclub and dance venue with three levels playing techno, hip hop and R&B. The Lost Arc is the neon-lit chill-out bar (undergoing renovations at the time of writing) opening on to Mitchell St, which starts to thaw after about 10pm.

CINEMAS

Deckchair Cinema   Cinema

(📞08-8981 0700; www.deckchaircinema.com; Jervois Rd, Waterfront Precinct; tickets adult/child $15/7; ⏲box office from 6.30pm Apr-Nov) During the Dry, the Darwin Film Society runs this fabulous outdoor cinema below the southern end of the Esplanade. Watch a movie under the stars while reclining in a deckchair. There's a licensed bar serving food or you can bring a picnic (no BYO alcohol). There are usually double features on Friday and Saturday nights (adult/child $22/10).

 Shopping

ARTS & CRAFTS

Aboriginal Fine Arts Gallery   Gallery

(www.aaia.com.au; 1st fl, cnr Mitchell & Knuckey Sts; ⏲9am-5pm) Displays and sells art from Arnhem Land and the Central Desert region.

Maningrida Arts & Culture   Gallery

(www.maningrida.com; 32 Mitchell St, Shop 1; ⏲9am-5pm Mon-Fri, 11.30am-4.30pm Sat) Features fibre sculptures, weavings and paintings from the Kunibidji community at Maningrida on the banks of the Liverpool River, Arnhem Land. Fully Aboriginal-owned.

Territory Colours   Gallery

(www.territorycolours.com; 46 Smith St Mall; ⏲10am-5pm Mon-Fri, to 3pm Sat & Sun) Contemporary paintings and crafts, including glass, porcelain and wood from local artists; features the work of contemporary Indigenous artist Harold Thomas.

ℹ Information

Medical Services

Royal Darwin Hospital (📞08-8920 6011; www. health.nt.gov.au; Rocklands Dr, Tiwi; ⏲24hr) Accident and emergency.

Travellers Medical & Vaccination Centre (📞08-8901 3100; www.traveldoctor.com.au; 43 Cavenagh St, 1st fl; ⏲8.30am-noon & 1.30-5pm Mon-Fri) GPs by appointment.

Tourist Information

Tourism Top End (📞1300 138 886, 08-8980 6000; www.tourismtopend.com.au; cnr Smith & Bennett Sts, Darwin, NT; ⏲8.30am-5pm Mon-Fri, 9am-3pm Sat & Sun) Hundreds of brochures; books tours and accommodation.

ℹ Getting There & Away

Air

Apart from the following major carriers arriving at Darwin International Airport (p281), smaller routes are flown by local operators; ask a travel agent.

Jetstar (www.jetstar.com) Direct flights to the eastern coast capitals and major hubs, as well as several South-East Asian cities.

Qantas (www.qantas.com.au) Direct flights to Perth, Adelaide, Canberra, Sydney, Brisbane, Alice Springs and Cairns.

Virgin Australia (www.virginaustralia.com) Direct flights between Darwin and Brisbane, Broome, Melbourne, Sydney and Perth.

Don't Miss
Litchfield National Park

It may not be as well known as Kakadu, but many Territory locals rate Litchfield even higher. In fact, there's a local saying that goes: 'Litchfield-do, Kaka-don't'. We don't entirely agree – we think Kaka-do-too – but this is certainly one of the best places in the Top End for **bushwalking**, **camping** and especially **swimming**, with waterfalls plunging into gorgeous, safe swimming holes.

The 1500-sq-km national park encloses much of the spectacular Tabletop Range, a wide sandstone plateau mostly surrounded by cliffs. The **waterfalls** that pour off the edge of this plateau are a highlight of the park, feeding crystal-clear cascades and croc-free plunge pools.

The two routes to Litchfield (115km south of Darwin) from the Stuart Hwy join up and loop through the park.

About 17km after entering the park from Batchelor, you come to what looks like tombstones. But only the very tip of these **magnetic termite mounds** is used to bury the dead; at the bottom are the king and queen, with workers in between.

Another 6km further along is the turn-off to **Buley Rockhole** (2km), where water cascades through a series of rock pools big enough to lodge your body in. This turn-off also takes you to **Florence Falls** (5km), accessed by a 15-minute, 135-step descent to a deep, beautiful pool surrounded by monsoon forest.

About 18km beyond the Florence Falls turn-off is the turn-off to the spectacular **Tolmer Falls** (pictured above), which is for looking only. A 1.6km loop track (45 minutes) offers beautiful views of the valley.

It's a further 7km along the main road to the turn-off for Litchfield's big-ticket attraction, **Wangi Falls** (pronounced *'wong*-guy'), 1.6km up a side road. The falls flow year-round, spilling either side of a huge orange-rock outcrop and filling an enormous swimming hole bordered by rainforest.

Bus

Greyhound Australia (www.greyhound.com.
au) operates long-distance bus services from
the **Transit Centre** (69 Mitchell St). There's at
least one service per day up/down the Stuart
Hwy, stopping at Pine Creek ($75, three hours),
Katherine ($94, 4½ hours), Mataranka ($132,
seven hours), Tennant Creek ($282, 14½ hours)
and Alice Springs ($391, 22 hours).

For Kakadu, there's a daily return service from
Darwin to Cooinda ($87, 4½ hours) via Jabiru
($62, 3½ hours).

Car & Campervan

For driving around Darwin, conventional vehicles
are cheap enough, but most companies offer only
100km free, which won't get you very far. Rates
start at around $40 per day for a small car with
100km per day.

There are also plenty of 4WD vehicles available
in Darwin, but you usually have to book ahead and
fees/deposits are higher than for 2WD vehicles.
Advance Car Rentals (www.advancecar.com.au;
86 Mitchell St) Local operator with some good
deals (ask about unlimited kilometres).

Train

The legendary *Ghan* train, operated by **Great
Southern Rail** (www.gsr.com.au), runs weekly
(twice weekly May to July) between Adelaide and
Darwin via Alice Springs.

ⓘ Getting Around

To/From the Airport

Darwin International Airport (www.darwin
airport.com.au; Henry Wrigley Dr, Marrara) is
12km north of the city centre, and handles both
international and domestic flights. **Darwin Airport
Shuttle** (☏1800 358 945, 08-8981 5066; www.
darwinairportshuttle.com.au) will pick up or drop
off almost anywhere in the centre for $15. When
leaving Darwin book a day before departure. A taxi
fare into the centre is about $30.

Public Transport

Darwinbus (www.nt.gov.au/transport) runs a
comprehensive bus network that departs from the
Darwin Bus Terminus (Harry Chan Ave), opposite
Brown's Mart.

A $2 adult ticket gives unlimited travel on
the bus network for three hours (validate your
ticket when you first get on). Daily ($5) and
weekly ($15) travel cards are also available from
bus interchanges, newsagencies and the visitor
information centre.

Alternatively, the privately run Tour Tub (p271)
is a hop-on, hop-off minibus touring Darwin's
sights throughout the day.

Scooter

Darwin Scooter Hire (www.esummer.com.
au; 9 Daly St) Rents out mountain bikes/50cc
scooters/motorbikes for $20/60/180 per day.

Taxi

Call **Darwin Radio Taxis** (☏13 10 08;
www.131008.com).

AROUND DARWIN

Territory Wildlife Park   Zoo

(www.territorywildlifepark.com.au; 960 Cox
Peninsula Rd; adult/child/family $26/13/45.50;
⊙8.30am-6pm, last admission 4pm) This excellent park showcases the best of Aussie
wildlife. Highlights include the Flight Deck,
where birds of prey display their dexter-
ity (free-flying demonstrations at 11am
and 2.30pm daily); the nocturnal house,
where you can observe nocturnal fauna
such as bilbies and bats; 11 different habitat aviaries; and a huge walk-through avi-
ary, representing a monsoon rainforest.
Pride of place must go to the aquarium,
where a clear walk-through tunnel puts
you among giant barramundi, stingrays,
sawfish and saratogas, while a separate
tank holds a 3.8m saltwater crocodile.

KAKADU NATIONAL PARK

Kakadu is a whole lot more than a
national park. It's also a vibrant, living
acknowledgment of the elemental link
between the Aboriginal custodians and
the country they have nurtured, endured
and respected for thousands of generations. Encompassing almost 20,000
sq km (about 200km north–south
and 100km east–west), it holds in its
boundaries a spectacular ecosystem and
a mind-blowing concentration of ancient
rock art.

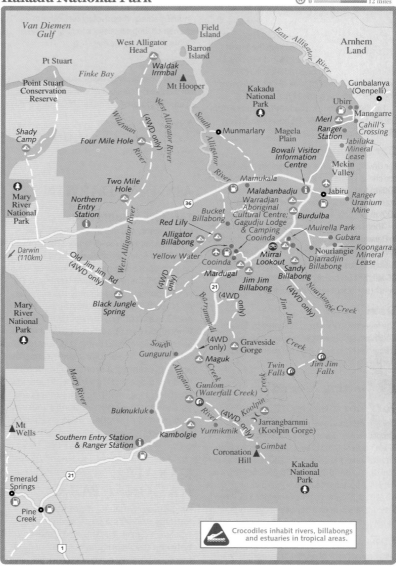

Crocodiles inhabit rivers, billabongs and estuaries in tropical areas.

In just a few days you can cruise on billabongs bursting with **wildlife**, examine 25,000-year-old rock paintings with the help of an Indigenous guide, swim in pools at the foot of tumbling **waterfalls** and hike through ancient sandstone escarpment country.

Kakadu has more than 60 species of mammals, more than 280 bird species, 120 recorded species of reptile, 25 species of frog, 55 freshwater fish species and at least 10,000 different kinds of insect.

Tours

Kakadu Animal Tracks Cultural Tour
(✆08-8979 0145; www.animaltracks.com.au; tours adult/child $205/135) 🏍 Based at Cooinda, this outfit runs seven-hour tours with an Indigenous guide combining a wildlife safari and Aboriginal cultural tour. You'll see thousands of birds, get to hunt, gather, prepare and consume bush tucker and crunch on some green ants.

Top End Explorer Tours Outdoors
(✆1300 556 609, 08-8979 3615; www.kakadutours.net.au; tours adult/child $195/150) Organises 4WD tours to Jim Jim Falls and Twin Falls from Jabiru and Cooinda.

Kakadu Air Scenic Flights
(✆1800 089 113; www.kakaduair.com.au) Offers 30-minute/one-hour fixed-wing flights for $140/230 per adult. Helicopter tours, though more expensive, give a more dynamic aerial perspective. They cost from $210 (20 minutes) to $460 (45 minutes) per person.

Yellow Water Cruises Cruise
(✆1800 500 401; www.gagudju-dreaming.com) Cruise the South Alligator River and Yellow Water Billabong spotting wildlife. Purchase tickets from Gagudju Lodge, Cooinda, where a shuttle bus will deliver you to the departure point. Two-hour cruises ($99/70 per adult/child) depart at 6.45am, 9am and 4.30pm; 1½-hour cruises ($68/47) leave at 11.30am, 1.15pm and 2.45pm.

Ubirr & Around

It'll take a lot more than the busloads of visitors here to disturb Ubirr's inherent majesty and grace. Layers of **rock-art paintings**, in various styles and from various centuries, command a mesmerising stillness.

The magnificent **Nardab Lookout** is a 250m scramble from the main gallery. Surveying the billiard-table-green

floodplain and watching the sun set and the moon rise, like they're on an invisible set of scales, is glorious, to say the least. **Ubirr** (⏱8.30am-sunset Apr-Nov, from 2pm Dec-Mar) is 39km north of the Arnhem Hwy via a sealed road.

Jabiru

It may seem surprising to find a town of Jabiru's size and structure in the midst of a wilderness national park, but it exists solely because of the nearby Ranger uranium mine.

Sleeping & Eating

Lakeview Park Cabins $$
(✆08-8979 3144; www.lakeviewkakadu.com.au; 27 Lakeside Dr; en suite powered sites $35, bungalows/d/cabins $120/130/235; ❄) Although there are no lake views as such, this Aboriginal-owned park is one of Kakadu's best with a range of tropical-design bungalows set in lush gardens. The doubles share a communal kitchen, bathroom and lounge, and also come equipped with their own TV and fridge, while the 'bush bungalows' are stylish elevated safari designs (no air-con) with private external bathroom that sleep up to four.

Gagudju Crocodile Holiday Inn Hotel $$$
(✆08-8979 9000; www.gagudju-dreaming.com; 1 Flinders St; d from $285; ❄ 🖥 ☲) Known locally as 'the Croc', this hotel is designed in the shape of a crocodile, which, of course, is only obvious when viewed from the air or Google Earth. The rooms are clean and comfortable if a little pedestrian for the price (which drops considerably during the Wet). Try for one on the ground floor opening out to the central pool. The **Escarpment Restaurant** (mains $24-38; ⏱breakfast, lunch & dinner) here is the best in Jabiru.

Nourlangie

The sight of this looming outlier of the Arnhem Land escarpment makes it easy to understand its ancient importance to

Detour:
Nitmiluk (Katherine Gorge) National Park

Spectacular **Katherine Gorge** forms the backbone of the 2920-sq-km **Nitmiluk (Katherine Gorge) National Park** (www.nt.gov.au/nreta/parks/find/nitmiluk.html), about 30km from Katherine. A series of 13 deep sandstone **gorges** have been carved out by the **Katherine River** on its journey from Arnhem Land to the Timor Sea. Plan to spend at least a full day canoeing or cruising on the river and bushwalking. Nothing beats exploring the gorges in your own boat, and lots of travellers canoe at least as far as the first or second gorge.

From April to November, **Nitmiluk Tours** (☏ 08-8972 1253, 1300 146 743; www.nitmiluktours.com.au) hires out single/double canoes for a half-day ($48/71, departing 8am and 1pm) or full day ($62/90, departing 8am), including the use of a splash-proof drum for cameras and other gear (it's not fully waterproof), a map and a life jacket.

An easy way to see far into the gorge is on a cruise, also with Nitmiluk Tours (breakfast cruise adult/child $88/58, sunset cruise $142/126). The **two-hour cruise** (adult/child $73/41) goes to the second gorge and visits a rock-art gallery (including 800m walk). The **four-hour cruise** (adult/child $91/46) goes to the third gorge and includes refreshments and a chance to swim.

Nitmiluk Tours also offers a variety of scenic flights ranging from an eight-minute buzz over the first gorge (per person $85) to an 18-minute flight over all 13 gorges ($232).

The **Nitmiluk Centre** (☏ 1300 146 743, 08-8972 1253; www.nitmiluktours.com.au; ⊙7am-6pm) has excellent displays and information on the park's geology, wildlife, the traditional owners (the Jawoyn) and European history.

It's 30km by sealed road from Katherine to the Nitmiluk Centre, and a few hundred metres further to the car park, where the gorge begins and the cruises start.

Daily transfers between Katherine and the gorge are run by **Nitmiluk Tours** (☏ 1300 146 743, 08-8972 1253; www.nitmiluktours.com.au; 27 Katherine Tce, Shop 2, Katherine; adult/child return $27/19), departing from the Nitmiluk Town Booking Office and also picking up at local accommodation places on request.

Aboriginal people. Its long red-sandstone bulk, striped in places with orange, white and black, slopes up from surrounding woodland to fall away at one end in stepped cliffs. Below is Kakadu's best-known collection of **rock art**.

The 2km looped walking track (open 8am to sunset) takes you first to the **Anbangbang Shelter**, used for 20,000 years as a refuge and canvas. Next is the **Anbangbang Gallery**, featuring Dreaming characters repainted in the 1960s. Look for the virile Nabulwinjbulwinj, a dangerous spirit who likes to eat females after banging them on the head with a yam. From here it's a short walk to **Gunwarddehwarde Lookout**, with views of the Arnhem Land escarpment.

Jim Jim Falls & Twin Falls

Remote and spectacular, these two falls epitomise the rugged Top End. **Jim Jim Falls**, a sheer 215m drop, is awesome after rain (when it can only be seen from the air), but its waters shrink to a trickle by about June. Twin Falls flows year-round (no swimming), but half the fun is getting there, involving a little **boat trip** (adult/child $2.50/free, running 7.30am to 5pm) and an over-the-water boardwalk.

Cooinda & Yellow Water

Cooinda is best known for the cruises (p283) on the wetland area known as Yellow Water, and has developed into a slick resort. About 1km from the resort, the **Warradjan Aboriginal Cultural Centre** (www.kakadu-attractions.com/warradjan; Yellow Water Area; ⏰9am-5pm) depicts Creation stories and has a great permanent exhibition that includes clap sticks, sugar-bag holders and rock-art samples.

Gagudju Lodge & Camping Cooinda (☏1800 500 401, 08-8979 0145; www.gagudjulodgecooinda.com.au; unpowered/powered sites $36/46, dm $57, budget/lodge r from $155/295; ✳@☀) is the most popular accommodation resort in the park. The budget air-con units share camping ground facilities and are compact and comfy enough (but for this money should be more than glorified sheds). The lodge rooms are spacious and more comfortable, sleeping up to four people. There's also a grocery shop, tour desk, fuel pump and the excellent open-air **Barra Bar & Bistro** (mains $15-36; ⏰breakfast, lunch & dinner) here too.

❶ Information

Admission to the park is via a 14-day Park Pass (adult/child $25/free): pick one up (along with the excellent *Visitor Guide* booklet) from Bowali visitor information centre, Tourism Top End in Darwin, Gagudju Lodge Cooinda, Goymarr Tourist Resort, or Katherine visitor information centre. Carry it with you at all times, as rangers conduct spot checks (penalties apply for nonpayment).

The excellent Bowali Visitor Information Centre (☏08-8938 1121; www.kakadu nationalparkaustralia.com/bowali_visitors_center.htm; Kakadu Hwy, Jabiru; ⏰8am-5pm) has walk-through displays that sweep you across the land, explaining Kakadu's ecology from Aboriginal and non-Aboriginal perspectives. The 'What's On' flier details where and when to catch a free and informative park ranger talk.

Kakadu National Park

BY RICK DELANDER, KAKADU TOUR GUIDE, ADVENTURE TOURS AUSTRALIA

1 WILDLIFE
On the way into Kakadu from Darwin, Fogg Dam is a wonderful spot which attracts lots of wildlife and birdlife. Billabongs like Yellow Water (p285) are a must if people want to see crocodiles.

2 WATERFALLS & SWIMMING HOLES
Whether it's Wet or Dry season, there are always places where you can swim. My favourite out-of-the-way spots are Maguk (Barramundi Gorge), Jim Jim Falls (p284), Gunlom Falls... There's a big plunge pool at the base of Jim Jim that stays fresh all Dry season – it's a wonderful place.

3 WALKS & LOOKOUTS
On the longer walks you can see waterfalls and have a nice refreshing swim! On the short walks around Ubirr (p283) and Nourlangie (p283) you can see rock art and some great views. Ubirr has a magnificent 360-degree lookout at the top: that's when people say they really feel they're in Kakadu.

4 INDIGENOUS KAKADU
Aboriginal culture is another big aspect of the park. Ubirr is a great spot to see some rock art and understand some of the culture. The Bowali Visitor Information Centre (p285) near Jabiru has a good display, but it's not really a one-on-one experience.

5 SCENIC FLIGHTS
You have to walk for an hour to get to some of the best spots, but if you can't do that, scenic flights are a quick option. Fixed-wing and helicopter flights operate out of Jabiru and Cooinda, but you can get them from Darwin as well.

Getting There & Around

Many people choose to access Kakadu on a tour, which shuffles them around the major sights with the minimum of hassles. But it's just as easy with your own wheels, if you know what kinds of road conditions your trusty steed can handle (Jim Jim Falls and Twin Falls, for example, are 4WD-access only).

Greyhound Australia (www.greyhound.com.au) runs a daily return coach service from Darwin to Cooinda ($89, 4½ hours) via Jabiru ($65, 3½ hours).

ALICE SPRINGS

This ruggedly beautiful town is shaped by its mythical landscapes, vibrant Aboriginal culture (where else can you hear six uniquely Australian languages in the main street?) and tough pioneering past. The town is a natural base for exploring central Australia, with Uluru-Kata Tjuta National Park a relatively close four-hour drive away.

Sights

Araluen Arts Centre · Gallery

For a small town, Alice Springs has a thriving arts scene and the Araluen Arts Centre is at its heart. There is a 500-seat theatre and four galleries with a focus on art from the central desert region.

Museum of Central Australia · Museum

(⏱10am-5pm, library 10am-4pm Mon-Fri) The natural history collection at this compact museum recalls the days of megafauna – when hippo-sized wombats and 3m-tall flightless birds roamed the land. Among the geological displays are meteorite fragments and fossils. There's a free audio tour, narrated by a palaeontologist, which helps bring the exhibition to life.

Tours

Alice Wanderer · Bus Tour

(☎1800 722 111; www.alicewanderer.com.au; Gregory Tce) Has the 'hop on/hop off' town tours aboard the Alice Explorer ($44), which continually loops around town

stopping at the major sights. The office is opposite the visitor information centre.

Dreamtime Tours · Cultural Tour

(☎08-8953 3739; www.rstours.com.au; adult/child $85/42, self-drive $66/33; ⏱8.30-11.30am) Runs the three-hour Dreamtime & Bushtucker Tour, where you meet Warlpiri Aboriginal people and learn a little about their traditions. As it caters for large bus groups it can be impersonal, but you can tag along with your own vehicle.

Foot Falcon · Walking Tour

(☎0427 569 531; www.footfalcon.com; tours $30; ⏱Mon & Thu 8.30am, Tue, Wed & Fri 4pm, Sun 3pm) Local historian, author and teacher Linda Wells leads two-hour walks around town with insights into Alice's indigenous and pioneering history.

Emu Run Tours · Outdoors

(☎1800 687 220, 08-8953 7057; www.emurun.com.au; 72 Todd St) Day tours to Uluru ($215) and two-day tours to Uluru and Kings Canyon ($520). Prices include park entry fees, meals and accommodation.

Sleeping

Alice Lodge Backpackers · Hostel $

(☎1800 351 925, 08-8953 1975; www.alicelodge.com.au; 4 Mueller St; dm $22-26, d/tr $65/80; ❄@🖥♿) Located in a lovely residential area across the Todd River, an easy 10-minute walk from town, this is a small, highly recommended, low-key hostel. The friendly staff are as accommodating as the variety of room options, which include mixed and female, three-, four- and six-bed dorms, as well as comfortable doubles and twins built around a central pool.

Alice on Todd · Apartments $$

(☎08-8953 8033; www.aliceontodd.com; cnr Strehlow St & South Tce; studio $128, 1-/2-bedroom apt $156/195, deluxe 1-/2-bedroom apt $170/210; ❄@🖥♿) This attractive and secure apartment complex on the banks of the Todd River offers one- and two- bedroom self-contained units with kitchen and lounge. The balconied units sleep up to six so they're a great option for families. The deluxe apartments are

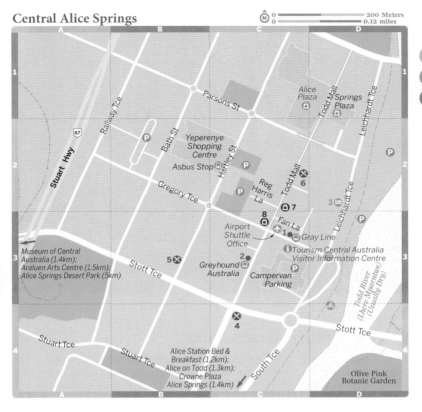

Central Alice Springs

🟢 Activities, Courses & Tours	
1 Alice Wanderer	C3
2 Emu Run Tours	C3

📖 Sleeping	
3 Aurora Alice Springs	D2

🍴 Eating	
4 Montes	C4
5 Overlanders Steakhouse	B3
6 Red Ochre Grill	C2

🛍 Shopping	
7 Aboriginal Art World	C2
8 Mbantua Gallery	C3

a step up in decor and comfort. The landscaped grounds enclose a BBQ area, playground and a games room.

Alice Station Bed & Breakfast
B&B **$$**

(☎ 08-8953 6600; www.alicestation.com; 25 The Fairway; s/d/ste from $180/195/260; ✳ @ 🛜 🌊) The host of this lovely B&B, which backs on to the bush, really does have kangaroos in her backyard. Made out of old *Ghan* railway sleepers, the whimsically designed home has a relaxed atmosphere with a communal lounge and stylishly decorated rooms with local Aboriginal art on the walls. Continental breakfasts get the thumbs up, as do the homemade cakes and eight different types of tea.

JASON EDWARDS/GETTY IMAGES ©

⭐ Don't Miss
Alice Springs Desert Park

If you haven't managed to glimpse a spangled grunter or a marbled velvet gecko on your travels, head to the Desert Park where the creatures of central Australia are all on display in one place. The predominantly open-air exhibits faithfully re-create the animals' natural environment in a series of habitats: inland river, sand country and woodland.

Try to time your visit with the terrific **birds of prey show**, featuring free-flying Australian kestrels, kites and awesome wedge-tailed eagles. To catch some of the park's rare and elusive animals such as the bilby, visit the excellent **nocturnal house**. If you like what you see, come back at night and spotlight endangered species on the guided **nocturnal tour** (booking essential).

It's an easy 2.5km cycle out to the park. Alternatively, **Desert Park Transfers** (📞1800 806 641, 08-8952 1731; www.tailormadetours.com.au; adult/child $48/33) operates five times daily during park hours, and the cost includes park entry and pick-up and drop-off at your accommodation.

NEED TO KNOW

www.alicespringsdesertpark.com.au; Larapinta Dr; adult/child $25/12.50, nocturnal tour adult/child $25/12.50; ⏱7.30am-6pm, last entry 4.30pm, birds of prey show 10am & 3.30pm, nocturnal tour 7.30pm

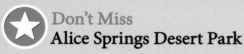

Crowne Plaza
Alice Springs   Hotel $$
(📞1300 666 545, 08-8950 8000; www.
crowneplaza.com.au; Barrett Dr; d from $150,

ste $188-328; ❄ @ 🛜 🏊) With its spacious resort-style facilities, this is widely considered Alice's top hotel. Choose from the garden-view rooms or the better mountain-range-view rooms – they're decked out with floor-to-ceiling windows, cane furniture and pastel colours. There's a lovely pool and spa, well-equipped gym and sauna, tennis courts and a house peacock. Alice's best restaurant, Hanuman, is in the lobby.

Aurora Alice Springs Hotel $$$
(📞1800 089 644, 08-8950 6666; www.aurora resorts.com.au; 11 Leichhardt Tce; standard/deluxe/executive d $210/230/299; ❄@🎧🐾) Right in the town centre – the 'back' door opens out onto Todd Mall, the front door looks over the Todd River – this modern hotel has a relaxed atmosphere and a great restaurant, the Red Ochre Grill. Standard rooms are comfortable and well appointed with fridge, phone and free in-house movies.

Eating

Hanuman Restaurant Thai $$
(📞08-8953 7188; Barrett Dr, Crowne Plaza Alice Springs; mains $18-36; 🕐12.30-2.30pm Mon-Fri, from 6.30pm daily; 🌿) You won't believe you're in the outback when you try the incredible Thai- and Indian-influenced cuisine at this stylish restaurant. The delicate Thai entrees are a triumph as are the seafood dishes, particularly the Hanuman prawns. Although the menu is ostensibly Thai, there are enough Indian dishes to satisfy a curry craving. There are several vegetarian offerings and a good wine list.

Montes Modern Australian $$
(cnr Stott Tce & Todd St; Mains $12-17; 🕐11am-late) A travelling circus meets outback homestead with a leafy beer garden (and range of beers) or intimate booth seating. Patio heaters keep patrons warm on a cool desert night. It's family friendly with a play area, and the food ranges from gourmet burgers, pizzas and tapas to curries and seafood.

Red Ochre Grill Modern Australian $$
(Todd Mall; mains $14-32; 🕐6.30am-9.30pm) Offering innovative fusion dishes with a focus on outback cuisine, the menu usually features traditional meats plus locally bred proteins, such as kangaroo and emu, matched with native herbs: lemon myrtle, pepper berries and bush tomatoes. The all-day brunch in the courtyard turns out more predictable dishes including excellent eggs Benedict.

Overlanders Steakhouse Steakhouse $$$
(📞08-8952 2159; 72 Hartley St; mains $21-40; 🕐6pm-late) The place for steaks, big succulent cuts of beef (and crocodile, camel, kangaroo or emu). Amid the cattle station decor (saddles, branding irons and the like) you can take the challenge of the Drover's Blowout, four courses including a platter of the aforementioned Aussie bush meats.

Shopping

Aboriginal Art World Indigenous Art
(📞08-8952 7788; www.aboriginalartworld.com.au; 89 Todd Mall) Specialises in art from about 70 artists living in South Australia and NT central deserts, particularly Pitjantjatjara lands. Most art pieces are sold with a DVD showing the artwork being created.

Mbantua Gallery Indigenous Art
(📞08-8952 5571; www.mbantua.com.au; 64 Todd Mall; 🕐9am-6pm Mon-Fri, 9.30am-3pm Sat) This privately owned gallery includes a cafe and extensive exhibits of works from the renowned Utopia region, as well as watercolour landscapes from the Namatjira school.

Information

Medical Services

Alice Springs Hospital (📞08-8951 7777; Gap Rd)

Tourist Information

Tourism Central Australia Visitor Information Centre (📞1800 645 199, 08-8952 5199; www.centralaustraliantourism.com; 60 Gregory Tce; 🕐8.30am-5pm Mon-Fri, 9.30am-4pm Sat & Sun) This helpful centre can load you up with stacks of brochures and the free visitor's guide. Ask about their unlimited kilometre deals if you are thinking of renting a car.

ℹ️ Getting There & Away

Air

Alice Springs is well connected, with Qantas (☎ 13 13 13, 08-8950 5211; www.qantas.com.au) operating daily flights to/from capital cities.

Bus

Greyhound Australia (☎ 1300 473 946; www.greyhound.com.au; 113 Todd St, shop 3; ⏰ office 8.30-11.30am & 1.30-4pm Mon-Fri) has regular services from Alice Springs (check website for timetables and discounted fares).

Emu Run (p286) runs the cheapest daily connections between Alice Springs and Yulara (adult/child $215/108) and between Kings Canyon and Alice Springs ($189/95). **Gray Line** (☎ 1300 858 687; www.grayline.com; Capricornia Centre 9 Gregory Tce) also runs between Alice Springs and Yulara (adult/child $226/113), and offers one-way option ($156/113).

Car & Motorcycle

All the major companies have offices in Alice Springs, and many have counters at the airport. Talk to the **visitor centre** (☎ 1800 645 199, 08-8952 5199) about its unlimited kilometres deal before you book. A conventional (2WD) vehicle will get you to most sights in the MacDonnell Ranges and out to Uluru and Kings Canyon via sealed roads.

Train

A classic way to enter or leave the Territory is by the *Ghan* which can be booked through **Great Southern Rail** (☎ 13 21 47; www.greatsouthernrail.com.au) or **Travelworld** (☎ 08-8953 0488; 40 Todd Mall).

ℹ️ Getting Around

To/From the Airport

Alice Springs airport is 15km south of the town. It's about $40 by taxi. The **airport shuttle** (☎ 08-8952 2111; Gregory Tce; 1/2 persons one-way $18.50/30 plus $10 each additional person) meets all flights and drops off passengers at city accommodation.

Bus

The public bus service, **Asbus** (☎ 08-8952 5611), departs from outside the Yeperenye Shopping Centre. The visitor information centre has timetables.

The **Alice Explorer** (☎ 1800 722 111, 08-8952 2111; www.alicewanderer.com.

au; adult/child $44/35; ⏰ 9am-4pm) is a hop-on, hop-off sightseeing bus that covers 11 major sites, including the Telegraph Station, School of the Air, Old Ghan Rail Museum and Araluen.

Taxi

Taxis congregate near the visitor information centre. To book, call ☎ 13 10 08 or 08-8952 1877.

ULURU-KATA TJUTA NATIONAL PARK

For many visitors, Australian and international, a visit to Uluru is high on the list of 'must-sees' and the World Heritage–listed icon has attained pilgrimage status.

ℹ️ Information

The **park** (www.environment.gov.au/parks/uluru; adult/child $25/free) is open from half an hour before sunrise to sunset daily (varying between 5am to 9pm November to March and 6am to 7.30pm April to October). Entry permits are valid for three days and available at the drive-through entry station on the road from Yulara.

Uluru-Kata Tjuta Cultural Centre (☎ 08-8956 1128; ⏰ 7am-6pm) is 1km before Uluru on the road from Yulara and should be your first stop. Displays and exhibits focus on tjukurpa (Aboriginal law, religion and custom) and the history and management of the national park. The information desk in the Nintiringkupai building is staffed by park rangers who supply the informative *Visitor Guide*, leaflets and walking notes. During the week a local Anangu ranger runs a presentation at 10am each morning on bush foods and Aboriginal history.

The Cultural Centre encompasses the craft outlet **Maruku Arts** (☎ 08-8956 2558; www.maruku.com.au; ⏰ 8.30am-5.30pm), owned by about 20 Anangu communities from across central Australia (including the local Mutitjulu community), selling hand-crafted wooden carvings, bowls and boomerangs.

Tours

BUS TOURS

Seit Outback Australia   Bus Tour

(☎ 08-8956 3156; www.seitoutbackaustralia.com.au) This small group tour operator has numerous options including a sunset tour

BETHUNE CARMICHAEL/GETTY IMAGES ©

Don't Miss
Kata Tjuta (The Olgas)

No journey to Uluru is complete without a visit to Kata Tjuta (the Olgas), a striking group of domed rocks huddled together about 35km west of the Rock. There are 36 boulders shoulder to shoulder, forming deep valleys and steep-sided gorges. Many visitors find them even more captivating than their prominent neighbour. The tallest rock, **Mt Olga** (546m, 1066m above sea level) is about 200m higher than Uluru.

The 7.4km **Valley of the Winds** loop (two to four hours) is one of the most challenging and rewarding bushwalks in the park. It winds through the gorges, giving excellent views of the surreal domes and traversing varied terrain. It's not particularly arduous, but wear sturdy shoes and take plenty of water. Starting this walk at first light often rewards you with solitude, enabling you to appreciate the sounds of the wind and bird calls carried up the valley.

The short signposted track beneath towering rock walls into pretty **Walpa Gorge** (2.6km return, 45 minutes) is especially beautiful in the afternoon, when sunlight floods the gorge.

Like Uluru, Kata Tjuta is at its glorious, blood-red best at sunset.

around Uluru (adult/child $139/110), and a sunrise tour at Kata Tjuta for the same price including breakfast and a walk into Walpa Gorge.

AAT Kings Bus Tour
(☑08-8956 2171; www.aatkings.com) Operating the biggest range of coach tours, AAT offers a range of half- and full-day tours

from Yulara. Check the website or enquire at the Tour & Information Centre in Yulara.

CULTURAL TOURS
Uluru Aboriginal Tours Cultural Tour
(☑0447 878 851; www.uluruaboriginaltours.com. au; guided tours starting from $45 per person) Owned and operated by Anangu from the

Mutitjulu community, this company offers a range of trips to give you an insight into the significance of the Rock through the eyes of the traditional owners. Tours operate and depart from the Cultural Centre, as well as from Yulara Ayers Rock Resort (through AAT Kings) and Alice Springs (through Adventure Tours Australia).

SCENIC FLIGHTS

Ayers Rock Helicopters   Scenic Flights
(☎08-8956 2077) A 15-minute buzz of Uluru costs $145; to include Kata Tjuta costs $275.

Ayers Rock Scenic Flights   Scenic Flights
(☎08-8956 2345; www.ayersrockflights.com.au) Prices start from $100 for a 20-minute flight over Uluru. Include Kata Tjuta and it's $200.

Uluru (Ayers Rock)

Nothing quite prepares you for the first sight of Uluru on the horizon – it will astound even the most jaded traveller. Uluru is 3.6km long and rises a towering 348m from the surrounding sandy scrubland (867m above sea level). Closer inspection reveals a wondrous contoured surface concealing numerous sacred sites of particular significance to the Anangu.

🏃 Activities

WALKING

There are walking tracks around Uluru, and ranger-led walks explain the area's plants, wildlife, geology and cultural significance.

The excellent *Visitor Guide & Maps* brochure, which can be picked up at the Cultural Centre, gives details on a few self-guided walks.

Base Walk   Walking
This track (10.6km, three to four hours) circumnavigates the rock, passing caves, paintings, sandstone folds and geological abrasions along the way.

Liru Walk   Walking
Links the Cultural Centre with the start of the Mala walk and climb, and winds

Uluru (Ayers Rock)

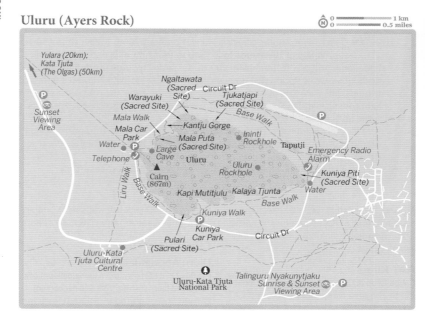

through strands of mulga before opening up near Uluru (4km return, 1½ hours).

Mala Walk   Walking

From the base of the climbing point (2km return, one hour), interpretive signs explain the tjukurpa of the Mala (hare-wallaby people), which is significant to the Anangu, as well as fine examples of rock art. A ranger-guided walk (free) along this route departs at 10am (8am from October to April) from the car park.

Kuniya Walk   Walking

A short walk (1km return, 45 minutes) from the car park on the southern side leads to the most permanent waterhole, Mutitjulu, home of the ancestral water-snake. Great birdwatching and some excellent rock art are highlights of this walk.

SUNSET & SUNRISE VIEWING AREAS

About halfway between Yulara and Uluru, the **sunset viewing area** has plenty of car and coach parking for that familiar postcard view. The **Talnguru Nyakunyt-jaku sunrise viewing area** is perched on a sand dune and captures both the Rock and Kata Tjuta in all their glory.

Yulara (Ayers Rock Resort)

Yulara is the service village for the national park and has effectively turned one of the world's least hospitable regions into a comfortable place to stay. Lying just outside the national park, 20km from Uluru and 53km from Kata Tjuta, the complex is the closest base for exploring the park. Yulara supplies the only accommodation, food outlets and other services available in the region.

Sleeping

All of the accommodation in Yulara, including the camping ground and hostel, is owned by the Ayers Rock Resort. Bookings can be made through **central reservations** (1300 134 044; www.ayers rockresort.com.au).

Local Knowledge

Uluru-Kata Tjuta National Park

BY TIM ROGERS, VISITOR SERVICES OFFICER, ULURU-KATA TJUTA NATIONAL PARK

1 ULURU ABORIGINAL TOURS

Make sure you go on a tour with a traditional owner and learn to see the landscape through Anangu eyes. You'll experience a land that's been sung about through story and law for generations, and hear a true Australian language that's been spoken throughout the desert regions for thousands of years.

2 ULURU'S CHANGING MOODS

I'm a keen photographer, so here are my tips. Winter months are best for great sunrise shots. If you come in summer, then sunset shots are your best bet. If you're really lucky, you'll get a rainbow with sun showers. When the heavens open and rain falls, Uluru (p292) suddenly has over 60 waterfalls cascading down – but only one in a hundred visitors gets to see this remarkable event.

3 YOUR OWN CONNECTION

If you want to be on your own at Uluru, slip off to one of the waterholes along the base walk an hour before sunset. While all the other guests are scrabbling for sunset photos, you'll have the whole rock to yourself. If you sit quietly, the birds will come in to drink and just on dusk the microbats will come out and snatch insects out of the air.

4 KATA TJUTA

My favourite activity is a sunrise walk at Kata Tjuta (p291). As the sun comes up it casts an array of hues, and you'll see the wildlife among the domes. Or, contrary to the crowd, you can visit the car sunset viewing area at sunrise. It's a nice spot to have breakfast, and you have a fantastic view of the mysterious silhouette of Uluru as dawn awakens.

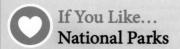

If You Like...
National Parks

If you like Uluru-Kata Tjuta National Park, take some time to explore these other superb national parks around the NT:

1 FINKE GORGE NATIONAL PARK
With its primordial landscape, the 4WD-accessible Finke Gorge National Park, about 140km west of Alice Springs, is one of central Australia's premier wilderness reserves. The top-billing attraction is Palm Valley, famous for its red cabbage palms, which exist nowhere else in the world.

2 WEST MACDONNELL NATIONAL PARK
This spectacular gorge country west of Alice Springs offers excellent camping and bushwalking, including the renowned Larapinta Trail. Day trips from Alice Springs are a good way to explore the region.

3 WATARRKA NATIONAL PARK
This park is centred on the grand chasm of Kings Canyon, about 300km north of Uluru on sealed roads. The 6km Kings Canyon Rim Walk is one of the best short walks in the NT.

4 ELSEY NATIONAL PARK
Near Mataranka between Katherine and Tennant Creek, the highlights of Elsey National Park are its amazing thermal springs. The almost unnatural blue-green colour of the 34°C water is due to dissolved limestone particles.

Emu Walk Apartments
Apartments **$$$**

(☎1300 134 044; 1-/2-bedroom apt from $380/480; ❄❙) The pick of the bunch for families looking for self-contained accommodation, Emu Walk has comfortable, modern apartments, each with a lounge room (with TV) and a well-equipped kitchen with washer and dryer. The one-bedroom apartment accommodates four people, while the two-bedroom version sleeps six.

Sails in the Desert
Hotel **$$$**

(☎1300 134 044; standard d $400, ste $780; ❄@🛜❙) Although refurbished in 2011/12, the rooms still seem overpriced and by far the best part of this hotel is the lovely (and exclusive) pool and surrounding lawn shaded by sails and trees. There are also tennis courts, a health spa, several restaurants and a piano bar. The best rooms have balcony views of the Rock – request one when you make a booking.

Eating

Geckos Cafe
Mediterranean **$$**

(Resort Shopping Centre; mains $18-28; ⊙11am-9pm; 🍴) For great value, warm atmosphere and tasty food head to this buzzing licensed cafe, which, it says, 'caters for everyone'. The wood-fired pizzas, salads and pasta go well with a carafe of sangria, and the courtyard tables are a great place to enjoy the desert night air. There are several veggie and gluten-free options plus meals can be made to takeaway.

Outback Pioneer Barbecue
Barbecue **$$**

(Outback Pioneer Hotel & Lodge; mains $20-35, salad only $16; ⊙6-9pm) For a fun, casual night out, this lively tavern is the popular choice for everyone from backpackers to grey nomads. Choose between kangaroo skewers, prawns, veggie burgers, steaks and emu sausages and grill them yourself at the communal BBQs.

Kuniya
Modern Australian **$$$**

(☎08-8956 2200; Sails in the Desert; mains $45-60; ⊙6.30-9.30pm) Yulara's most sophisticated restaurant, Kuniya is the place for romantic dinners and special occasions. The walls are adorned with contemporary Australian art and the inspired menu features Aussie cuisine infused with native ingredients that complement the extensive Australian wine list. Reservations are essential.

A Question of Climbing

Many visitors consider climbing Uluru a highlight – even a rite of passage – of a trip to the Centre. But for the traditional owners, the Anangu, Uluru is a sacred place. The path up the side of the Rock is part of the route taken by the Mala ancestors on their arrival at Uluru and has great spiritual significance – and is not to be trampled by human feet.

The Anangu are the custodians of Uluru and take responsibility for the safety of visitors. Any injuries or deaths that occur are a source of distress and sadness to them. For similar reasons of public safety, Parks Australia would prefer that people didn't climb.

ℹ Information

Tour & Information Centre (☎08-8957 7324; **Resort Shopping Centre**; ⊙8am-8pm) Most tour operators and car-hire firms have desks at this centre.

Visitor Information Centre (☎08-8957 7377; ⊙8.30am-4.30pm) Contains displays on the geography, wildlife and history of the region. There's a short audio tour ($2) if you want to learn more. It also sells books and regional maps.

ℹ Getting There & Away

Air

Connellan airport is about 4km north from Yulara. **Qantas** (☎13 13 13; www.qantas.com.au) has direct flights from Alice Springs, Melbourne, Perth, Adelaide and Sydney. **Virgin Australia** (☎13 67 89; www.virginaustralia.com) has daily flights from Sydney.

Bus

Daily shuttle connections (listed as mini tours) between Alice Springs and Yulara are run by **AAT Kings** (☎1300 556 100; www.aatkings.com) and cost adult/child $150/75. Emu Run (p286) runs the cheapest daily connections between Alice Springs and Uluru ($215/108).

Car & Motorcycle

One route from Alice to Yulara is sealed all the way, with regular food and petrol stops. It's 200km from Alice to Erldunda on the Stuart Hwy, where you turn west for the 245km journey along the Lasseter Hwy. The journey takes about four to five hours.

ℹ Getting Around

A free shuttle bus meets all flights and drops off at all accommodation points around the resort; pick-up is 90 minutes before your flight.

Uluru Express (☎08-8956 2152; www.uluruexpress.com.au) falls somewhere between a shuttle-bus service and an organised tour. It provides return transport from the resort to Uluru (adult/child $50/30, $60/30 for the sunrise and sunset shuttles). Morning shuttles to Kata Tjuta cost $80/45; afternoon shuttles include a stop at Uluru for sunset and cost $90/45. Fares do not include the park entry fee.

Hiring a car will give you the flexibility to visit the Rock and the Olgas whenever you want. **Hertz** (☎08-8956 2244) has a desk at the Tour & Information Centre, which also has direct phones to the **Avis** (☎08-8956 2266) and **Thrifty** (☎08-8956 2030) desks at Connellan Airport.

Perth & the West Coast

Western Australia (WA) is seriously big – almost four times the size of Texas! With swaths of gloriously empty outback, a small population hugging the coast and Perth's distinction as the world's most isolated capital city, WA is Australia at its most 'frontier'. Backed by a booming economy fuelled by mining, Western Australians are defiantly independent and happily distinct from that 'other' Australia on the east coast.

To the north of Perth, Shark Bay delivers a watery wildlife spectacle like no other. South of the city is the effervescent port of Fremantle, beyond which you'll find uncrowded beaches, expanses of wildflowers and lush green forests.

Around Margaret River, the fruit of the vine keeps winemakers busy, vineyard restaurants offer the freshest food and artisans of all sorts make inspired craft from the salvaged wood of stunning karri, marri and jarrah trees.

Perth (p306) at night
ORIEN HARVEY/GETTY IMAGES ©

Ningaloo Marine Park (p317)

Perth & the West Coast

Exmouth &
Ningaloo
Marine Park
(310km)

Carnarvon
Dorre
Island
*Shark
Bay*
Monkey
Mia
François Peron
National Park
5
Dirk Hartog
Island
Denham

North West Coastal Hwy

1 **Perth**
2 **Fremantle**
3 **Margaret River**
4 **Valley of the Giants**
5 **Monkey Mia**

Kalbarri

Northampton
Mullewa
Geraldton
Pelsaert
Island
Dongara - Port Denison

*Mongers
Lake*
Great Northern Hwy
*Lake
Moore*

*Lake
Barlee*

WESTERN
AUSTRALIA

*INDIAN
OCEAN*

Cervantes
Moora
*Cowcowing
Lakes*

Brand Hwy

Yanchep
Northam
Great Eastern Hwy
Merredin
Southern
Cross

1 Perth
Perth
York
Rottnest Island
Fremantle
2
Rockingham
Mandurah

Albany Hwy

Pingelly

Narrogin

0   100 km
0   50 miles

Wagin

Bunbury
Cape
Naturaliste
Collie
Dunsborough
Yallingup
Donnybrook
Busselton

30

*Lake
Magenta*
Ravensthorpe

Katanning

1
*Esperance
(120km)*

Margaret River
Bridgetown
3
Augusta
Manjimup
Cape Leeuwin
Pemberton
Mount
Barker
Doubtful
Islands

D'Entrecasteaux
National Park
Valley of the
Giants

South Coast Hwy

Walpole
4
Denmark
Point
D'Entrecasteaux
Nornalup
Albany

*SOUTHERN
OCEAN*

Perth & the West Coast Highlights

Perth

If you think Perth (p306) feels a bit shy and embarrassed about being so isolated, think again! This is a town with spirit, enthusiasm and a progressive 'go get them' attitude. And really, who needs the east coast when the beaches, beer and BBQ weather are so good here? Cap it off with beaut museums, restaurants, bars and clubs and Perth proves to be a real winner.

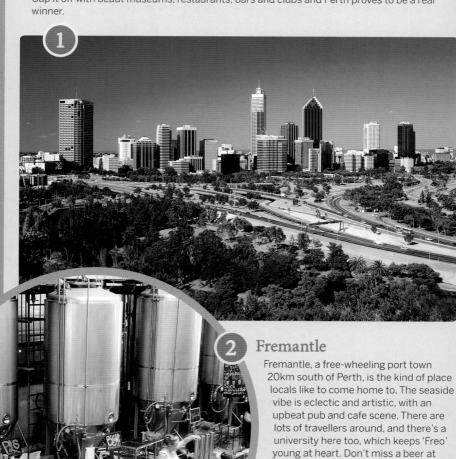

Fremantle

Fremantle, a free-wheeling port town 20km south of Perth, is the kind of place locals like to come home to. The seaside vibe is eclectic and artistic, with an upbeat pub and cafe scene. There are lots of travellers around, and there's a university here too, which keeps 'Freo' young at heart. Don't miss a beer at Little Creatures (p324) brewery near the harbour, or an hour or two at Fremantle Markets (p321). Little Creatures

ORIEN HARVEY/GETTY IMAGES ©

Margaret River

3

Wildly popular Margaret River (p328) serves up some of the best surfing in Australia, along with coastal caves, sophisticated restaurants, and internationally acclaimed vineyards scattered throughout richly forested land. The town itself, affectionately known as 'Margs', is an affable enclave of cafes and accommodation that satisfies both surfies and affluent weekend escapees travelling down the coast from Perth.

Surfers Point

4

Valley of the Giants

Giant tingle trees live for up to 400 years, can grow to 60m tall and 16m around the base, and are unique to this region of southwestern WA. For years folks would come to the Valley of the Giants (p333), eager to walk among the stoic 'Ancient Empire' stand of trees. Now you can explore the elevated realm of the canopy on the magical Tree Top Walk.

5

Monkey Mia

World-renowned Monkey Mia (p338) needs little introduction: the friendly wild dolphins that visit daily have really put it on the map! Dolphins started interacting with humans here when local Aboriginal fishermen Jimmy Poland and Laurie Bellotti began handing them fish after their fishing expeditions. Then, in the 1960s, a visitor called Nin Watts started feeding the dolphins from the beach...and now you can too!

Perth & the West Coast's Best…

Wildlife & Wilderness

⊙ Shark Bay Compelling marine wonderland surrounded by starkly beautiful landforms. (p339)

⊙ Ningaloo Marine Park Highly accessible coral reef sustaining abundant marine life. (p317)

⊙ Valley of the Giants Be humbled by the grandeur of mighty tingle trees. (p333)

⊙ Kings Park & Botanic Garden It mightn't be remote, but the indigenous plants and flowers here are wild indeed. (p308)

Urban Experiences

⊙ Eating out in Perth Superb seafood with river views or Indian Ocean sunsets. (p311)

⊙ Live music in Fremantle The sounds of Freo: buskers on the streets and rockin' bands in the pubs. (p324)

⊙ Art Gallery of Western Australia Outstanding Indigenous art from across the state. (p306)

⊙ Drinking in Northbridge Sometimes rough, often trashy…but never boring! (p315)

Places to Unwind

⊙ Margaret River Lose the kids and treat yourself to some wining and dining or a quiet country drive. (p328)

⊙ Esperance A long way from anywhere (just how the locals like it). (p336)

⊙ Denmark No, not next to Sweden…WA's version is a beachy, laid-back, alt-lifestyle haven. (p332)

⊙ Rottnest Island (Wadjemup) The perfect old-fashioned swimmin' and fishin' beach holiday. (p326)

Need to Know

Diving & Snorkelling

○ **Ningaloo Marine Park** One of the world's premier places to dive with whale sharks and manta rays. (p317)

○ **Rottnest Island (Wadjemup)** Family-friendly, with protected reef and wreck snorkelling sites and dive lessons. (p326)

○ **Monkey Mia** Strap on a snorkel and Monkey Mia's famously friendly dolphins may join you. (p338)

○ **Aquarium of Western Australia** Muster some nerve and snorkel or dive with sharks. (p306)

ADVANCE PLANNING

○ **One month before** Plan your route across vast WA: book accommodation and rental vehicles.

○ **Two weeks before** Book regional flights to Denham (for Shark Bay), and Exmouth if Ningaloo Marine Park is on your hit list.

○ **One week before** Book a diving lesson or whale-swim tour, and a table at Harvest (p324) restaurant in Fremantle or Greenhouse (p312) in Perth.

RESOURCES

○ **Tourism Western Australian** (www.westernaustralia.com) The official website for general statewide info. Most country towns have their own helpful visitor centres.

○ **Western Australian Visitor Centre** (www.bestofwa.com.au) Website for the downtown Perth visitor centre: accommodation, tours, events and deals.

○ **Department of Environment & Conservation** (www.dec.wa.gov.au) Government department responsible for WA's national parks.

○ **Royal Automobile Club of Western Australia** (RAC; www.rac.com.au) Driving info and emergency roadside assistance.

GETTING AROUND

○ **Boat** To Rottnest Island, or down the Swan River from Perth to Fremantle.

○ **Walk** Beneath giant tingle trees or amid WA's famed wildflower blooms.

○ **Swim** With whale sharks and dolphins.

○ **Train** Across the continent to/from Sydney: slow but scenic.

○ **Fly** To Denham (for Monkey Mia) or Exmouth (for Ningaloo): cover WA's massive distances in a short time.

BE FOREWARNED

○ **Rottnest Island** Summer and school-holiday accommodation on 'Rotto' gets booked out months in advance.

○ **Ningaloo Marine Park** The whale sharks arrive in May and depart in July.

Left: Quokka, Rottnest Island (Wadjemup); **Above:** Denmark (p332)

Perth & the West Coast Itineraries

Perth and Fremantle offer urban enticements, while Western Australia's southwestern corner is strewn with beaches, vineyards and tall forests. Add a long hop north and you can swim with dolphins at Shark Bay.

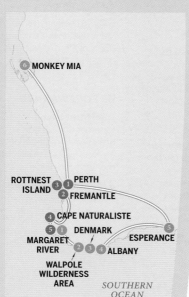

3 DAYS

PERTH TO MARGARET RIVER

City to the Sea

Kick-start your Western Australian adventure in ❶ **Perth** (p306) and expend your urban urges in the city's great pubs, galleries, bars and restaurants. Don't miss the Indigenous galleries at the Art Gallery of Western Australia, and a dip at Cottesloe Beach.

Pay a quick visit to happening ❷ **Fremantle** (p319) for some maritime history and busker appreciation. From Freo you can catch the ferry out to pedal-powered ❸ **Rottnest Island** (p326) for a car-free, care-free day.

Back on the mainland, head south to the awesome beaches of ❹ **Cape Naturaliste** (p330), then roll into ❺ **Margaret River** (p328), a richly forested region with award-winning wineries and upmarket B&Bs. 'Margs' also has some of the country's best surf: hire a long board and go for a paddle.

Top Left: Art Gallery of Western Australia (p306); **Top Right:** Southern right whale and calf

5 DAYS

MARGARET RIVER TO MONKEY MIA

Whales, Wilderness & Wild Dolphins

Surfing, exploring caves, wine quaffing... You could hang around ❶**Margaret River** (p328) for weeks, but there's much more to see around here!

At the ❷**Walpole Wilderness Area** (p331), walk through a lofty canopy of magnificent tingle trees. Alt-lifestyle ❸**Denmark** (p332) is a chilled-out spot to spend the night and explore the Great Southern wine region.

Next stop is the old whaling port of ❹**Albany** (p334), WA's oldest European settlement. The whales have forgiven and forgotten: spot them from the beaches between July and mid-October.

Roll east along Hwy 1 to beachy ❺**Esperance** (p336) for a night. From here, take the long drive back to Perth via quirky Kalgoorlie, or catch a flight.

If you have time, hop another flight north to Denham, gateway to the astonishing Shark Bay. Take an Indigenous cultural tour and splash around with wild dolphins at ❻**Monkey Mia** (p338).

Discover Perth & the West Coast

At a Glance

○ **Perth** (p306) Capital of Australia's Wild West.

○ **Fremantle** (p319) Hip, arty port town south of Perth.

○ **Margaret River** (p328) Wineries, surf beaches and foodie culture in southwest WA.

○ **South Coast** (p331) Forests, hippie towns and old whaling ports.

○ **Shark Bay** (p339) Watery wonderland with Monkey Mia's famous dolphins.

PERTH

Planted by a river and beneath an almost permanent canopy of blue sky, the city of Perth is a modern-day boomtown, stoking Australia's economy from its glitzy central business district. Yet it remains as relaxed as the sleepy Swan River – black swans bobbing atop – which winds past the sky-scrapers and out to the Indian Ocean.

◉ Sights

Art Gallery of Western Australia
Gallery

(www.artgallery.wa.gov.au; Perth Cultural Centre; ⊙10am-5pm Wed-Mon) **FREE** Founded in 1895, this excellent gallery houses the state's pre-eminent art collection, with the Indigenous galleries providing the highlight. The annual WA Indigenous Art Awards entries are displayed here from August to December.

Free tours take place at 11am and 1pm on Sundays, Mondays, Wednesdays and Thursdays, at 12.30pm and 2pm on Fridays, and at 1pm on Saturdays.

Western Australian Museum – Perth
Museum

(www.museum.wa.gov.au; Perth Cultural Centre; ⊙9.30am-5pm) **FREE** This branch of the state's six-headed museum includes dinosaur, mammal, butterfly and bird galleries, a children's discovery centre, and an excellent WA Land and People display that covers Indigenous and colonial history. The complex includes Perth's original jail (1856).

Aquarium of Western Australia
Aquarium

(AQWA; ☏08-9447 7500; www.aqwa.com.au; Hillarys Boat Harbour; adult/child $28/16; ⊙10am-

Western Australian Museum – Perth
ANDREW WATSON/GETTY IMAGES ©

5pm) AQWA offers the chance to enjoy the state's underwater treasures without getting wet...or eaten, stung or poisoned. You can wander through a 98m underwater tunnel as gargantuan stingrays, turtles, fish and sharks stealthily glide over the top of you. The daring can snorkel or dive with the sharks; book in advance ($159 with your own gear; hire snorkel/dive gear $20/40; 1pm and 3pm).

Perth Institute of Contemporary Arts
Gallery

(PICA; www.pica.org.au; Perth Cultural Centre; ⏰11am-6pm Tue-Sun) FREE Commonly referred to by its acronym, PICA (pee-kah) may have a traditional wrapping (it's housed in an elegant 1896 red-brick former school) but inside it's anything but, being one of Australia's principal platforms for cutting-edge contemporary art – installations, performance, sculpture, video works and the like.

Swan Valley
Wineries, Craft Beer

Perthites visit this semirural valley on the city's eastern fringe to partake in booze, nosh and the great outdoors. Perhaps in a tacit acknowledgement that its wines will never compete with the state's more prestigious regions (it doesn't really have the ideal climate), the Swan Valley compensates with galleries, breweries, providores and restaurants.

The gateway is National Trust–classified Guildford, established in 1829. Heritage buildings, one housing the **visitor centre** (☎08-9379 9400; www.swanvalley.com.au; Old Courthouse, cnr Swan & Meadow Sts; ⏰9am-4pm), make it the logical starting place for day trippers. Guildford is 12km from central Perth by suburban trains.

Cottesloe Beach
Beach

The safest swimming, cafes, pubs, pine trees and fantastic sunsets.

 Activities

Surf Sail Australia
Windsurfing, Kitesurfing

(☎1800 686 089; www.surfsailaustralia.com.au; 260 Railway Pde; ⏰10am-5pm Mon-Sat)

When the afternoon sea breeze blusters in, windsurfers take to the Swan River, Leighton and beaches north of Perth. Hire or buy gear here.

Oceanic Cruises
Whale Watching

(☎08-9325 1191; www.whalewatching.com.au; adult/child $77/34) Departs Barrack St Jetty at 8.30am, returning at 5.45pm after spending the afternoon in Fremantle. Daily departures during the school holidays, otherwise Wednesday and Friday to Sunday only.

Cycle Centre
Bicycle Rental

(☎08-9325 1176; www.cyclecentre.com.au; 313 Hay St; per day/week $25/65; ⏰9am-5.30pm Mon-Fri, to 3pm Sat, 1-4pm Sun) See the website for recommended rides.

Surfschool
Surfing

(☎08-9447 5637; www.surfschool.com; Scarborough Beach; adult/child $55/50) Two-hour lessons at Scarborough Beach, including boards and wetsuits.

Tours

Indigenous Tours WA
Cultural Tour

(www.indigenouswa.com) See Perth through the eyes of the local Wadjuk people. Options include the **Indigenous Heritage Tour** (☎08-9483 1106; adult/child $25/15; ⏰1.30pm) – a 90-minute guided walk around Kings Park – and an indigenous-themed stroll (p321) around Fremantle.

City Sightseeing Perth Tour
Bus Tour

(☎08-9203 8882; www.citysightseeingperth.com; adult/child $28/10) Hop-on, hop-off double-decker bus tour, with loop routes taking in the central city, Kings Park and the Burswood Entertainment Complex. Tickets are valid for two days. The Kings Park section can be purchased separately (adult/child $6/3).

Captain Cook Cruises
Cruise

(☎08-9325 3341; www.captaincookcruises.com.au) Cruises to the Swan Valley or Fremantle.

PHILIP GAME/GETTY IMAGES ©

Don't Miss
Kings Park & Botanic Garden

The bush-filled 400-hectare expanse of Kings Park is where the city's good burghers head for a picnic under the trees or to let the kids off the leash in one of the playgrounds. Its numerous tracks are popular with walkers and joggers.

At the park's heart is the 17-hectare Botanic Garden, containing more than 2000 indigenous plant species. In spring there's an impressive display of the state's famed wildflowers. A highlight is the **Lotterywest Federation Walkway**, a 620m path through the gardens including a 222m-long, glass-and-steel bridge that passes through the canopy of a stand of eucalypts. Free guided walks leave from the **Kings Park Visitor Centre** (🕙9.30am-4pm).

NEED TO KNOW

www.bgpa.wa.gov.au; 🕙Lotterywest Federation Walkway 9am-5pm, guided walks 10am, noon & 2pm

---

**Two Feet &
A Heartbeat**   Walking Tour
(📞1800 459 388; www.twofeet.com.au; per person $40-50) Daytime walking tours of Perth, and a popular after-dark 'Small Bar Tour'.

Rottnest Air Taxi   Scenic Flights
(📞08-9292 5027; www.rottnest.de) Thirty-minute joy flights over the city, Kings Park and Fremantle ($88 to $115).

 Sleeping

City Centre

Regal Apartments   Apartment $$
(📞08-9221 8614; www.regalapartments.com.au; 11 Regal Pl; apt from $230; ❄@) Tucked in behind good-value Asian restaurants east of the city centre, these recently

redecorated one- and two-bedroom apartments are spacious and modern. Fully equipped kitchens make them ideal for families watching their dollars.

Medina Executive Barrack Plaza
Apartments $$

(☏08-9267 0000; www.medina.com.au; 138 Barrack St; apt from $229; ❄ 🏊) The Medina's meticulously decorated apartment-sized hotel rooms are minimalist yet welcoming. All one-bedrooms have balconies. Rooms on Barrack St have more natural light.

Riverview on Mount Street
Apartments $$

(☏08-9321 8963; www.riverviewperth.com.au; 42 Mount St; apt from $140; ❄ @ 🛜) There's a lot of brash new money up here on Mount St, but character-filled Riverview stands out as the best personality on the block. Its refurbished 1960s bachelor pads sit neatly atop a modern foyer and a relaxed cafe.

Pensione Hotel
Boutique Hotel $$

(☏08-9325 2133; www.pensione.com.au; 70 Pier St; d from $155; ❄ 🛜) The Pensione's standard rooms definitely veer to cosy and (very) compact, but classy decor and a good location are two definite pluses in an expensive city.

City Waters
Motel $$

(☏08-9325 1566; www.citywaters.com.au; 118 Terrace Rd; s/d $130/150; ❄) Rooms are small, simple and face onto the car park, but they're clean, airy and the waterfront location is top-notch. Top-floor rooms are best; river views exist but are difficult to secure.

Northbridge, Highgate & Mt Lawley

Emperor's Crown
Hostel $

(☏08-9227 1400; www.emperorscrown.com.au; 85 Stirling St; dm $36, r with/without bathroom from $130/110; ❄ @ 🛜) One of Perth's best hostels has a great position (close to the Northbridge scene without being in the thick of it), friendly staff and high house-keeping standards.

Durack House
B&B $$

(☏08-9370 4305; www.durackhouse.com.au; 7 Almondbury Rd; s $160, d $175-190; 🛜) Set on a peaceful suburban street, the three rooms here have plenty of old-world charm, paired with thoroughly modern bathrooms. It's only 250m from Mt Lawley station; turn left onto Railway Pde and then first right onto Almondbury Rd.

Pension of Perth
B&B $$

(☏08-9228 9049; www.pensionperth.com.au; 3 Throssell St; s/d from $150/165; ❄ @ 🛜) Pension of Perth's French belle-époque-style lays luxury on thick: chaise lounges, rich floral rugs, heavy brocade curtains, open fireplaces and gold-framed mirrors. Two doubles with bay windows (and small bathrooms) look out onto the park, and there are two rooms with spa baths. It's adjacent to gorgeous Hyde Park.

Above Bored
B&B $$

(☏08-9444 5455; www.abovebored.com.au; 14 Norham St; d $190-200; ❄ 🛜) In a quiet residential neighbourhood, this 1927 Federation house is owned by a friendly TV scriptwriter. Two themed rooms in the main house have eclectic decor, there's also a cosy self-contained cottage with a kitchenette.

Subiaco & Kings Park

Eight Nicholson
Boutique Hotel $$$

(☏08-9382 1881; www.8nicholson.com.au; 8 Nicholson Rd; r from $369; ❄ 🛜) This stylish heritage house is one part luxury boutique hotel and one part welcoming bed and breakfast. Hip but elegant decor and interesting artworks are evidence of the well-travelled owners' eclectic tastes.

Beaches

Trigg Retreat
B&B $$

(☏08-9447 6726; www.triggretreat.com; 59 Kitchener St; r $190; ❄ @ 🛜) Quietly classy, this three-room B&B offers attractive and comfortable queen bedrooms in a modern house a short drive from Trigg

Central Perth

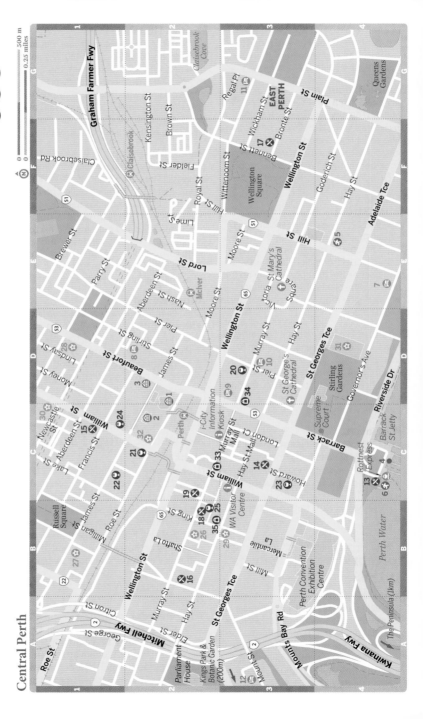

Central Perth

Beach. A cooked breakfast is included in the rates.

Other Areas

Peninsula Apartment **$$**
(☏08-9368 6688; www.thepeninsula.net; 53 South Perth Esplanade; apt from $205; ❄@🤖) While only the front few apartments have full-on views, the Peninsula's waterfront location lends itself to lazy ferry rides and sunset riverside strolls along the river. It's a sprawling, older-style complex but kept in good nick.

 Eating

City Centre

Mama Tran Vietnamese **$**
(www.mamatran.com.au; 36-40 Milligan St; snacks & mains $8-12; ❤7am-4pm) The hip

Mama Tran does hearty bowls of *pho* (Vietnamese noodle soup), excellent coffee, fresh rice-paper rolls, and Asian salads.

Tiger, Tiger Cafe **$**
(☏08-9322 8055; www.tigertigercoffeebar.com; Murray Mews; mains $8-20; ❤7am-5pm Mon & Sat, to 8pm Tue-Thu, to midnight Fri; 🤖) In a laneway off Murray St, the shabby-chic interior isn't as popular as the outdoor setting. The free wi-fi's a drawcard, but the food is also excellent – all the regular breakfast favourites, along with pasta, curry, tarts, soups and baguettes on the lunch menu.

Annalakshmi Indian **$**
(☏08-9221 3003; www.annalakshmi.com.au; 1st fl, Western Pavilion; pay by donation; ❤noon-2.30pm & 6.30-9pm Tue-Sun; 🍴) While the 360-degree views of the Swan River are worth a million dollars, the food's literally priceless. Run by volunteers you pay by donation. An eclectic clientele lines up for spicy vegetarian curries and fragrant

dhal, and chilled coconut-milk and cardamom desserts cleanse the palate.

Venn Cafe & Bar
Cafe $$

(www.venn.net; 16 Queen St; mains $13-28, pizza $15; ⏰7am-5pm Mon & Tue, to midnight Wed-Fri, 9am-midnight Sat) Equal parts design store, gallery, bar and cafe. Breakfast and lunch team with good coffee – try the quinoa and banana pancakes or carpaccio of Margaret River Wagyu beef – and later at night pizza and charcuterie combine with wine and craft beers from around Australia.

Greenhouse
Tapas $$

(☎08-9481 8333; www.greenhouseperth.com; 100 St Georges Tce; tapas $10-19; ⏰7am-midnight Mon-Sat) 🍃 Groundbreaking design combines with excellent food at this hip tapas-style eatery. Asian and Middle Eastern influences inform a sustainably sourced menu including spiced lamb with yoghurt and quinoa, or lamb with pistachio and pomegranate.

Restaurant Amusé
Modern Australian $$$

(☎08-9325 4900; www.restaurantamuse.com.au; 64 Bronte St; degustation $125; ⏰6.30pm-late Tue-Sat) The critics have certainly been amused by this degustation-only establishment, regularly rated as WA's finest. The latest gong was for Perth's Restaurant of the Year in the 2013 *Good Food Guide*. Book well ahead.

Northbridge, Highgate & Mt Lawley

Little Willy's
Cafe $

(267 William St; mains $5-14; ⏰6am-6pm Mon-Fri, 8am-4pm Sat & Sun) Grab a sidewalk table and tuck into robust treats like the city's best breakfast burrito and bircher museli. It's also a preferred coffee haunt for the hip Northbridge indie set. BYO skinny jeans.

Cantina 663
Mediterranean $$

(☎08-9370 4883; www.cantina663.com; 663 Beaufort St; lunch $12-28, dinner $26-34;

Left: Must Winebar; **Below:** Tiger, Tiger (p311)
(LEFT & BELOW) ORIEN HARVEY/GETTY IMAGES ©

8am-late Mon-Sat, to 3pm
Sun) Spanish, Portuguese and Italian flavours all feature at this chic but casual cantina. Service can be a bit too cool for school, but it's worth waiting for dishes like Ortiz anchovies with lemon and charred bread.

Beaufort St Merchant   Cafe $$
(☎08-9328 6299; www.beaufortmerchant. com; 488 Beaufort St; breakfast $13-22, lunch & dinner $24-37; ⊘7am-10pm) Our favourite cafe in Mt Lawley, and one of our favourite cafes in Perth – especially for a leisurely breakfast over the papers and a couple of coffees. Go for the chorizo and manchego-cheese tortilla, and work out what you'd order if you came back for dinner. Maybe the lime-baked ocean trout or crab linguini, we reckon.

Namh Thai   Thai $$$
(☎08-9328 7500; 223 Bulwer St; mains $22-40; ⊘6-10pm Mon-Sat) Namh Thai experiments with interesting taste combinations – duck with lychees is the speciality – and

serves them in an elegant candlelit dining room. Fridays and Saturdays are given over to banquet-style dining.

Must Winebar   French $$$
(☎08-9328 8255; www.must.com.au; 519 Beaufort St; mains $39-46; ⊘noon-midnight) Not content with being Perth's best wine bar, Must is one of its best restaurants as well. The Gallic vibe is hip, slick and a little bit cheeky, and the menu marries classic French bistro flavours with the best local produce.

Mt Hawthorn & Leederville

Kitsch   Asian $$
(www.kitschbar.com.au; 229 Oxford St; small plates $5-19; ⊘5pm-midnight Tue-Sat) Southeast Asian–style street food, Thai beers and an eclectic garden make Kitsch a great spot for a few laidback hours of

313

Perth for Children

With a usually clement climate and plenty of open spaces and beaches to run around on, Perth is a great place to bring children. Of the beaches, Cottesloe is the safest. If the kids are old enough, take advantage of the bike tracks that stretch along the river and the coast. Kings Park has playgrounds and walking tracks.

Many of Perth's big attractions cater well for young audiences, especially AQWA, the WA Museum and the Art Gallery of Western Australia.

Part of the fun of **Perth Zoo** (www.perthzoo.wa.gov.au; 20 Labouchere Rd; adult/child $28/14; 9am-5pm) is getting there by ferry. **Scitech** (www.scitech.org.au; Sutherland St, City West Centre; adult/child $14/9; 10am-4pm) has more than 160 hands-on, large-scale science and technology exhibits.

Adventure World (www.adventureworld.net.au; 179 Progress Dr; adult/child $51/43; 10am-5pm Thu-Mon late Sep-early May, daily in school holidays) has rides, pools, waterslides and a castle. It's open daily during school holidays and through December.

At 26 sq km, **Whiteman Park** (www.whitemanpark.com; enter from Lord St or Beechboro Rd, West Swan; 8.30am-6pm) is Perth's biggest, with more than 30km of walkways and bike paths, and numerous picnic and barbecue spots. Within its ordered grounds are **Caversham Wildlife Park** (www.cavershamwildlife.com.au; adult/child $23/10; 9am-5.30pm, last entry 4.30pm), **Bennet Brook Railway** (www.whitemanpark.com; adult/child $8/4; 11am-1pm Wed, Thu, Sat & Sun), **tram rides** (www.pets.org.au; adult/child $5/2.50; noon-2pm Tue & Fri-Sun) and the **Motor Museum of WA** (www.motormuseumofwa.asn.au; adult/child $10/7; 10am-4pm).

---

tasty grazing. Standout dishes include the son-in-law eggs with tamarind and pork crackling, or the five-spice pork with plums and ginger chilli caramel.

Duende
Tapas $$

(08-9228 0123; www.duende.com.au; 662 Newcastle St; tapas & mains $14-29; 7.30am-late) Stellar modern-accented tapas are served, so make a meal of it or call in for a late-night glass of dessert wine and *churros* (Spanish doughnuts). We're also partial to Duende's crab and chorizo omelette for brunch.

Sayers
Cafe $$

(www.sayersfood.com.au; 224 Carr Pl; mains $10-27; 7am-3pm) This classy cafe has a counter groaning under the weight of an alluring cake selection. The breakfast menu includes eggy treats like a beetroot-cured salmon omelette, and

lunch highlights include a zingy calamari, watermelon and fresh mint salad.

Subiaco & Kings Park

Subiaco Hotel
Gastropub $$

(08-9381 3069; www.subiacohotel.com.au; 465 Hay St; mains $19-34; 7am-late) The Subi's buzzy dining room showcases classy fare including Asian-inspired pork belly, perfectly cooked steaks, and excellent fish dishes.

Drinking & Nightlife

City Centre

Greenhouse
Cocktail Bar

(www.greenhouseperth.com; 100 St Georges Tce; 7am-midnight Mon-Sat) In a city so in love with the great outdoors, it's surprising that nobody's opened a rooftop bar in the central city before now. Hip, eco-conscious Greenhouse is leading the way, mixing up a storm amid the greenery with great cocktails and an interesting beer and wine list.

Helvetica
Bar

(www.helveticabar.com.au; rear 101 St Georges Tce; ⏱3pm-midnight Tue-Thu, 6pm-midnight Fri, 6pm-midnight Sat) Clever artsy types tap their toes to alternative pop in this bar named after a typeface and specialising in whisky and cocktails. The concealed entry is off Howard St: look for the chandelier in the lane behind Andaluz tapas bar.

Wolfe Lane
Cocktail Bar

(www.wolflane.com.au; Wolfe Lane; ⏱4pm-midnight Tue-Sat) Exposed bricks, classic retro furniture and high ceilings create a pretty decent WA approximation of a New York loft. A serious approach to cocktails and wine combines with an eclectic beer selection, and bar snacks include shared plates of cheese and chorizo.

Ambar
Club

(www.boomtick.com.au/ambar; 104 Murray St; ⏱10pm-5am Fri & Sat) Perth's premier club for breakbeat, drum'n'bass and visiting international DJs.

Geisha
Club

(www.geishabar.com.au; 135a James St; ⏱11pm-6am Fri & Sat) A small-and-pumping DJ-driven, gay-friendly club.

....

Northbridge, Highgate & Mt Lawley

Mechanics Institute
Bar

(www.mechanicsinstitute bar.com.au; 222 William St; ⏱noon-midnight Tue-Sun) Negotiate the laneway entrance around the corner on James St to discover one of Perth's most down-to-earth small bars. Share one of the big tables on the deck or nab a stool by the bar. You can also order in a gourmet burger from **Flipside** (www.flipsideburgerbar.com.au; 222 William St; burgers $10.50-14.50; ⏱11.30am-10pm Tue-Sat, to 9pm Sun) downstairs.

Five Bar
Craft Beer, Cafe

(www.fivebar.com.au; 560 Beaufort St; ⏱11am-midnight) More than 50 international and Australian craft beers – and a few inter-esting ciders – make Mt Lawley's Five Bar worth seeking out by the discerning drinker. Wine lovers are also well catered for, and the menu leans towards classy comfort food.

Ezra Pound
Bar

(www.epbar.com.au; 189 William St; ⏱1pm-midnight Thu-Tue) Down a much graffitied lane leading off William St, Ezra Pound is favoured by Northbridge's bohemian set. Earnest conversations about Kerouac and Kafka are strictly optional.

His Majesty's Theatre (p316)
CHRIS MELLOR/GETTY IMAGES ©

Brisbane
Pub

(www.thebrisbanehotel.com.au; 292 Beaufort St; ⏱11.30am-late) This classic corner pub (1898) is now a thoroughly modern venue, where each space seamlessly blends into the next. Best of all is the large courtyard where the phoenix palms and ponds provide a balmy holiday feel.

Bird
Bar

(http://williamstreetbird.com; 181 William St; ⏱1pm-midnight) Grungy indie bar that's always worth a look for local bands and DJs. Upstairs there's a brick-lined deck with city views.

Subiaco & Kings Park

Honey Lounge
Bar

(663 Newcastle St; ⏱Tue-Sun) Ladies only on Queen Bee nights the first Thursday of every month.

Beaches

Cottesloe Beach Hotel
Pub

(www.cottesloebeachhotel.com.au; 104 Marine Pde; ⏱11am-midnight Mon-Sat, to 10pm Sun) Grab a spot on the lawn in the massive beer garden, or watch the sun set from the balcony. A recent trendy makeover has installed a specialist craft beer bar downstairs.

⭐ Entertainment

LIVE MUSIC

Ellington Jazz Club
Jazz

(www.ellingtonjazz.com.au; 191 Beaufort St; ⏱7pm-1am Mon-Thu, to 3am Fri & Sat, 5pm-midnight Sun) Live jazz nightly in this handsome, intimate venue.

Bakery
Live Music

(www.nowbaking.com.au; 233 James St; ⏱7pm-late) Popular indie gigs are held almost every weekend.

Amplifier
Live Music

(www.amplifiercapitol.com.au; rear 383 Murray St) Live (mainly indie) bands. Adjaecent is Capitol, used mainly for DJ gigs.

Moon
Live Music

(www.themoon.com.au; 323 William St; ⏱6pm-late Mon-Tue, 11am-late Wed-Sun) Low-key, late-night cafe with singer-songwriters on Wednesdays, jazz on Thursdays, and poetry on Saturday afternoons.

THEATRE & CLASSICAL MUSIC

State Theatre Centre
Theatre

(www.statetheatrecentrewa.com.au; 174 William St) Includes the Heath Ledger Theatre and the smaller Studio Underground, and home to the Black Swan State Theatre Company and Perth Theatre Company.

His Majesty's Theatre
Theatre

(www.hismajestystheatre.com.au; 825 Hay St) Home to the **West Australian Ballet** (www.waballet.com.au) and **West Australian Opera** (www.waopera.asn.au).

Perth Concert Hall
Concert Venue

(www.perthconcerthall.com.au; 5 St Georges Tce) Home to the **Western Australian Symphony Orchestra** (WASO; www.waso.com.au).

CINEMA

Somerville Auditorium
Cinema

(www.perthfestival.com.au; 35 Stirling Hwy; ⏱Dec-Mar) The Perth Festival's film program is held on beautiful grounds surrounded by pine trees.

Luna
Cinema

(www.lunapalace.com.au; 155 Oxford St) Art-house cinema with Monday double features.

Moonlight Cinema
Cinema

(www.moonlight.com.au; Synergy Parklands, Kings Park) Movies are shown during summer only.

🔒 Shopping

City Centre

Wheels & Doll Baby
Clothing

(www.wheelsanddollbaby.com; 26 King St; ⏱10am-6pm Mon-Sat, 11am-5pm Sun) Punky rock chick chic with a bit of baby doll mixed in. Perhaps Perth fashion's coolest

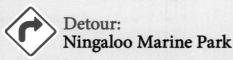

Detour:
Ningaloo Marine Park

A two-hour flight north of Perth, Ningaloo is Australia's largest fringing reef, in places only 100m offshore, and this accessibility and the fact that it's home to a staggering array of **marine life** is what makes it so popular. Sharks, manta rays, humpback whales, turtles, dugongs and dolphins complement more than 500 species of fish.

There's excellent marine activity to enjoy year-round:

November to March Turtles – three endangered species nestle and hatch in the dunes.

March Coral spawning – an amazing event seven days after the full moon.

Mid-March to July Whale sharks – the biggest fish on the planet arrive for the coral spawning.

May to November Manta rays – present year-round; their numbers increase dramatically over winter and spring.

June to November Humpback whales – they breed in the warm tropics, then head back south to feed in the Antarctic.

More than 220 species of hard **coral** have been recorded in Ningaloo, ranging from bulbous brain corals found on bommies, to delicate branching staghorns and the slow-growing massive coral. Spawning, where branches of hermaphroditic coral simultaneously eject eggs and sperm into the water, occurs after full and new moons between February and May, but the peak action is usually six to 10 days after the March full moon.

It's this spawning that attracts the park's biggest drawcard, the solitary speckled **whale shark** (*Rhiniodon typus*). You can upload your amazing whale-shark pics to **Ecocean** (www.whaleshark.org), which will identify and track your whale shark.

Most travellers visit Ningaloo Marine Park to snorkel. Stop at **Milyering visitor centre** (☏ 08-9949 2808; Yardie Creek Rd; ☺ 9am-3.45pm) for maps and information on the best spots and conditions. The shop next to the park office sells and rents snorkelling equipment ($10 per day, $15 overnight).

export, and worn by Courtney Love, Katy Perry and Debbie Harry.

78 Records   Music
(www.78records.com.au; upstairs 255 Murray St Mall; ☺ 9am-5pm Mon-Sat, from 11am Sun) Independent record shop with a massive range of CDs and lots of specials. Also good for vinyl and tickets to rock and indie gigs.

Pigeonhole   Clothing, Accessories
(www.pigeonhole.com.au; Shop 16, Bon Marche Arcade, 80 Barrack St; ☺ 10am-5.30pm

Mon-Sun) Hip clothing, and stylish retro accessories and gifts. There are five stores around the city – the main store is adjacent to the associated **Cabin Fever** (88 Barrack St, Bon Marche Arcade; snacks $5-10; ☺ 7am-5pm Mon-Fri, 10am-5pm Sat; ☎) cafe in Bon Marche Arcade.

Leederville

Oxford St Books   Books
(119 Oxford St) Knowledgeable staff, great range of fiction and a travel section.

If You Like...
The Underwater World

If you like diving and snorkelling at Ningaloo Marine Park, here are some other beaut places to explore the underwater world:

1 GERALDTON
The Abrolhos archipelago of 122 coral islands is about 60km off the coast of Geraldton, itself three hours south of Shark Bay. Here Acropora genus corals abound and, thanks to the warm Leeuwin Current, a rare and spectacular mix of tropical and temperate fish species thrives.

2 BUSSELTON
Take the plunge into Geographe Bay at Busselton, 230km south of Perth. Don't miss Four Mile Reef (a 40km limestone ledge about 6.5km off the coast) and the scuttled navy vessel HMAS *Swan* off Dunsborough.

3 ALBANY
Albany has been a top-class diving destination since the warship HMAS *Perth* was scuttled in 2001, creating an artificial reef. Natural reefs here feature temperate corals, home to the bizarre and wonderful leafy and weedy sea dragons.

4 ESPERANCE
In the amazing Recherche Archipelago off Esperance you can bubble beneath the surface to the wreck of the *Sanko Harvest*. Keep an eye out for dolphins.

Subiaco & Kings Park

Indigenart Indigenous Art
(www.mossensongalleries.com.au; 115 Hay St; ⊙10am-5pm Mon-Fri, 11am-4pm Sat) Reputable Indigenart carries art from around the country, with a particular focus on WA.

ℹ Information

Medical Services

Royal Perth Hospital (☎08-9224 2244; www. rph.wa.gov.au; Victoria Sq) In the CBD.

Travel Medicine Centre (☎08-9321 7888; www. travelmed.com.au; 5 Mill St; ⊙8am-5pm Mon-Fri)

Tourist Information

i-City Information Kiosk (Murray St Mall; ⊙9.30am-4.30pm Mon-Thu & Sat, to 8pm Fri, 11am-3.30pm Sun) Volunteer-run walking tours.

WA Visitor Centre (☎08-9483 1111, 1800 812 808; www.bestofwa.com.au; 55 William St; ⊙9am-5.30pm Mon-Fri, 9.30am-4.30pm Sat, 11am-4.30pm Sun) Information on all of WA.

ℹ Getting There & Away

Air
For details on flights to Perth from international, interstate and other Western Australian destinations, see Transport (p396).

ℹ Getting Around

To/From the Airport
The domestic and international terminals of Perth's airport are 10km and 13km east of Perth respectively, near Guildford. Taxi fares to the city are around $40 from the domestic/ international terminal, and about $60 to Fremantle.

Connect (☎1300 666 806; www. perthairportconnect.com.au) runs shuttles to and from hotels and hostels in the city centre (one way/return $18/30, every 50 minutes) and in Fremantle (one way/return $33/58, every 2½ hours).

Transperth bus 37 travels to the domestic airport from St Georges Tce, near William St ($4.55, 44 minutes, every 10 to 30 minutes, hourly after 7pm).

Public Transport
Transperth (☎13 62 13; www.transperth.wa.gov. au) operates Perth's public buses, trains and ferries. There are Transperth information offices at Perth Station (Wellington St), Wellington St Bus Station, Perth Underground Station (off Murray St) and the Esplanade Busport (Mounts Bay Rd). There's also a journey planner on the website.

From the central city, the following fares apply for all public transport:

Free Transit Zone (FTZ) Central commercial area, bounded (roughly) by Fraser Ave, Kings Park Rd, Thomas St, Newcastle St, Parry St, Lord St and the river (including City West and

Claisebrook train stations, to the west and east respectively).

Zone 1 City centre and inner suburbs ($2.70).

Zone 2 Fremantle, Guildford and the beaches as far north as Sorrento ($4).

DayRider Unlimited travel after 9am weekdays and all day on the weekend in any zone ($11).

FamilyRider Lets two adults and up to five children travel for a total of $1 on weekends, after 6pm weekdays and after 9am on weekdays during school holidays.

Bus

As well as regular buses the FTZ is well covered during the day by the three free CAT (Central Area Transit) services. The Yellow and Red CATs operate east–west routes, Yellow sticking mainly to Wellington St and Red looping roughly east on Murray and west on Hay. The Blue Cat does a figure eight through Northbridge and the south end of the city; this is the only one to run late – until 1am on Friday and Saturday nights only.

The metropolitan area is serviced by a wide network of Transperth buses. Pick up timetables from any of the Transperth information centres or use the 'journey planner' on its website.

Ferry

The only ferry runs every 20 to 30 minutes between Barrack St Jetty and Mends St Jetty in South Perth – use it to get to the zoo or for a bargain from-the-river glimpse of the Perth skyline.

Train

Transperth operates five train lines from around 5.20am to midnight weekdays and until about 2am Saturday and Sunday. Your rail ticket can also be used on Transperth buses and ferries within the ticket's zone.

Taxi

The two main companies are Swan Taxis (☏13 13 30; www.swantaxis.com.au) and Black & White (☏13 10 08; www.bwtaxi.com.au), both of which have wheelchair-accessible cabs.

FREMANTLE

Perth has sprawled to enfold Fremantle within its suburbs, yet the port city maintains its own distinct personality – proud of its nautical ties, working-class roots, bohemian reputation and, especially, its football team.

Fremantle Markets (p321)

RICHARD I'ANSON/GETTY IMAGES ©

There's a lot to enjoy here – fantastic museums, edgy galleries, pubs thrumming with live music and a thriving coffee culture.

◉ Sights

Fremantle Prison
Historic Building

(☏08-9336 9200; www.fremantleprison.com.au; 1 The Terrace; torchlight tours $25/21; ⊘9am-5.30pm) With its foreboding 5m-high walls enclosing a nearly 6-hectare site, the old convict-era prison still dominates present-day Fremantle. In 2010 its cultural status was recognised, along with 10 other penal buildings, as part of the Australian Convict Sites entry on the Unesco World Heritage list.

To enter the prison proper, you'll need to take a tour. During the day there are two fascinating 1¼-hour tours on offer (Doing Time and Great Escapes), timed so that you can take one after the other on a combined ticket (single tour adult/child $19/10, combined $26/17).

Bookings are required for the two more intense experiences on offer. Torchlight Tours (90 minutes, adult/child $25/21, Wednesday and Friday evenings) are designed to chill. The 2½-hour Tunnels Tour (adult/child over 12 $60/40) takes you 20m underground to tunnels and includes an underground boat ride.

Western Australian Museum – Maritime
Museum

(www.museum.wa.gov.au; Victoria Quay; adult/child museum $10/3, submarine $10/3, museum & submarine $16/5; ⊘9.30am-5pm) Housed in an intriguing sail-shaped building on the harbour, just west of the city centre, this is a fascinating exploration of WA's relationship with the ocean. Various boats are on display and, if you're not claustrophobic, you can take an hour-long tour of the Australian Navy submarine HMAS *Ovens* (departing every half-hour from 10am to 3.30pm).

Western Australian Museum – Shipwreck Galleries
Museum

(www.museum.wa.gov.au; Cliff St; admission by donation; ⊘9.30am-5pm) Housed in an 1852 commissariat store, the Shipwreck Galleries are considered the finest display of maritime archaeology in the southern hemisphere. The highlight is the Batavia Gallery, where a section of the hull of Dutch merchant ship the *Batavia*, wrecked in 1629, is displayed.

Fremantle Arts Centre
Gallery

(www.fac.org.au; 1 Finnerty St; ⊘10am-5pm) FREE An impressive neo-Gothic building surrounded by lovely elm-shaded gardens, the Fremantle Arts Centre was constructed by convict labourers as a lunatic asylum in the 1860s. Saved from demolition in the 1960s, it houses interesting exhibitions and the excellent Canvas (p323) cafe.

Fremantle Prison
GREG ELMS/GETTY IMAGES ©

During summer, there's concerts, courses and workshops.

Fremantle Markets Market

(www.fremantlemarkets.com.au; cnr South Tce & Henderson St; ⊗8am-8pm Fri, to 6pm Sat & Sun) FREE Originally opened in 1897, these colourful markets were reopened in 1975 and today draw slow-moving crowds, combing over souvenirs such as plastic boomerangs and swan-shaped magnets. The fresh produce section is a good place to stock up on snacks.

Tours

Fremantle Tram Tours City

(☑08-9433 6674; www.fremantletrams.com.au; Ghostly Tour adult/child $70/50, Lunch & Tram adult/child $79/42, Triple Tour adult/child $85/40, Tram & Prison adult/child $42/13) Looking like a heritage tram, this bus departs from the Town Hall on an all-day hop-on, hop-off circuit around the city (adult/child $24/5). The **Ghostly Tour** runs 6.45pm to 10.30pm Fridays and visits the prison, Round House and Fremantle Arts Centre (former asylum) by torchlight.

Captain Cook Cruises Cruise

(☑08-9325 3341; www.captaincookcruises.com.au; C Shed) Cruises between Fremantle and Perth (adult/child $25/15). A three-hour lunch cruise departs at 12.45pm (adult/child $62/41).

Fremantle Indigenous Heritage Tours Walking Tour

(☑08-9431 7878; www.indigenouswa.com; adult/child $25/15; ⊗10.30am) Highly regarded tour covering the history of Fremantle and the Nyoongar and Wadjuk people. Book at the Fremantle visitor centre.

Sleeping

Fothergills of Fremantle B&B $$

(☑08-9335 6784; www.fothergills.net.au; 18-22 Ord St; r $175-225; ❄ 🤶) Naked bronze women sprout from the front garden, while a life-size floral cow shelters on the verandah of these neighbouring

mansions on the hill. Inside, the decor is in keeping with their venerable age (built 1892), aside from the contemporary art scattered about.

Terrace Central B&B Hotel B&B $$

(☑08-9335 6600; www.terracecentral.com.au; 79-85 South Tce; d $190-215; ❄ @ 🤶) Terrace Central may be a character-filled B&B at heart, but its larger size gives it the feel of a boutique hotel. The main section is created from an 1888 bakery and an adjoined row of terrace houses, and there are also modern one- and two-bedroom apartments.

Port Mill B&B B&B $$

(☑08-9433 3832; www.portmillbb.com.au; 3/17 Essex St; r $179-299; ❄ 🤶) One of the most luxurious B&Bs in town, this is clearly the love child of Paris and Freo. Crafted from local limestone (it was built in 1862 as a mill), inside it's all modern Parisian-style, with gleaming taps, contemporary French furniture and wrought-iron balconies. French doors open out to the sun-filled decks, where you can tinkle the china on your breakfast platter.

Norfolk Hotel Hotel $$

(☑08-9335 5405; www.norfolkhotel.com.au; 47 South Tce; s/d without bathroom $100/140, d with bathroom $180; ❄ 🤶) Far above your standard pub digs, they've all been tastefully decorated in muted tones and crisp white linen, and there's a communal sitting room. It can be noisy on weekends, but the bar closes at midnight .

Bannister Suites Fremantle Hotel $$

(☑08-9435 1288; www.bannistersuitesfremantle.com.au; 22 Bannister St; r from $199; ❄) Modern and fresh, boutiquey Bannisters is a stylish highlight of central Fremantle's accommodation scene. It's worth paying extra for one of the suites with balconies, where you can enjoy views over the rooftops.

Quest Harbour Village Apartments $$$

(☑08-9430 3888; www.questharbourvillage.com.au; Mews Rd, Challenger Harbour; apt from

Fremantle

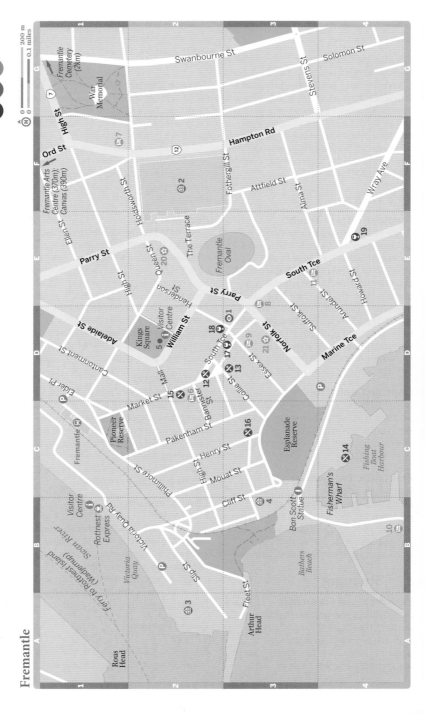

Fremantle

$292; ❋ 🛜) At the end of a wharf, this attractive, two-storey, sandstone and brick block of one- to three-bedroom apartments makes the most of its nautical setting; one-bedroom units have views over the car park to the Fishing Boat Harbour, while the others directly front the marina.

 Eating

City Centre & South Fremantle

Moore & Moore
Cafe $

(www.mooreandmoorecafe.com; 46 Henry St; mains $8-22; ⏱8am-4pm; 🛜) An urban-chic cafe that spills into the adjoining art gallery and overflows into a flagstoned courtyard. With great coffee, good cooked breakfasts, pastries, wraps and free wi-fi, it's a great place to linger.

iPho
Vietnamese $

(1/25 Collie St; mains $12.50-22; ⏱11.30am-9.30pm Tue-Sun) Settle into the mod-Asian decor and multitask your way through the menu including crispy *cha gio* (spring rolls), plump *banh xeo* (Vietnamese crepes), and hearty noodle-filled bowls of *pho*.

Canvas
Cafe $$

(www.canvasatfremantleartscentre.com; Fremantle Arts Centre; mains $12-25; ⏱8.30am-4pm) Located in the Fremantle Arts Centre, Freo's best cafe channels Middle Eastern, Spanish and North African culinary influences. Breakfast highlights are the baked-egg dishes – you should try the Israeli-style Red Shakshuka or the Spanish eggs Flamenco – while lunch presents everything from citrus-cured salmon to scallops.

Maya
Indian $$

(📞08-9335 2796; www.mayarestaurant.com.au; 77 Market St; mains $18-29; ⏱6pm-late Tue-Sun, noon-3pm Fri) Maya's white tablecloths and wooden chairs signal classic style without the pomp. Its well-executed meals have made it a popular local spot for years, earning it the reputation of WA's best Indian restaurant.

Gino's
Cafe $$

(www.ginoscafe.com.au; 1 South Tce; mains $15-30; ⏱6am-late; 🛜) Old-school Gino's is Fremantle's most famous cafe, and while it has become a tourist attraction in its own right, the locals still treat it as their second living room, only with better coffee.

Fishing Boat Harbour

Little Creatures   Pub $$

(www.littlecreatures.com.au; 40 Mews Rd; pizzas $18-34, shared plates $9-24; ⏰10am-midnight) Little Creatures is classic Freo: harbour views, fantastic brews (made on the premises) and excellent food. In a cavernous converted boatshed overlooking the harbour, it can get chaotic at times, but a signature Pale Ale with a wood-fired pizza will be worth the wait. More substantial shared plates include chick pea tagine and pork belly with fennel. No bookings.

North Fremantle

Harvest   Modern Australian $$$

(📞08-9336 1831; www.harvestrestaurant.net.au; 1 Harvest Rd; mains $38-42; ⏰6pm-late Tue-Thu, noon-late Fri, 8am-late Sat, 8am-3pm Sun) Swing through the heavy, fuchsia-painted metal doors and into the dark-wood dining room lined with artworks and curios. Then settle down to comforting Mod Oz dishes cooked with a dash of panache. Breakfast and lunch are less expensive.

 Drinking & Entertainment

Sail & Anchor   Pub

(www.sailandanchor.com.au; 64 South Tce; ⏰11am-midnight Mon-Sat, to 10pm Sun) More than 40 different taps delivering a stunning range of local and international beers. Welcome to the best destination for the travelling beer geek in Western Australia. Occasional live music and decent pub meals complete the picture.

Little Creatures   Brewery

(www.littlecreatures.com.au; 40 Mews Rd, Fishing Boat Harbour; ⏰10am-midnight) Try the Pale Ale and Pilsner, and other beers and ciders under the White Rabbit and Pipsqueak labels. Creatures Loft is an adjacent lounge bar with regular live entertainment and DJs. Live jazz kicks off at 4pm on Sundays.

Who's Your Mumma   Bar

(cnr Wray Ave & South Tce; ⏰4pm-late Mon-Thu, 8am-late Fri-Sun) Industrial-chic lightbulbs and polished-concrete floors are softened by recycled timber at the laid-back

Sail & Anchor

Who's Your Mumma. An eclectic crew of South Freo locals crowd in for great-value combo specials (around $15) including 'Taco Tuesdays' and 'Schnitzel Mondays'.

Norfolk Hotel   Pub
(www.norfolkhotel.com.au; 47 South Tce; ⊙11am-midnight Mon-Sat, to 10pm Sun) Slow down to Freo pace and take your time over one of the many beers on tap at this 1887 pub. Lots of interesting guest brews create havoc for the indecisive drinker, and the pub food and pizzas are very good.

Monk   Craft Beer
(www.themonk.com.au; 33 South Tce; ⊙11.30am-late) Enjoy occasional guest beers or the the Monk's own brews (kolsch, mild, wheat, porter, rauch, pale ale). The bar snacks and pizzas are also good.

Fly by Night
Musicians Club   Live Music
(www.flybynight.org; Parry St) Variety is the key at Fly by Night, a not-for-profit club that's been run by musos for musos for years. Many local bands made a start here.

Mojo's   Live Music
(www.mojosbar.com.au; 237 Queen Victoria St, North Fremantle; ⊙7pm-late) Mojo's is one of Freo's longstanding live-music venues. Local and national bands and DJs play at this small venue, and there's a sociable beer garden out the back.

Luna on SX   Cinema
(www.lunapalace.com.au; Essex St) Art-house films; set back in a lane between Essex and Norfolk Sts.

ℹ️ Information

Fremantle Hospital (☎08-9431 3333; www.fhhs.health.wa.gov.au; Alma St)

Visitor Centre (☎08-9431 7878; www.fremantlewa.com.au; Kings Sq, Town Hall; ⊙9am-5pm Mon-Fri, 10am-3pm Sat, 11.30am-2.30pm Sun) Free maps and brochures, and bookings for accommodation and tours.

> ## Local Knowledge

Fremantle

BY PHOEBE PHILLIPS, FREMANTLE LOCAL

1 LITTLE CREATURES
You never know what you're going to get at Little Creatures (p324)! Dress-up days, theme days... The main bar is really buzzy and has wicked views, and the Loft next door is more of a chilled-out lounge bar. The beer brewed here is awesome, and the food is great, too.

2 LIVE MUSIC
Mojo's (p325) in North Freo has gigs or open-mic nights each night: every hippie and his guitar has heard about Mojo's! The Basement at the Norfolk Hotel (p325) has really good bands, and DJs upstairs on Sunday and Friday. The Monk (p325) has live musicians on weekends, and there are heaps of buskers around.

3 EATING & DRINKING
Fremantle does cafe and pub culture really well. Moore & Moore (p323) in the West End is a cool little cafe attached to an art gallery. Harvest (p324) in North Fremantle is great for an upmarket dinner. Pub-wise, on the cafe strip there's the Monk, which is another microbrewery, and the Norfolk Hotel.

4 FISHING BOAT HARBOUR
There didn't used to be much here, but now there's Little Creatures and a string of fish restaurants along the boardwalk. It's all very laid-back, with lots of boat yards and yachts around.

5 ROTTNEST ISLAND
Ferries to Rottnest Island (p326) also leave from Perth, but it's a shorter ride from Fremantle. There's good surf, the snorkelling is amazing, or take a tour in a glass-bottom boat.

ℹ️ Getting There & Around

Fremantle sits within Zone 2 of the Perth public-transport system. Transperth (☎13 62 13; www.

transperth.wa.gov.au), and is only 30 minutes away by train. There are numerous buses between Perth's city centre and Fremantle, including routes 103, 106, 107, 111 and 158.

Another very pleasant way to get here from Perth is by the 1¼-hour river cruise run by Captain Cook Cruises (p321).

It's easy enough to travel by foot or on the free CAT bus service, which takes in all the major sites on a continuous loop every 10 minutes from 7.30am to 6.30pm on weekdays, until 9pm on Fridays, and from 10am to 6.30pm on the weekend.

Bicycles (Kings Sq, Fremantle Visitor Centre; ⊙9.30am-4.30pm Mon-Fri, to 3.30pm Sat, 10.30am-3.30pm Sun) can be rented for free at the visitor centre, an ideal way to get around Freo's storied streets. A refundable bond of $200 applies.

AROUND PERTH

Rottnest Island (Wadjemup)

'Rotto' has long been the family-holiday playground of choice for Perth locals. Although it's only about 19km offshore from Fremantle, this car-free, off-the-grid slice of paradise, ringed by secluded beaches and bays, feels a million miles from the metropolis.

Cycling round the 11km-long, 4.5km-wide car-free island is a real pleasure; just ride around and pick your own bit of beach to spend the day on.

If you fancy further diversions, snorkelling, fishing, surfing and diving are all excellent on the island.

Sights

Quod & Aboriginal Burial Ground
Historic Site

(Kitson St) This octagonal 1864 building with a central courtyard was once the Aboriginal prison block but is now part of a hotel. During its time as a prison, several men would sleep in each 3m by 1.7m cell with no sanitation (most of the deaths were due to disease). Immediately adjacent to the Quod is a **wooded area** where hundreds of Aboriginal prisoners were buried in unmarked graves.

Rottnest Museum
Museum

(Kitson St; admission by gold coin donation; ⊙11am-3.30pm) Housed in the old hay-store building, this little museum tells the island's natural and human history.

Activities

Excellent visibility in the temperate waters, coral reefs and shipwrecks makes Rottnest a top spot for **scuba diving** and **snorkelling**. There are snorkel trails with underwater plaques at **Little Salmon Bay** and **Parker Point**.

The best surfing breaks are at **Strickland**, **Salmon** and **Stark Bays**, at the west end of the island.

Rottnest Island Bike Hire
Bicycle Hire

(☏08-9292 5105; www.rottnestisland.com; cnr Bedford Ave & Welch Way; ⊙8.30am-4pm, to 5.30pm summer) Rents masks, snorkels and fins (per day $20) and surfboards (per day $50).

Tours

Rottnest Voluntary Guides
Walking Tour

(☏08-9372 9757; www.rvga.asn.au) FREE Themed walks leave from the Salt Store daily. Guides also run tours of **Wadjemup Lighthouse** (adult/child $7/3) and Oliver Hill Gun & Tunnels (adult/child $8/3.50); you'll need to make your own way there.

Discovery Coach Tour
Bus Tour

(www.rottnestisland.com; adult/child $35/17; ⊙departs 11.20am, 1.40pm & 1.50pm) Leaves from Thomson Bay three times daily (book at the visitor centre); includes commentary and a stop at West End.

Rottnest Adventure Tour
Cruise

(www.rottnestexpress.com.au; adult/child $50/25; ⊙late Sep-early Jun) Ninety-minute cruises around the coast with an emphasis on spotting wildlife, including whales in season from October to November. Pack-

Quokkas

Once found throughout the southwest, quokkas are now confined to forest on the mainland and a population of 8000 to 10,000 also remains on Rottnest Island. These cute, docile little marsupials have suffered a number of indignities over the years. First de Vlamingh's crew mistook them for rats. Then the British settlers misheard and mangled their name (the Noongar word was probably *quak-a* or *gwaga*). But worst of all, a cruel trend for 'quokka soccer' by sadistic louts in the 1990s saw many kicked to death before a $10,000 fine was imposed.

ages also available from Perth (adult/child $130/67) and Fremantle ($115/57).

Sleeping & Eating

Rottnest Lodge   Hotel $$
(☏08-9292 5161; www.rottnestlodge.com.au; Kitson St; r $190-300, mains $27-34;) It's claimed there are ghosts in this comfortable complex, which is based around the former Quod and boys' reformatory school. If that worries you, ask for a room in the new section, looking onto a salt lake.

Rottnest Island Authority Cottages   Accommodation Services $$
(☏08-9432 9111; www.rottnestisland.com; cottages $100-228) There are more than 250 villas and cottages for rent around the island. Some have magnificent beachfront positions and are palatial; others are more like beach shacks. Prices rise by around $60 for Friday and Saturday nights, and they shoot up by up to $120 in peak season (late September to April).

Hotel Rottnest   Hotel $$$
(☏08-9292 5011; www.hotelrottnest.com.au; 1 Bedford Ave; r $270-320;) Based around the former summer holiday pad for the state's governors (built in 1864), the former Quokka Arms has been transformed by a stylish renovation. The whiter-than-white rooms are smart and modern, if a tad pricey. A big glass pavilion creates an open and inviting space,

and bistro-style food (mains $19 to $38) is reasonably priced given the location.

Riva   Seafood $$
(Kitson St, Rottnest Lodge; mains $27-34; ☾noon-late) Classy Italian restaurant with a strong focus on local seafood. Prawns, squid, mussels and oysters all receive an elegant touch of the Med, and there are also wood-fired pizzas and interesting spins on duck, chicken and lamb.

ℹ Information

Visitor Centre (www.rottnestisland.com) Thomson Bay (☏08-9372 9732; www.rottnestisland.com; ☾7.30am-5pm Sat-Thu, to 7pm Fri, extended in summer) Fremantle (☏08-9432 9300; www.rottnestisland.com; E Shed, Victoria Quay) Handles check-ins for all the island authority's accommodation. There's a bookings counter at the Fremantle office, near where the ferry departs.

ℹ Getting There & Away

Air

Rottnest Air-Taxi (☏0411 264 547; www.rottnest.de) Flies from Jandakot airport in four-seater (one way/same-day return/extended return $230/330/430) or six-seater planes (one way/extended return $350/550).

Boat

Rottnest Express (☏1300 467 688; www.rottnestexpress.com.au) Fremantle (B Shed, Victoria Quay; adult/child $72.50/40) Northport

(1 Emma Pl, Northport, Rous Head; adult/child $72.50/40) Perth (Pier 2, Barrack St Jetty; adult/child $92.50/50) The prices listed are for return day trips and include the island admission fee; add $10 for an extended return. Ferry schedules are seasonal, though those listed here are roughly the minimum: Perth (1¾ hours, twice daily), Fremantle (30 minutes, five times daily) and North Fremantle (30 minutes, three times daily).

Rottnest Fast Ferries (☑08-9246 1039; www.rottnestfastferries.com.au; adult/child $83/45) Departs from Hillarys Boat Harbour (40 minutes; three times daily). Packages also available. Hillarys Boat Harbour is around 40 minutes-drive north of Perth.

ⓘ Getting Around

Bikes can be booked in advance online or on arrival from **Rottnest Island Bike Hire** (☑08-9292 5105; www.rottnestisland.com; cnr Bedford Ave & Welch Way; per hour/1/2/3/4/5 days $16/28/45/56/67/79; ⊗8.30am-4pm, to 5.30pm in summer). Rottnest Express also hires bikes (per 1/2/3 days $28/41/56).

A free shuttle runs between Thomson Bay and the main accommodation areas. The Bayseeker (day pass adult/child $14/6) does an hourly loop around the island.

THE SOUTHWEST

The farmland, forests, rivers and coast of the lush southwestern corner of WA contrast vividly with the stark, sunburnt terrain of much of the state. On land, world-class wineries beckon and tall trees provide shade for walking trails and scenic drives, while offshore, bottlenose dolphins and whales frolic, and devoted surfers search for – and often find – their perfect break.

Margaret River Wine Region

With its blissful country roads shaded by mature trees, crashing surf beaches, and, of course, excellent chardonnays and Bordeaux-style reds, Margaret River is our favourite Australian wine region and a highlight of any trip to WA.

YALLINGUP & AROUND

Beachside Yallingup is as much a mecca for salty-skinned surfers as it is for wine aficionados. You're permitted to let a 'wow' escape when the surf-battered coastline first comes into view.

◉ Sights & Activities

Wardan Aboriginal Centre Gallery
(☑08-9756 6566; www. wardan.com.au; Injidup Springs Rd, Yallingup; ⊗10am-4pm daily 15 Oct-15 Mar, closed Tue & Sat 15 Mar-15 Oct, experiences Sun, Mon, Wed & Fri) ⚑ **FREE**
Offers a window into the

Margaret River vineyard

Surfing the Southwest

Known to surfers as 'Yals' (around Yallingup) and 'Margs' (around the mouth of the Margaret River), the beaches between Capes Naturaliste and Leeuwin offer powerful reef breaks, mainly left-handers.

Around Dunsborough, the better locations are between Eagle and Bunker Bays. Near Yallingup are the Three Bears, Rabbits (a beach break towards the north of Yallingup Beach), Yallingup, Injidup Car Park and Injidup Point. You'll need a 4WD to access Guillotine/Gallows, north of Gracetown. Also around Gracetown are Huzza's, South Point and Lefthanders. The annual surfer pro is held around Margaret River Mouth and Southside ('Suicides').

---

lives of the local Wardandi people. There's a gallery, an interpretive display on the six seasons which govern the Wardandi calendar (admission $5) and the opportunity to take part in various **experiences** (experiences adult/child $20/10) such as stone-tool-making and boomerang and spear throwing. Guided bushwalks explore Wardandi spirituality and the uses of plants for food, medicine and shelter.

Ngilgi Cave Caving
(☏08-9755 2152; www.geographebay.com; Yallingup Caves Rd; adult/child $21/11; ⏱9.30am-4.30pm) Between Dunsborough and Yallingup, this 500,000-year-old cave is known for its limestone formations. Entry is by semiguided tours departing every half-hour.

 Sleeping & Eating

Wildwood Valley Cottages & Cooking School Cottages $$
(☏08-9755 2120; www.wildwoodvalley.com.au; 1481 Wildwood Rd; cottages from $220; 🛜) Luxury cottages trimmed by native bush are arrayed across 120 acres, and the property's main house also hosts the Mad About Food Cooking School with Sioban and Carlo Baldini.

Studio Bistro Modern Australian $$$
(☏08-9756 6164; www.thestudiobistro.com.au; 7 Marrinup Dr; mains $35, degustation menu with/without wine matches $125/90; 🍴) 🖼 The gallery focuses on Australian artists, while the restaurant showcases subtle dishes like pan-fried fish with cauliflower cream, radicchio, peas and crab meat. Five-course degustation menus are offered on Friday and Saturday nights. Bookings recommended.

COWARAMUP & WILYABRUP

Cowaramup is little more than a couple of blocks of shops lining Bussell Hwy. That a significant percentage of those are devoted in one way or another to eating or drinking is testament to its position at the heart of the wine region. The rustic area to the northwest known as Wilyabrup is where, in the 1960s, the Margaret River wine industry was born.

 Activities

Margaret River Regional Wine Centre Wine Shop
(www.mrwines.com; 9 Bussell Hwy, Cowaramup; ⏱10am-7pm) A one-stop shop for Margaret River wine, with daily tastings rotating between smaller wineries without cellar doors.

 Sleeping

Noble Grape Guesthouse B&B $$
(☏08-9755 5538; www.noblegrape.com.au; 29 Bussell Hwy, Cowaramup; s $135-155, d $150-190; ❄🛜) Noble Grape is more like an upmarket motel than a traditional B&B. Rooms offer a sense of privacy and each has a well-tended garden courtyard.

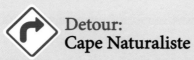

Detour:
Cape Naturaliste

Northwest of Dunsborough, Cape Naturaliste Rd leads to the excellent beaches of **Meelup**, **Eagle Bay** and **Bunker Bay**, and on to Cape Naturaliste. Bunker Bay is also home to **Bunkers Beach Cafe** (www.bunkersbeachcafe.com.au; Farm Break Lane; breakfast $14-24, lunch $16-34; ⏱11.30am-4pm), which serves an adventurous menu from a spot only metres from the sand.

The **Cape Naturaliste lighthouse** (adult/child $13/7; ⏱tours every 30min 9.30am-4pm), built in 1903, can be visited, and Above and Below packages (adult/child $27/14) incorporate entry to Ngilgi Cave (p329) near Yallingup.

Craft beer fans should definitely divert to the **Eagle Bay Brewing Co** (www.eaglebaybrewing.com.au; Eagle Bay Rd, Dunsborough; ⏱11am-5pm) for sublime rural views, great beer and wine, and woodfired pizzas.

 Eating & Drinking

Providore Deli **$**
(www.providore.com.au; 448 Tom Cullity Dr, Wilyabrup; ⏱9am-5pm) Voted one of Australia's Top 100 Gourmet Experiences by *Australian Traveller* magazine – and, given its amazing range of artisan produce including organic olive oil, tapenades and preserved fruits, we can only agree.

Vasse Felix Winery Restaurant **$$$**
(📞08-9756 5050; www.vassefelix.com.au; cnr Caves Rd & Harmans Rd S, Cowaramup; mains $29-39; ⏱10am-3pm) Vasse Felix is considered by many to have the finest restaurant in the region. The grounds are peppered with sculptures, while the gallery displaying works from the Holmes à Court collection is worth a trip in itself.

MARGARET RIVER

Although tourists might outnumber locals much of the time, Margaret River still feels like a country town. The advantage of basing yourself here is that after 5pm, once the surrounding wineries shut up shop, it's one of the few places with any vital signs.

 Sleeping

Edge of the Forest Motel **$$**
(📞08-9757 2351; www.edgeoftheforest.com.au; 25 Bussell Hwy; r $120-180; ❄🛜) New

owners have re-energised this motel a pleasant stroll from Margaret River township. The six rooms have all been recently renovated, several with a chic Asian theme.

Burnside Organic Farm Bungalows **$$$**
(📞08-9757 2139; www.burnsideorganicfarm.com.au; 287 Burnside Rd; d $275; ❄) Rammed-earth and limestone bungalows have spacious decks and designer kitchens, and the surrounding farm hosts a menagerie of animals and organic avocado and macadamia orchards.

 Eating & Drinking

Margaret River Bakery Cafe **$**
(89 Bussell Hwy; mains $10-18; ⏱7am-4pm Mon-Sat; 📷) 🥬 Elvis on the stereo, retro furniture, and kitsch needlework 'paintings' – the MRB has a rustic, playful interior. It's the perfect backdrop to the bakery's honest home-style baking, often with a vege or gluten-free spin.

Settler's Tavern Pub **$$**
(www.settlerstavern.com; 114 Bussell Hwy; mains $15-29; ⏱11am-midnight Mon-Sat, to 10pm Sun) There's live entertainment Thursday to Sunday at Settler's, so pop in for good pub grub and a beer or wine from the extensive list. Dinner options are limited

PERTH & THE WEST COAST MARGARET RIVER WINE REGION

in Margaret River, and Settler's is often wildly popular with locals and visitors.

 Information

Visitor centre (☏08-9757 2911; www.margaret river.com; Bussell Hwy; ◷9am-5pm) This sleek visitor centre includes an on-site wine centre.

 Getting Around

Margaret River Beach Bus (☏08-9757 9532; www.mrlodge.com.au) Minibus linking the township and the beaches around Prevelly ($10, three daily); summer only, bookings essential.

SOUTH COAST

Standing on the cliffs of the wild south coast as the waves pound below is an elemental experience. And on calm days, when the sea is varied shades of aquamarine and the glorious white-sand beaches lie pristine and welcoming, it's an altogether different type of magnificent.

Getting There & Away

Virgin Australia (☏13 67 89; www. virginaustralia.com) flies daily from Perth to Albany (75 minutes) and Esperance (1¾ hours).

Walpole & Nornalup

The peaceful twin inlets of Walpole and Nornalup make good bases from which to explore the heavily forested Walpole Wilderness Area – an immense wilderness incorporating a rugged coastline, several national parks, marine parks, nature reserves and forest-conservation areas – covering a whopping 3630 sq km.

Tours

WOW Wilderness Ecocruises
Cruise

(☏08-9840 1036; www.wowwilderness.com. au; adult/child $40/15) The magnificent landscape and its ecology are brought to life with anecdotes about Aboriginal settlement, salmon fishers and shipwrecked pirates. The 2½-hour cruise through the inlets and river systems leaves at 10am daily; book at the visitor centre.

Naturally Walpole Eco Tours
Ecotour

(☏08-9840 1019; www.naturallywalpole.com. au) Half-day tours through the Walpole Wilderness (adult/child $75/40), and customised winery and wildflower tours.

 Sleeping & Eating

Riverside Retreat
Chalets $$

(☏08-9840 1255; www.riversideretreat.com.au; South Coast Hwy, Nornalup; chalets $140-200) Set up off the road and on the banks of the beautiful Frankland River, these spotless and well-equipped chalets are great value, with pot-bellied stoves for cosy winter warmth, and tennis and canoeing as outdoor pursuits. Frequent visits from local wildlife make Riverside Retreat a good option for families.

Nornalup Riverside Chalets
Chalets $$

(☏08-9840 1107; www.walpole.org.au/nornalup riversidechalets; Riverside Dr, Nornalup; chalets

---

The Road to Mandalay

About 13km west of Walpole, at Crystal Springs, is an 8km gravel road to **Mandalay Beach**, where the *Mandalay,* a Norwegian barque, was wrecked in 1911. Every 10 years or so, as the sand gradually erodes with storms, the wreck eerily appears in shallow water that is walkable at low tide. The beach is glorious, often deserted, and accessed by an impressive boardwalk across sand dunes and cliffs.

$110-180) Stay a night in sleepy Nornalup in these comfortable, colourful self-contained chalets, just a rod's throw from the fish in the Frankland River.

Thurlby Herb Farm Cafe **$$**
(www.thurlbyherb.com.au; 3 Gardiner Rd; mains $15-20; ☺9am-4.30pm Mon-Fri) Apart from distilling its own essential oils and making herb-based products including soap, Thurlby serves up tasty light lunches and cakes accompanied by fresh-picked herbal teas.

 Information

Visitor Centre (☏08-9840 1111; www.walpole.com.au; South Coast Hwy, Walpole; ☺9am-5pm)

Denmark

The first wave of alternative lifestylers landed in idyllic Denmark about 20 years ago, attracted by its beaches, river, sheltered inlet, forested backdrop and rolling hinterland.

The town is located in the cool-climate Great Southern wine region and has some notable wineries, including **Howard Park** (www.howardparkwines.com.au; Scotsdale Rd; ☺10am-4pm) and **Forest Hill** (www.foresthillwines.com.au; cnr South Coast Hwy & Myers Rd; ☺10am-5pm).

Sights & Activities

Surfers and anglers usually waste no time in heading to ruggedly beautiful **Ocean Beach**. If you're keen to try surfing, accredited local instructor Mike Neunuebel gives **surf lessons** (☏0401 349 854; www.southcoastsurfinglessons.com.au; 2hr lessons incl equipment from $50).

To get your bearings, walk the **Mokare Heritage Trail** (3km circuit along the Denmark River) or the **Wilson Inlet Trail** (12km return, starting at the river mouth), which forms part of the longer **Nornalup Trail**. Put everything into perspective at **Mt Shadforth Lookout**, with its view of fine coastal scenery. The lush **Mt Shadforth Road**, running from the centre of town and finishing up on the South

Coast Hwy west of town, makes a great scenic drive, as does the longer pastoral loop of **Scotsdale Road**. Potter along these, taking your pick of attractions including alpaca farms, wineries, cheese farms, and art and craft galleries.

William Bay National Park, about 20km west of town, offers sheltered swimming in gorgeous **Greens Pool** and **Elephant Rocks**, and has good walking tracks. Swing by **Bartholomews Meadery** for a post-beach treat of homemade ice cream.

Tours

Out of Sight! Outdoors
(☏08-9848 2814; www.outofsighttours.com) Nature trips into the Walpole Wilderness (three hours, adult/child $90/45), West Cape Howe (six hours, adult/child $150/75) or Stirling Range (eight hours, adult/child $200/100); sightseeing around Denmark (two hours, adult/child $50/25); or sampling tours of the local wineries (full day $100).

Sleeping

Cape Howe Cottages Cottages **$$**
(☏08-9845 1295; www.capehowe.com.au; 322 Tennessee Rd S; cottages $170-280; ❄) For a remote getaway, these five cottages in bushland southeast of Denmark really make the grade. They're all different, but the best is only 1.5km from dolphin-favoured Lowlands Beach and is properly plush – with a BBQ on the deck, a dishwasher in the kitchen and laundry facilities.

Eating & Drinking

Mrs Jones Cafe **$$**
(☏0467 481 878; www.mrsjonescafe.com; 12 Mt Shadforth Rd; breakfast $9-18, lunch $14-21; ☺7am-4pm) Denmark's best coffee is at this spacious spot with high ceilings and exposed beams. Settle in for interesting cafe fare including Turkish eggs with roasted pumpkin, chorizo and lentils, or Asian-style duck pancakes with a plum sauce.

ANDREW BAIN/GETTY IMAGES ©

Don't Miss
Walpole-Nornalup National Park

The giant trees of this park include red, yellow and Rates tingle trees, and, closer to the coast, the red flowering gum.

In the **Valley of the Giants** the **Tree Top Walk** (pictured above) is Walpole's main drawcard. A 600m-long ramp rises from the floor of the valley, allowing visitors access high into the canopy of the giant tingle trees. At its highest point the ramp is 40m above the ground. It's on a gentle incline so it's easy to walk and is even accessible by assisted wheelchair. At ground level the **Ancient Empire** boardwalk meanders around and through the base of veteran red tingles, some of which are 16m in circumference.

There are numerous good walking tracks around, including a section of the **Bibbulmun Track**, which passes through Walpole to Coalmine Beach. Scenic drives include the **Knoll Drive**, 3km east of Walpole; the **Valley of the Giants Road**; and the drive through pastoral country to **Mt Frankland**, 29km north of Walpole. Here you can climb to the summit for panoramic views or walk around the trail at its base. Opposite Knoll Dr, Hilltop Rd leads to a **giant tingle tree**; this road continues to the **Circular Pool** on the Frankland River, which is a popular canoeing spot. You can also hire canoes from Nornalup Riverside Chalets (see p331).

Midway between Nornalup and Peaceful Bay, check out **Conspicuous Cliffs**. It's a great spot for whale watching from July to November, with a boardwalk, hilltop lookout and steepish 800m walk to the beach.

NEED TO KNOW

www.valleyofthegiants.com.au; Valley of the Giants Tree Top Walk adult/child $12.50/5; ⊗Valley of the Giants Tree Top Walk 9am-4.15pm

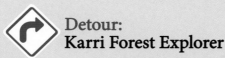

Detour:
Karri Forest Explorer

Punctuated by glorious walks, magnificent individual trees, picnic areas and lots of interpretive signage, this tourist drive wends its way along 86km of scenic (partly unsealed) roads through three national parks (vehicle entry $11).

Popular attractions include the **Gloucester Tree**; if you're feeling fit and fearless, make the 58m climb to the top. The **Dave Evans Bicentennial Tree**, tallest of the 'climbing trees' at 68m, is in Warren National Park, 11km south of Pemberton. The Bicentennial Tree one-way loop passes through 250-year-old karri stands.

Pick up a brochure from Pemberton's visitor centre.

Pepper & Salt
Modern Australian **$$$**
(☏08-9848 3053; www.matildasestate.com; 18 Hamilton St, Matilda's Estate; mains $35-40; ⊙noon-10pm) Highlights include chilli-and-coconut prawns, or the great-value tasting platter ($48), which effortlessly detours from Asia to the Middle East. Buy some wine from the adjacent Matilda's Estate before settling in for a foodies adventure. Bookings recommended.

Boston Brewery
Craft Beer
(www.willoughbypark.com.au; Willoughby Winery, South Coast Hwy; pizzas $18-23, mains $24-32; ⊙10am-7pm Mon-Thu, to 10pm Fri & Sat, to 9pm Sun) The industrial chic of the brewery gives way to an absolute edge-of-vineyard location, and wood-fired pizzas, meals and bar snacks go well with Boston's four beers. There's also live music from 4pm to 8pm every second Saturday afternoon.

Information

Visitor Centre (☏08-9848 2055; www.denmark.com.au; 73 South Coast Hwy; ⊙9am-5pm) Ask for *The Wine Lovers' Guide to Denmark* brochure and get exploring.

Albany

Established shortly before Perth in 1826, the oldest European settlement in the state is now the bustling commercial centre of the southern region. Albany is a mixed bag, comprising a stately colonial quarter, a waterfront in the midst of redevelopment and a hectic sprawl of malls and fast-food joints. Less ambivalent is its coastline, which is uniformly spectacular.

◉ Sights

Western Australian Museum – Albany
Museum
(www.museum.wa.gov.au; Residency Rd; admission by donation; ⊙10am-4.30pm) This branch of the state museum is split between two neighbouring buildings. The newer Eclipse building has a kids' discovery section, a lighthouse exhibition, a gallery for temporary exhibitions and a gift shop. The restored 1850s home of the resident magistrate illuminates Minang Noongar history, local natural history, and seafaring stories.

Brig Amity
Ship
(www.historicalbany.com.au; adult/child $5/2; ⊙9am-4pm) This full-scale replica of the brig which carried Albany's first British settlers from Sydney in 1826 was completed for the city's 150th anniversary. Self-guided audio tours bring to life the ship's history.

 Activities

Albany Dolphin & Whale Cruises
Whale Watching
(☏0428 429 876; www.whales.com.au; adult/child $80/45; ⊙Jul–mid-Oct) Runs regular whale-watching cruises in season.

Sleeping

Albany Harbourside Apartments **$$**
(☏08-9842 1769; www.albanyharbourside.
com.au; 8 Festing St; d $159-219; ❄) Albany
Harbourside's portfolio includes spacious
and spotless apartments on Festing St,
and three other self-contained options
arrayed around central Albany. Decor is
modern and colourful, and some apart-
ments have ocean views.

**Beach House at
Bayside** Boutique Hotel **$$$**
(☏08-9844 8844; www.thebeachhouseat
bayside.com.au; 33 Barry Ct, Collingwood Park;
r $249-335; ❄) Positioned right by the
beach and the golf course in a quiet
cul-de-sac, midway between Middleton
Beach and Emu Point, this modern block
distinguishes itself with absolutely wonderful service.

Eating & Drinking

York Street Cafe Cafe **$$**
(www.184york.com; 184 York St; lunch $10-22,
dinner $22-36; ⊙7.30am-3pm Mon-Tue, to late
Wed-Fri, 8.30am-2.30pm Sat & Sun) Lunch
includes roasted tomato and prosciutto
salad or chicken pot pie, while at dinner
the attention turns to bistro items like
prawns with pasta and a hearty goat
tagine. It's BYO wine.

White Star Hotel Pub **$$**
(72 Stirling Tce; mains $16-34; ⊙11am-late)
With 20 beers on tap (including its own
Tanglehead brews) and excellent pub
grub, this old pub gets a gold star. Sunday
night folk and blues gigs are a good opportunity to share a pint with Albany's
laid-back locals.

Liberté Cafe, Bar
(162 Stirling Tce, London Hotel; ⊙8.30am-5pm
Mon & Tue, till late Wed-Sat) Channelling a
louche Parisian cafe and a velvet-trimmed
speakeasy, Liberté's Gallic-inspired versa-
tility includes good coffee and cake during
the day, and craft beer, potent cocktails
and Med-inspired tapas later at night.

Information

Visitor Centre (☏08-9841 9290; www.
amazingalbany.com; Proudlove Pde; ⊙9am-5pm)
In the old train station.

Replica of the Brig Amity

ANDREW WATSON/GETTY IMAGES ©

Around Albany

◎ Sights

Whale World Museum   Museum

(☎08-9844 4019; www.whaleworld.org; French-man Bay Rd; adult/child $29/10; ☺9am-5pm)
When the Cheynes Beach Whaling Station ceased operations in November 1978, few could predict its gore-covered decks would be covered in tourists, craning to see passing whales. The museum screens several films about marine life and whaling operations, and displays giant skeletons, harpoons, whaleboat models and scrimshaw (etchings on whalebone). Free guided tours depart hourly from 10am to 3pm.

Torndirrup
National Park   National Park

(Frenchman Bay Rd) FREE Covering much of the peninsula enclosing the southern reaches of King George Sound, this national park is known for its windswept, ocean-bashed cliffs. The Gap is a natural cleft in the rock, channelling surf through walls of granite, and close by is the Natural Bridge.

Further east, the spectacular Blowholes are worth the 78 steps down and back up.

Esperance

Esperance sits on the Bay of Isles, a seascape of aquamarine waters and squeaky white beaches. Despite its southeastern isolation, Esperance still has devotees who make the intrepid pilgrimage from Perth to melt into the low-key, community-oriented vibe.

◎ Sights & Activities

Esperance Museum   Museum

(cnr James & Dempster Sts; adult/child $6/2; ☺1.30-4.30pm) Glass cabinets are crammed with sea shells, frog ornaments, tennis rackets and bed pans. Bigger items include boats, a train carriage and the remains of the USA's spacecraft *Skylab*, which made its fiery re-entry at Balladonia, east of Esperance, in 1979.

Great Ocean Drive   Scenic Drive

Many of Esperance's most dramatic sights can be seen on this well-signposted

Blue whale skeleton, Whale World Museum

40km loop. Starting from the waterfront it heads southwest past breathtaking and popular surfing and swimming spots including **Blue Haven Beach** and **Twilight Cove**. Stop at rugged **Observatory Point** and the lookout on **Wireless Hill**. A turn-off leads to the **wind farm**, supplying 23% of Esperance's electricity. Walking among the turbines is surreal when it's windy.

Tours

Esperance Island Cruises   Cruise
(☎08-9071 5757; www.woodyisland.com.au; 72 The Esplanade; ☼daily late Sep-May) Tours include Esperance Bay and Woody Island in a power catamaran (half-/full day $95/150), getting close to fur seals, sea lions, Cape Barren geese and (with luck) dolphins. In January there's a ferry to Woody Island (adult/child return $60/30).

Kepa Kurl Eco Cultural Discovery Tours   Cultural Tour
(☎08-9072 1688; www.kepakurl.com.au; Museum Village) 🚗 Explore the country from an Aboriginal perspective: visit rock art and waterholes, sample bush food and hear ancient stories (adult/child $105/90; minimum two).

Eco-Discovery Tours   Driving Tour
(☎0407 737 261; www.esperancetours.com.au) Runs 4WD tours along the sand to Cape Le Grand National Park (half-/full day $95/165, minimum two/four) and two-hour circuits of the Great Ocean Drive (adult/child $55/40).

Sleeping

Esperance B&B by the Sea   B&B $$
(☎08-9071 5640; www.esperancebb.com; 34 Stewart St; s/d $120/170; ❄) This great-value beachhouse has a private guest wing and breathtaking views overlooking Blue Haven Beach. It's just a stroll from the ocean and a five-minute drive from Dempster St.

♥ If You Like... Discovering National Parks

If you like Walpole-Nornalup National Park, we think you'll also like these detour-worthy national parks:

1 YALGORUP NATIONAL PARK
This beautiful coastal region of woodlands, lakes and sand dunes is 50km south of Mandurah (itself 70km south of Perth). The park is an internationally significant wetland for migrating waterbirds. Rock hounds will want to see the globular thrombalites at Lake Clifton.

2 D'ENTRECASTEAUX NATIONAL PARK
This quiet gem of a national park, named after French Admiral Bruny d'Entrecasteaux, stretches for 130km along the coast 60km south of Pemberton. It's a complete contrast to the tall forests of WA's southwest, with its five rivers and wild stretches of coastal heath, sand dunes, cliffs and beaches.

3 BEEDELUP NATIONAL PARK
This enchanting park, 15km west of Pemberton on the Vasse Hwy (Rte 104), shouldn't be missed. There's a short, scenic walk that crosses Beedelup Brook near Beedelup Falls. North of town, Big Brook Arboretum features big trees from all over the world.

4 STIRLING RANGE NATIONAL PARK
Rising abruptly from the plains 80km north of Albany, this 1156-sq-km national park consists of a single 65km-long chain of peaks pushed up by plate tectonics. Bluff Knoll (Bular Mai) is the highest point in the southwest (1095m).

5 FITZGERALD RIVER NATIONAL PARK
Midway between Albany and Esperance, this national park is a Unesco biosphere reserve. Its 3300 sq km contain 22 mammal species, 200 species of bird and 1700 species of plant (20% of WA's described species). Wildflowers bloom throughout the year.

/GETTY IMAGES ©

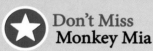

Don't Miss
Monkey Mia

Watching the wild dolphins arrive each morning in the shallow waters of Monkey Mia, 26km northeast of Denham, is a highlight of every traveller's trip. The first feed is around 7.45am, but the dolphins will normally arrive earlier. The pier is a good vantage point. Hang around after the first session, as the dolphins routinely come back a second and sometimes a third time.

Monkey Mia visitor centre (☎08-9948 1366; ⊕8am-4pm) has a range of publications and books tours. Recommended ones include **Wula Guda Nyinda Aboriginal Cultural Tours** (☎0429 708 847; www.wulaguda.com.au; 90min tours adult/child from $50/25): pick up some local Malgana language and identify bush tucker and indigenous medicine on these amazing bushwalks led by local Aboriginal guide Darren 'Capes' Capewell. The evening 'Didgeridoo Dreaming' tours (adult/child $60/30) are magical. **Wildsights** (☎1800 241 481; www.monkeymiawildsights.com.au) take you out on a small Shotover catamaran where you're close to the action; 2½-hour cruises start from $79.

For lodgings, **Monkey Mia Dolphin Resort** (☎1800 653 611; www.monkeymia.com.au; tent sites per person $15, van sites from $39, dm/d $30/89, garden units $223, beachfront villas $315; ❄@🛜🏊) has a stunning location, friendly staff and good-value backpacker doubles.

NEED TO KNOW
adult/child/family $8/3/16

Clearwater Motel Apartments   Motel $$
(☎08-9071 3587; www.clearwatermotel.com.au; 1a William St; s $110, d $140-195; ❄)

The bright and spacious rooms and apartments here have balconies and are fully self-contained, and there's a well-equipped shared barbecue area. It's just a short walk from both waterfront and town.

Eating

Taylor's Beach Bar & Cafe   Cafe $$
(Taylor St Jetty; lunch $7-24, dinner $24-32; 🕓7am-2pm Wed, to 9pm Thu-Mon; 🛜) This attractive, sprawling cafe by the jetty serves cafe fare, tapas, seafood and salads. Locals hang out at the tables or read on the covered terrace. Sandwiches ($6.50 to $9.50) are good value if you're heading for the beach, and it's good for a chilled pint of Little Creatures Pale Ale.

Pier Hotel   Pub $$
(www.pierhotelesperance.net.au; 47 The Esplanade; mains $20-35; 🕓11.30am-late) Lots of beers on tap, wood-fired pizzas and tasty bistro meals conspire to make the local pub a firm favourite.

Information

Visitor Centre (☎08-9083 1555; www. visitesperance.com; cnr Kemp & Dempster Sts; 🕓9am-5pm Mon-Fri, to 2pm Sat, to noon Sun)

SHARK BAY

World Heritage–listed Shark Bay, with more than 1500km of pristine coastline, barren peninsulas, white-sand beaches and bountiful marine life, draws tourists from around the world. The sheltered turquoise waters and skinny fingers of stunted land at the westernmost edge of the continent are one of WA's most biologically rich habitats.

ℹ️ Getting There & Away

Shark Bay airport is located between Denham and Monkey Mia. Skippers flies to Perth six times weekly, with some return flights via Kalbarri.

The closest Greyhound and Integrity approach is the Overlander Roadhouse, 128km away on the North West Coastal Hwy. **Shark Bay Car Hire** (☎0427 483 032; www.carhire.net.au; 65 Knight Terrace, Denham; shuttle $67, car/4WD hire per day $95/185) runs a connecting shuttle (book ahead!).

Denham

Beautiful, laid-back Denham, with its aquamarine sea and palm-fringed beach-front, makes a great base for trips to the surrounding Shark Bay Marine Park, nearby François Peron and Dirk Hartog Island National Parks, and Monkey Mia, 26km away.

Sights & Activities

Shark Bay World Heritage Discovery Centre   Museum
(☎08-9948 1590; www.sharkbayvisit.com; 53 Knight Tce; adult/child $11/6; 🕓9am-5pm Mon-Fri, 10am-4pm Sat & Sun) Informative and evocative displays of Shark Bay's ecosystems, marine and animal life, Indigenous culture, early explorers, settlers and shipwrecks.

Ocean Park   Aquarium
(☎08-9948 1765; www.oceanpark.com.au; Shark Bay Rd; adult/child $20/12; 🕓9am-5pm) On a headland just before town, this family-run aquaculture farm features an artificial lagoon where a 60-minute guided tour observes feeding sharks, turtles, stingrays and fish. The licensed cafe has sensational views.

Tours

Aussie Off Road Tours   Driving Tour
(☎0429 929 175; www.aussieoffroadtours. com.au) Culture, history, wildlife and bush tucker feature in these excellent Indigenous-owned and -operated 4WD tours, including twilight wildlife ($90), full day/overnight François Peron National Park ($189/$300) and overnight to Steep Point ($390).

Shark Bay Scenic Flights   Scenic Flights
(☎0417 919 059; www.sharkbayair.com.au) Offers various scenic flights, including 15-minute Monkey Mia flyovers ($59) and a sensational 40-minute trip over Steep Point and the Zuytdorp Cliffs ($175).

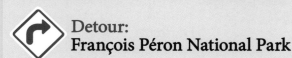

Detour:
François Péron National Park

Covering the whole peninsula north of Denham is an area of low scrub, salt lakes and red sandy dunes, home to the rare bilby, mallee fowl and woma python. Don't miss the fantastic **Wanamalu Trail** (3km return), which follows the cliff top between Cape Peron and Skipjack Point, from where you can spot marine life in the crystal waters below. Park entry is $11 per vehicle. Tours start at around $180 from Denham or Monkey Mia, but if you're in a group, consider hiring your own 4WD from Denham for the same price.

Shark Bay Coaches & Tours
Bus Tour

(☎08-9948 1081; www.sbcoaches.com; bus/quad bike $80/$90) Half-day bus tours to all key sights and two-hour quad bike tours to Little Lagoon.

 ## Sleeping & Eating

Bay Lodge
Hostel $

(☎08-9948 1278; www.baylodge.info; 113 Knight Tce; dm/d from $26/68; ❄@⛵) Every room at this YHA hostel has its own en suite, kitchenette and TV/DVD. Ideally located across from the beach, it also has a pool, common kitchen, and a shuttle bus to Monkey Mia.

Oceanside Village
Cabins $$

(☎1800 680 600; www.oceanside.com.au; 117 Knight Tce; cabins $160-200; ❄🛜⛵) These neat self-catering cottages with sunny balconies are perfectly located directly opposite the beach.

Old Pearler Restaurant
Seafood $$$

(☎08-9948 1373; 71 Knight Tce; meals $30-49; ◷dinner Mon-Sat) Built from shell bricks, this atmospheric nautical haven does fantastic seafood. The exceptional seafood platter features local snapper, whiting, cray, oysters, prawns and squid – all grilled, not fried. BYO.

❶ Information

Shark Bay Visitor Centre (☎08-9948 1590; www.sharkbayvisit.com; 53 Knight Tce; ◷9am-5pm Mon-Fri, 10am-4pm Sat & Sun) Located in the Discovery Centre foyer, the very informative staff handle accommodation and tour bookings and issue bush-camping permits for South Péron.

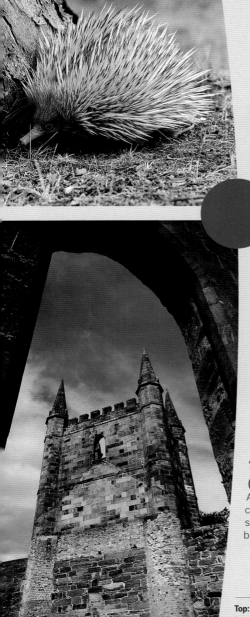

Best of the Rest

Canberra (p342)
'Our nation's capital' is a lot more than just bureaucracy, public servants and filing cabinets (...try the museums and galleries, for starters).

Adelaide, Kangaroo Island & the Barossa Valley (p344)
Adelaide has dignity, culture, poise... and plenty of pubs to help you forget all that stuff. Offshore, Kangaroo Island is a wildlife spectacular, while an hour north of Adelaide the Barossa Valley is one of the planet's greatest wine regions.

Tasmania & Port Arthur (p349)
Australia's island state, 'Tassie' delivers convict sites, photogenic wilderness and a show-stopping art museum that's making a big international splash.

Top: Echidna, Kangaroo Island
Bottom: Port Arthur Historic Site (p353)

Canberra

HIGHLIGHTS

1 **Australian War Memorial** (p342)
Pay your respects, or stand silently
for the *Last Post*.

2 **National Gallery of Australia**
(p342) Stroll the corridors of
creativity.

3 **Parliament House** (p342) Politics
and politicians – plenty of both.

Parliament House
CHRISTOPHER GROENHOUT/GETTY IMAGES ©

The city of Canberra has an urban landscape that is expertly designed to show
off the nation's democratic and cultural
institutions. It is an excellent destination
for museum addicts, with wonderful fine
art and historical collections.

◉ Sights

Australian War Memorial   Museum
(📞02-6243 4211; www.awm.gov.au; Treloar
Cres, Campbell; ⊙10am-5pm) **FREE** The War
Memorial provides a fascinating insight
into how war has forged Australia's
national identity, and in so doing delivers
Canberra's most rewarding museum
experience. Free volunteer-led 90-minute
guided tours leave from the **Orientation Gallery** next to the main entrance
at 10am, 10.15am, 10.30am, 11am, noon,
1pm, 1.30pm, 2pm, 2.30pm and 3pm;
45-minute tours leave at 10.45am and
1.15pm. Alternatively, purchase the *Self-
Guided Tour* leaflet with map ($5)..

**National Gallery of
Australia**   Gallery
(📞02-6240 6502; www.nga.gov.au; Parkes Pl,
Parkes; permanent collection admission free;
⊙10am-5pm) On entering this impressive gallery, you will be confronted with
one of its most extraordinary exhibits,
an Aboriginal Memorial from Central
Arnhem Land that was created for the
nation's bicentenary in 1988. Also on
show is Australian art from the colonial to
contemporary period and three galleries
showcasing art from the Indian Subcon-
tinent, Southeast Asia and China, Japan
and Central Asia.

Consider taking advantage of a free
guided tour – check the website for
details.

Parliament House   Notable Building
(📞02-6277 5399; www.aph.gov.au; ⊙from
9am Mon & Tue & from 8.30am Wed & Thu
sitting days, 9am-5pm nonsitting days) **FREE**
Opened in 1988 after a 10-year, $1.2
billion construction project, the national
parliament building is dug into Capital
Hill, its roof covered in grass and topped
by an 81m-high flagpole. Underneath is a
complex of five buildings that incorporate

17 courtyards, a striking entrance foyer, a Great Hall, the House of Representatives, the Senate and 2300km of corridors. All can be visited on a free guided tour (30-minutes on sitting days, 45 minutes on nonsitting days). These set off at 10am, 1pm and 3pm daily.

Sleeping

Diamant Hotel
Boutique Hotel **$$**

(📞02-6175 2222; www.diamant.com.au; 15 Edinburgh Ave, Civic; r $160-320, apt $350-650; P❄️📶) Located in the up-and-coming New Acton precinct near Civic, the Diamant has a sheen of Sydney-style sophistication. Eight types of rooms and apartments occupy a handsome 1926 apartment block, all totally renovated and featuring amenities including iPod docks, CD players and spacious bathrooms with rain showers.

East Hotel
Hotel **$$$**

(📞02-6295 6925, 1800 816 469; www.easthotel.com.au; 69 Canberra Ave, Kingston; studio r $265-320, apt $315-270; P❄️@📶) Cleverly straddling the divide between boutique and business, this new hotel offers thoughtfully planned and stylishly executed spaces. Rooms feature amenities including a work desk, iPod dock, espresso machine and equipped kitchenette – we were particularly impressed with the 'luxe studios' and with the family rooms, which come complete with X-box and beanbags.

Eating

Italian & Sons
Italian **$$**

(📞02-6162 4888; www.italianandsons.com.au; Shop 7, 7 Lonsdale St, Braddon; mains $24-33; ⏰6-10pm Mon, noon-2.30pm & 6-10pm Tue-Fri, 6-10pm Sat) As hip as Canberra gets, this bustling trattoria serves thin-crust pizzas, perfectly al dente pastas and one dish of the day to an appreciative and loyal clientele. Book ahead.

ℹ️ Information

Canberra & Region Visitor Centre (📞1300 554 114, 02-6205 0044; www.visitcanberra.com.au; 330 Northbourne Ave, Dickson; ⏰9am-5pm Mon-Fri, to 4pm Sat & Sun) Head to this centre north of Civic for a wealth of information about the city and the region.

ℹ️ Getting There & Away

Air

Canberra International Airport (📞02-6275 2226; www.canberraairport.com.au) is serviced by **Qantas** (📞13 13 13, 1800 652 660; www.qantas.com.au; Northbourne Ave, Jolimont Centre, Civic) and **Virgin Australia** (📞13 67 89; www.virginaustralia.com), with direct flights to Adelaide, Brisbane, Melbourne and Sydney.

Bus

The **interstate bus terminal** is at the Jolimont Centre.

Train

Kingston train station (Wentworth Ave) is the city's rail terminus. CountryLink trains run to/from Sydney ($56, 4½ hours, two daily).

Adelaide, Kangaroo Island & the Barossa Valley

HIGHLIGHTS

❶ **Central Market** (p344) Explore Adelaide's amazing multicultural food market.

❷ **Seal Bay Conservation Park** (p345) Get up close to some Kangaroo Island locals.

❸ **Barossa Valley** (p347) Sip your way around the winery cellar doors.

Central Market, Adelaide
OLIVER STREWE/GETTY IMAGES ©

ADELAIDE

Multicultural flavours infuse Adelaide's restaurants; there's a great pub, arts and live-music scene here; and the city's festival calendar has vanquished dull Saturday nights.

◉ Sights

Central Market Market
(www.adelaidecentralmarket.com.au; Gouger St; ⏰7am-5.30pm Tue, 9am-5.30pm Wed & Thu, 7am-9pm Fri, 7am-3pm Sat) Satisfy both obvious and obscure culinary cravings at the 250-odd stalls in Adelaide's superb Central Market. A sliver of salami from the Mettwurst Shop, some English stilton from the Smelly Cheese Shop, a tub of blueberry yoghurt from the Yoghurt Shop – you name it, it's here.

Art Gallery of South Australia Gallery
(www.artgallery.sa.gov.au; North Tce; ⏰10am-5pm) **FREE** Spend a few hushed hours in the vaulted, parquetry-floored gallery that represents the big names in Australian art. Permanent exhibitions include Australian, modern Australian, contemporary Aboriginal, Asian, Islamic and European art (19 bronze Rodins!). Free guided tours (11am and 2pm daily) and lunchtime talks (12.30pm daily).

National Wine Centre of Australia Winery
(www.wineaustralia.com.au; cnr Botanic & Hackney Rds; ⏰9am-5pm) **FREE** Check out the free self-guided, interactive Wine Discovery Journey exhibition, paired with tastings of Australian wines (from $10), at this very sexy wine centre (actually a research facility for the University of Adelaide, more than a visitor centre per se). Free 30-minute tours run at 11.30am daily.

🛏 Sleeping

Hotel Richmond Hotel $$
(☎08-8215 4444; www.hotelrichmond.com.au; 128 Rundle Mall; d from $165; P ❄ 🛜) This opulent hotel in a grand 1920s building

in the middle of Rundle Mall has mod-minimalist rooms with king-sized beds, marble bathrooms and American oak and Italian furnishings. Oh, and that hotel rarity – opening windows.

Clarion Hotel Soho   Hotel $$

(☑08-8412 5600; www.clarionhotelsoho.com.au; 264 Flinders St; d $145-590; P ❀ 🛜 🏊) Attempting to conjure up the vibe of London's Soho district, these 30 very plush suites (some with spas, most with balconies) are complimented by sumptuous linen, 24-hour room service, iPod docks, Italian marble bathrooms, jet pool, a fab restaurant...

 Eating

Press   Modern Australian $$$

(☑08-8211 8048; www.pressfoodandwine.com.au; 40 Waymouth St; mains $16-46; ☺noon-9pm Mon-Sat) Super-stylish (brick, glass, lemon-coloured chairs) and not afraid of offal (pan-fried lamb's brains, grilled calf's tongue) or things raw (beef carpaccio, gravlax salmon) and confit (duck leg, onion, olives). Try the house-made spicy beef sausages, or the tasting menu ($68 per person).

 Information

South Australian Visitor Information Centre (☑1300 764 227; www.southaustralia.com; 108 North Tce, Adelaide, SA; ☺9am-5pm Mon-Fri, to 2pm Sat, 10am-3pm Sun) Abundantly stocked with info (including fab regional booklets) on Adelaide and SA.

 Getting There & Away

Air

Adelaide Airport (ADL; ☑08-8308 9211; www.aal.com.au; 1 James Schofield Dr, Adelaide Airport) Has direct flights to/from the big Australian cities capitals and many regional centres.

Bus

Adelaide Central Bus Station (www.sa.gov.au; 85 Franklin St; ☺6am-9.30pm) For interstate and statewide buses.

Train

Adelaide's interstate train terminal is **Adelaide Parklands Terminal** (www.gsr.com.au; Railway Tce, Keswick; ☺6am-1.30pm Mon, Wed & Fri, 7am-6.30pm Tue, 9am-7pm Thu, 5.15-6.30pm Sat, 8.30am-7pm Sun), 1km southwest of the city centre.

KANGAROO ISLAND

Long devoid of tourist trappings, Kangaroo Island (KI) these days is a booming destination for wilderness and wildlife fans – it's a veritable zoo of seals, birds, dolphins, echidnas and (of course) kangaroos.

 Sights

Seal Bay
Conservation Park   Nature Reserve

(☑08-8553 4460; www.environment.sa.gov.au/sealbay; Seal Bay Rd; self-guided tours adult/child/family $15/9/40, guided $32/18/80, twilight $60/36/165; ☺tours 9am-4.15pm year-round, extra tours Dec-Feb) 🍃 'Observation, not interaction' is the mentality. Guided tours stroll along the beach (or board-walk on self-guided tours) to a colony of (mostly sleeping) Australian sea lions. Twilight tours December and January. Bookings advised.

Kangaroo Island
Penguin Centre   Ecotour

(www.kipenguincentre.com.au; Kingscote Wharf; adult/child/family $17/6/40, pelican feeding adult/child $5/3; ☺tours 8.30pm & 9.30pm Oct-Jan & Mar, 7.30pm & 8.30pm Apr-Oct, closed Feb, pelican feeding 5pm) Runs one-hour tours of its saltwater aquariums and the local penguin colony, plus some stargazing if the sky is clear. It also runs informative (and comical) **pelican feeding** sessions at the adjacent wharf.

 Sleeping & Eating

Aurora Ozone Hotel   Hotel $$

(☑1800 083 133, 08-8553 2011; www.aurora resorts.com.au; cnr Commercial St & Kingscote Tce; d pub/motel from $129/165, 1-/2-/3-bed apt from $190/340/540; ❀ @ 🛜 🏊) Opposite

 Don't Miss
Flinders Chase National Park

Occupying the western end of the island, Flinders Chase is one of South Australia's top national parks.

Once a farm, **Rocky River** is a rampant hotbed of wildlife, with kangaroos, wallabies and Cape Barren geese competing for your affections.

From Rocky River, a road runs south to a remote 1906 lighthouse atop wild **Cape du Couedic**. A boardwalk weaves down to **Admirals Arch**, a huge archway ground out by heavy seas, and passes a colony of New Zealand fur seals (sweet-smelling they ain't...).

At Kirkpatrick Point, a few kilometres east of Cape du Couedic, the **Remarkable Rocks** (pictured above) are a cluster of hefty, weather-gouged granite boulders atop a rocky dome that arcs 75m down to the sea.

Flinders Chase Visitor Information Centre (☎08-8559 7235; www.environment. sa.gov.au/parks; South Coast Rd, Flinders Chase; ⏲9am-5pm) has info, maps and camping/accommodation bookings, plus a cafe and displays on island ecology.

the foreshore with killer views, the 100-year-old Ozone pub has quality pub rooms upstairs, motel rooms, and stylish deluxe apartments in a new wing across the street. The eternally busy bistro (mains $20 to $48) serves meaty grills and seafood, and you can pickle yourself on KI wines at the bar.

Kangaroo Island Wilderness Retreat Hotel, Resort $$
(☎08-8559 7275; www.kiwr.com; Lot 1, South Coast Rd, Flinders Chase; d $176-360; ❄@ 🛜)
A low-key, log-cabin-style resort on the Flinders Chase doorstep with resident grazing wallabies. Accommodation ranges from basic motel-style rooms to

flashy spa suites. There's a petrol pump, a bar and a restaurant here too (breakfast mains $17 to $25, 7.30am to 9.30am) and dinner (mains $28 to $35, 6pm to 8.30pm).

Information

Kangaroo Island Gateway Visitor Centre (☏08-8553 1185; www.tourkangarooisland. com.au; Howard Dr; ☺9am-5pm Mon-Fri, 10am-4pm Sat & Sun) Just outside Penneshaw on the road to Kingscote, this centre is stocked with brochures and maps. It also books accommodation and sells park entry tickets and passes.

ⓘ Getting There & Away

Air
Regional Express (Rex; www.regionalexpress. com.au) flies daily between Adelaide and Kingscote.

Bus
Sealink (☏13 13 01; www.sealink.com.au) operates a morning and afternoon bus service between Adelaide Central Station and Cape Jervis.

Ferry
Sealink (☏13 13 01; www.sealink.com.au) operates a car ferry between Cape Jervis and Penneshaw on KI, with at least three ferries each way daily.

BAROSSA VALLEY

With hot, dry summers and cool, moderate winters, the Barossa is one of the world's great wine regions – an absolute must for anyone with even the slightest interest in a good drop. The towns here have a distinctly German heritage, dating back to 1842.

 Sights

Keg Factory   Factory Tours
(www.thekegfactory.com.au; Lot 10, St Hallett Rd; ☺10am-4pm) **FREE** Watch honest-to-goodness coopers make and repair wine barrels, 4km south of Tanunda.

Tours

Barossa Epicurean Tours   Food, Wine
(☏08-8564 2191; www.barossatours.com.au; full-/half-day tours $100/70) Good-value, small-group tours visiting the wineries of your choice and Mengler Hill Lookout.

Barossa Classic Cycle Tours   Bike Tour
(☏0427 000 957; www.bccycletours.com.au; tours per person per day from $260) One- and two-day cycling tours of the valley, covering about 30km per day. Cheaper rates for bigger groups.

Sleeping & Eating

Whistler Farm   B&B $$
(☏0415 139 758; www.whistlerfarm.com.au; 616 Samuel Rd; d incl breakfast $195; ❄ 🛜) Surrounded by vineyards and native shrubs, this farmhouse B&B has a private guest wing with exposed timber beams, separate guest entry and two country-style rooms. Snooze on the wide verandah and contemplate a day's successful (or imminent) wine touring. It's near Nuriootpa.

Ferment Asian   Southeast Asian $$
(☏08-8563 0765; www.fermentasian.com.au; 90 Murray St; mains $22-26; ☺noon-2.30pm Tue-Sun, 6pm-9.30pm Wed-Sat) Having recently featured in the *Weekend Australian* magazine's 'Top 50 Restaurants' listings, Tanunda's Ferment is hot property right now. What sounds exotic is actually refreshingly simple: *goi bo den* = grilled Barossa Angus beef with herb salad; *ca ri vit* = red duck curry with lychees and pineapple. Modern Vietnamese in a lovely old stone villa.

ⓘ Information

Barossa Visitor Information Centre (☏1300 852 982, 08-8563 0600; www.barossa.com; 66-68 Murray St, Tanunda; ☺9am-5pm Mon-Fri, 10am-4pm Sat & Sun; 🛜) The lowdown on the valley, plus internet, bike hire and accommodation and tour bookings. Stocks the *A Town Walk of Tanunda* brochure.

MILTON WORDLEY/GETTY IMAGES ©

Don't Miss
Barossa Valley Wineries

The valley is best known for shiraz, with riesling the dominant white. There are around 80 vineyards here and 60 cellar doors, ranging from boutique wine rooms to monstrous complexes. Three of the best:

Rockford Wines (www.rockfordwines.com.au; Krondorf Rd, Tanunda; ⊙11am-5pm) This 1850s cellar door sells traditionally made, small-range wines, including sparkling reds. The Black Shiraz is a smooth and spicy killer.

Henschke (www.henschke.com.au; Henschke Rd, Keyneton; ⊙9am-4.30pm Mon-Fri, to noon Sat) Henschke, about 10km southeast of Angaston in the Eden Valley, is known for its iconic Hill of Grace red, but most of the wines here are classics.

Penfolds (www.penfolds.com.au; 30 Tanunda Rd, Nuriootpa; ⊙10am-5pm) You know the name. Book ahead for the 'Make your own Blend' tour ($65), or 'Taste of Grange' tour ($150) which allows you to slide some Grange Hermitage across your lips.

Getting There & Away

Bus & Train

Adelaide Metro (www.adelaidemetro.com.au) operates daily trains to Gawler ($4.90, one hour), from where you can catch **LinkSA** (www.linksa.com.au) buses to Tanunda ($9.50, 45 minutes), Nuriootpa ($12, one hour) and Angaston ($14.50, 1¼ hours).

Tasmania & Port Arthur

HIGHLIGHTS

1 **MONA** (p351) Hobart's Museum of Old & New Art is awesome!

2 **Salamanca Market** (p349) Meander lazily through the labyrinth of Saturday-morning stalls.

3 **Port Arthur** (p352) Contemplate the contrast between melancholy silence and beautiful scenery.

Salamanca Market, Hobart
RICHARD I'ANSON/GETTY IMAGES ©

HOBART

Australia's second-oldest city and southernmost capital lies at the foothills of Mt Wellington on the banks of the Derwent River. The town's rich colonial heritage and natural charms are accented by a spirited, rootsy atmosphere: festivals, superb restaurants and hip urban bars abound.

Sights

Salamanca Place   Historic Area

This picturesque row of four-storey sandstone warehouses on Sullivans Cove is Australia's best-preserved historic urban precinct. Salamanca Place was the hub of old Hobart Town's trade and commerce, but by the mid-20th century many of these 1830s whaling-era buildings had become decrepit ruins. The 1970s saw the dawning of Tasmania's sense of 'heritage', which helped to reinvigorate the warehouses as restaurants, cafes, bars and shops.

Don't miss the **Salamanca Market** every Saturday morning (see www.salamanca.com.au).

Tasmanian Museum & Art Gallery   Museum

(www.tmag.tas.gov.au; 40 Macquarie St; ⏰10am-5pm) **FREE** Reopened in early 2013 after a $30 million redevelopment, this superb museum includes the Commissariat Store (1808; the state's oldest building), colonial relics and art, and excellent Aboriginal displays. There are free guided tours at 2.30pm from Wednesday to Sunday. Take in the *Islands to Ice: Antarctica* exhibition before recharging in the museum's cafe.

Penitentiary Chapel Historic Site   Historic Site

(www.penitentiarychapel.com; cnr Brisbane & Campbell Sts; tours adult/child/family $10/8/20; ⏰tours 10am, 11.30am, 1pm & 2.30pm Sun-Fri, 1pm & 2.30pm Sat) Ruminating over the court rooms, cells and gallows here, writer TG Ford mused, 'As the Devil was going through Hobart Gaol, he saw a solitary cell; and the Devil was pleased for it gave him a hint, for improving the prisons in hell.' Take the excellent National Trust–run tour or the one-hour Penitentiary Chapel Ghost Tour (☎03-6231 0911; www.hobart ghosts.com; adult/child/family $15/10/40; ⏰8.30pm Mon & Fri), held most nights (bookings essential).

Mt Wellington   Park

(www.wellingtonpark.org.au) Cloaked in winter snow,Mt Wellington peaks at 1270m, towering above Hobart like a benevolent overlord. The citizens find reassurance in its constant, solid presence, while outdoors types find the space to hike and bike on its leafy flanks. And the view from the top is unbelievable! Don't be deterred if the sky is overcast – often the peak rises above cloud level and looks out over a magic carpet of cotton-topped clouds.

Some bus-tour companies include Mt Wellington in their itineraries. Another option is the Mt Wellington Shuttle Bus Service (☎0408 341 804; per person return $25), departing the visitor centre at 10.15am and 1.30pm daily. City pick-ups by arrangement; call to book and confirm times.

Sleeping

Astor Private Hotel   Hotel $$

(☎03-6234 6611; www.astorprivatehotel.com.au; 157 Macquarie St; s from $77, d $93-140, all incl breakfast; 🛜) A rambling, 1920s charmer, the Astor features stained-glass windows, old furniture, ceiling roses and the ir-repressible Tildy at the helm. Older-style rooms have shared facilities, and newer en-suite rooms are also excellent value.

Henry Jones
Art Hotel   Boutique Hotel $$$

(☎03-6210 7700; www.thehenryjones.com; 25 Hunter St; d $255-399; @🛜) ✐ Since opening in 2004, super-swish HJs has become a beacon of sophistication. Abso-lute waterfront in a restored jam factory, it oozes class but is far from intimidat-ing. Modern art enlivens the walls, while facilities and downstairs distractions (bar, restaurant, cafe) are world class. The hotel also makes smart use of recycled materials.

The Islington   Boutique Hotel $$$

(☎03-6220 2123; www.islingtonhotel.com; 321 Davey St; d $395-595; 🛜) One of Hobart's best, the Islington effortlessly combines a heritage building with interesting antique furniture, contemporary art and a glorious garden. Service is attentive but understated, and breakfast is served in an expansive conservatory. Private dinners are also available.

✖ Eating & Drinking

Pigeon Hole   Cafe $

(93 Goulburn St; mains $10-13; ⏰8am-4.30pm Mon-Sat) This funky and friendly cafe is the kind of place every inner-city neighbour-hood should have. The freshly baked panini are the best you'll have, and the foodie owners always concoct innova-tive spins on traditional cafe fare. Try the baked eggs *en cocotte* with serrano ham for a lazy brunch.

Sidecar   Tapas Bar $$

(129 Bathurst St; small plates $10-18; ⏰5pm-late daily, lunch from noon Fri) ✐ Originally set up for diners waiting for a table at nearby Ga-ragistes, the sleek and industrial Sidecar is now one of Hobart's best small bars in its own right. Conversation comes natu-rally at the shared zinc counter, further enhanced by an excellent wine and beer list and small plates including charcuterie, spicy pigs ears and wagyu hot dogs.

Garagistes   Modern Australian $$$

(☎03-6231 0558; www.garagistes.com.au; 103 Murray St; shared plates $19-36; ⏰from 6pm Wed-Thu, from 5pm Fri-Sat) ✐ The very fine Garagistes delivers innovative small plates in a simple, yet dramatic, dining room. Owner Luke Burgess pushes the culinary envelope with dishes including salted cabbage, ricotta and barley salad and raw jack mackerel with pickles, young elderberries and rhubarb. Sunday lunch is four highly recommended courses. Book-ings essential.

Knopwood's Retreat   Pub

(www.knopwoods.com; 39 Salamanca Pl; ⏰10am-late) Adhere to the 'when in Rome...' dictum and head for Knoppies, Hobart's

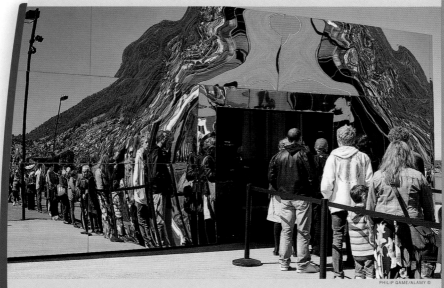

PHILIP GAME/ALAMY ©

★ Don't Miss
MONA

Fast becoming Tasmania's biggest attraction is MONA, the $75-million Museum of Old & New Art, described by owner David Walsh as 'a subversive adult Disneyland'. The extraordinary installation is arrayed across three underground levels concealed inside a sheer rock face. Ancient antiquities are showcased next to more recent works by Sir Sidney Nolan and British enfant terrible, Damien Hirst.

To get to MONA catch a fast ferry or bus from the MONA Brooke St Ferry Terminal (30 minutes, per person return $20).

NEED TO KNOW

📞 03-6277 9900; www.mona.net.au; 655 Main Rd, Berriedale; adult/concession/child under 18 $20/18/free; ⏰ 10am-6pm Wed-Mon, also Tue in Jan

best pub, which has been serving ales to seagoing types since the convict era. For most of the week it's a cosy watering hole with an open fire. On Friday nights the city workers swarm and the crowd spills across the street.

ℹ Information

Hobart Visitor Centre (📞 1800 990 440; www. hobarttravelcentre.com.au; cnr Davey & Elizabeth Sts; ⏰ 8.30am-5.30pm Mon-Fri, 9am-5pm

Sat-Sun) Information and state-wide tour and accommodation bookings.

ℹ Getting There & Away

Air

Hobart Airport (📞 03-6216 1600; www. hobartairpt.com.au) is at Cambridge, 16km east of town. Airlines flying between Tasmania and mainland Australia include **Jetstar** (📞 13 15 38; www.jetstar.com.au), **Qantas** (📞 13 13 13; www.qantas.com.au) and **Virgin Australia** (📞 13 67 89; www.virginaustralia.com).

ANDREW BAIN/GETTY IMAGES ©

 Don't Miss
Cradle Mountain-Lake St Clair National Park

Tasmania is world-famous for the stunning 168,000-hectare World Heritage area of Cradle Mountain-Lake St Clair National Park. Its southern Lake St Clair section is 175km northwest of Hobart, and the northern Cradle Mountain section is 155km west of Launceston. It was one of Australia's most heavily glaciated areas, and includes Tasmania's highest peak, Mt Ossa (1617m), and Australia's deepest natural freshwater lake, Lake St Clair (167m).

There are plenty of day walks here, but it's the spectacular 80.5km walk between the Cradle Valley and Cynthia Bay regions – known as the Overland Track – that has turned this park into a bushwalkers' mecca.

The **Cradle Mountain visitor information centre** (☎03-6492 1110; www.parks. tas.gov.au; Cradle Mountain Rd; ⏲8am-5pm, reduced hours in winter) provides extensive bushwalking information (including national park and Overland Track passes and registration), and informative flora, fauna and park history displays.

Boat

The **Spirit of Tasmania** (☎1800 634 906, 03-6421 7209; www.spiritoftasmania.com.au) operates two car and passenger ferries that cruise nightly between Melbourne and Devonport (on Tasmania's northwest coast) in both directions.

PORT ARTHUR

From 1830 to 1877, 12,500 convicts did hard, brutal prison time at Port Arthur, a 95km day-trip southeast of Hobart. Although Port Arthur is a hugely popular tourist site – over 300,000 visitors annually – it remains a sombre, confronting and haunting place.

Sights

Port Arthur
Historic Site   Historic Site

(☑03-6251 2310, Historic Ghost Tour 1800 659 101; www.portarthur.org.au; Arthur Hwy; adult/child from $32/16, Historic Ghost Tour adult/child $25/15); ☺tours & buildings 9am-5pm, grounds 8.30am-dusk) The visitor centre includes an information counter, cafe, restaurant and gift shop. Downstairs is an excellent interpretation gallery, where you can follow the convicts' journey from England.

Worthwhile guided tours (included in admission) leave regularly from the visitor centre. You can visit all the restored buildings, including the Old Asylum (now a museum and cafe) and the Model Prison. Admission tickets, valid for two consecutive days, also entitle you to a short harbour cruise circumnavigating (but not stopping at) the **Isle of the Dead**. For an additional $12/8 per adult/child, you can visit the island on 40-minute guided tours – count headstones and listen to some stories. Or you can tour to **Point Puer** boys' prison for the same additional prices.

Extremely popular is the 90-minute, lantern-lit **Historic Ghost Tour**, which leaves from the visitor centre nightly at dusk. Bookings are essential.

Tours

Gray Line   Bus Tour

(☑1300 858 687; www.grayline.com.au; full-day tour adult/child from $108/54) Coach tours ex-Hobart, including a harbour cruise around the Isle of the Dead, Port Arthur admission and guided tour, and pit stops at Tasman Arch and the Devils' Kitchen.

Navigators   Cruise

(☑03-6223 1914; www.navigators.net.au; Brooke St Pier; full-day tour from adult/child $159/128; ☺Wed, Fri & Sat Oct-May) Cruises from Hobart to Port Arthur, returning on a coach. Includes entrance to the historic site, guided tour and morning tea. Also running is a cruise around Tasman Island from Port Arthur.

Tasman Island Cruises   Cruise

(☑03-6250 2200; www.tasmancruises.com.au; full-day tour from adult/child $210/140) Take a bus to Port Arthur for a three-hour ecocruise around Tasman Island, then explore the Port Arthur Historic Site and bus it back to town. Includes morning tea, lunch and Port Arthur admission. You can also take just the cruise from Port Arthur (adult/child $100/55).

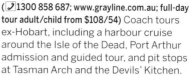

Australia

In Focus

Nullarbor Plain road sign, South Australia
ELENA MARTINELLO/GETTY IMAGES ©

Australia Today

Bondi Beach (p74), Sydney

66

Cities here are in a constant state of growth, reinvention and flux

99

belief systems
(% of population)

64	19	2	2	1	12
Christian	Agnostic	Buddhist	Muslim	Hindu	Other

if Australia were 100 people

79 would speak English at home
3 would speak Chinese at home
2 would speak Italian at home
1 would speak Vietnamese at home
15 would speak another language at home

population per sq km

= 3 people

AUS   NZ   USA

Great Southern Land

Australia's geographic identity has been forged by millennia of survival and isolation. This rugged resilience is evident in its people, hiding behind larrikin wit and amicable informality. The local economy has also proved robust in recent times, riding out the GFC on the back of a mining boom.

Talk of the Town

The talk around the country is invariably about the weather, which seems to have gone haywire in recent years. A decade of drought – the shocking nadir of which were the 2009 'Black Saturday' bushfires in Victoria – came to an end in 2010 with mass flooding across eastern Australia. This continued into 2011 with yet more floods and the sweeping devastation brought by category-five Tropical Cyclone Yasi in Queensland. In 2013 southeast Queensland was again inundated, this time by the tail-end of Tropical Cyclone Oswald, which immersed Bundaberg and

OLIVER STREWE/GETTY IMAGES ©

broke the hearts of many residents who had just rebuilt after the 2011 disaster.

In Victoria, conservative premier Ted Ballieu fell on his sword in 2013 after a protracted period of wavering leadership and debate over his bullish communication style. New state premier Denis Napthine has seen it all before – he was conservative leader back in 2002.

In Tasmania, green-minded organisations and government logging and hydro-electric authorities have been at each other's throats for decades. Trees or jobs? Jobs or trees?

In South Australia (SA) – the driest state – the lower lakes at the mouth of the Murray River, Australia's version of the Mississippi, have been revived by flow-on effects of the big rains further north.

In the Northern Territory (NT), the Indigenous population continues its parlous existence. Substance abuse, domestic violence, suicide and infant mortality rates in Indigenous communities remain significantly higher than in the nonindigenous realm. Darwin is booming, with apartment towers going up apace.

WA is enigmatic: still bound by drought, but blessed with phenomenal mineral wealth that continues to put a rocket under the local (and national) economy.

parts of Brisbane in river water. At the same time Tasmania was being ravaged by bushfires and drought was persisting across parts of Western Australia (WA).

The political landscape has also been red-hot, with the 2013 federal election anointing a new conservative Liberal-National Party Coalition government after six years of left-wing Labor. Outgoing Prime Minister Kevin Rudd seemed only mildly surprised; his successor Tony Abbott has yet to convince many.

States of Mind

Of course, state by state, local issues dominate. In New South Wales (NSW) the limp state of the economy, transport system and general infrastructure is causing ructions. But aside from mourning the demise of the kitsch-but-lovable Darling Harbour monorail in 2013, the mood isn't grim.

Queensland is still wringing itself dry after the 2013 floods closed airports and

City Life

Australia is an urbanised country: around 90% of Australians live in cities and towns. Cities here are in a constant state of growth, reinvention and flux, absorbing fresh influences from far corners of the globe. Multiculturalism prevails and cities here remain distinct: Sydney is a luscious tart, Melbourne an arty glamour puss, Brisbane a blithe playmate, Adelaide a gracious dame and Perth a free spirit. Not to mention bookish Hobart, hedonistic Darwin and museum-fixated Canberra.

357

History

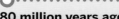
TOM COCKREM/GETTY IMAGE

Dr Michael Cathcart

*Australia is an ancient continent –
rocks here have been dated back
beyond the Archean eon 3.8 billion
years ago. Its Indigenous people
have been here more than 50,000
years. Given this backdrop, 'history' as we describe it can seem
somewhat fleeting...but it sure
makes an interesting read! For
more indigenous history, see Aboriginal Australia (p371).*

Europeans Arrive

By sunrise, the storm had passed. Zach-
ary Hicks was keeping sleepy watch on
the British ship *Endeavour* when suddenly he was wide awake. He summoned
his commander, First Lieutenant James
Cook. Ahead lay an uncharted country
of wooded hills and gentle valleys. It was
19 April 1770. In the coming days Cook
began to draw the first European map of
Australia's eastern coast.

80 million years ago
Continental Australia
breaks free from the
Antarctic landmass and
drifts north.

Two weeks later Cook led a party of men onto a narrow beach. The local Aboriginal people called the place Kurnell, but Cook gave it a foreign name: he called it Stingray Bay and later Botany Bay.

Cook's ship *Endeavour* was a floating annexe of London's leading scientific organisation, the Royal Society. The ship's gentlemen passengers included technical artists, scientists, an astronomer and a wealthy botanist named Joseph Banks. As Banks and his colleagues strode about the Aboriginal peoples' territory, they were delighted by the mass of new plants they collected.

When the *Endeavour* reached the northern tip of Cape York, Cook and his men could smell the sea-route home. And on a small, hilly island (Possession Island), Cook raised the Union Jack. Amid volleys of gunfire, he claimed the eastern half of the continent for King George III.

Cook's intention was not to steal land from the Aboriginal peoples. In fact he rather idealised them. 'They are far more happier than we Europeans', he wrote. 'They think themselves provided with all the necessaries of Life and that they have no superfluities.'

Convict Beginnings

Eighteen years after Cook's arrival, in 1788, the English were back to stay. They arrived in a fleet of 11 ships, packed with supplies including weapons, tools, building materials and livestock. The ships also contained 751 convicts and more than 250 soldiers, officials and their wives. This motley 'First Fleet' was under the command of a humane and diligent naval captain, Arthur Phillip. As his orders dictated, Phillip dropped anchor at Botany Bay. But the paradise that had so delighted Joseph Banks filled Phillip with dismay. So he left his floating prison and embarked in a small boat to search for a better location. Just a short way up the coast his heart leapt as he sailed into the finest harbour in the world. There, in a small cove, in the idyllic lands of the Eora people, he established a British penal settlement. He renamed the place after the British Home Secretary, Lord Sydney.

Phillip's official instructions urged him to colonise the land without doing violence to the local inhabitants. Among the Indigenous people he used as intermediaries was an Eora man named Bennelong, who adopted many of the white people's customs and manners. But Bennelong's people were shattered by the loss of their lands. Hundreds died of smallpox, and many of the survivors, including Bennelong himself, succumbed to alcoholism and despair.

In 1803, English officers established a second convict settlement in Van Diemen's Land (now Tasmania). Soon, reoffenders filled the grim prison at Port Arthur on the beautiful and wild coast near Hobart.

50,000 years ago
The first Australians arrive by sea to northern Australia.

1606
Dutch Navigator Willem Janszoon makes the first authenticated European landing on Australian soil.

1770
First Lieutenant James Cook claims the entire east coast of Australia for England.

The Best...
Convict History

From Shackles to Freedom

At first, Sydney and the smaller colonies depended on supplies brought in by ship. Anxious to develop productive farms, the government granted land to soldiers, officers and settlers. After 30 years of trial and error, the farms began to flourish. The most irascible and ruthless of these new landholders was John Macarthur.

Macarthur was a leading member of the Rum Corps, a clique of powerful officers who bullied successive governors (including William Bligh of *Bounty* fame) and grew rich by controlling much of Sydney's trade, notably rum. But the Corps' racketeering was ended in 1810 by a tough new governor named Lachlan Macquarie. Macquarie laid out the major roads of modern-day Sydney, built some fine public buildings (many of which were designed by talented convict-architect Francis Greenway) and helped to lay the foundations for a more civil society. Macquarie also championed the rights of freed convicts, granting them land and appointing several to public office.

Southern Settlements

In the cooler grasslands of Van Diemen's Land, sheep farmers were thriving. In the 1820s they waged a bloody war against the island's Indigenous population, driving them to the brink of extinction. Now these settlers were hungry for more land.

In 1835 an ambitious young man named John Batman sailed to Port Phillip Bay on mainland Australia. On the banks of the Yarra River, he chose the location for Melbourne, famously announcing 'This is the place for a village'. Batman persuaded local Aboriginal peoples to 'sell' him their traditional lands (a whopping 250,000 hectares) for a crate of blankets, knives and knick-knacks. Back in Sydney, Governor Bourke declared the contract void, not because it was unfair, but because the land officially belonged to the British Crown.

At the same time, a private British company settled Adelaide in South Australia. Proud to have no links with convicts, these God-fearing folk instituted a scheme under which their company sold land to well-heeled settlers, and used the revenue to assist poor British labourers to emigrate. When these worthies earned enough to buy land from the company, that revenue would in turn pay the fare of another shipload of labourers.

1788
Captain Arthur Phillip and the First Fleet – 11 ships and about 1350 people – arrive at Botany Bay.

1851
A gold rush in central Victoria brings settlers from across the world. Democracy is introduced in the eastern colonies.

1880
Bushranger Ned Kelly is hanged as a criminal – and remembered as a folk hero. Ned Kelly's armour, Old Melbourne Gaol

Gold & Rebellion

Transportation of convicts to eastern Australia ceased in the 1840s. This was just as well: in 1851 prospectors discovered gold in New South Wales and central Victoria, including at Ballarat. The news hit the colonies with the force of a cyclone. Young men and some women from every social class headed for the diggings. Soon they were caught up in a great rush of prospectors, publicans and prostitutes. In Victoria the British governor was alarmed – both by the way the Victorian class system had been thrown into disarray, and by the need to finance the imposition of law and order on the goldfields. His solution was to compel all miners to buy an expensive monthly licence.

But the lure of gold was too great and in the reckless excitement of the goldfields, the miners initially endured the thuggish troopers who enforced the government licence. After three years, though, the easy gold at Ballarat was gone, and miners were toiling in deep, water-sodden shafts. They were now infuriated by a corrupt and brutal system of law which held them in contempt. Under the leadership of a charismatic Irishman named Peter Lalor, they raised their own flag, the Southern Cross, and swore to defend their rights and liberties. They armed themselves and gathered inside a rough stockade at Eureka, where they waited for the government to make its move.

In the predawn of Sunday 3 December 1854, a force of troopers attacked the stockade. It was all over in 15 terrifying minutes. The brutal and one-sided battle claimed the lives of 30 miners and five soldiers. But democracy was in the air and public opinion sided with the miners. The eastern colonies were already in the process of establishing democratic parliaments, with the full support of the British authorities.

Meanwhile, in the West...

Western Australia lagged behind the eastern colonies by about 50 years. Though Perth was settled by genteel colonists back in 1829, its material progress was handicapped by isolation, Aboriginal resistance and the arid climate. It was not until the 1880s that

The Long Walk to Ballarat

During the 1850s gold rush in Victoria, the town of Robe in South Australia came into its own when the Victorian government whacked a $10-per-head tax on Chinese gold miners arriving to work the goldfields. Thousands of Chinese miners dodged the tax by landing at Robe instead, then walking the 400-odd kilometres to Bendigo and Ballarat: 10,000 arrived in 1857 alone. But the flood stalled as quickly as it started when the SA government instituted its own tax on the Chinese.

1901
The Australian colonies form a federation of states. The federal parliament sits in Melbourne.

1915
The Anzacs join a British invasion of Turkey: this military disaster spawns a nationalist legend.

DAVID WALL PHOTO/GETTY IMAGES ©

the discovery of remote goldfields promised to gild the fortunes of the isolated colony. At the time, the west was just entering its own period of self-government, and its first premier was a forceful, weather-beaten explorer named John Forrest. He saw that the mining industry would fail if the government did not provide a first-class harbour, efficient railways and reliable water supplies. Ignoring the threats of private contractors, he appointed the brilliant engineer CY O'Connor to design and build each of these as government projects.

Nationhood

On 1 January 1901, Australia became a federation. When the members of the new national parliament met in Melbourne, their first aim was to protect the identity and values of a European Australia from an influx of Asians and Pacific Islanders. The solution was a law which became known as the White Australia Policy. It became a racial tenet of faith in Australia for the next 70 years.

For whites who lived inside the charmed circle of citizenship, this was to be a model society, nestled in the skirts of the British Empire. Just one year later, white

Anzac Square war memorial, Brisbane
MOMORAD/GETTY IMAGES ©

1942
The Japanese bomb Darwin, the first of numerous air strikes on the northern capital.

1945
Australia's motto: 'Populate or Perish!'. Over the next 30 years more than two million immigrants arrive.

1956
The Olympic Games are held in Melbourne: the flame is lit by running champion Ron Clarke.

women won the right to vote in federal elections. In a series of radical innovations, the government introduced a broad social welfare scheme and it protected Australian wage levels with import tariffs.

Entering the World Stage

Living on the edge of a dry and forbidding land, isolated from the rest of the world, most Australians took comfort in the knowledge that they were a dominion of the British Empire. When war broke out in Europe in 1914, thousands of Australian men rallied to the Empire's call. They had their first taste of death on 25 April 1915, when the Australian and New Zealand Army Corps (the Anzacs) joined thousands of other British and French troops in an assault on the Gallipoli Peninsula in Turkey. It was eight months before the British commanders acknowledged that the tactic had failed. By then 8141 young Australians were dead. Before long the Australian Imperial Force was fighting in the killing fields of Europe. By the time the war ended, 60,000 Australians had died.

In the 1920s Australia embarked on a decade of chaotic change. The country careered wildly through the 1920s until it collapsed into the abyss of the Great Depression in 1929. World prices for wheat and wool plunged. Unemployment brought its shame and misery to one in three households.

War with Japan

After 1933, the economy began to recover. Daily life was hardly dampened when Hitler hurled Europe into a new war in 1939. Though Australians had long feared Japan, they took it for granted that the British navy would keep them safe. In December

Sticky Wicket

The year 1932 saw accusations of treachery on the cricket field. The English team, under captain Douglas Jardine, employed a violent new bowling tactic known as 'bodyline'. The aim was to unnerve Australia's star batsman, the devastatingly efficient Donald Bradman. The bitterness of the tour provoked a diplomatic crisis with Britain and became part of Australian legend. Bradman batted on. When he retired in 1948 he had a still-unsurpassed career average of 99.94 runs.

1965
Menzies commits Australian troops to the American war in Vietnam, and divides the nation.

1967
In a national referendum, white Australians vote overwhelmingly to give citizenship to Indigenous people.

1975
Against a background of reform and inflation, Governor General Sir John Kerr sacks the Whitlam government.

The Best...
History Museums

1941, Japan bombed the US Fleet at Pearl Harbor. Weeks later, the 'impregnable' British naval base in Singapore crumbled.

As the Japanese swept through Southeast Asia and into Papua New Guinea, the British announced that they could not spare any resources to defend Australia. But US commander General Douglas MacArthur saw that Australia was the perfect base for American operations in the Pacific. In fierce sea and land battles, Allied forces turned back the Japanese advance. Importantly, it was the USA, not the British Empire, who saved Australia. The days of alliance with Britain alone were numbered.

Visionary Peace

When WWII ended, a new slogan rang out: 'Populate or Perish!'. The Australian government embarked on a scheme to attract thousands of immigrants. People flocked from Britain and non-English-speaking countries. They included Greeks, Italians, Serbs, Croatians and Dutch, followed by Turks and many others.

In addition to growing world demand for Australia's primary products (wool, meat and wheat), there were jobs in manufacturing and on major public works, notably the mighty Snowy Mountains Hydro-Electric Scheme in the mountains near Canberra.

This era of growth and prosperity was dominated by Robert Menzies, the founder of the Liberal Party of Australia, and Australia's longest-serving prime minister. Menzies was steeped in British tradition, and was also a vigilant opponent of communism. As Asia succumbed to the chill of the Cold War, Australia and New Zealand entered a formal military alliance with the USA – the 1951 Anzus security pact. When the USA jumped into a civil war in Vietnam, Menzies committed Australian forces to battle. The following year Menzies retired, leaving his successors a bitter legacy.

In an atmosphere of youthful rebellion and new-found nationalism, the Labor Party was elected to power in 1972 under an idealistic lawyer named Gough Whitlam. In four short years his government transformed the country, ending conscription and abolishing university fees. He introduced a free universal health scheme, no-fault divorce, and the principles of Indigenous land rights and equal pay for women.

By 1975, the Whitlam government was rocked by inflation and scandal. At the end of 1975 his government was infamously dismissed from office by the governor general.

1992
The High Court of Australia recognises the principle of native title in the Mabo decision. High Court, Canberra

2000
The Sydney Olympic Games are a triumph of spectacle and goodwill.

DAVID MESSENT/GETTY IMAGES ©

Today

Today Australia faces new challenges. After two centuries of development, the strains on the environment are starting to show – on water supplies, forests, soil and the oceans.

Under John Howard, Australia's second-longest serving prime minister (1996–2007), the country grew closer to the USA, joining the Americans in their war in Iraq. The government's harsh treatment of asylum seekers, its refusal to acknowledge the reality of climate change, its anti-union reforms and the prime minister's lack of empathy with Indigenous peoples dismayed many liberal-minded Australians. But Howard presided over a period of economic growth and won continuing support in middle Australia.

In 2007, Howard was defeated by the Labor Party's Kevin Rudd, an ex-diplomat who immediately issued a formal apology to Indigenous Australians for the injustices they had suffered over the past two centuries. Though it promised sweeping reforms in environment and education, the Rudd government found itself faced with a crisis when the world economy crashed in 2008; by June 2010 it had cost Rudd his position. Incoming prime minister Julia Gillard, the first woman to hold the position, battled slow economic recovery and diminishing party support, eventually losing her job to a resurgent Rudd in June 2013. Rudd was then ousted again by his right-wing adversary Tony Abbott and the Liberal-National Party Coalition in the 2013 federal election.

2007

Kevin Rudd is elected prime minister and says 'Sorry' to Australia's Indigenous peoples.

2010

Kevin Rudd is ousted as prime minister by Julia Gillard. Rudd then ousts Gillard in mid-2013. Touché!

2013

A federal election installs a new conservative Liberal-National Party Coalition government after six years of left-wing Labor.

Family Travel

RICHARD I'ANSON/GETTY IMAGES

'Are we there yet?' As anyone with kids knows, getting from A to B is the biggest threat to everyone enjoying themselves. Don't underestimate vast distances in Australia: the open road may be just the tonic for stressed-out parents, but it's probably not numero uno on the kids' hit-list. Australia's cities, however, abound with attractions designed for bright young minds and bodies of limitless energy.

Practicalities

Lonely Planet's *Travel with Children* contains a wealth of useful information, hints and tips.

Most shopping centres and all cities and major towns have public baby change facilities; ask the local tourist office or city council for details. It is your legal right to publicly breastfeed anywhere in Australia.

Top-end hotels and many (but not all) midrange hotels cater for children. B&Bs, however, often market themselves as sanctuaries from all things child related. Many cafes, pubs and restaurants have dedicated kids' menus or will provide small serves from the main menu.

If you want to leave Junior behind for a few hours, many of Australia's licensed childcare agencies offer casual care. Check under 'Baby Sitters' and 'Child Care Centres' in the *Yellow Pages*, or contact the local council for listings.

Child and family concessions often apply to accommodation, tours, admission fees and transport, with discounts as high as 50% off the adult rate. However, the definition of 'child' varies from under 12 to under 18 years. Accommodation concessions generally apply to children under 12 years sharing the same room as adults. On the major airlines, infants travel free provided they don't occupy a seat – child fares usually apply between the ages of two and 11 years.

Australia has high-standard medical services and facilities: items such as baby formula and disposable nappies are widely available. Major hire-car companies supply baby capsules and booster seats, charging around $18 for up to three days' use, with an additional daily fee for longer periods.

Sights & Activities

There's no shortage of active, interesting or amusing things for children to focus on in Australia. Museums, zoos, aquariums, science centres and pioneer villages have historical, natural or interactive exhibits to get kids involved. And of course, outdoor destinations are always a winner. This guide has hot tips for keeping kids occupied in Sydney, Melbourne, Perth and Brisbane...and when in doubt, take them to the beach!

The Best... For Kids

1 Gold Coast theme parks (p138)

2 SEA LIFE Sydney Aquarium (p69)

3 AFL footy at the Melbourne Cricket Ground (p221)

4 Territory Wildlife Park (p281)

5 Australia Zoo (p156)

6 Sydney Harbour ferries (p102)

Need to Know

- **Changing facilities** In most towns and shopping malls
- **Cots** Usually available in midrange and top-end accommodation
- **Health** High first-world standards
- **High chairs** Widely available in restaurants and cafes
- **Kids' menus** Widely available in less-formal restaurants and cafes
- **Nappies (diapers)** Widely available
- **Strollers** Even on public transport you'll get a helping hand
- **Transport** All public transport caters for young passengers

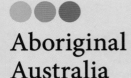

Aboriginal Australia

Aboriginal dot painting, Northern Territory

OLIVER STREWE/GETTY IMAGES ©

Cathy Craigie

A visit to Australia would not be complete without experiencing the rich cultures of Aboriginal and Torres Strait Islander peoples. Visitors have an opportunity to learn and interact with the oldest continuous cultures in the world and share a way of life that has existed for over 50,000 years.

Aboriginal Culture

Aboriginal cultures have evolved over thousands of years with strong links between the spiritual, economic and social lives of the people. This heritage has been kept alive from one generation to the next by the passing of knowledge through rituals, arts, cultural material and language.

Aboriginal culture has never been static, and continues to evolve with the changing times and environment. New technologies and mediums are now used to tell Aboriginal stories, and cultural tourism and hospitality ventures where visitors can experience an Aboriginal perspective have been established. You can learn about ancestral beings at particular natural landmarks, look at rock art that is thousands of years old, taste traditional foods or attend an Aboriginal festival or performance.

Land

Aboriginal land ethic is based on humans fitting into the ecology and not living outside of it. Everything is connected and not viewed as just soil and rocks but as a whole environment that sustains the spiritual, economic and cultural lives of the people. In turn, Aboriginal people have sustained the land by conducting ceremonies, rituals, songs and stories. For Aboriginal people land is intrinsically connected to identity and spirituality. Sacred sites can be parts of rocks, hills, trees or water and are associated with an ancestral being or an event that occurred. Often these sites are part of a Dreaming story and link people across areas.

The Arts

Aboriginal art has impacted the Australian landscape and is now showcased at national and international events and celebrated as a significant part of Australian culture. Exhibited in state institutions, independent theatres and galleries, Aboriginal art has slowly grown in its visibility. It still retains the role of passing on knowledge but today it is also important for economic, educational and political reasons.

Rock Art

Rock art is the oldest form of human art and Aboriginal rock art stretches back thousands of years. Rock art is found in every state of Australia and many sites are thousands of years old. There are a number of different styles of rock art across Australia. These include engravings in sandstone and stencils, prints and drawings in rock shelters.

Some of the oldest examples of engravings can be found in the Pilbara in Western Australia (WA) and in Olary in South Australia (SA) where there is an engraving of a crocodile. All national parks surrounding Sydney have rock engravings and can be easily accessed and viewed. At Gariwerd (the Grampians) in Victoria there are hand prints and hand stencils.

The Best...
Indigenous Art Encounters

1 National Gallery of Australia (p342)

2 Rock art in Kakadu National Park (p281)

3 Art Gallery of NSW (p63)

4 Koorie Heritage Trust (p217)

5 Art Gallery of Western Australia (p306)

Torres Strait Islanders

Indigenous societies in Australia are diverse, meaning there's not one homogenous group but several hundred different sovereign nations. Torres Strait Islanders are a Melanesian people with a separate culture to that of Aboriginal Australians; however, they have a shared history with Aboriginal people and together these two groups constitute Australia's Indigenous peoples.

Gurrumul

Described by *Rolling Stone* magazine as 'Australia's Most Important Voice', blind singer Geoffrey Gurrumul Yunupingu (www.gurrumul.com) sings in the Yolngu language from Arnhem Land. His angelic voice tells of identity, connecting with land and ancestral beings. Gurrumul has entranced Australian and overseas audiences and reached platinum with his two albums.

In the Northern Territory (NT) many of the rock-art sites have patterns and symbols that appear in paintings, carvings and other cultural material. Kakadu National Park has over 5000 recorded sites but many more are thought to exist.

Contemporary Art

The National Gallery of Australia in Canberra has a fantastic collection, but contemporary Aboriginal art can also be viewed at any public art gallery or in one of the many independent galleries dealing in Aboriginal work. The central desert area is still a hub for Aboriginal art and Alice Springs is one of the best places to see and buy art. Cairns is another hot spot for innovative Aboriginal art.

Music

Music has always been a vital part of Aboriginal culture. Songs were important for teaching and passing on knowledge and musical instruments were often used in healing, ceremonies and rituals. The most well known instrument is the Yidaki or didgeridoo, which was traditionally only played by men in northern Australia.

This rich musical heritage continues today with a very strong contemporary music industry. Contemporary artists such as Dan Sultan and Jessica Mauboy have crossed over successfully into the mainstream and have won major music awards and can be seen regularly on popular programs and at major music festivals.

Performing Arts

Dance and theatre are a vital part of social and ceremonial life and important elements in Aboriginal culture. Historically, dances often told stories to pass on knowledge. Like other art forms, dance has adapted to the modern world and contemporary dance companies and groups have merged traditional forms into a modern interpretation. The most well-known dance company is the internationally acclaimed Bangarra Dance Theatre.

Theatre also draws on the storytelling tradition. Currently there are two major Aboriginal theatre companies, Ilbijerri in Melbourne and Yirra Yakin in Perth. Traditionally drama and dance came together in ceremonies or corroborees and this still occurs in many contemporary productions.

TV, Radio & Film

Aboriginal people have quickly adapted to electronic broadcasting and have developed an extensive media network of radio, print and television services. There are more than 120 Aboriginal radio stations and programs operating across Australia in cities, rural areas and remote communities.

There is a thriving Aboriginal film industry and in recent years feature films including *The Sapphires*, *Bran Nue Day* and *Samson and Delilah* have had mainstream success. Since the first Aboriginal television channel, NITV, was launched in 2007, there has been a growth in the number of film-makers wanting to tell their stories.

History of Aboriginal Australia

First Australians

Many academics believe Aboriginal people came from somewhere else, and scientific evidence places Aboriginal people on the continent at least 40,000 to 50,000 years ago. However, Aboriginal people believe they have always inhabited the land.

At the time of European contact the Aboriginal population was grouped into 300 or more different nations with distinct languages and land boundaries. From the desert to the sea Aboriginal people shaped their lives according to their environments and developed different skills and a wide body of knowledge about their territory.

Colonised

The effects of colonisation started immediately after the Europeans arrived. Right from the start there was appropriation of land and water resources and an epidemic of diseases. Smallpox killed around 50% of Sydney Harbour's Indigenous population. A period of resistance occurred as Aboriginal people fought back to retain their land and way of life. As violence and massacres swept the country, many Aboriginal people were pushed further and further away from their traditional lands. In a period of just a hundred years, the Aboriginal population was decimated by 90%.

Rights & Reconciliation

The relationship between Indigenous and 'white' Australia hasn't been an easy one. Aboriginal people had to adapt to the new culture but were treated like second-class citizens. Employment opportunities were scarce. This disadvantage has continued and even though successive government policies and programs have been implemented, there is still great disparity between Indigenous and other Australians, including lower standards of education, employment, health and living conditions, high incarceration and suicide rates, and a lower life expectancy.

Over the years several systematic policies have been put in place to aid reconciliation, but these have often had an underlying purpose including control over the land, decimating the population, protection, assimilation, self-determination and self-management. The history of forced resettlement, removal of children and the loss of land and culture cannot be erased even with governments addressing some of the issues. Current policies are focused on 'closing the gap' and centre on better delivery of essential services to improve lives.

The Stolen Generations

When Australia became a Federation in 1901, a government policy known as the 'White Australia policy' was put in place. It was implemented to restrict nonwhite immigration to Australia but the policy also impacted on Indigenous Australia. Assimilation into the broader society was 'encouraged' by all sectors of government. An official policy of forcibly removing Aboriginal and Torres Strait Islander children from their families operated from 1909 to 1969. The generations of children who were taken from their families became known as the stolen generations. Today many still suffer from the trauma this policy inflicted. On 13 February 2008 the then prime minister of Australia, Kevin Rudd, offered a national apology to the stolen generations.

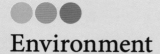

Environment

Female eastern grey kangaroo with joey in pouch

MITCH REARDON/GETTY IMAGES ©

Dr Tim Flannery

Australia's plants and animals are just about the closest things to alien life you are likely to encounter on earth. That's because Australia has been isolated from the other continents for a very long time – at least 45 million years. Places like Sydney have preserved extraordinary fragments of the original environment that are relatively easy to access.

Fundamentally Different

There are two big factors that go a long way towards explaining nature in Australia: its soils and its climate. Both are unique.

On other continents in recent geological times, processes such as volcanism, mountain building and glacial activity have been busy creating new soil. All of these processes have been almost absent from Australia. Under such conditions no new soil is created and the old soil is leached of all its goodness by the rain, and is blown and washed away. Australia is an old, infertile land, and life here has been adapting to these conditions for aeons.

Australia's misfortune in respect to soils is echoed in its climate. Most of Australia experiences seasons – sometimes very severe ones – yet life does not respond solely to them. This can clearly be seen in the fact that although there's plenty of snow and cold country in Australia, there are almost no native trees that shed their leaves in winter, nor do any Australian animals hibernate. Instead there is a far more potent climatic force that Australian life must obey: El Niño.

El Niño is a complex climatic pattern that can cause major weather shifts around the South Pacific. The cycle of flood and drought that El Niño brings is profound. Australia's rivers – even the mighty Murray River, the nation's largest waterway – can be miles wide one year, yet you can literally step over its flow the next. This is the power of El Niño, and its effect, when combined with Australia's poor soils, manifests itself compellingly. As you might expect, relatively few of Australia's birds are seasonal breeders, and few migrate. Instead, they breed when the rain comes, and a large percentage are nomads, following the rain across the breadth of the continent.

Fuel-Efficient Fauna

Australia is famous as the home of the kangaroo and other marsupials. Have you ever wondered why roos hop? It turns out that hopping is the most efficient way of getting about at medium speeds. This is because the energy of the bounce is stored in the tendons of the legs – much like in a pogo stick – while the intestines bounce up and down like a piston, emptying and filling the lungs without needing to activate the chest muscles.

Marsupials are so energy-efficient that they need to eat one-fifth less food than equivalent-sized placental mammals (everything from bats to rats, whales and ourselves). But some have taken energy efficiency much further: if you visit a wildlife park or zoo you might notice that faraway look in a koala's eyes. Several years ago biologists announced that koalas are the only living creatures with brains that don't fit their skulls. Instead they have a shrivelled walnut of a brain that rattles around in a fluid-filled cranium. There is no doubt that the koala is no Einstein of the animal world, and we now believe that it has sacrificed its brain to energy efficiency. Brains cost a lot to run – our brains typically weigh 2% of our body weight, but use 20% of the energy we consume. Koalas eat gum leaves, which are so toxic that koalas use 20% of their energy just detoxifying their food, leaving little energy for the brain.

The peculiar constraints of the Australian environment have not made everything dumb. The koala's nearest relative, the wombat (of which there are three species), has a large brain for a marsupial. These creatures live in complex burrows and can weigh up to 35kg, making them the largest herbivorous burrowers on earth.

Two unique monotremes (egg-laying mammals) live in Australia: the bumbling echidna, something akin to a hedgehog but bigger and spikier; and the platypus, a bit like an otter, with webbed feet and a duck-like bill. Echidnas are common along bushland trails, but platypuses are elusive, seen at dawn and dusk in quiet rivers and streams.

Shark!

Despite media hype, Australia has averaged just one shark-attack fatality per year since 1791 – a remarkably low number considering how many beaches there are around the coastline. Sydney in particular has a bad rep. Attacks here peaked between 1920 and 1940, but since shark net installation began in 1937 there's only been one fatality (1963), and dorsal-fin sightings are rare enough to make the nightly news. Realistically, you're more likely to get hit by a bus – so look both ways before crossing the road on the way to the beach!

Food & Wine

'Mod Oz' seafood dish

GREG ELMS/GETTY IMAGES ©

Once upon a time in a decade not so far away, Australians proudly survived and thrived on a diet of 'meat and three veg'. Fine fare was a Sunday roast cooked to carcinogenic stages and lasagne was considered exotic. Fortunately, the country's culinary sophistication has evolved and, mirroring the population's cheeky and disobedient disposition, contemporary Australian cuisine now thrives on breaking rules and conventions.

Variety is the Spice of Life

Australian cuisine may not have a high international profile, but visitors will find a huge range and wealth of food available in city restaurants, markets, delicatessens and cafes. Competition for the custom of savvy tastebud-owners is increasingly fierce, and standards are high (as are sometimes prices). This is most evident in Sydney, Melbourne and Brisbane, but also in the other capital cities and tourist destinations. In regional areas, variety diminishes along with the population.

Mod Oz?

The Australian propensity to absorb global influences is spurred by an inquisitive public willing to try new things. The result is dynamic and surprising cuisine, and what's hot this morning may be dated by tomorrow – or reinvented and improved.

Immigration has been the key to Australia's culinary rise. A significant influx of migrants in the last 70 years, from Europe, Asia, the Middle East and Africa, has introduced new ingredients and new ways to use existing staples. Anything other countries do, Australia does too: Vietnamese, Japanese, Fijian – no matter where it's from, there's an expat community here cooking and eating it. Dig deep enough and you'll find Jamaicans using scotch-bonnet peppers and Tunisians making tajine.

With this wealth of inspiration, urban Australians have become culinary snobs. In order to wow the socks off diners, restaurants must succeed in fusing contrasting ingredients and traditions into ever more innovative fare. The phrase Modern Australian (Mod Oz) has been coined to classify this unclassifiable technique: a melange of East and West, a swirl of Atlantic and Pacific Rim, and a dash of authentic French and Italian.

If this sounds overwhelming, fear not. Dishes are characterised by bold and interesting flavours, and fresh ingredients rather than fuss or clutter. Spicing ranges from gentle to extreme, seafood is plentiful and meats are tender and full flavoured. The range of food in Australia is its greatest culinary asset: all palates – timid or brave, shy or inquisitive – are well catered for.

The Best...
Wine Tasting

1 National Wine Centre of Australia (p344), Adelaide, South Australia

2 Hunter Valley, New South Wales (p105)

3 Margaret River, Western Australia (p328)

4 Yarra Valley, Victoria (p246)

Cheers!

No matter what your poison, you're in the right country if you're after a drink.

Wine

Long recognised as some of the finest in the world, wine is now one of Australia's top exports. In fact, if you're in the country's cooler southern climes (or even in southeast Queensland), you're probably not far from a wine region. Some regions have been producing wines from the early days of settlement more than 220 years ago. Most wineries have small cellar door sales where you can taste for a nominal fee (or often free). Although plenty of good wine comes from big producers with economies of scale on their side, the most interesting wines are usually made by smaller, family-run wineries.

Beer

As the public develops a more demanding palate, Aussie beers are rising to the occasion, with a growing wealth of microbrewed flavours and varieties available. Have a look at www.brew.com.au and www.findabrewery.com.au for brewery listings. Most beers have an alcohol content between 3.5% and 5.5% – less than many European beers but more than most in North America.

The terminology used when ordering beer varies state by state. In New South Wales you ask for a 'schooner' (425mL) if you're thirsty and a 'middy' (285mL) if you're not quite so dry. In Victoria a 285mL glass is a 'pot' and in Tasmania it's a '10 ounce' – but in most of the country you can just ask for a beer and wait to see what turns up. Pints (425mL or 568mL, depending on where you are) tend to warm quickly on a summer's day but are popular with the 'upsize' generation.

Your shout!

At the bar, 'shouting' is a revered custom, where people take turns to pay for a round of drinks. Leaving before it's your turn to buy won't win you many friends! Once the drinks are distributed, a toast of 'Cheers!' is standard practice: everyone should touch glasses and look each other in the eye as they clink – failure to do so purportedly results in seven years' bad sex.

Coffee

Coffee has become a nationwide addiction: there are Italian-style espresso machines in virtually every cafe, boutique roasters are all the rage and, in urban areas, the qualified barista (coffee-maker) is the norm. Sydney, Melbourne and even subtropical Brisbane have borne generations of coffee snobs, but Melbourne takes top billing as Australia's caffeine capital. The cafe scene here rivals the most vibrant in the world: the best way to dunk yourself in it is by wandering the city centre's cafe-lined lanes.

Sport

AFL Grand Final, Melbourne Cricket Ground (p221)

TOM COCKREM/GETTY IMAGES ©

Although Australia is relatively small population-wise (just over 22 million), its inhabitants constantly vie for kudos by challenging formidable sporting opponents around the globe in just about any event they can attempt. This has resulted in some extraordinary successes on the world stage. But it's the local football codes that really excite Aussies and tap into primal passions.

Australian Rules Football

Australia's number-one-watched sport is Australian Rules football. Originally exclusive to Victoria, the Australian Football League (AFL; www.afl.com.au) has expanded into South Australia, Western Australia and even rugby-dominated New South Wales and Queensland. Long kicks, high marks and brutal collisions whip crowds into fevered frenzies: the roar of 50,000-plus fans yelling 'Carn the [insert team nickname]' and '*Baaalll!!!*' upsets dogs in suburban backyards for kilometres around.

Rugby

The National Rugby League (NRL; www.nrl.com.au) is the most popular football code north of the Murray, with the season highlight the annual State of Origin series between New South Wales and Queensland.

The Best...
Sporting Experiences

To witness an NRL game is to fully appreciate Newton's laws of motion – bone-crunching!

Meanwhile, the national rugby union (www.rugby.com.au) team, the Wallabies, won the Rugby World Cup in 1991 and 1999 and were runners-up in 2003, but couldn't make the semifinals in 2007. Third place in 2011 was some consolation. In between World Cups, Bledisloe Cup games against New Zealand are hotly contested.

Soccer

Australia's star-studded national soccer team, the Socceroos, qualified for the 2006 and 2010 World Cups after a long history of almost-but-not-quite getting there. Results were mixed, but national pride in the team remains undiminished. The national A-League (www.a-league.com.au) has enjoyed increased popularity in recent years.

Cricket

The Aussies dominated world test and one-day cricket for much of the naughties, but things aren't looking so rosy these days. The retirements of once-in-a-lifetime players like Shane Warne and Ricky Ponting exposed a leaky pool of second-tier talent, and recent test series losses to arch-rivals England have caused nationwide misery.

Tennis

Every January tennis shoes melt in the Melbourne heat at the Australian Open (www.australianopen.com), one of tennis' four Grand Slam tournaments. In the men's comp, Lleyton Hewitt has been Australia's great hope in recent years, but the former world No 1's best playing days are behind him. In the women's game, Australian Sam Stosur won the US Open in 2011 and has been hovering around the top 10 in the player rankings ever since.

Horse Racing

Australian's love to bet on the 'nags' – in fact, betting on horse racing is almost a national hobby! On the first Tuesday in November the nation stops for a world-famous horse race, the Melbourne Cup (www.melbournecup.com). In Victoria it's cause for a holiday. Australia's most famous cup winner was Phar Lap, who won in 1930, and later died of a mystery illness in the USA. Makybe Diva is a more recent star, winning three Melbourne Cups in a row before retiring in 2005.

Australia Outdoors

Larapinta Trail, West MacDonnell National Park (p294), Northern Territory

TONY WHEELER/GETTY IMAGES ©

Australia is a natural adventure playground and its sheer size means there is an incredible range of outdoor activities. The easy-on-the-eye landscape, so much of it still refreshingly free from the pressures of overpopulation, lends itself to any number of energetic pursuits and pure natural fun, whether you're on a wilderness trail or ski slope, under the sea beside a coral reef, or catching a wave.

Bushwalking

Bushwalking is supremely popular in Australia, with national parks and vast tracts of untouched scrub and forest providing ample opportunity. June to August are the best walking months up north; in the south, summer months are better.

Lonely Planet's *Walking in Australia* provides detailed information and trail notes for Australia's best bushwalks. Online, look at www.bushwalkingaustralia. org. The book *Sydney's Best Harbour & Coastal Walks* details the excellent 5.5km Bondi to Coogee Clifftop Walk and the 10km Manly Scenic Walkway, in addition to wilder walks.

Other good sources of bushwalking information and trail descriptions are

The Best...
Sydney Bushwalks

1 Sydney Harbour
National Park (p60)

2 Bondi to Coogee
Clifftop Walk (p74)

3 Royal National Park
(p104)

4 Ku-ring-gai Chase
National Park (p77)

outdoor stockists and the websites of the various state government national parks departments.

Cycling

Avid cyclists have access to great routes and can tour the country for days, weekends or even on multi-week trips.

Victoria is a super state for on- and off-road cycling and mountain biking. Standout routes for longer rides in this state include the Murray to the Mountains Rail Trail and the East Gippsland Rail Trail. In Western Australia (WA), the Munda Biddi Mountain Bike Trail offers 900km of pedal power; you can tackle the same distance on the Mawson Trail in South Australia (SA). There's also a whole network of routes around the country that follow disused railway and tram lines: www.railtrails.org.au describes these and other routes.

Rates charged by most bike-hire companies for renting road or mountain bikes are usually around $20 per hour and $40 per day. Security deposits can range from $50 to $200, depending on the rental period.

Online, www.bicycles.net.au is a useful resource; in print, there's Lonely Planet's *Cycling Australia*.

Mt Buller, Victoria

RICHARD NEBESKY/GETTY IMAGES

Diving & Snorkelling

Professional Association of Diving Instructors (PADI) dive courses are offered throughout the country. Learning here is fairly inexpensive: PADI courses range from two to five days and cost anything between $350 and $800. Also, don't forget you can enjoy the marine life by snorkelling; hiring a mask, snorkel and fins is an affordable way to get underwater.

In Queensland, the Great Barrier Reef has more dazzling dive sites than you can poke a fin at. There are coral reefs off some mainland beaches and around several of the islands, and many day trips to the Great Barrier Reef provide snorkelling gear for free.

North of Sydney in New South Wales (NSW), try Broughton Island near Port Stephens. Further north, Fish Rock Cave off South West Rocks has excellent diving, with shells, schools of clownfish and humpback whales. You can swim with grey nurse sharks at the Pinnacles near Forster, and leopard sharks at Julian Rocks Marine Reserve off Byron Bay. On the NSW south coast popular diving spots are Jervis Bay, Montague Island and Merimbula.

In WA, Ningaloo Reef is every bit as interesting as the east-coast coral reefs, without the tourist numbers.

Check out www.diveoz.com.au for nationwide information.

The Best... Surf Spots

1 Byron Bay, New South Wales (p126)

2 Bells Beach, Victoria (p252)

3 Burleigh Heads, Queensland (p135)

4 Margaret River, Western Australia (p329)

5 Sydney's Northern Beaches, New South Wales (p77)

Skiing & Snowboarding

Australia has a small but enthusiastic skiing industry, with snowfields straddling the NSW–Victoria border. The season is relatively short, however, running from about mid-June to early September, with unpredictable snowfalls. The top places to ski are in the Snowy Mountains in NSW (Perisher and Thredbo snowfields), and Mt Buller, Falls Creek and Mt Hotham in Victoria's High Country. Cross-country skiing is popular and most resorts offer lessons and equipment.

See www.ski.com.au for ski-cams, and www.ski-australia.com.au for info on the Perisher, Falls Creek, Mt Buller and Thredbo snowfields.

Surfing

World-class waves can be found all around Australia, from Queensland's subtropical Gold Coast, along the NSW coast and at beaches in Victoria, Tasmania, SA and WA. Visit surf shops for board hire and surf school info. If you've never surfed before, a lesson or two will get you started.

In NSW, Sydney is strewn with ocean beaches that offer decent breaks. Further north, Crescent Head is the longboard capital of Australia, and there are brilliant breaks at Lennox Head and Byron Bay. The NSW south coast also has great surf beaches – try Wollongong and Merimbula.

There are some magical breaks along Queensland's southeastern coast, most notably at Coolangatta, Burleigh Heads, Surfers Paradise, North Stradbroke Island and Noosa.

A Whale of a Time

A driving economic force across much of southern Australia from the time of colonisation, whaling was finally banned in Australia in 1979. Before then, humpback, blue, southern right and sperm whales were culled in huge numbers for their oil and bone.

Over recent years, whale watching has emerged as a lucrative tourist activity in migratory hot spots such as Victor Harbor and Head of Bight in South Australia, Warrnambool in Victoria, Hervey Bay in Queensland and out on the ocean beyond Sydney Harbour. If you're lucky enough to be out on the water with whales, give them a wide berth – humanity owes them a little peace and quiet.

Victoria's Southern Ocean coastline has impressive surf. Local and international surfers head to Torquay, while Bells Beach hosts the annual Rip Curl Pro competition. For the less experienced, there are surf schools in Victoria at Anglesea, Lorne and Phillip Island. Elsewhere, southern WA is a surfing mecca (head for Margaret River), while Tasmania has some remote cold-water surf spots.

See www.coastalwatch.com for forecasts and surf-cams.

Wildlife Watching

Wildlife is one of Australia's top selling points. Most national parks are home to native fauna, although much of it is nocturnal so you may need good flashlight skills to spot it. Australia is also a twitcher's haven, with a wide variety of birdlife, particularly water birds.

In NSW there are platypuses and gliders in New England National Park, and 120 bird species in Dorrigo National Park. The Border Ranges National Park is home to a quarter of all of Australia's bird species. Willandra National Park is World Heritage–listed and has dense temperate wetlands and wildlife, and koalas are everywhere around Port Macquarie. In Victoria, Wilsons Promontory National Park teems with wildlife – in fact, wombats seem to have right of way.

In Queensland, head to Malanda for birdlife, turtles and pademelons (small wallabies); Cape Tribulation for even better birdlife; Magnetic Island for koala spotting; Fraser Island for dingoes; and the Daintree for cassowaries. In SA, make a beeline for Flinders Chase National Park on Kangaroo Island where you can see platypuses, kangaroos and New Zealand fur seals.

In Tasmania, Maria Island is another twitcher's paradise, while Mt William and Mt Field National Parks and Bruny Island teem with native fauna. In the Northern Territory (NT), head for Kakadu National Park where birdlife is abundant and you can spot crocodiles. WA also has ample birdwatching hot spots, while Canberra has the richest birdlife of any Australian capital city.

Survival
Guide

Kings Canyon, Watarrka National Park (p294), Northern Territory
TED MEAD/GETTY IMAGES ©

Directory

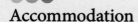

Accommodation

During the high season over summer (December to February) and at other peak times, particularly school holidays and Easter, prices are usually at their highest. Outside these times you'll find useful discounts and lower walk-in rates. Notable exceptions include central Australia, the Top End and Australia's ski resorts, where summer is the low season and prices drop substantially.

B&Bs

Local bed-and-breakfast options include everything from restored miners' cottages, converted barns, rambling old houses, upmarket country manors and beachside bungalows to a simple bedroom in a family home. In areas that attract weekenders – historic towns, wine regions, accessi-ble forest regions such as the Blue Mountains in New South Wales and the Dandenongs in Victoria – B&Bs are often upmarket, charging small fortunes for weekend stays in high season. Tariffs are typically in the midrange bracket, but can be higher. Local tourist offices can usually provide a list of places. Online resources include:

○ **Bed & Breakfast Accommodation in Australia** (BABS; www.babs.com.au)

○ **Hosted Accommodation Australia** (www.australianbedandbreakfast.com.au)

○ **OZ Bed & Breakfast** (www.ozbedandbreakfast.com)

Holiday Apartments

Costs For a two-bedroom flat, you're looking at anywhere from $140 to $200 per night, but you will pay much more in high season and for serviced apartments in major cities.

Facilities Self-contained holiday apartments range from simple, studio-like rooms with small kitchenettes, to two-bedroom apartments with full laundries and state-of-the-art entertainment systems: great value for multinight

Book Your Stay Online

For more accommodation reviews by Lonely Planet authors, check out http://hotels.lonelyplanet.com/australia. You'll find independent reviews, as well as recommendations on the best places to stay. Best of all, you can book online.

Sleeping Price Ranges

The following price ranges refer to a double room with bathroom in high season (summer):

○ **$** less than $100

○ **$$** $100 to $200

○ **$$$** more than $200

Expect to pay $20 to $50 more in expensive areas – notably Sydney, Perth and parts of northern Western Australia.

stays. Sometimes they come in small, single-storey blocks, but in tourist hot spots such as the Gold Coast expect a sea of high-rises.

Hotels

Hotels in Australian cities or well-touristed places are generally of the business or luxury-chain variety (midrange to top end): offering comfortable, anonymous, mod-con-filled rooms in multistorey blocks. For these hotels we quote 'rack rates' (official advertised rates – usually more than $150 a night), though significant discounts can be offered when business is quiet.

Motels

Drive-up motels offer comfortable midrange accommodation and are found all over Australia. They rarely offer a cheaper rate for singles, so are better value for couples or groups of three. You'll mostly pay between $100 and

$150 for a simple room with a kettle, fridge, TV, air-con and bathroom.

Pubs

Hotels in Australia – the ones that serve beer – are commonly known as pubs (from the term 'public house'). Many were built during boom times, so they're often among the largest, most extravagant buildings in town. Some have been restored but, generally, rooms remain small and weathered, with a long amble down the hall to the bathroom. They're usually central and cheap – singles/doubles with shared facilities from $50/80, more if you want a private bathroom – but if you're a light sleeper, avoid booking a room above the bar and check whether a band is playing downstairs that night.

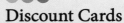

Customs Regulations

For detailed information on customs and quarantine regulations, contact the **Australian Customs & Border Protection Service** (📞1300 363 263, 02-6275 6666; www.customs.gov.au) and the **Department of Agriculture, Fisheries & Forestry** (www.daff.gov.au).

When entering Australia you can bring most articles in free of duty provided that customs is satisfied they are for personal use and that you'll be taking them with you when you leave. Duty-free quotas per person:

Alcohol 2.25L (over the age of 18)

Cigarettes 50 cigarettes (over the age of 18)

Dutiable goods Up to the value of $900 ($450 for people under 18)

Narcotics, of course, are illegal, and customs inspectors and their highly trained hounds are diligent in sniffing them out. Quarantine regulations are strict, so you must declare all goods of animal or vegetable origin – wooden spoons, straw hats, the lot. Fresh food (meat, cheese, fruit, vegetables etc) and flowers are prohibited. There

are disposal bins located in airports where you can dump any questionable items if you don't want to bother with an inspection. You need to declare currency in excess of $10,000 (including foreign currency).

Discount Cards

Travellers over 60 with some form of identification (eg a Seniors Card – www.seniorscard.com.au) are often eligible for concession prices. Overseas pensioners are entitled to discounts of at

Climate

Cairns

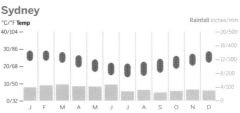

Sydney

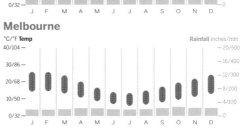

Melbourne

least 10% on most express-bus fares with Greyhound.

The internationally recognised **International Student Identity Card** (ISIC; www.isic.org) is available to full-time students aged 12 and over. The card gives the bearer discounts on accommodation, transport and admission to various attractions. The same organisation also produces the International Youth Travel Card (IYTC), issued to people under 26 years of age who are not full-time students, and has benefits equivalent to the ISIC.

Electricity

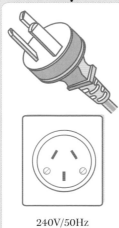

240V/50Hz

Food

For information on eating and drinking in Australia, see the Food & Wine chapter (p374).

Gay & Lesbian Travellers

Australia is a popular destination for gay and lesbian travellers, with the so-called 'pink tourism' appeal of Sydney especially big, thanks largely to the city's annual, high-profile and spectacular Sydney Gay & Lesbian Mardi Gras. In general, Australians are open-minded about homosexuality, but the further into the country you get, the more likely you are to run into overt homophobia.

Same-sex acts are legal in all states but the age of consent varies.

Major Gay & Lesbian Events

Midsumma Festival (www.midsumma.org.au; ⊘ Jan-Feb) Melbourne's annual gay-and-lesbian arts festival features more than 100 events from mid-January to mid-February, with a Pride March finale.

Sydney Gay & Lesbian Mardi Gras (www.mardigras.org.au) The highlight of this world-famous, month-long festival is the over-the-top, sequined Oxford St parade. February to March.

Pridefest (www.pridewa.asn.au) In October in Perth.

Feast Festival (www.feast.org.au) Three weeks in November in Adelaide, with a carnival, theatre, dialogue and dance.

Publications & Contacts

Major cities have gay newspapers, available from clubs, cafes, venues and newsagents. Gay and lesbian lifestyle magazines include *DNA, Lesbians on the Loose (LOTL)* and the Sydney-based *SX.* In Melbourne look for *MCV;* in Queensland look for *Queensland Pride.* Perth has the free *OutinPerth* and Adelaide has *Blaze.*

Gay and Lesbian Counselling & Community Services of Australia (GLCCS; www.glccs.org.au) Telephone counselling.

Gay & Lesbian Tourism Australia (GALTA; www.galta.com.au) A wealth of information about gay and lesbian travel in Australia.

Same Same (www.samesame.com.au) News, events and lifestyle features.

Health

Healthwise, Australia is a remarkably safe country in which to travel, considering that such a large portion of it lies in the tropics. Few travellers to Australia will experience anything worse than an upset stomach or a bad hangover and, if you do fall ill, the standard of hospitals and health care is high.

Vaccinations

Visit a physician four to eight weeks before departure. Ask your doctor for an International Certificate of Vaccination (aka the 'yellow booklet'), which will list the vaccinations you've received.

If you're entering Australia within six days of having stayed overnight or longer in a yellow-fever-infected country, you'll need proof of yellow-fever vaccination. For a full list of these countries visit the website of **Centers for Disease Control & Prevention** (www.cdc.gov/travel).

The **World Health Organization** (WHO; www.who.int/wer) recommends that all travellers should be covered for diphtheria, tetanus, measles, mumps, rubella, chicken pox and polio, as well as hepatitis B, regardless of their destination. While Australia has high levels of childhood vaccination coverage, outbreaks of these diseases do occur.

Insurance

Health insurance is essential for all travellers; see p388 for more details.

Internet Resources

There's a wealth of travel health advice on the internet: **Lonely Planet** (www.lonelyplanet.com) is a good place to start. The **World Health Organization** (WHO; www.who.int/ith) publishes *International Travel and Health*, revised annually and available free online. **MD Travel Health** (www.mdtravelhealth.com) provides complete travel health recommendations for every country, updated daily. A selection of government travel health websites:

○ **Australia** (www.smartraveller.gov.au)

○ **Canada** (www.hc-sc.gc.ca)

○ **UK** (www.nhs.uk/livewell/travelhealth)

○ **USA** (www.cdc.gov/travel)

Availability & Cost of Health Care

Facilities Australia has an excellent health-care system. It's a mixture of privately run medical clinics and hospitals alongside a system of public hospitals funded by the Australian government. There are also excellent specialised public-health facilities for women and children in major centres.

Medicare This system covers Australian residents for some health-care costs. Visitors from countries with which Australia has a reciprocal health-care agreement are eligible for benefits specified under the Medicare program. Agreements are currently in place with Finland, Italy, Malta, the Netherlands, Norway, Sweden and the UK – check the details before departing these countries. For further details, visit www.humanservices.gov.au/customer/enablers/medicare/medicare-card/new-arrivals-and-visitors-to-australia.

Medications Painkillers, antihistamines for allergies, and skincare products are widely available at chemists throughout Australia. You may find that medications readily available over the counter in some countries are only available in Australia by prescription. These include the oral contraceptive pill, some medications for asthma and all antibiotics.

Environmental Hazards

Heat Exhaustion & Heatstroke

Symptoms of heat exhaustion include dizziness, fainting, fatigue, nausea or vomiting. The skin is usually pale, cool and clammy. Treatment consists of rest in a cool, shady place and fluid replacement with water or diluted sports drinks.

Heatstroke is a severe form of heat illness and is a true medical emergency, with heating of the brain leading to disorientation, hallucinations and seizures. Prevent heatstroke by maintaining an adequate fluid intake to ensure the continued passage of clear and copious urine, especially during physical exertion.

Hypothermia

More bushwalkers in Australia die of cold than in bushfires. Even in summer, particularly in highland Tasmania, Victoria and NSW, conditions can change quickly, with temperatures dropping below freezing and blizzards blowing in. Hypothermia is a real risk. Early signs include the inability to perform fine movements (eg doing up buttons), shivering

Practicalities

○ **Currency** The Australian dollar comprises 100 cents. There are 5c, 10c, 20c, 50c, $1 and $2 coins, and $5, $10, $20, $50 and $100 notes.

○ **DVDs** Australian DVDs are encoded for Region 4, which includes Mexico, South America, Central America, New Zealand, the Pacific and the Caribbean.

○ **Newspapers** Leaf through the daily *Sydney Morning Herald*, Melbourne's *Age* or the national *Australian* broadsheet newspapers.

○ **Radio** Tune in to ABC radio; check out www.abc.net.au/radio.

○ **Smoking** Banned on public transport, in pubs, bars and eateries, and in some public outdoor spaces.

○ **TV** The main free-to-air TV channels are the government-sponsored ABC, multicultural SBS and the three commercial networks – Seven, Nine and Ten – plus numerous additional channels from these main players.

○ **Weights and measures** Australia uses the metric system.

and a bad case of the 'umbles' (fumbles, mumbles, grumbles, stumbles). Get out of the cold, change out of wet clothing and into dry stuff, and eat and drink to warm up.

Insect-Borne Illnesses

Various insects in Australia may be the source of specific diseases (dengue fever, Ross River fever, viral encephalitis). For protection wear loose-fitting, long-sleeved clothing, and apply 30% DEET to all exposed skin.

Insurance

Worldwide travel insurance is available at www.lonelyplanet.com/travel_services. You can buy, extend and claim

online anytime – even if you're already on the road.

Level of cover A good travel insurance policy covering theft, loss and medical problems is essential. Some policies specifically exclude designated 'dangerous activities' such as scuba diving, skiing and even bushwalking. Make sure the policy you choose fully covers you for your activity of choice.

Health You may prefer a policy that pays doctors or hospitals directly rather than requiring you to pay on the spot and claim later. If you have to claim later make sure you keep all documentation. Check that the policy covers ambulances and emergency medical evacuations by air.

Car See p399 for information on vehicle insurance.

Internet Access

Accessing Terminals

There are fewer internet cafes around these days than there were five years ago (thanks to the advent of iPhones/iPads and wi-fi) but you'll still find them in most sizable towns. Hourly costs range from $6 to $10. Most youth hostels have both internet kiosks and wi-fi, as do many hotels and caravan parks.

Most public libraries have internet access, but generally it's provided for research needs, not for travellers to check Facebook – so book ahead or tackle an internet cafe.

BYO

ISPs If you're bringing your palmtop or laptop, check with your Internet Service Provider (ISP) for access numbers you can dial into in Australia. Some major Australian ISPs:

○ **Australia On Line** (☑ 1300 650 661; www.ozonline.com.au)

○ **Dodo** (☑ 13 36 36; www.dodo.com)

○ **iinet** (☑ 13 19 17; www.iinet.net.au)

○ **iPrimus** (☑ 13 17 89; www.iprimus.com.au)

○ **Optus** (www.optus.com.au)

○ **Telstra BigPond** (☑ 13 76 63; www.bigpond.com)

Plugs Australia primarily uses the RJ-45 telephone plugs although you may see Telstra EXI-160 four-pin plugs – electronics shops such as Tandy and Dick Smith can help.

Modem Keep in mind that your PC-card modem may not work in Australia. The safest option is to buy a reputable 'global' modem before you leave home or buy a local PC-card modem once you get to Australia.

Wi-Fi

It's still rare in remote Australia, but wireless internet access is increasingly the norm in Australia's big-city accommodation, with cafes, bars and even some public gardens also providing wi-fi access (often free for customers/guests). For locations, visit www.freewifi.com.au.

Legal Matters

Most travellers will have no contact with Australia's police or legal system; if they do, it's most likely to be while driving.

Driving There's a significant police presence on central Australian roads, and police have the power to stop your car, see your licence (you're required to carry it), check your vehicle for roadworthiness, and insist that you take a breath test for alcohol (and sometimes illicit drugs).

Drugs First-time offenders caught with small amounts of illegal drugs are likely to

Where the Wild Things Are

Australia's profusion of dangerous creatures is legendary: snakes, spiders, sharks, crocodiles, jellyfish... Travellers needn't be alarmed, though – you're unlikely to see many of these creatures in the wild, much less be attacked by one.

● **Crocodiles** Around the northern Australian coastline, saltwater crocodiles (salties) are a real danger. They also inhabit estuaries, creeks and rivers, sometimes a long way inland. Observe safety signs or ask locals whether that inviting-looking waterhole or river is croc-free before plunging in.

● **Jellyfish** With venomous tentacles up to 3m long, box jellyfish (aka sea wasps or stingers) inhabit Australia's tropical waters. You can be stung during any month, but they're most common during the wet season (October to March) when you should stay out of the sea in many places. Stinger nets are in place at some beaches, but never swim unless you've checked. 'Stinger suits' (full-body Lycra swimsuits) prevent stinging, as do wetsuits. If you are stung, wash the skin with vinegar then get to a hospital. The box jellyfish also has a tiny, lethal relative called an irukandji though, to date, only two north-coast deaths have been directly attributed to it.

● **Sharks** Despite extensive media coverage, the risk of shark attack in Australia is no greater than in other countries with extensive coastlines. Check with surf life-saving groups about local risks.

● **Snakes** There's no denying it: Australia has plenty of venomous snakes. Most common are brown and tiger snakes, but few species are aggressive. Unless you're messing around with or accidentally standing on one, it's extremely unlikely that you'll get bitten. The golden rule: if you see a snake, do a Beatles and let it be. If you are bitten, prevent the spread of venom by applying pressure to the wound and immobilising the area with a splint or sling before seeking medical attention.

● **Spiders** Australia has several poisonous spiders, bites from which are usually treatable with antivenins. The deadly funnel-web spider lives in New South Wales (including Sydney) – bites are treated as per snake bites (pressure and immobilisation before transferring to a hospital). Redback spiders live throughout Australia; bites cause pain, sweating and nausea. Apply ice or cold packs, then transfer to hospital. White-tailed spider bites may cause an ulcer that's slow and difficult to heal. Clean the wound and seek medical assistance. The disturbingly large huntsman spider is harmless, though seeing one can affect your blood pressure and/or underpants.

Interstate Quarantine

When travelling within Australia, whether by land or air, you'll come across signs (mainly in airports and interstate train stations and at state borders) warning of the possible dangers of carrying fruit, vegetables and plants from one area to another. Certain pests and diseases (fruit fly, cucurbit thrips, grape phylloxera...) are prevalent in some areas but not in others: authorities would like to limit them spreading.

There are quarantine inspection posts on some state borders and occasionally elsewhere. While quarantine control often relies on honesty, many posts are staffed and officers are entitled to search your car for undeclared items. Generally they will confiscate all fresh fruit and vegetables, so it's best to leave shopping for these items until the first town past the inspection point.

receive a fine rather than go to jail, but the recording of a conviction against you may affect your visa status.

Visas If you remain in Australia beyond the life of your visa, you'll officially be an 'overstayer' and could face detention and then be prevented from returning to Australia for up to three years.

Arrested? It's your right to telephone a friend, lawyer or relative before questioning begins. Legal aid is available only in serious cases; for Legal Aid office info see www.nla.aust.net.au. However, many solicitors do not charge for an initial consultation.

●●●

Money

See the Need to Know chapter (p48) for exchange rates and costs. In this book, prices refer to the (very stable) Australian dollar.

ATMs & Eftpos

ATMs Australia's 'big four' banks – ANZ, Commonwealth, National Australia Bank and Westpac – and affiliated banks have branches all over Australia, and many provide 24-hour automated teller machines (ATMs). But don't expect to find ATMs *everywhere,* certainly not off the beaten track or in small towns. Most ATMs accept cards issued by other banks (for a fee) and are linked to international networks.

Eftpos Most service stations, supermarkets, restaurants, cafes and shops have Electronic Funds Transfer at Point of Sale (Eftpos) facilities these days, allowing you to make purchases and even draw out cash with your credit or debit card. Just don't forget your PIN (Personal Identification Number)!

Fees Bear in mind that withdrawing cash via ATMs or

Eftpos may attract significant fees – check the associated costs with your bank first.

Credit Cards

Credit cards such as Visa and MasterCard are widely accepted for everything from a hostel bed or a restaurant meal to an adventure tour, and are pretty much essential (in lieu of a large deposit) for hiring a car. They can also be used to get cash advances over the counter at banks and from many ATMs, depending on the card, though these transactions incur immediate interest. Diners Club and American Express (Amex) are not as widely accepted.

Lost credit-card contact numbers:

- **American Express** (☎1300 132 639; www.americanexpress.com.au)

- **Diners Club** (☎1300 360 060; www.dinersclub.com.au)

- **MasterCard** (☎1800 120 113; www.mastercard.com.au)

- **Visa** (☎1800 450 346; www.visa.com.au)

Debit Cards

A debit card allows you to draw money directly from your home bank account using ATMs, banks or Eftpos machines. Any card connected to the international banking network – Cirrus, Maestro, Plus and Eurocard – should work with your PIN. Expect substantial fees.

Companies such as Travelex offer debit cards (Travelex calls them 'Cash Passport' cards) with set withdrawal fees and a balance you can top up from your personal bank account while on the road.

Exchanging Money

Changing foreign currency or travellers cheques is usually no problem at banks throughout Australia, or at licensed moneychangers such as Travelex or AmEx in cities and major towns.

Taxes & Refunds

The goods and services tax (GST) is a flat 10% tax on all goods and services – accommodation, eating out, transport, electrical and other goods, books, furniture, clothing etc. There are exceptions, such as basic foods (milk, bread, fruit and vegetables etc). By law the tax is included in the quoted or shelf price, so all prices are GST-inclusive.

International air and sea travel to/from Australia is GST-free, as is domestic air travel when purchased outside Australia by nonresidents.

If you purchase new or secondhand goods with a total minimum value of $300 from any one supplier no more than 30 days before you leave Australia, you are entitled under the Tourist Refund Scheme (TRS) to a refund of any GST or WET (wine equalisation tax) paid. The scheme doesn't apply to all goods, and those that do qualify must be worn or taken as hand luggage onto the plane or ship. Also note that the refund is valid for goods bought from more than one supplier, but only if at least $300 is spent in each. For more details, see the website of the Australian Customs & Border Protection Service (p385).

Travellers Cheques

○ The ubiquity and convenience of internationally linked credit and debit card facilities in Australia means that travellers cheques are virtually redundant.

○ AmEx and Travelex will exchange their associated travellers cheques, and major banks will change travellers cheques also.

○ In all instances you'll need to present your passport for identification when cashing them.

●●●●
Opening Hours

Business hours do vary from state to state, but use the following as a guide. Note that nearly all attractions across Australia are closed on Christmas Day; many also close on New Years Day and Good Friday.

Banks 9.30am to 4pm Monday to Thursday; until 5pm on Friday. Some large city branches open 8am to 6pm weekdays; a few also till 9pm Friday.

Cafes All-day affairs opening from around 7am until around 5pm, or continuing their business into the night.

Petrol stations and roadhouses Usually open 8am to 10pm. Some urban service stations open 24 hours.

Post offices 9am to 5pm Monday to Friday; some from 9am to noon on Saturday. You can also buy stamps from newsagents and some delis.

Pubs Usually serve food from noon to 2pm and from 6pm to 8pm. Pubs and bars often open for drinking at lunchtime and continue well into the evening, particularly from Thursday to Saturday.

Restaurants Open around noon for lunch and from 6pm for dinner, typically serving until at least 2pm and 8pm respectively, often later. Big-city eateries keep longer hours.

Shops and businesses 9am to 5pm or 6pm Monday to Friday, until either noon or 5pm on Saturday. Sunday trading operates in major cities, urban areas and tourist towns. There is late-night shopping till 9pm in major towns (usually Thursday or Friday night).

Supermarkets Generally open from 7am until at least 8pm; some open 24 hours. Delis (general stores) also open late.

●●●●
Public Holidays

Timing of public holidays can vary from state to state: check locally for precise dates (* indicates holidays that are only observed locally within each state).

National

New Year's Day 1 January

Australia Day 26 January

Easter (Good Friday to Easter Monday inclusive) late March/ early April

Anzac Day 25 April

Queen's Birthday (except WA) Second Monday in June

Queen's Birthday (WA) Last Monday in September

Christmas Day 25 December

Boxing Day 26 December

Australian Capital Territory

Canberra Day Second Monday in March

Bank Holiday First Monday in August

Labour Day First Monday in October

New South Wales

Bank Holiday First Monday in August

Labour Day First Monday in October

Northern Territory

May Day First Monday in May

Show Day* (Alice Springs) First Friday in July; (Tennant Creek) second Friday in July; (Katherine) third Friday in July; (Darwin) fourth Friday in July

Picnic Day First Monday in August

Queensland

Labour Day First Monday in May

Royal Queensland Show Day* (Brisbane) Second or third Wednesday in August

South Australia

Adelaide Cup Day Third Monday in May

Labour Day First Monday in October

Proclamation Day Last Monday or Tuesday in December

Tasmania

Regatta Day* (Hobart) 14 February

Launceston Cup Day* Last Wednesday in February

Eight Hours Day First Monday in March

Bank Holiday Tuesday following Easter Monday

King Island Show* First Tuesday in March

Launceston Show Day* Thursday preceding second Saturday in October

Hobart Show Day* Thursday preceding fourth Saturday in October

Recreation Day* (Northern Tasmania) First Monday in November

Victoria

Labour Day Second Monday in March

Melbourne Cup Day First Tuesday in November

Western Australia

Labour Day First Monday in March

Foundation Day First Monday in June

School Holidays

❂ The Christmas/summer school holiday season runs from mid-December to late January.

❂ Three shorter school holiday periods occur during the year, varying by a week or two from state to state. They fall roughly from early to mid-April, late June to mid-July, and late September to early October.

Safe Travel

Australia is a relatively safe place to travel by world standards – crime- and war-wise at any rate – but natural disasters have been wreaking havoc of late. Bushfires, floods and cyclones regularly decimate parts of most states and territories, but if you pay attention to warnings from local authorities and don't venture into affected areas, you should be fine.

At the Beach

Undertows (or rips) are a problem in the surf, but popular beaches are patrolled by surf life-savers. Patrolled areas are indicated by red-and-yellow flags. If you find yourself being carried out by a rip, swim parallel to the shore until you're out of the rip, then head for the beach.

Several people are paralysed every year by diving into shallow waves and hitting sand bars: look before you leap.

Bushfires

Bushfires happen regularly across Australia. In hot, dry and windy weather and on total-fire-ban days, be extremely careful with naked flames (including cigarette butts) and don't use camping stoves, campfires or BBQs. Bushwalkers should delay trips until things cool down. If you're out in the bush and you see smoke, take it seriously: find the nearest open space (downhill if possible). Forested ridges are dangerous places to be.

●●●●
Telephone

Australia's main telecommunication companies:

Telstra (www.telstra.com.au) The main player – landline and mobile phone services.

Optus (www.optus.com.au) Telstra's main rival – landline and mobile phone services.

Vodafone (www.vodafone.com.au) Mobile phone services.

Virgin (www.virginmobile.com.au) Mobile phone services.

Toll-Free & Information Calls

○ Many businesses have either a toll-free 1800 number, dialled from anywhere within Australia for free, or a 13 or 1300 number, charged at a local call rate. None of these numbers can be dialled from outside Australia.

○ To make a reverse-charge (collect) call from any public or private phone, dial ☎1800 738 3773 or 12 550.

Maintaining Perspective

There's approximately one shark-attack and one croc-attack fatality per year in Australia. Blue-ringed-octopus deaths are rarer – only two in the last century. Jellyfish do better – about two deaths annually – but you're still more than 100 times more likely to drown. Spiders haven't killed anyone in the last 20 years. Snake bites kill one or two people per year, as do bee stings, but you're about a thousand times more likely to perish on the nation's roads.

○ Numbers starting with 190 are usually recorded information services, charged at anything from 35c to $5 or more per minute (more from mobiles and payphones).

Important Numbers

Country code	☎61
International access code	☎0011
Emergency (ambulance, fire, police)	☎000
Directory assistance	☎1223
Road Conditions (NSW)	☎13 27 01

International Calls

From payphones Most payphones allow International Subscriber Dialling (ISD) calls, the cost and international dialling code of which will vary depending on which international phonecard provider you are using. International phone cards are readily available from internet cafes and convenience stores.

From landlines International calls from landlines in Australia are also relatively

cheap and often subject to special deals; rates vary with providers.

Codes When calling overseas you will need to dial the international access code from Australia (0011 or 0018), the country code and then the area code (without the initial 0). So for a London telephone number you'll need to dial ☎0011-44-20, then the number. In addition, certain operators will have you dial a special code to access their service. If dialling Australia from overseas, the country code is 61 and you need to drop the 0 in state/territory area codes. Country codes:

COUNTRY	CODE
France	☎33
Germany	☎49
Ireland	☎353
Japan	☎81
Netherlands	☎31
New Zealand	☎64
UK	☎44
USA & Canada	☎1

Local Calls

Calls from private phones cost 15c to 30c, while local calls from public phones cost 50c; both involve unlimited talk time. Calls to mobile phones attract higher rates and are timed.

Long-Distance Calls & Area Codes

Long-distance calls (over around 50km) are timed. Australia uses four Subscriber Trunk Dialling (STD) area codes. These STD calls can be made from any public phone and are cheaper during off-peak hours (generally between 7pm and 7am, and on weekends). Broadly, the main area codes are as follows.

STATE/ TERRITORY	AREA CODE
ACT	☎ 02
NSW	☎ 02
NT	☎ 08
QLD	☎ 07
SA	☎ 08
TAS	☎ 03
VIC	☎ 03
WA	☎ 08

Area code boundaries don't necessarily coincide with state borders; for example some parts of NSW use the neighbouring states' codes.

Mobile Phones

Numbers Numbers with the prefix 04xx belong to mobile phones.

Networks The GSM and 3G mobile networks service more than 90% of the population but leave vast tracts of the country uncovered. Australia's digital network is compatible with GSM 900 and 1800 (used in Europe), but generally not with the systems used in the USA or Japan.

Reception The east coast, southeast and southwest get good reception, but elsewhere (apart from major towns) it can be haphazard or nonexistent. Things are improving, however.

New accounts It's easy and cheap enough to get connected short-term, with prepaid mobile systems offered by the main providers.

Phonecards & Public Phones

A variety of phonecards can be bought at newsagents, hostels and post offices for a fixed dollar value (usually $10, $20 etc) and can be used with any public or private phone by dialling a toll-free access number and then the PIN number on the card.

Most public phones use phonecards; some also accept credit cards. Old-fashioned coin-operated public phones are becoming increasingly rare (and if you do find one, chances are the coin slot will be gummed up or vandalised beyond function).

Time

Zones Australia is divided into three time zones: Western Standard Time (GMT/UTC plus eight hours), covering WA; Central Standard Time (plus 9½ hours), covering NT and SA; and Eastern Standard Time (plus 10 hours), covering Tasmania, Victoria, NSW, the ACT and Queensland. There are minor exceptions – Broken Hill (NSW), for instance, is on Central Standard Time.

For international times, see www.timeanddate.com/worldclock.

Daylight saving Clocks are put forward an hour. This system operates in some states during the warmer months (October to early April), but things can get pretty confusing, with WA, NT and Queensland staying on standard time, while in Tasmania daylight saving starts a month earlier than in SA, Victoria, ACT and NSW.

Tourist Information

The **Australian Tourist Commission** (ATC; www.australia.com) is the national government tourist body, and has a good website for pre-trip research. The website also lists reliable travel agents in countries around the world to help you plan your trip, plus visa, work and customs information.

Within Australia, tourist information is disseminated by various regional and local offices. Almost every major town in Australia seems to maintain a tourist office of some type and in many cases they are very good, with chatty staff (often retiree volunteers) providing local info not readily available from the state offices.

Travellers with Disabilities
◦ Disability awareness in Australia is high and getting higher.

Legislation requires that new accommodation meets accessibility standards for mobility-impaired travellers, and discrimination by tourism operators is illegal.

Many of Australia's key attractions, including many national parks, provide access for those with limited mobility and a number of sites also address the needs of visitors with visual or aural impairments. Contact attractions in advance to confirm the facilities.

Tour operators with vehicles catering to mobility-impaired travellers operate from most capital cities.

Facilities for wheelchairs are improving in accommodation, but there are still many older establishments where the necessary upgrades haven't been done.

Resources

Deaf Australia (www.deafau. org.au)

Easy Access Australia (www.easyaccessaustralia. com.au) A publication by Bruce Cameron available from various bookshops. Details accessible transport, accommodation and attraction options.

e-Bility (www.ebility.com) Classifieds, resources and links for people with disabilities.

National Information Communication & Awareness Network (NICAN; www.nican.com.au) Australia-wide directory providing information on access issues, accessible

accommodation, sporting and recreational activities, transport and specialist tour operators.

National Public Toilet Map (www.toiletmap.gov. au) Lists more than 14,000 public toilets around Australia, including those with wheelchair access.

Spinal Cord Injuries Australia (SCIA; www. spinalcordinjuries.com.au)

Vision Australia (www. visionaustralia.org.au)

Air Travel

Qantas (www.qantas.com.au) entitles a disabled person and the carer travelling with them to a discount on full economy fares; contact NICAN for eligibility and an application form. Guide dogs travel for free on Qantas, Jetstar (p397) and Virgin Australia (p396), and their affiliated carriers. All of Australia's major airports have dedicated parking spaces, wheelchair access to terminals, accessible toilets, and skychairs to convey passengers onto planes via airbridges.

Train Travel

In NSW, CountryLink's XPT trains have at least one carriage (usually the buffet car) with a seat removed for a wheelchair, and an accessible toilet. Queensland Rail's *Tilt Train* from Brisbane to Cairns has a wheelchair-accessible carriage.

Melbourne's suburban rail network is accessible; guide and hearing dogs are permitted on all public

transport in Victoria. **Metlink** (http://ptv.vic.gov.au) offers a free travel pass to visually impaired people in Melbourne.

Visas

All visitors to Australia need a visa – only New Zealand nationals are exempt, and even they sheepishly receive a 'special category' visa on arrival. Application forms for the several types of visa are available from Australian diplomatic missions overseas, travel agents or the website of the **Department of Immigration & Citizenship** (www.immi.gov.au).

eVisitor (651)

A three-month visa (free) for many European passport holders. They are electronically stored and linked to individual passport numbers, so no stamp in your passport is required. It's advisable to apply at least 14 days prior to your proposed date of travel to Australia.

Electronic Travel Authority (ETA; 601)

A three-month visa (free) for citizens of 34 countries, including Brunei, Canada, Hong Kong, Japan, Malaysia, Singapore, South Korea and the USA.

Tourist Visas (600)

A three-, six- or 12-month visa ($115) for citizens of countries other than those listed above, or for people from the above countries who want to stay longer than three months.

Women Travellers

Australia is generally a safe place for women travellers, although the usual sensible precautions apply.

Night-time Avoid walking alone late at night in any of the major cities and towns – keep enough money aside for a taxi back to your accommodation.

Pubs Be wary of staying in basic pub accommodation unless it looks safe and well managed.

Sexual harassment Rare, though some macho Aussie males still slip – particularly when they've been drinking.

Rural areas Stereotypically, the further you get from the big cities, the less enlightened your average Aussie male is probably going to be about women's issues. Having said that, many women travellers say that they have met the friendliest, most down-to-earth blokes in outback pubs and remote roadhouse stops.

Hitchhiking Hitching is not recommended for anyone. Even when travelling in pairs, exercise caution at all times.

Drugged drinks Some pubs in Sydney and other big cities post warnings about drugged or 'spiked' drinks: probably not cause for paranoia, but play it safe if someone offers you a drink in a bar.

Transport

Getting There & Away

Australia is a long way from just about everywhere – getting there usually means a long-haul flight. If you're short on time on the ground, consider internal flights – they're affordable (compared with petrol and car-hire costs), can usually be carbon offset, and will save you some *looong* days in the saddle. Flights, tours and rail tickets can be booked online at www.lonelyplanet.com/bookings.

Entering the Country

Arrival in Australia is usually straightforward and efficient, with the usual customs declarations. There are no restrictions for citizens of any particular foreign countries entering Australia – if you have a current passport and visa (see p395), you should be fine.

 Air

High season (with the highest prices) for flights into Australia is roughly over the country's summer (December to February); low season generally tallies with the winter

months (June to August), though this is actually peak season in central Australia and the Top End. Australia's international carrier is **Qantas** (www.qantas.com.au), which has an outstanding safety record (...as Dustin Hoffman said in *Rainman*, 'Qantas never crashed').

International Airports

Australia has numerous international gateways, with Sydney and Melbourne being the busiest. Other than the big-city airports listed here, some smaller cities (notably the Gold Coast) also offer international flights.

- **Adelaide Airport** (www.aal.com.au)

- **Brisbane Airport** (www.bne.com.au)

- **Cairns Airport** (www.cairnsairport.com)

- **Darwin Airport** (www.darwinairport.com.au)

- **Melbourne Airport** (Tullamarine; www.melbourneairport.com.au)

- **Perth Airport** (www.perthairport.net.au)

- **Sydney Airport** (Kingsford Smith; www.sydneyairport.com.au)

Getting Around

 Air

Airlines in Australia

Australia's main (and highly safe and professional) domestic airlines are **Qantas** (www.qantas.com.au) and **Virgin Australia** (www.virginaustralia

.com), servicing all the main centres with regular flights. **Jetstar** (www.jetstar.com. au) (a subsidiary of Qantas) and **Tiger Airways** (www. tigerairways.com) (partially owned by Singapore Airlines) are generally a bit cheaper and fly between most Australian capital cities. See regional chapters for info on airlines operating locally within Australia's states and territories.

Air Passes

Qantas offers a discount-fare **Walkabout Air Pass** for passengers flying into Australia from overseas with Qantas or American Airlines. The pass allows you to link up around 80 domestic Australian destinations for less than you'd pay booking flights individually.

Bicycle

Australia has much to offer cyclists, from bike paths winding through most major cities, to thousands of kilometres of good country roads where you can wear out your sprockets. There's lots of flat countryside and gently rolling hills to explore and, although Australia is not as mountainous as, say, Switzerland or France, mountain bikers can find plenty of forest trails and high country. If you're really keen, outback cycling might also be an option.

Hire Bike hire in cities is easy, but if you're riding for more than a few hours or even a day, it's more economical to invest in your own wheels.

Legalities Bike helmets are compulsory in all states and territories, as are white front-lights and red rear-lights for riding at night.

Maps You can get by with standard road maps, but to avoid low-grade unsealed roads, the government series is best. The 1:250,000 scale is suitable, though you'll need lots of maps if you're going far. The next scale up is 1:1,000,000 – widely available in map shops.

Weather In summer carry plenty of water. Wear a helmet with a peak (or a cap under your helmet), use sunscreen and avoid cycling in the middle of the day. Beware summer northerlies that can make a north-bound cyclist's life hell. South-easterly trade winds blow in April, when you can have (theoretically) tail winds all the way to Darwin. It can get very cold in Victoria, Tasmania, southern South Australia and the New South Wales mountains, so pack appropriate clothing.

Transport If you're bringing in your own bike, check with your airline for costs and the degree of dismantling or packing required. Within Australia, bus companies require you to dismantle your bike and some don't guarantee that it will travel on the same bus as you.

Information

The national cycling body is the **Bicycle Federation of Australia** (www.bicycles.net. au). Each state and territory has a touring organisation that can also help with cycling information and put you in touch with touring clubs.

Climate Change & Travel

Every form of transport that relies on carbon-based fuel generates CO_2, the main cause of human-induced climate change. Modern travel is dependent on aeroplanes, which might use less fuel per kilometre per person than most cars but travel much greater distances. The altitude at which aircraft emit gases (including CO_2) and particles also contributes to their climate change impact. Many websites offer 'carbon calculators' that allow people to estimate the carbon emissions generated by their journey and, for those who wish to do so, to offset the impact of the greenhouse gases emitted with contributions to portfolios of climate-friendly initiatives throughout the world. Lonely Planet offsets the carbon footprint of all staff and author travel.

○ **Bicycle Network Victoria** (www.bicyclenetwork. com.au)

○ **Bicycle NSW** (www. bicyclensw.org.au)

○ **Bicycle Queensland** (www.bq.org.au)

○ **Bicycle SA** (www.bikesa. asn.au)

○ **Bicycle Tasmania** (www. biketas.org.au)

○ **Bicycle Transportation Alliance** (www.btawa.org.au) In WA.

○ **Cycling Northern Territory** (www.nt.cycling. org.au)

○ **Pedal Power ACT** (www. pedalpower.org.au)

Bus

Australia's extensive bus network is a reliable way to get around, though bus travel isn't always cheaper than flying and it can be tedious over huge distances. Most buses are equipped with air-con, toilets and videos; all are smoke-free. There are no class divisions on Australian buses (very democratic), and the vehicles of the different companies all look pretty similar.

Small towns eschew formal bus terminals for a single drop-off/pick-up point (post office, newsagent, corner shop etc).

Greyhound Australia (www.greyhound.com.au) runs a national network (notably not across the Nullarbor Plain, between Adelaide and Perth). Book online for the cheapest fares. Other operators:

Firefly Express (www.fireflyexpress.com.au) Runs between Sydney, Canberra, Melbourne and Adelaide.

Premier Motor Service (www.premierms.com.au) Runs along the east coast between Cairns and Melbourne.

V/Line (www.vline.com.au) Connects Victoria with NSW, SA and the ACT.

Bus Passes

Greyhound offers a slew of passes geared towards various types and routes of travel: see www.greyhound.com.au/ australia-bus-pass for details. Many offer a 10% discount for members of YHA, VIP, Nomads and other approved organisations.

Kilometre Pass

Under the banner of 'Oz-Flexi Travel', these are the simplest passes, giving you specified amounts of travel starting at 500km ($108), going up in increments of 1000km to a maximum of 25,000km ($2600). A 5000km pass costs $814; 10,000km is $1397. Passes are valid for 12 months (90 days for 500km and 1000km passes), and you can travel where and in what direction you please, stopping as many times as you like. Use the online kilometre chart to figure out which pass suits you. Phone at least a day ahead to reserve your seat.

Mini Traveller Passes

In the 'Oz-Choice Travel' pass category, these 90-day, hop-on/hop-off passes cover a couple of dozen popular routes, mostly on the east coast. Travel is in one direction. Melbourne to Cairns is $450; Perth to Broome is $405; Sydney to Brisbane is $147.

Costs

Following are the average, nondiscounted, one-way bus fares along some well-travelled routes:

ROUTE	ADULT/ CHILD/ BACKPACKER
Adelaide–Darwin	$631/532/575
Adelaide–Melbourne	$90/78/83
Brisbane–Cairns	$292/249/267
Cairns–Sydney	$470/398/430
Sydney–Brisbane	$178/150/162
Sydney–Melbourne	$100/88/94

Car & Motorcycle

Driving Licence

To drive in Australia you'll need to hold a current driving licence issued in English from your home country. If the licence isn't in English, you'll also need to carry an International Driving Permit, issued in your home country.

Choosing a Vehicle

2WD Depending on where you want to travel, a regulation 2WD vehicle might suffice. They're cheaper to hire, buy and run than 4WDs and are more readily available. Most are fuel efficient, and easy to repair and sell. Downsides: no off-road capability and no room to sleep!

4WD Four-wheel drives are good for outback travel as they can access almost any track you get a hankering for. And there might even be space to sleep in the back. Downsides: poor fuel economy, awkward to park and more expensive to hire/buy.

Campervan Creature comforts at your fingertips: sink, fridge, cupboards, beds, kitchen and space to relax. Downsides: slow and often not fuel-efficient, not great on dirt roads and too big for nipping around the city.

Motorcycle The Australian climate is great for riding, and bikes are handy in city traffic. Downsides: Australia isn't particularly bike-friendly in terms of driver awareness, there's limited luggage capacity, and exposure to the elements.

Renting a Vehicle

Larger car-rental companies have drop-offs in major cities and towns. Most companies require drivers to be over the age of 21, though in some cases it's 18 and in others 25.

Suggestions to assist in the process:

○ Read the contract cover to cover.

○ Bond: some companies may require a signed credit-card slip, others may actually charge your credit card; if this is the case, find out when you'll get a refund.

○ Ask if unlimited kilometres are included and, if not, what the extra charge per kilometre will be.

○ Find out what excess you'll have to pay if you have a prang, and if it can be lowered by an extra charge per day (this option will usually be offered to you whether you ask or not). Check if your personal travel insurance covers you for vehicle accidents and excess.

○ Check for exclusions (hitting a kangaroo, damage on unsealed roads etc) and whether you're covered on unavoidable unsealed roads (eg accessing camp sites). Some companies also exclude parts of the car from cover, such as the underbelly, tyres and windscreen.

○ At pick-up inspect the vehicle for any damage. Make a note of anything on the contract before you sign.

○ Ask about breakdown and accident procedures.

○ If you can, return the vehicle during business hours and insist on an inspection in your presence.

The usual big international companies all operate in Australia (Avis, Budget, Europcar, Hertz, Thrifty). The following websites offer last-minute discounts:

○ **Carhire.com** (www.carhire.com.au)

○ **Drive Now** (☑1300 547 214; www.drivenow.com.au)

○ **Webjet** (www.webjet.com.au)

4WDs

Having a 4WD is essential for off-the-beaten-track driving into the outback. The major car-hire companies have 4WDs.

Renting a 4WD is affordable if a few people get together: something like a Nissan X-Trail (which can get you through most, but not all, tracks) costs around $100 to $150 per day; for a Toyota Landcruiser you're looking at around $150 up to $200, which should include unlimited kilometres.

Check the insurance conditions, especially the excess (which can be up to $5000), as they can be onerous and policies might not cover damage caused when travelling off-road. A refundable bond is also often required – this can be as much as $7500.

Campervans

Companies for campervan hire – with rates from around $90 (two-berth) or $150 (four-berth) per day, usually with minimum five-day hire and unlimited kilometres – include the following:

○ **Apollo** (☑1800 777 779; www.apollocamper.com)

○ **Britz** (☑1800 331 454; www.britz.com.au)

○ **Jucy Rentals** (☑1800 150 850; www.jucy.com.au)

○ **Maui** (☑1300 363 800; www.maui.com.au)

○ **Mighty Cars & Campers** (☑1800 670 232; www.mightycampers.com)

○ **Spaceships** (☑1300 132 469; www.spaceshipsrentals.com.au)

○ **Travelwheels** (☑1800 289 222; www.travelwheels.com.au)

○ **Wicked Campers** (☑1800 246 869; www.wickedcampers.com.au)

One-Way Relocations

Relocations are usually cheap deals, although they don't allow much time flexibility. Most of the large hire companies offer deals, or try the following operators. See also www.drivenow.com.au.

○ **Relocations2Go** (☑1800 735 627; www.relocations2go.com)

○ **imoova** (☑1300 789 059; www.imoova.com)

○ **Transfercar** (☑02-8011 1870; www.transfercar.com.au)

Insurance

Rental vehicles When it comes to hire cars, understand your liability in the event of an accident. Rather than risk paying out thousands of dollars, consider taking out comprehensive car insurance or paying an additional daily amount to the rental company for excess reduction (this reduces the excess payable in the event of an accident from between $2000 and $5000 to a few hundred dollars).

Exclusions Be aware that if travelling on dirt roads you usually will not be covered by insurance unless you have a 4WD (read the fine print). Also, many companies' insurance won't cover the cost of damage to glass (including the windscreen) or tyres.

Auto Clubs

Under the auspices of the **Australian Automobile Association** (AAA; ☎02-6247 7311; www.aaa.asn.au) are automobile clubs in each state, handy when it comes to insurance, regulations, maps and roadside assistance. Club membership (around $100 to $150) can save you a lot of trouble if things go wrong mechanically. If you're a member of an auto club in your home country, check if reciprocal rights are offered in Australia. The major Australian auto clubs generally offer reciprocal rights in other states and territories.

○ **AANT** (Automobile Association of the Northern Territory; ☎08-8925 5901; www.aant.com.au)

○ **NRMA** (☎13 11 22; www.mynrma.com.au) NSW and the ACT.

○ **RAC** (Royal Automobile Club of WA; ☎13 17 03; www.rac.com.au)

○ **RACQ** (Royal Automobile Club of Queensland; ☎13 19 05; www.racq.com.au)

○ **RACT** (Royal Automobile Club of Tasmania; ☎13 27 22; www.ract.com.au)

○ **RACV** (Royal Automobile Club of Victoria; ☎13 72 28; www.racv.com.au)

Road Rules

Australians drive on the left-hand side of the road and all cars are right-hand drive.

Give way An important road rule is 'give way to the right' – if an intersection is unmarked (unusual) and at roundabouts, you must give way to vehicles entering the intersection from your right.

Speed limits The general speed limit in built-up and residential areas is 50km/h (or sometimes 40km/h). Near schools, the limit is usually 25km/h in the morning and afternoon. On the highway it's usually 100km/h or 110km/h; in the NT it's either 110km/h or 130km/h. Police have speed radar guns and cameras and are fond of using them in strategic locations.

Seatbelts and car seats It's the law to wear seatbelts in the front and back seats; you're likely to get a fine if you don't. Small children must be belted into an approved safety seat.

Drink-driving Random breath-tests are common. If you're caught with a blood-alcohol level of more than 0.05% expect a fine and the loss of your licence. Police can randomly pull any driver over for a breathalyser or drug test.

Mobile phones Using a mobile phone while driving is illegal in Australia (excluding hands-free technology).

Hazards & Precautions

Fatigue Be wary of driver fatigue; driving long distances (particularly in hot weather) can be utterly exhausting. Falling asleep at the wheel is not uncommon. On a long haul, stop and rest every two hours or so – do some exercise, change drivers or have a coffee.

Road trains Be careful overtaking road trains (trucks with two or three trailers stretching for as long as 50m); you'll need distance and plenty of speed. On single-lane roads get right off the road when one approaches.

Unsealed roads Unsealed road conditions vary wildly and cars perform differently when braking and turning on dirt. Don't exceed 80km/h on dirt roads; if you go faster you won't have time to respond to a sharp turn, stock on the road or an unmarked gate or cattle grid.

ANIMAL HAZARDS

○ Roadkill is a huge problem in Australia, particularly in the NT, Queensland, NSW, SA and Tasmania. Many Australians avoid travelling once the sun drops because of the risks posed by nocturnal animals on the roads.

○ Kangaroos are common on country roads, as are cows and sheep in the unfenced outback. Kangaroos are most active around dawn and dusk and often travel in groups: if you see one hopping across the road, slow right down, as its friends may be just behind it.

○ If you hit and kill an animal while driving, pull it off the road, preventing the next car from having a potential accident. If the animal is only injured and is small, perhaps an orphaned joey (baby kangaroo), wrap it in a towel or blanket and call the relevant wildlife rescue line.

Department of Environment & Conservation (☏ 08-9474 9055; www.dec.wa.gov.au) WA

Department of Environment & Heritage Protection (☏ 1300 130 372; www.ehp.qld.gov.au) Queensland

Fauna Rescue of South Australia (☏ 08-8289 0896; www.faunarescue.org.au)

NSW Wildlife Information, Rescue & Education Service (WIRES; ☏ 1300 094 737; www.wires.org.au)

NT Wildlife Rescue Wildlife Rescue Darwin (☏ 0409 090 840; www.wildlifedarwin.com.au); Katherine Wildlife Rescue Service (☏ 0407 934 252; www.fauna.org.a); Wildcare Inc Alice Springs (☏ 0419 221 128; www.fauna.org.au)

Wildlife Care (☏ 03-6233 6556; www.fnpw.org.au) Tasmania

Wildlife Victoria (☏ 1300 094 535; www.wildlifevictoria.org.au)

Fuel

Fuel types Unleaded and diesel fuel is available from service stations sporting well-known international brand names. LPG (liquefied petroleum gas) is not always stocked at more remote roadhouses; if you're on gas it's safer to have dual-fuel capacity.

Costs Prices vary from place to place, but at the time of writing unleaded was hovering between $1.30 and $1.50 in the cities. Out in the country, prices soar – in outback NT, WA and Queensland you can pay as much as $2.20 per litre.

Availability In cities and towns petrol stations proliferate, but distances between fill-ups can be long in the outback. That said, there are only a handful of tracks where you'll require a long-range fuel tank. On main roads there'll be a small town or roadhouse roughly every 150km to 200km. Many petrol stations, but not all, are open 24 hours.

Resources

Australian Bureau of Meteorology (www.bom.gov.au) Weather information.

Green Vehicle Guide (www.greenvehicleguide.gov.au) Rates Australian vehicles based on greenhouse and air-pollution emissions.

Live Traffic NSW (☏ 13 27 01; http://livetraffic.rta.nsw.gov.au) NSW road conditions.

Main Roads Western Australia (☏ 13 81 38; www.mainroads.wa.gov.au) WA road conditions.

Motorcycle Riders Association of Australia (MRAA; www.mraa.org.au)

Road Report (☏ 1800 246 199; www.roadreport.nt.gov.au) NT road conditions.

Traffic & Travel Information (☏ 13 19 40; http://highload.131940.qld.gov.au) Queensland road conditions.

Department of Planning, Transport & Infrastructure (☏ 1300 361 033; www.transport.sa.gov.au) SA road conditions.

Local Transport

All of Australia's major towns have reliable, affordable public bus networks, and there are suburban train lines in Sydney, Melbourne, Brisbane, Adelaide and Perth. Melbourne also has trams (Adelaide has one!), and Sydney has harbour ferries and

---

Carbon Offsetting

Various organisations use 'carbon calculators' that allow travellers to offset the greenhouse gases they are responsible for with financial contributions.

Carbon Neutral (www.carbonneutral.com.au)

Carbon Planet (www.carbonplanet.com)

Elementree (www.elementree.com.au)

Greenfleet (www.greenfleet.com.au)

a light rail line. Taxis operate Australia-wide.

See regional chapters for detailed info.

🚃 Train

Long-distance rail travel in Australia is something you do because you really want to – not because it's cheap, convenient or fast. That said, trains are more comfortable than buses, and there's a certain long-distance 'romance of the rails' that's alive and kicking. Shorter-distance rail services within most states are run by state rail bodies, either government or private.

The three major interstate services in Australia are operated by **Great Southern Rail** (☏13 21 47; www.gsr. com.au), namely the *Indian Pacific* between Sydney and Perth, the *Overland* between Melbourne and Adelaide, and the *Ghan* between Adelaide and Darwin via Alice Springs. There's also the *Sunlander* service between Brisbane and Cairns, operated by **Queensland Rail** (☏1800 872 467; www.queenslandrail. com.au). Trains from Sydney to Brisbane, Melbourne and Canberra are operated by **CountryLink** (www. countrylink.info).

Costs

Following are standard internet-booked one-way train fares. Note that cheaper seat fares are readily available but are generally nonrefundable with no changes permitted. Backpacker discounts are also available.

....

Adelaide–Darwin Adult/ child seated $862/403; from $2290/1582 in a cabin

Adelaide–Melbourne Adult/ child seated from $116/60

....

Adelaide–Perth Adult/ child seated $553/310; from $1750/1202 in a cabin

....

Brisbane–Cairns Adult/child seated from $269/135; from $349/215 in a cabin

....

Sydney–Canberra Adult/ child seated $57/28

....

Sydney–Brisbane Adult/ child seated $130/65; cabin $271/180

....

Sydney–Melbourne Adult/ child seated $130/65; cabin $271/180

....

Sydney–Perth Adult/child seated $783/575, from $2178/1936 in a cabin.

Train Passes

For international visitors only, the **Ausrail Pass** offered by Great Southern Rail permits unlimited travel on the interstate rail network (including CountryLink and *Sunlander* services) over a three- or six-month period (seated, not in cabins). The three-/six-month pass costs $795/1045 per adult – inexpensive considering the amount of ground you could cover. Present your passport to qualify.

Great Southern Rail offers international visitors a couple of other passes, the pick of which is probably the **Rail Explorer Pass**, costing $495/649 per adult for three/ six months. Travel is on the *Ghan*, the *Overland* and the *Indian Pacific* (again, seated, not in cabins).

CountryLink offers several passes covering various regions, some utilising Great Southern Rail services. The **East Coast Discovery Pass** allows one-way economy travel between Melbourne and Cairns (in either direction) with unlimited stopovers, and is valid for six months – the full trip costs $450, while Sydney to Cairns is $370 and Brisbane to Cairns is $280. The **Backtracker Pass**, which is available only to international visitors, permits travel on the entire CountryLink network and has four versions: a 14-day/one-/ three-/six-month pass costing $232/275/298/420.

Behind the Scenes

Author Thanks
Charles Rawlings-Way

Huge thanks to Maryanne for the gig, and to my highway-addled coauthors, who covered a helluva lot of kilometres in search of the perfect review. Thanks also to the all-star inhouse Lonely Planet production staff, and in Brisbane thanks to Christian, Lauren, Rachel, Brett and all the kids. Special thanks as always to Meg, my road-trippin' sweetheart, and our daughters Ione and Remy, who provided countless laughs, unscheduled pit-stops and ground-level perspectives along the way.

Acknowledgments

Climate map data adapted from Peel MC, Finlayson BL & McMahon TA (2007) 'Updated World Map of the Köppen-Geiger Climate Classification', *Hydrology and Earth System Sciences*, 11, 163344.

Illustration p64-5 by Javier Zarracina.

Cover photographs: Front: Sydney Harbour skyline, Shaun Egan/AWL Library; Back: Uluru-Kata Tjuta National Park, Wibowo Rusli/Getty Images.

Our Readers

Many thanks to the travellers who used the last edition and wrote to us with helpful hints, useful advice and interesting anecdotes:

Cameron Mason, Islay-Mavora Christophers, Janeen Turano

This Book

This 3rd edition of Lonely Planet's *Discover Australia* was coordinated by Charles Rawlings-Way, and researched and written by Charles Rawlings-Way, Brett Atkinson, Lindsay Brown, Jayne D'Arcy, Anthony Ham, Shawn Low, Virginia Maxwell, Tom Spurling, Steve Waters and Meg Worby, with contributions from Michael Cathcart, Cathy Craigie and Tim Flannery. This guidebook was commissioned in Lonely Planet's Melbourne office, and produced by the following:

Commissioning Editors Maryanne Netto, William Gourlay
Coordinating Editor Branislava Vladisavljevic
Senior Cartographers Diana von Holdt, Julie Sheridan
Coordinating Layout Designer Carlos Solarte
Managing Editors Brigitte Ellemor, Annelies Mertens
Managing Layout Designer Chris Girdler
Assisting Editors Erin Richards, Ross Taylor
Assisting Cartographer Fatima Basic
Cover Research Naomi Parker
Internal Image Research Aude Vauconsant
Thanks to Anita Banh, Adrian Blackburn, Laura Crawford, Bruce Evans, Ryan Evans, Larissa Frost, Genesys India, Bronwyn Hicks, Jouve India, Andi Jones, Clara Monitto, Wayne Murphy, Trent Paton, Martine Power, Alison Ridgway, Dianne Schallmeiner, Kerrianne Southway, Gerard Walker

SEND US YOUR FEEDBACK

We love to hear from travellers – your comments keep us on our toes and help make our books better. Our well-travelled team reads every word on what you loved or loathed about this book. Although we cannot reply individually to postal submissions, we always guarantee that your feedback goes straight to the appropriate authors, in time for the next edition. Each person who sends us information is thanked in the next edition, the most useful submissions are rewarded with a selection of digital PDF chapters.

Visit **lonelyplanet.com/contact** to submit your updates and suggestions or to ask for help. Our award-winning website also features inspirational travel stories, news and discussions.

Note: We may edit, reproduce and incorporate your comments in Lonely Planet products such as guidebooks, websites and digital products, so let us know if you don't want your comments reproduced or your name acknowledged. For a copy of our privacy policy visit lonelyplanet.com/privacy.

Index

000 Map pages

000 Map pages

How to Use This Book

These symbols give you the vital information for each listing:

☑	Telephone Numbers	☎	Wi-Fi Access	☒	Bus
☺	Opening Hours	☒	Swimming Pool	☒	Ferry
℗	Parking	☒	Vegetarian Selection	Ⓜ	Metro
⊖	Nonsmoking	☒	English-Language Menu	Ⓢ	Subway
✳	Air-Conditioning	⊕	Family-Friendly	⊖	London Tube
@	Internet Access	☒	Pet-Friendly	☒	Tram

Look out for these icons:

 No payment required

🍃 A green or sustainable option

Our authors have nominated these places as demonstrating a strong commitment to sustainability – for example by supporting local communities and producers, operating in an environmentally friendly way, or supporting conservation projects.

All reviews are ordered in our authors' preference, starting with their most preferred option. Additionally:

Sights are arranged in the geographic order that we suggest you visit them, and within this order, by author preference.

Eating and Sleeping reviews are ordered by price range (budget, mid-range, top end) and within these ranges, by author preference.

Map Legend

Sights
- 🏖 Beach
- ☸ Buddhist
- 🏰 Castle
- ✝ Christian
- 🕉 Hindu
- ☪ Islamic
- ✡ Jewish
- ⊙ Monument
- 🏛 Museum/Gallery
- ⊙ Ruin
- ⊙ Winery/Vineyard
- 🐾 Zoo
- ⊙ Other Sight

Activities, Courses & Tours
- ⊙ Diving/Snorkelling
- ⊙ Canoeing/Kayaking
- ⊙ Skiing
- ⊙ Surfing
- ⊙ Swimming/Pool
- ⊙ Walking
- ⊙ Windsurfing
- ⊙ Other Activity/Course/Tour

Sleeping
- ⊙ Sleeping
- ⊙ Camping

Eating
- ⊗ Eating

Drinking
- ⊙ Drinking
- ⊙ Cafe

Entertainment
- ⊙ Entertainment

Shopping
- ⊙ Shopping

Information
- ⊙ Post Office
- ⊙ Tourist Information

Transport
- ⊙ Airport
- ⊗ Border Crossing
- ⊙ Bus
- ⊕ Cable Car/Funicular
- ⊙ Cycling
- ⊙ Ferry
- ⊙ Monorail
- ℗ Parking
- ⓢ S-Bahn
- ⊙ Taxi
- ⊕ Train/Railway
- ⊕ Tram
- ⊙ Tube Station
- Ⓤ U-Bahn
- Ⓜ Underground Train Station
- ● Other Transport

Routes
- Tollway
- Freeway
- Primary
- Secondary
- Tertiary
- Lane
- Unsealed Road
- Plaza/Mall
- Steps
- ⊃⊂ Tunnel
- Pedestrian Overpass
- Walking Tour
- Walking Tour Detour
- Path

Boundaries
- ――― International
- ――― State/Province
- ――― Disputed
- ――― Regional/Suburb
- Marine Park
- Cliff
- Wall

Population
- ⊗ Capital (National)
- ◉ Capital (State/Province)
- ⊙ City/Large Town
- ⊙ Town/Village

Geographic
- ⊙ Hut/Shelter
- ⊙ Lighthouse
- ⊙ Lookout
- ▲ Mountain/Volcano
- ⊙ Oasis
- ⊙ Park
-)(Pass
- ⊙ Picnic Area
- ⊙ Waterfall

Hydrography
- River/Creek
- Intermittent River
- Swamp/Mangrove
- Reef
- Canal
- Water
- Dry/Salt/Intermittent Lake
- Glacier

Areas
- Beach/Desert
- Cemetery (Christian)
- Cemetery (Other)
- Park/Forest
- Sportsground
- Sight (Building)
- Top Sight (Building)

ANTHONY HAM

Sydney & the Blue Mountains Anthony was born in Melbourne, grew up in Sydney and spent much of his adult life travelling the world. He recently returned to Australia after 10 years living in Madrid. In NSW he found a perfect fit for his passion for wild landscapes – coastal rainforests, vast sweeps of sand and the endless outback horizon reminded him just how much he missed the land of his birth. He brings to the book the unique perspective of knowing the land intimately, yet seeing it anew as if through the eyes of an outsider.

SHAWN LOW

Tropical North Queensland Good things come to those who wait. So the cliché goes. After missing out on a chance to work on the previous edition of the *Australia* guide, Shawn filled in his time with research trips to Singapore, Korea and China instead. His patience was rewarded and aside from a wicked tan, Shawn now has a new bagload of travel stories to enthral (or bore) his mates with at the next pub session. Find out where he's currently travelling via Twitter @shawnlow.

VIRGINIA MAXWELL

Sydney & the Blue Mountains, Best of the Rest Despite being born, bred and based in Melbourne, Virginia knows Sydney well and loves it to bits. Having lived there in the past and visited frequently ever since, she has a good grasp of where to swim, sightsee, sleep and party. She resolutely refuses to engage in the age-old Sydney vs Melbourne rivalry – both are wonderful cities, especially now that Sydney has finally added a vibrant coffee culture to its many charms.

TOM SPURLING

Tropical North Queensland Tom has written 10 guidebooks about countries on five continents for Lonely Planet. He lives dangerously close to a trotting track in Perth, Western Australia. For this book he returned to Queensland with his wife and two children, driving 3000km of near-coastal highway listening to nonstop nursery rhymes. He escaped just days before mass floods. Tom also drove the outback with his dad, who snored a lot but bought most of the beer.

STEVE WATERS

Perth & the West Coast From the corrugations of the Tanami to Nambung's ghostly Pinnacles, Steve covered 15,000km in Ezy, his Subaru L-series. Driving lights dropped off, shockers, tyres, drive shafts all shattered and they both almost drowned entering Purnululu. It only caught fire once. Slept in, eaten on, buried in Dampier Peninsula pindan, covered in Pilbara dust, pulled over by Cervantes cops, Ezy kept going. Steve's also coauthored previous editions of *Australia*, as well as *Indonesia* and *Great Adventures*, and while not on the road, he frequents Lonely Planet's Melbourne office.

MEG WORBY

Brisbane & the East Coast Beaches, Best of the Rest Meg's first foray into Queensland introduced her to a green turtle, face-to-face underwater. Twenty-eight years and six trips later, Queensland's inhabitants are still as naturally charming and a lot more cosmopolitan. Meanwhile, writing about South Australia was an honour as always. Meg is a former member of Lonely Planet's languages, editorial and publishing teams, and this is her seventh Australian guidebook for Lonely Planet.

CONTRIBUTING AUTHORS

Michael Cathcart Michael teaches history at the Australian Centre, University of Melbourne. He is well known as a broadcaster on ABC Radio National and has presented history programs on ABC TV. Michael wrote the History chapter.

Cathy Craigie Cathy is a Gamilaori/Anaiwon woman from northern New South Wales. She is a freelance writer and cultural consultant and has extensive experience in Aboriginal Affairs. Cathy wrote the Aboriginal Australia chapter.

Tim Flannery Tim is a scientist, explorer and writer. He has written several award-winning books including *The Future Eaters*, *Throwim Way Leg* (an account of his work as a biologist in New Guinea) and *The Weather Makers*. He lives in Sydney where he is a professor in the faculty of science at Macquarie University. Tim wrote the Environment chapter.

Our Story

A beat-up old car, a few dollars in the pocket and a sense of adventure. In 1972 that's all Tony and Maureen Wheeler needed for the trip of a lifetime – across Europe and Asia overland to Australia. It took several months, and at the end – broke but inspired – they sat at their kitchen table writing and stapling together their first travel guide, *Across Asia on the Cheap*. Within a week they'd sold 1500 copies. Lonely Planet was born.

Today, Lonely Planet has offices in Melbourne, London and Oakland, with more than 600 staff and writers. We share Tony's belief that 'a great guidebook should do three things: inform, educate and amuse'.

Our Writers

CHARLES RAWLINGS-WAY

Coordinating Author, Brisbane & the East Coast Beaches, Best of the Rest As a likely lad, Charles suffered in shorts through Tasmanian winters, and in summer counted the days till he visited his grandparents in Adelaide. With desert-hot days, cool swimming pools, pasties with tomato sauce squirted into the middle and four TV stations, this flat South Australian city held paradisiacal status. Little did he know that southeast Queensland was just as alluring – a fact confirmed by more recent encounters with Brisbane's bookshops, bars and band rooms. An underrated rock guitarist and proud father of daughters, Charles has penned 20-something guidebooks for Lonely Planet.

BRETT ATKINSON

Perth & the West Coast, Best of the Rest Brett's previous visits to Western Australia involved museum- and bar-hopping in Fremantle, and taking on the mighty Nullarbor Plain. This time he expanded his WA horizons by immersing himself in Perth's restaurants and cafes, 'researching' craft breweries in the Swan Valley, and jumping from beach to forest and back to beach throughout Margaret River and the southwest. Brett's covered more than 45 countries as a guidebook author and travel and food writer. See www.brett-atkinson.net for where he's travelling to next.

LINDSAY BROWN

Darwin, Uluru & the Red Centre A former conservation biologist and publishing manager of outdoor activity guides at Lonely Planet, Lindsay enjoys nothing more than heading into the outback in his trusty old 4WD to explore and photograph Australia's heartland. As a Lonely Planet author, Lindsay has contributed to several titles including *Australia, Central Australia, Northern Territory, Queensland & the Great Barrier Reef, East Coast Australia, Sydney & New South Wales* and *Walking in Australia*.

JAYNE D'ARCY

Melbourne & the Great Ocean Road Melbourne strikes a new pose every day and Jayne does her best to snap it in words and photos. A fan of cycling around the city, she's learnt that you can't look at anything in Melbourne at face value, you've got to look up (for the rooftop bars), down (for the graffiti) and along that grimy laneway (for the glitzy restaurant). Jayne's lived on the Mornington Peninsula and Great Ocean Road but is now happier than ever in Melbourne.

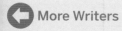

More Writers

Published by Lonely Planet Publications Pty Ltd
ABN 36 005 607 983
3rd edition – Jan 2014
ISBN 978 1 74220 560 1